Cultural Contestation in Ethnic Conflict

Ethnic conflict often focuses on culturally charged symbols and rituals that evoke strong emotions from all sides. Marc Howard Ross examines battles over diverse cultural expressions and enactments, including Islamic headscarves in France, parades in Northern Ireland, holy sites in Jerusalem and Confederate flags in the American South, to propose a psychocultural framework for understanding ethnic conflict, as well as barriers to, and opportunities for, its mitigation. His analysis explores how culture frames interests, structures demand-making and shapes how opponents can find common ground to produce constructive outcomes to long-term disputes. He focuses on participants' accounts of conflict to identify emotionally significant issues, and the power of cultural expressions to link individuals to larger identities and shape action. Ross shows that, contrary to popular belief, culture does not necessarily exacerbate conflict; rather, the constructed nature of psychocultural narratives can facilitate successful conflict mitigation through the development of more inclusive narratives and identities.

Marc Howard Ross is William Rand Kenan Jr. Professor of Political Science at Bryn Mawr College where he has taught since 1968. He has had a long term interest in social science theories of conflict management and has done research in East Africa, France, Northern Ireland, the Middle East, Spain, South Africa, and the United States. Professor Ross has written or edited six books including *The Culture of Conflict* (1993) and *The Management of Conflict* (1993).

Cambridge Studies in Comparative Politics

General Editor
Margaret Levi, *University of Washington, Seattle*

Assistant General Editor
Stephen Hanson, *University of Washington, Seattle*

Associate Editors
Robert H. Bates, *Harvard University*
Helen Milner, *Princeton University*
Frances Rosenbluth, *Yale University*
Susan Stokes, *Yale University*
Sidney Tarrow, *Cornell University*
Kathleen Thelen, *Northwestern University*
Erik Wibbels, *University of Washington, Seattle*

(Continues after the index)

Cultural Contestation in Ethnic Conflict

MARC HOWARD ROSS

Bryn Mawr College

 CAMBRIDGE
UNIVERSITY PRESS

CAMBRIDGE UNIVERSITY PRESS
Cambridge, New York, Melbourne, Madrid, Cape Town, Singapore,
São Paulo, Delhi, Dubai, Tokyo

Cambridge University Press
The Edinburgh Building, Cambridge CB2 8RU, UK

Published in the United States of America by Cambridge University Press, New York

www.cambridge.org
Information on this title: www.cambridge.org/9780521690324

First published 2007

A catalogue record for this publication is available from the British Library

ISBN 978-0-521-87013-9 Hardback
ISBN 978-0-521-69032-4 Paperback

Transferred to digital printing 2009

To Katherine with love
for all the joys we share including
Katherine, Thomas
and the future members of their generation

Contents

Figures

Figures

Every effort has been made to trace all the copyright holders, but if any have been inadvertently overlooked, Cambridge University Press will be pleased to make the necessary acknowledgments at the first opportunity.

Preface

A decade ago I began puzzling about why, and how, what to some people are innocent cultural expressions are to others provocative, aggressive, politically significant acts. At one level, I had known this was the case for a long time from personal observations and experiences as well as the analyses of scholars such as Murray Edelman and Abner Cohen, both of whom, in different ways, focused my attention on the political uses of culture. My own investigation of culture and politics started thirty years ago when I began a cross-cultural study of conflict that examined differences between high- and low-conflict societies. This project led me to articulate ideas concerning the complementary roles of structural and psychocultural mechanisms that create societal dispositions toward particular forms and levels of conflict and violence. Next I utilized the same framework to explore how any given theory of conflict has crucial implications for the theory and practice of conflict management. For example, if a conflict is viewed as one over resource competition, people trying to end it will seek to negotiate an agreement to divide the resources in a manner that all sides can accept, while those who attribute the same conflict to incompatible identities will make bridging these differences central to their conflict management efforts.

As part of my work on conflict management, I asked why some conflicts are managed more successfully than others, and a case I investigated in depth was the 1989 conflict in France that arose when three Muslim junior high students were expelled for wearing headscarves in school (Ross 1993b). I was living in France with my family at the time and was astounded at how quickly the conflict expanded, at the intensity of emotion it generated, and at how inadequate the outcome was as it failed to address the deep identity needs of those involved. Several years later I began studying Protestant Loyal Order parades in Northern Ireland where sometimes thousands of police and army troops are mobilized to separate Protestant marchers and Catholic protesters.

Once I began looking at, and talking about, intense conflict involving expressive culture, more and more examples that seemed especially relevant in long-term ethnic conflicts became apparent, or were recounted to me. In these conflicts, while there are always substantive, tangible issues dividing the parties, it is also the case that cultural assertion of exclusive identities invariably contributes significantly to heightened tensions, intransigent positions and, sometimes, to violence. As a result, conflict often persisted over what seems to outsiders, but not to the parties themselves, to be the most trivial of differences.

At some point, I realized how much I didn't understand about the psychocultural dynamics of conflict expansion in enduring conflicts, and why and how small incidents engage so many people so passionately, why these conflicts are so resistant to resolution, and decided that there was a need for concepts to better analyze them, as well as for hypotheses about why some cultural conflicts take a more constructive turn than others.

The result is this book, a long answer to a short question that political scientists have struggled to explain: why are many ethnic conflicts so intense and so hard to settle? The most common answer to this question is that clashing interests over tangible resources such as land, jobs, or control of the state, create zero-sum conflicts that endure when the parties believe losing them can have disastrous consequences. As a result, institutions are unable to provide adequate security guarantees and the parties are unable to overcome commitment problems to find ways to share power and deescalate conflict. While such answers are useful, I also find them incomplete. What they lack is thoughtful consideration of where interests come from in the first place, how interests get defined in specific cultural contests, and the ways that culture structures appropriate ways to pursue them. The theories and language of interest and institutional analyses that are the bases for most political analyses make too little space for identity and culture and pay too little attention to how they directly affect conflict.

My starting point is different – namely that rich analyses of the politics of identity and culture provide an explanatory power that cannot simply be incorporated into a rationalist framework. The analysis of identity politics requires other tools. We need to investigate the power of culture to order priorities, define enemies and allies, and offer meaning to large numbers of people under stress, threat, and uncertainty. In this book I emphasize the importance of psychocultural narratives and dramas and the power of cultural expressions and enactments to shape how people understand their group and its interests, to promote particular actions, and to create a society's symbolic landscape. Widely shared narratives matter because they offer emotionally meaningful accounts of the world, defining groups and explaining their motives and actions. Because they frame the world and shape action, powerful narratives must be central to the analysis of ethnic conflict and steps taken to mitigate it. Finally, politically relevant psychocultural analysis not only examines group narratives, but also considers the many ways in which they are enacted in daily life and in a community's sacred rituals. Enactment matters because participation affirms core elements of a narrative and strengthens attachment to it and to the group while linking present conflicts and people across time and space.

I emphasize identities and psychocultural dynamics because political scientists have paid too little attention to them; I believe they are central to analyzing core political questions about conflict, authority, and community. Our theories of conflict, and in particular its management, would be richer if we expanded our understanding of conflict and articulated more effectively how interests and identities interact and shape each other rather than the position that one is necessarily determinant of the other. Many conflict resolution practitioners understand this complementary relationship intuitively, and have integrated this into their practice. For them this book may be less relevant in terms of making explicit the role of culture in ethnic conflict than in spelling out the theoretical basis for what they already do, and providing some comparative examples.

This project involved field research in six countries and inspiration during visits to at least five more. As the project evolved, I sharpened and limited the cases I would examine and what I needed to know about each. Having engaged primarily in quantitative comparative research in the past, the methodological issues of what constituted not only evidence but comparable data in the qualitative case studies was not always easy to conceptualize let alone collect.

Two of the cases I included pressed me to separate my preconceptions from my analysis, and to be particularly rigorous in applying the tools the book offers. The first was the case of the Confederate flag controversies in the United States. When I began the research I didn't plan to include race in the United States as one of my cases but I changed my mind for three reasons. One was a comment from political psychologist Dan Bar-On who pushed me to focus attention on US racial conflict and not just think about ethnic conflict in other societies. Bringing the tools of my analysis back home would, he argued, perhaps provide important insights and would engage me differently than the study of other societies had. Second, my wife Katherine not only agreed with Bar-On's points but added that including my own society (and eventually my own city) along with others in my project would be the best way to communicate to readers that the problems of ethnic and racial conflicts are not just found in far-away lands. Third, for some time I had followed the Confederate flag conflicts in the South and realized that these were quite comparable to the cultural contestation I had been examining elsewhere.

The second case that challenged my objectivity and my capacity to separate my own preconceptions and emotions from the analysis was the work I did in France, where I have lived a great deal in the past thirty-five years. To me, the argument that French culture is at risk from head-scarves in schools did not seem plausible. I saw no threat in ten, twenty, or even a thousand young girls wearing a scarf on their head in school, and I was impatient with the lack of respect that many in power have demonstrated, and the refusal of many French officials to think through their positions in constructive ways. However, as with the other cases, the point is not which side is "right" and which one is "wrong." My reaction to the French narratives was no better than telling someone their feelings are wrong or than an analyst telling a patient they had a stupid dream. Dismissal of passionately held positions does not help us understand why people feel as they do and what the significance of these strong feelings is for political and social action; neither does it suggest useful steps to address the conflict constructively.

What I found especially difficult in studying conflicts in the societies I know best was listening actively to all the parties – a crucial first step in my methodological approach, which is based on my belief that you don't have to accept someone's position, but you do need to be clear what it is and then ask why they hold it so passionately. This is clear to me in theory, but, for example, given my own upbringing and experiences, when the object was the Confederate battle flag, it was not easy for me to see it as anything but a symbol of racial oppression. Explanations that it represented heritage and alternative constitutional principles (at least for some people) first struck me as false consciousness, if not deception. To do the research and analysis effectively, I had to set aside these prior, and deeply held, personal positions to take seriously the question of why attachment to the flag is so strong, and to consider ways in which heritage primarily concerns the present rather than the past. Because this conflict was close to home and so connected to my life experience and values I had to be rigorous in applying the method that had been so much easier to use in more unfamiliar cultures in order to understand that for blacks as well as whites the heritage issues related to the Confederate battle flag are about recognition and loss as well as race, and that I owed them the same acknowledgment, not just rejection, that I urge on theorists and practitioners working on conflict in other cultures. My experience with the French case was similar, if less intense.

Let me close by saying that finishing this book has been very difficult because none of the cases I have examined sit still. Since the completion of early drafts, one of the cases has heated up considerably, while some that had been volatile have become more contained. I note this to make the point that I am not in the business of making predictions but rather of trying to understand both escalating conflict and the potential for conflict mitigation, and of identifying tools that help theorists to analyze ethnic conflict and practitioners to move toward "good enough" solutions. What I hope readers will take away from this book is a sense that even when ethnic conflict is intense, or when groups that appeared to have found a way to coexist return to violence, we should not simply wring our hands and believe that ancient hatreds make ongoing violent conflict inevitable.

Undertaking this research and writing required help from more than a few people and several grants that paid my research expenses, providing time to read, think and write as I explored new theoretical problems and literatures. A grant from the United States Institute for Peace got me started and I hope that the people who awarded it to me will recognize the core questions I promised to examine in this book despite the many changes in cases and concepts. A generous grant from the Mellon Foundation's New Directions Program and regular sabbatical and research support from Bryn Mawr College provided the time and resources needed to do field work in six different countries and the time needed for writing. Students in my Culture and Ethnic Conflict Management class that I have taught since 1999 continually obliged me to sharpen my ideas and to make explicit the connection between the case studies and my larger argument.

I benefited from comments I received at professional meetings where I presented parts of this work and at seminar presentations at Harvard, Hebrew University, INCORE, Ohio State's Mershon Center, Syracuse, George Mason, the University of Pennsylvania, Complutense University of Madrid, the Peace and Conflict Studies at the University of Granada, and at the University of the Western Cape in South Africa.

I am deeply grateful to Kevin Avruch, Stuart Kaufman, and Lou Kriesberg who commented on the entire manuscript, making a number of very detailed and helpful suggestions as I struggled through the problem of making connections among the cases in a theoretically useful way. Many other people in many places have talked and corresponded with me about parts of this project and I want to thank them for their time and comments: Miguel Rodrigo Alsina, Eileen Babbitt, Gabriel Barkay, Dan Bar-On, Yaacov Bar Siman-Tov, Dani Bar-Tal, Zvi Beckerman, Meir Ben-Dov, Philip Bonner, Dominic Bryan, David Bunn, Ariane Chebel d'Apollonia, John Coski, John Darby, Lionel Davis, Fannie du Toit, Roy Eidelson, Mari Fitzduff, Tanya Gallagher, Mathias Gardet, Harvey Glickman, Gershom Gorenberg, Deborah Harrold, Ron Hassner, Neil Jarman, Riva Kastoryano, Herb Kelman, Cynthia Kros, Cecelia Kruger, Yehezekial Landau, Ned Lebow, Ed Linenthal, Ian Lustick, Jannie Malan, Charles Malcolm, Sabine Marschall, Clark McCauley, Siobhan McEvoy-Levy, Hlengiwe Mkhize, Ifat Moaz, Rob Mortimer, Bob Mulvihill, Dorothy Noyes, Brendan O'Leary, Gert Operman, Ciraj Rassool, Nadim Rouhanna, Paul Rozin, Hal Saunders, Stuart Saunders, Astrid Schwenke, Sandra Scham, Lee Smithey, Robin Wagner-Pacifici, Catherine Withol de Wenden, Leslie Witz, and Alan Zuckerman. Many others made useful suggestions for readings and gave me ideas about directions to pursue.

Lastly, I want to thank my family, and especially Katherine, for all the help and support they provided me while I worked on this project, listening to my stories, reactions to accounts of what I was reading, and always pushing me to think more clearly about what I was doing. Kim and Warren talked to me about Southern culture, the Civil War and reenactors; Aaron kept giving me new websites where I could find material about the latest conflict from a non-American perspective; Kristin told me that if I wanted just one more case it should be Rwanda, preferably when she was working there; and Ethan listened, nodded, and would ask questions that really made me think hard about what I was doing. Katherine visited each of the countries in which I did research, and read and commented on more drafts of more chapters than I can remember having written. What is more incredible to me is that she never stopped giving me her reactions, telling me what she thought needed changing, highlighting, recasting and always doing it with care and love. No one can be luckier than I have been to have had such a terrific partner with whom to share a project. I can never tell her enough how meaningful this has been to me, but at some deep level I think she knows. For that I am incredibly grateful.

1

Introduction: easy questions and hard answers, what are they fighting about?

What are long-term ethnic conflicts about? How do they develop? Why are they so intense and hard to settle? Why do opposing sides view and describe what are ostensibly the same events so differently? How does identity shape why and how ethnic conflict is waged? What do good settlements look like?

Over the past thirty years, political analyses have offered very diverse answers to these apparently straightforward questions. In general, political scientists approaching ethnic conflict have focused on the interests motivating contending groups and the strategies by which these interests are pursued. Some answers from this perspective are interesting and non-obvious. On the whole, however, they are partial, and fail to address some important issues, thereby limiting our understanding of ethnic conflict and its management. For example, most existing work has little to say about how interests are developed and defined in different societies. In addition, there is little effort to deal with the puzzles that arise when what are apparently the same competing interests in two different settings result in intense conflict and violence in one but not the other. Often, interest-based accounts cannot explain why hypothesized preconditions for intense conflict, such as ethnic group inequalities, produce high conflict in some places but very little in others. Nor do they help us understand why some societies with relatively little intergroup inequality, such as Northern Ireland, have a great deal of conflict and violence, while others with high inequalities, such as post-apartheid South Africa, have far less intergroup conflict than many expected.

What is missing from many rationalist political analyses is attention to group identity and the role it plays in ethnic conflict. Group identity is a collective process that connects individuals to groups and defines shared worldviews and interests (Northrup 1989). It is tied to culture and cultural expressions that mark groups as distinct from each other. Identities are frequently articulated through, and contested around, collective memories and mundane, everyday cultural practices such as parades, flag displays, language, clothing, religious practices, and public monuments that symbolically connect the past and present and are visible in a region's symbolic landscape. Mundane practices that represent one group to its members become polarizing when their expression is felt as a threat by a second group, and/or when attempts to limit the practices are perceived as a threat by the group performing them.

Before I go further, a brief mention of how I am using a few key terms is in order. By culture I refer to the shared system of meaning that people use to make sense of the world (Geertz 1973a; Ross 1997; 2002). Culture is expressed in a wide variety of symbolic forms, some highly formalized (e.g., religious and national rituals), others less formal but widespread (e.g. language, clothing, food, games). Sometimes culture is expressed in physical forms that define the symbolic landscape such as monuments, murals, or banners or at sacred sites; some of these are natural like rivers or mountains; other forms are human constructions such as holy places or battleground memorials. Attention to symbols, rituals, and the narratives that members of a group use to make sense of the world is key to understanding how culture shapes their lives and their collective behaviors. I have sought a single phrase that encompasses the many different forms of cultural conflict of interest here and often the term "cultural expression" is appropriate but sometimes I use the terms "cultural performance" and "cultural enactment." What they share is that each refers to contextually significant activities, objects, and/or symbols that have strong emotional meaning and become focal points of intergroup conflict. Analyzing the dynamics of these conflicts and their settlement can provide us with useful insights about the roots of ethnic conflict and its mitigation.

To examine contestation over cultural expressions and performance, I extend my earlier work to develop and utilize the concepts of psychocultural narratives and dramas; those help offer a more complete understanding of ethnic conflict than an interest-base approach alone can provide. The analysis links collective psychological and social processes, placing identity issues and their cultural enactments at the center of ethnic conflict. It examines cultural expressions in ethnic conflict as markers of divisive identity and mutually exclusive positions. At the same time, the socially and contextually constructed nature of cultural expressions and identities, and the redefinition of, or changes in, the meaning of cultural narratives, offer opportunities for conflict mitigation between former opponents, and allow them to develop a greater sense of interdependence and mutually beneficial cooperative relations.

Cultural expressions are not just surface phenomena. They are *reflectors* of groups' worldviews and on-going conflict that can help us better comprehend what a group's deepest hopes and fears are, how it understands an opponent's actions and motives, and what a good enough agreement with an adversary would provide. Cultural expressions play a *causal* role in conflict, when they make certain action possibilities more plausible, and therefore more probable, than others as they direct collective understandings of the motives, interests, and behaviors of the in-group and of opponents. In addition, cultural expressions serve as *exacerbaters* or *inhibiters* of conflict. Cultural expressions and the narratives associated with them communicate a worldview that ranges from highly exclusive to highly inclusive. The more that exclusivity and mutual incompatibility are expressed, the harder it is for opponents to alter their relationship; conversely, the more that cultural expressions are, or become, inclusive, the more likely it is that the parties can deal successfully with differences.

Cultural identities, from this perspective, are both barriers to, and opportunities for, the mitigation of ethnic conflict. The argument developed here is that movement toward constructive conflict management in long-term intergroup conflicts is facilitated through the development of inclusive narratives, symbols, rituals, and other cultural expressions in contexts where mutually exclusive claims previously predominated. Signed agreements between long-standing opponents, such as Protestants and Catholics in Northern Ireland, are only one step in a peace process. A cultural perspective obliges us to go beyond formal agreements to recognize ritual and symbol as crucial to the implementation of agreements for peacemaking and peacebuilding. Before opposing parties can come to the table to renegotiate their incompatible interests and change their behaviors and relationship, there often needs to be bridging in the form of inclusive cultural expressions that link formerly opposing communities or redefine older rituals to be less threatening and exclusive.

Cultural expressions that become the focal points in ethnic conflicts take many forms; the chapters that follow offer extended cases that include contested issues of parades, festivals, language, archeology, and holy sites, flags, monuments, museums, and clothing from Northern Ireland, England, Catalonia, Québec, Jerusalem, India, the US, South Africa, and France. The cases range from ones such as the Israeli–Palestinian conflict in which violence has been high to those such as Québec or France where it is low; in addition, they vary in the extent to which the conflict is currently intense and bitter, such as Northern Ireland, to those in which it has moved in a more constructive direction, such as Catalonia.

The roots of this inquiry lie in an earlier study I conducted on cross-cultural differences in conflict and conflict management in 90 pre-industrial societies (Ross 1993a; 1993b). That analysis showed, first, how both structurally rooted interests and psychoculturally based identities independently explain a society's level and targets of conflict and violence, and second, that both also matter in conflict mitigation. Despite being a political scientist I became particularly interested in the psychocultural side of conflict and its management and argued in my conclusions that interpretations are central to conflict behavior because conflict evokes deep-seated emotions in situations that are highly ambiguous and often unstructured. The combination of emotion and ambiguity readily produces psychic threat, leading to regression with a return to earlier experiences, and shapes how participants react to a conflict. Such interpretations are cultural, not just personal, when they are nurtured and socially reinforced, linking individuals in a collective process (1993b: 192). I hypothesized that especially in long-term intractable conflicts a prerequisite to constructive conflict management is modifying competing psychocultural interpretations or narratives so that the parties in conflict come to believe that there are people on the other side with whom they can negotiate, and issues that are negotiable. After completing the cross-cultural study, I began asking myself why in so many ethnic conflicts expressive practices and sacred places produce intense disputes that outsiders quickly dismiss as irrational, and how a better understanding of this phenomenon could help us manage these conflicts more effectively. This volume brings together my answers to these questions, placing at center stage the competing accounts of participants in conflict. I ask little about whether or not they are "true" and a lot about how they shape beliefs and behaviors about one's own side, an opponent, and what constitutes appropriate and inappropriate action.

The goal of this book is to offer an alternative way to think about successful and unsuccessful ethnic conflict mitigation to enrich more well-known structural and interest-based approaches. It is intended to help people studying ethnic conflict make better sense of it and to aid participants and third parties seeking constructive outcomes. The key points I emphasize include: taking seriously participants' own accounts to identify emotionally significant elements that must be part of any settlement; making sense of why and how the narratives are emotionally powerful; examining how the narratives shape beliefs that facilitate the choice of some actions over others; analyzing the power of collective memories in linking individuals to larger social and political identities; emphasizing the widespread use of imaginative and politically effective culturally grounded expressions and enactments to make claims, build commitment, and mobilize action; considering the ways that political actions shape identity, culture, and interests; identifying psychocultural narratives about peoplehood; and recognizing how the constructed nature of narratives makes possible successful conflict mitigation. To begin, the next section of this chapter introduces two conflicts that are treated in greater length later: parade conflicts in Northern Ireland, and language conflict between Catalonia and Spain. The subsequent section outlines core questions in the psychocultural analysis of ethnic conflict and specification of some limits to the cultural analysis of conflict; and the final section explains my use of the concepts of culture, identity, and ethnic conflict in this book.

Getting started: Northern Ireland and Catalonia

Northern Ireland

After generations of violent conflict, both Catholic and Protestant paramilitary groups have since 1994 (mostly) observed a ceasefire in Northern Ireland. In 1998 the major political parties, along with the British and Irish governments, reached a negotiated agreement, variously called the Good Friday Agreement (by most Catholics) or the Belfast Agreement (by most Protestants). It called for a return to self-rule, and was ratified through a referendum by a majority of citizens in each group. However, implementation of the agreement has been slow and incomplete. Conflict did not disappear overnight, although it has taken new, less violent forms with particular focus on cultural expressions such as parades and official insignias. Listening to the parties describe what is at stake in these conflicts quickly reveals the deepest fears and insecurities that still divide the people of the region, and the divergent narratives about Protestant Loyal Order[1] parades and other cultural expressions.[2]

Following time-honored traditions, throughout the "marching season" in Northern Ireland Protestant men in dark suits and bowler hats assemble at local lodges, attend church services, and hold parades to mark various sacred days, with a particular emphasis on two dates in the first half of July: July 1, the anniversary of the Battle of the Somme in 1916, in which many soldiers from Northern Ireland died; and July 12, the day when, in 1690, William of Orange's Protestant forces defeated Catholic King James' troops at the Battle of the Boyne. Protestant accounts of the parades stress their solemn, religious nature and the occasions they mark (Lucy and McClure 1997). Banners celebrate key events in Protestant history and highlight important religious themes, symbols, and persons. Bands accompany the marchers playing familiar music, and at significant parades important politicians address the crowd (Bryan 1997; Fraser 2000a; Jarman 1997).

Catholic narratives about the parades emphasize their celebration of the Protestant triumphalism and the oppression that marked centuries of British rule and Protestant domination in the region. The aggressive music of the "blood and thunder" bands made up of young men often clad in paramilitary symbols, and the viciously anti-Catholic lyrics of some of their songs are further evidence to Catholics that the parades are acts of aggression. Catholics in many parts of Northern Ireland have organized and demanded changes in the parades, and especially in parade routes passing through Catholic neighborhoods.

Parading identity in Northern Ireland has a long history and often raises sectarian tensions (Fraser 2000a). As a result, any parade in Northern Ireland can easily become an emotionally charged, exclusive political expression. The Loyal Order parades have been going on for generations, with periods of greater and lesser vigor, and more and less strife. In 1997, the British government took steps which led to the creation of a Parades Commission, charged with developing procedures for overseeing parades generally and especially for contentious ones.

[1] The term Loyal Order indicates the parades' expression of support for the continuing link between Northern Ireland and Britain and their ongoing allegiance to the British crown.
[2] A brief note on terms: Protestants are generally referred to as either Unionists because they favor the continued union of Northern Ireland and Great Britain or Loyalists because they are loyal to the crown. Catholics are variously called Nationalists or Republicans and favor reuniting the island into one political unit.

Even though there are only a little over 1.5 million people in the region, the Parades Commission reported that in 2003 there were over 3100 parades of which about 7 percent to 8 percent are "contentious," i.e. that they were brought before the Parades Commission, which holds a hearing before deciding whether they can proceed as planned or require modification.[3] The vast majority of parades are exclusively Protestant (70%) or Catholic (4%) affairs that mark, celebrate, or commemorate events of significance to each community,[4] are typically celebrations of in-group solidarity, and are widely perceived as statements of domination or resistance (Bryan 1997; Jarman 1997). While Catholics living on or near the Loyal Order parade routes strongly resent the parades, and the often-aggressive behavior of the participants, Protestants contend that restrictions on parading along "traditional" routes are an infringement of their religious and political rights. In recent years there have been confrontations with police, and violence and death associated with parades, especially those in South Belfast and Portadown.

The annual parade in Portadown in County Armagh, long a site of sectarian violence, has been especially contentious for quite some time. In the 1980s, the police rerouted it away from a Catholic area near the start of the route after several years of severe violence (Bryan 1997). From 1995 through 1997, following the IRA and other paramilitary ceasefires, the police announced a ban on the last part of the parade down the Garvaghy Road through another Catholic neighborhood; and each year they then reversed their position and allowed the parade to proceed. Angry Catholics attacked the police. In 1998, the first year of its existence, the new Parades Commission addressed the Portadown situation, insisting on dialogue between the Orange Order and the Catholic Residents' Association; when the Orange Order refused to negotiate, the Commission prohibited the marchers from returning to their Lodge along the Garvaghy Road. Protestant violence in Portadown and deaths in other parts of the province followed. Though the violence has since decreased,

---

[3] http://cain.ulst.ac.uk/issues/parade/pc/pc231204ar.pdf. The Parades Commission also reported that in 2002 they rerouted forty-six loyalist parades and imposed various restrictions on others. In addition, there were twenty-six disorderly incidents involving Loyalist parades, most typically involving clashes between marchers and their supporters and nationalist protesters. Jarman (1997: 118–19) and Fraser (2000:4) report data from the mid 1990s on the number of parades in Northern Ireland that are quite similar.

[4] The remaining 407 parades are not classified as either Loyalist (Protestant) or Nationalist (Catholic) and include such events as May Day parades held by trade unions and Salvation Army parades. More details on parades in Northern Ireland are provided in Chapter 4.

the annual confrontation has produced a yet unresolved stalemate and seven years later each July in Portadown there are still large numbers of security forces, including army units who flood the fields beneath Drumcree church and string barbed wire to prohibit the marchers from completing their circuit.

The Portadown District Orange Order Lodge insists the issue is a matter of free speech and the "right to walk the King's highway." For years, their "civil rights website" has proclaimed support for equality, justice, tolerance, and respect; it prominently displays the words of Martin Luther King, "Somewhere I read of the freedom of assembly. Somewhere I read of the freedom of the press. Somewhere I read that the greatness of America is the right to protest for right. And so just as I say, we aren't going to let any injunction turn us around. We are going on."[5] To dramatize their position, in 1998 a small group of Orangemen camped out in the field next to Drumcree church vowing not to leave until they were allowed to walk down the Garvaghy Road to return to their lodge. "Here we stand. We can do no other," proclaims the sign next to the church where they have since been camped symbolically.

Catholic opposition to the present parade route emphasizes their experiences of long-term victimization, and their right to be free from intimidation, and asks why the parade route isn't simply changed as many have been in other towns and cities, including some in the early 1980s in Portadown (Bryan 1997). Catholic residents' associations in Portadown and elsewhere (which Protestants often dismiss as Sinn Féin fronts)[6] have demanded that parade organizers negotiate contentious questions surrounding parades with them and have declared, "No consent, no parade." For Catholics (and for the Parades Commission), dialogue and negotiations are the proper mechanism for managing differences over parades; they point to other places in Northern Ireland where negotiations have produced agreements around parades that have allowed them to proceed in ways that each side has accepted. (An important example of this conflict mitigation process, found in Londonderry/Derry, is discussed in Chapter 4.) In contrast, many Orangemen, such as those in Portadown, reject the idea that their basic, traditional right to parade needs to be negotiated, let alone with Sinn Féin and former IRA members.

---

[5] http://www.orangenet.org/civilrights/
[6] Sinn Féin, currently the largest Catholic political party in the region, is the political wing of the Irish Republican Army (IRA).

Introduction

The Parades Commission has pushed the Orange Order to enter into negotiations and asserts that it considers the essence of engagement to be attempts at genuine communication between protagonists to a particular parading dispute.

This on-going conflict around parades is so polarized and so stuck because conflicts about parades in Northern Ireland are not fundamentally about freedom of speech or religion or protection from intimidation, but about the threatened identities of people in the region. "Put simply, the parades issue goes to the heart of the deeply fractured society that, sadly, Northern Ireland represents" (North 1997: 41). The importance of social identity and its expression in ethnic conflicts, how it is symbolized and communicated, and how it affects political behavior and beliefs is central to the analysis that follows (Ross 1997). Focusing on identity is especially useful in explaining ethnic conflict's intensity, and how the content and salience of identity variously resists and yields to change (Ross 1993a; 1997; 2001a). Understanding identity directs our attention to the deepest fears that drive ethnic conflict, as for example when an Orange Order website proclaims, "If Orange parades continue to be stopped, then over the years, Protestant culture will be slowly strangled."[7]

Catalonia

Catalonia is a region of 6 million people in northeast Spain that includes Barcelona. There is a long history of tension between the Spanish state and the region which was once independent politically and linguistically. Today Catalans are bilingual, speaking Catalan, a romance language closely related to Provençal, and Castilian (Spanish). Catalonia was incorporated into the Spanish state over several centuries[8] and Castilian came to be spoken more and more, especially among the region's elites (Laitin 1989). Industrialization, in-migration, and a Catalan linguistic and cultural revival marked the nineteenth century as Catalans pressed for regional autonomy. However, in the 1920s Spanish dictator Primo de Rivera restricted Catalan cultural expression and political liberty, both of which were revived briefly during the Republic in the early 1930s. The region was a site of intense fighting and brutal violence during Spain's

---

[7] http://ulsterloyal.freeservers.com/parades_culture_tradition.html
[8] Catalans solemnly mark September 11 as the day when they finally lost their autonomy through their defeat in the Battle of Malplaquet in which they were on the losing side in one of the many wars of Spanish Succession.

civil war (1936–39) and under Francisco Franco (1939–75) Catalan autonomy and cultural expressions were severely curtailed. His regime banned the use of the language in education and government, prohibited publication in Catalan, and burned books written in the language.[9]

There was a slow, unofficial revival of Catalan as a spoken language in the later years of Franco's rule, and when he died in 1975 Catalans were poised to demand political and linguistic autonomy for the region, and the return to the use of Catalan in schools. At the time, many observers expected that the strong emotions surrounding these issues would spark conflict and violence between the Spanish state and hard-line Catalan nationalists. Although there was a good deal of tension and tough talk exchanged between the parties, there was no significant violence on either side. Catalan cultural expression is often strident and even aggressive but never violent. There have been repeated requests for direct representation in European Community organizations, for example, that annoy, and even exasperate, the Madrid government, but the dueling visions of Spain have not clashed violently.

Two competing narratives have long existed here, but since 1975 the opposing sides have found ways to bridge them to avoid stalemate. Since a good theory of ethnic conflict needs to account for the absence of violence and conflict as well as its presence, we have as much of an obligation to explain the success of the Spanish government and Catalan nationalists in developing a mutually acceptable solution without resort to violence as we have to explain the failure to do so in Northern Ireland.

There is a long history of tension between the Spanish state and the demands for linguistic and cultural autonomy from the historical nationalities in Spain,[10] and there have been periodic violence and wars pitting the regions against the center, which is located, geographically and politically, in Madrid. At various times, including during Franco's rule, the center's wishes dominated. However, following Franco's death, the new Spanish government, including many who had served under Franco, realized that change was needed both within the country and in Spain's relationship with its Common Market neighbors. Democratization and

---

[9] The regime moved quickly against those expressing Catalan nationalist sentiments. For example, in 1960 the future Catalan leader Jordi Pujol was sentenced to seven years in prison and served two and a half for having led a Catalan nationalist campaign that included singing the Catalan anthem in Barcelona's Opera House at a time when Franco was visiting Barcelona.

[10] The term refers to the Catalans, Basques, and Galicians.

liberalization were seen as essential, and the new constitution provided for significant regional autonomy including linguistic rights in ways that recognized multiple identities – Catalan nationality and Spanish citizenship. King Juan Carlos, Franco's chosen successor, strongly supported these efforts and the country's transition to democracy (Linz, Stephan, and Gunther 1995).

Catalan quickly returned to the schools and media in Catalonia, while Castilian remained the official language of Spain. The result was official bilingualism in the region that the Spanish state accepted. Making this work took some time given that even among those who spoke Catalan during the Franco years, most did not know how to read or write it. Three decades later, however, this has changed; both languages are now used in schools and universities, the media, and government. What is even more striking is that many Catalan speakers today are either immigrants from other parts of Spain (and especially Andalusia) or their descendants, who have been willing to learn and use Catalan. In great part this is because Catalans have emphasized an inclusive, non-racial definition of what it means to be Catalan. As the Catalan nationalist leader, Jordi Pujol has said, "A Catalan is someone who lives and works in Catalonia."[11]

The negotiated relationship between Madrid and Catalonia produced a mutually acceptable arrangement in contrast to the situation between the Spanish state and the Basques, although the Basques have even more autonomy than the Catalans.[12] All but the most hardline Catalans are more or less satisfied with the arrangements and despite tensions at several points in the past twenty-five years, there has been no violence. Barcelona has prospered both economically and culturally and it is referred to as one of the four motors of southern Europe. Nonetheless, since 1980 the relationship between the center-right Catalan government and Madrid has sometimes been complicated. At times, both the right and the left in Madrid have found the Catalans insufficiently attentive to the needs of Spain as a whole and complain that Catalans look north toward Europe too much and south too little.

---

[11] Many add that the unstated premise here is that the person speaks Catalan. Of course, in practice the designations are more nuanced.

[12] A number of authors have sought to explain differences in the two cases. Most focus on the very different nature of Catalan and Basque identity – the former as more cultural and inclusive and the latter as more genealogical and exclusive – and differences in the social organization of the two communities (see for example, Conversi 1997; Laitin 1995).

Many of these tensions came to a head symbolically when in the mid-1980s Barcelona was awarded the 1992 Summer Olympic Games. Putting on the games required complex cooperation between the city, the region, and the Spanish state and raised a number of identity issues. Perhaps the most striking illustration of this was a two-page advertisement that appeared in major North American and European papers a few months prior to the games, asking on the left-hand page "Where is Barcelona?" On the right-hand page came the response, "In Catalonia." Needless to say, the Spanish government, which was paying the most money to host the games, as well as many non-Catalans in Spain, was not pleased.

There were, however, pressures that limited the conflict to symbolic expressions. The Catalans wanted to show they could put on such a visible world-class event without any problems and to present Barcelona as a dynamic world-class city, while the Spanish hoped the games would showcase their country's economic growth and political accomplishments since Franco. In the run-up to the games, conflicts arose continually concerning the designation of official languages, the flags to be displayed, and the anthems to be played. These issues came to a head prior to the games at the 1989 inauguration of the Olympic stadium – one that had originally been built to hold an alternative games to Hitler's Berlin Olympics in 1936 – when the Catalans jeered long and hard as King Juan Carlos entered. It was clear that symbolic issues threatened how the world would view Spain and Catalonia.

In the six months leading up to the July 1992 games there were extensive Catalan symbolic displays and a marked rise in tension that never became violent. In the end, Castilian and Catalan were given equal status among the official languages and both flags and anthems were featured in a way that all sides felt was balanced. During the opening ceremonies, the king entered the stadium while the Catalan anthem was playing – to inhibit jeers from the crowd – and then pronounced the games open in Catalan and drew a huge warm response from the crowd. He was visible throughout the games and served as a symbol of the Spanish state but also through his presence and the nature of his involvement offered a clear legitimation of the expression of Catalan identity. Catalan flags and cultural expressions were ever present during the games, but there were no violent incidents. In the end, when the games were over, both Catalans and people throughout the rest of Spain believed the Olympics had been successful and expressed pride in the achievement (Hargreaves 2000). There was increased support for the idea that people could be both Catalan and Spanish and that these two identities were not mutually exclusive.

When hearing about long-standing conflicts in Northern Ireland, such as those involving the parades, there is a tendency for outsiders to simply dismiss them as unavoidable and irrational and to symbolically seal off the region as "a place apart." In contrast, reactions to the accommodation between Catalan nationalism and the Spanish state are sometimes explained in a different way – as examples of the pragmatism and rationality of the Catalans and the reasonableness of the post-Franco Spanish state. Simply to accept this explanation is also a mistake for there was no inevitability to the outcome that was reached; many contemporary observers expected considerable disarray and violence. Despite a reputation for reasonableness, Catalan resistance to the Spanish state has sometimes been strong, and the violence in Barcelona around social issues in the nineteenth and early in the twentieth centuries has been far from simply pragmatic on many occasions. The fact that the conflict evolved in a deescalatory direction didn't mean that this resolution, or others described in this book, was inevitable or that initial differences between the parties were not great.

Neither of these common responses to conflict or its absence offers any real explanation for why and how differences on some cultural issues turn bitter and violent and others are managed constructively. Nor do they recognize that two decades ago few observers would have predicted either that in Northern Ireland cultural questions such as parades would move to the center of the conflict, or that the post-Franco state would effectively negotiate extensive linguistic and cultural rights and meaningful levels of political autonomy for the country's historical nationalities.

Cultural expressions and ethnic conflict: initial questions

What are ethnic conflicts about?

It would be foolish to suggest there is a single short answer to this question, for ethnic conflicts are about competing interests, constitutional arrangements, and political power, as well as about incompatible identities. Evaluating competing theories of ethnic conflict is not a goal here as I have treated this question in prior publications emphasizing the differences between structural theories that focus on interests and psychocultural theories that stress incompatible identities (Ross 1993a;

2000a; 2001a). Interests and identities are often highly interconnected (Bates, Rui J. P. de Figueiredo, and Weingast 1998).[13]

Identity issues are not just peripheral concerns; they are at the core of long-term conflicts such as in Northern Ireland and Catalonia. In these intense conflicts, the contending parties present mutually exclusive positions in which if one side wins the other necessarily loses. In conflicts like these each side deeply fears that recognizing the claims of the other invalidates their own. As a result there is an escalation of demands and actions and an increase in claims that leave little room for compromise or mutual recognition.

In Northern Ireland, opposing identities continue to be defined in mutually exclusive terms. Each side continues to fear the other and sees them as seeking total victory. For Catholics this means fears of a return to unfettered Protestant rule in which Northern Ireland was "a Protestant state for a Protestant people," as Northern Ireland's first Prime Minister James Craig put it. For Protestants, the fear is that if Ireland is reunited as most Catholics would like, they will become a small minority whose rights will be ignored. To date, despite the signed agreement that insures protections against both of these outcomes without majority consent, many on each side remain distrustful and the self-government that the 1998 agreement promised has functioned for only a fraction of the eight years since the agreement was signed. The problem, it seems, lies not in the arrangements which constitutional scholars have saluted for their ingeniousness, but in the mutual distrust that makes the present-day stalemate preferable to the risks of cooperation.

During Franco's reign, conflict between the central government in Madrid and the Catalans was framed in mutually exclusive terms and Franco refused to recognize that Catalan or Basque identity could be compatible with a Spanish one. In contrast, the ability of post-Franco

---

[13] The distinction between the two is analytic, and people caught up in conflicts intuitively understand their empirical linkage. For example, it is easy to see how the achievement of certain interest goals, such as gaining a political office or improved job opportunities, can, at the same time, address a group's identity and recognition concerns. To the extent that interest claims are "tests" of a group's acceptance as a legitimate political player, then achievement of the interest claims also addresses concerns about identity. However, there are times when a group may be ready to drop or alter an interest claim if identity needs can be met in another manner, especially when identity-based fears of exclusion diminish. Understanding intense ethnic conflict as involving both interests and identities thus increases not only our analytical understanding but also our options for constructive conflict management (Ross 1993a; 1993b).

Spain to recognize its citizens' multiple identities and to develop political arrangements for their expression provided the space for the redefinition of the conflict in more inclusive directions and isolated the remaining hard core on either side – those who sought either Catalan independence or Franco-like centralization – as is explained at greater length in Chapter 6.

Why the intensity?

A striking feature of many identity-based ethnic conflicts is the emotional investment parties make in what to outsiders often seem unimportant matters. The fact is, however, that any matter invested with emotional significance is no longer trivial to those involved, and intransigent intergroup disputes quickly become characterized by perceived threats to group self-esteem and legitimation (Ross 1995). In this, dynamic identity issues and threats to the group are at the core of peoples' concerns. Furthermore, the conflict becomes such a central part of their identity that giving it up is giving up a part of oneself (Kaufman 2001; Kelman 1999; Northrup 1989). Such emotion-laden conflicts are especially difficult to settle. Often the fact that each side feels the same intense emotions makes it difficult to recognize their common experiences and shared parts of their narratives (Nic Craith 2002), and promotes a "double minority" view of the conflict in which each side feels vulnerable. For example, Protestants and Catholics in Northern Ireland each see themselves as threatened and have trouble acknowledging the other's parallel perceptions. This is because each party's emotional concerns make it very difficult to hear, let alone acknowledge, the other's account, especially when their own actions may be the root cause of an adversary's feelings and behavior. Battles over cultural expressions and the symbolic landscape are central to group recognition and identity; it should not be surprising that conflicts around cultural questions are intense when they raise basic issues concerning a group's legitimacy and deep fears about threats to its existence. Central to understanding the intensity of some identity conflicts is uncovering the existential fears group narratives evoke as they try to explain the social and political world.

Why does each party offer such different accounts of the same conflict?

How can people who have been in intense interaction and conflict with each other for so long have such different ideas about what the conflict is

symbols, a system of inherited conceptions expressed in symbolic forms by means of which men [*sic*] communicate, perpetuate, and develop their knowledge about and attitudes toward life" (Geertz 1973a: 89).[15] Culture can be examined through the narratives people recount to explain their own and others' actions as well as the institutions and practices found in a society (Ross 1997; 2002). This definition of culture emphasizes public, shared meanings. Behaviors, values, institutions, and social structure are understood not as culture itself but as culturally constituted phenomena (Spiro 1984). These behaviors include emotionally significant ritual actions that link people across time and space while distinguishing between in-group and out-group members. Within-group connections are preserved in group memory through oral, written, and visual accounts and reenacted through social action and ritual performance. Culture from this perspective is a worldview that includes cognitive and affective beliefs about social reality and assumptions about when, where, why, and how people in one's culture and those in other cultures are likely to act in particular circumstances (Avruch 1998; Chabal and Daloz 2006; Ross 1997). In sum, culture is a framework for interpreting the world that marks "a distinctive way of life" characterized in the subjective we-feelings among group members, and expressed though specific behaviors including customs and rituals – both sacred and mundane – that mark the daily, yearly, and lifecycle rhythms that connect people across time and space.

Cultures and cultural differences do not themselves cause conflict (Eller 1999; Posner 2004) but are the lenses through which the causes of conflict are refracted (Avruch and Black 1993: 133–34). People begin conflicts, often for what they believe are only economic and political reasons; but it is important to understand how leaders and groups evoke cultural meanings and the deep feelings they evoke in organizing collective action. Eller (1999: 48) describes culture as a code for authentic and alternative groupness, and the basis of context-specific political claims. Cultural meanings and the emotions associated with them are not invariant and inter-group interaction and contestation affect them. For example, in the Middle East and South Asia there are sacred sites that different religious communities have at times shared; at other times as conflict between the groups has intensified, exclusive claims for

---

[15] D'Andrade (1984: 88) points out the radical shift in the social sciences after the 1950s from the view of culture as behavior that could be understood within a stimulus-response framework to culture as a system of meaning. For a more complete discussion of culture as meanings and symbols see Schweder and LeVine (1984).

their use has increased. Cultural conflicts are not just out there ready to happen as Kaplan's (1993) "ancient hatreds" argument would have us believe. Rather, as conflicts evolve the intensity of emotions surrounding cultural expressions and enactments as well as their meanings often shift (Weeden 2002).

Many people have an image of culture as unified and monolithic. This is a serious mistake. The definition of culture I am using emphasizes only that people within a given cultural group understand, but not that they always agree with, one another (Avruch 1998; 2003). Understanding shared meanings is not the same as agreement in values or engagement in the same behaviors (Chabal and Daloz 2006; Cohen 1991). As LeVine argues, "Culture represents a consensus on a wide variety of meanings among members of an interacting community approximating that of the consensus on language among members of a speech-community" (1984: 68). This does not mean there is unity in thoughts, feelings, behavior and even conceptions of the social order. This point is crucial for my analysis for it helps us understand that within the cultural communities discussed in the following chapters there is frequent intragroup conflict and competition such as one finds between religious and secular Jews in Israel, federalists and supporters of independence in Québec, Republicans and Nationalists among Catholics in Northern Ireland, and integrationists and pluralists in France (Eller 1999). Culture, and its narratives, offer in-group agreement about meaning but not necessarily about substance. As a result conflict and its management is a two (at least) level game, with one level focusing on within group competition and the second on what occurs between groups. Finally, we need to recognize that what people who share a group identity *believe* is shared is often greater than what is *actually* shared, and is over-stated in the interest of presenting a unified, strong group to outsiders.

In a similar fashion, we often imply that cultures and ethnic groups are bounded, unified, and purposive entities, when in fact as Brubaker says "'Groupness' is a variable" (Brubaker 2004: 4). Ethnic and national groups are not organizations that charge dues and issue membership cards, and who is included and who is not can be murky and contested. Rather, they are affinity groups whose boundedness, unity and coordination vary across time and space (Barth 1969; Eller 1999). Our language gets in the way here however since we readily employ collective nouns to talk about large groups that are internally differentiated and often have more trouble acting collectively than the term "group" implies. We write "Israelis think ... " when it is the case that what we mean is "a good

19

number of Israelis, perhaps, an overwhelming majority of Israelis think …" But if we put in all the qualifying language to capture internal variation in every sentence a manuscript would quickly be unreadable. The point is that even though culture and ethnic identity are not bounded entities, they are nonetheless important concepts in understanding many social and political conflicts, and studying them has its own methodological complexity.

Identity-affirming cultural activities and institutions can play a central role in the pursuit of political goals, as anthropologist Abner Cohen (1969) observed over three decades ago. He pointed out that in many settings where explicit political organization is either not possible or not likely to be effective, cultural organizations build or maintain in-group solidarity and organize collective action. Cohen realized that intensive participation in shared cultural activities and organizations increased feelings of group distinctiveness, facilitated within-group communication, enhanced group decisionmaking, increased within-group authority, spread shared ideology, and promoted within-group discipline (1969: 201–11); these all facilitate ethnic groups behaving like interest groups.

Cohen's emphasis on culture is quite different from Samuel Huntington's (1993) often cited clash of civilizations. Whereas Huntington emphasizes political divisions built on broad-based long-standing cultural differences, Cohen is more interested in the shifting nature of culturally defined groups and cultural expression in response to changing contexts. For example, in Ibadan, a city in western Nigeria, he analyzes the rise of an Islamic brotherhood as a mechanism for political and economic coordination among Northern Nigerians whose numbers were too small to form an effective political party. In a more recent study, he uses the contested nature of the Notting Hill Carnival in London to examine the changing nature of the relationship between West Indians and native British in London (Cohen 1993).

Cohen's studies explore culture as a resource that groups, not always consciously, use strategically, although he also recognized culture's expressive power.[16] In his study of the Carnival in London, Cohen examines changing cultural meanings, contestation over the "ownership"

---

[16] While David Laitin (1986) contrasts this strategic use of culture with that of Clifford Geertz, his reading of Cohen is in my view too limited. Cohen, like Geertz, is also interested in how people construct meaning.

20

of cultural production (music and the instruments on which it is played), and conflict over cultural expression as mechanisms for the management of within- and between-group relationships. His analysis differs sharply from Huntington in that Cohen emphasizes the fact that many conflicts Huntington calls cultural or civilizational are, in fact, political, even though they are often framed in cultural terms and cultural issues play a central role in them (Eller 1999: 141, Ross 2002). While there is often an important linkage between culture and politics, as Huntington suggests, cultural differences themselves are not at the core of these conflicts. Culture is neither the root cause of ethnic conflict nor an epiphenomenon. Rather, conflict is about both material interests and collective cultural identities (Ross 1993a, 1997; Bates, Figueiredo, and Weingast 1998), and understanding a conflict's cultural frames is a central challenge to the analysis and constructive management of them. Rejecting as too simple the hypothesis that conflicts are *about* cultural differences is not incompatible with the proposition that culture plays a significant role in conflict and that cultural issues often encapsulate and symbolize the differences between the contending parties as cultural performance and memory become hotly contested and intertwined with strongly held political positions (Ross 1997).

Cultural enactment and performance refer to behavioral expressions that evoke central meanings, images, and metaphors rooted in collective memories that are emotionally significant for a group and its members. Obvious examples include celebration of national holidays, display of emblems such as flags, sacred music, funerals, and religious ceremonies in sacred locations. Cultural enactment is powerful because it is linked to cultural memory, and serves to renew memories across generations by expressing a group's most basic hopes and fears. Cultural enactment renews links among members while emphasizing distinctions between group members and outsiders. Performance and memory create emotional realities, making accompanying narratives seem truthful to group members though they often puzzle outsiders. The need for these tools for weaker or minority communities is obvious, but we must understand that dominant groups use culture as well to define the playing field and the rules of the game, to articulate and assert political claims, to mobilize supporters, justify their dominant position, and to control minorities, as for example in the development and implementation of state language policy (Laitin 1998). Dominant and subordinate groups that feel threatened can use performance to communicate identities that define

21

boundaries between themselves and outsiders and can make it more or less difficult to become a group member or hold multiple identities.

Conflict and identity

Cultural identities, such as ethnicity, connect individuals through perceived common past experiences and expectations of shared future ones. In linking people across time and space, identity both defines and reinforces social categories that organize a good deal of behavior. People sharing a group identity possess, to a greater or lesser degree, a sense of common fate including expectations of common treatment, joint fears of survival/extinction, and beliefs about group worth, dignity, and recognition. Identity involves group judgments and judgments about groups and their motives. For example, Horowitz (1985: 147–92) discusses the power of assigning the labels "backward" and "advanced" to ethnic groups in colonial and post-colonial settings and claims of entitlement that groups do or do not make as a consequence of such a designation.

Humans have an evolved predisposition for sociality and a well-developed capacity to form cohesive social groups (Howell and Willis 1989), and in-group identity provides the basis for a fundamental paradox of human existence. It facilitates physical and emotional survival and within-group cooperation; at the same time, strong in-group solidarity promotes out-group competition and conflict (LeVine and Campbell 1972).[17] Social identity, including attachment to a group, begins to develop at the earliest stages of the lifecycle and its intensity is crucial in explaining why people are willing to make great personal sacrifices in its name (Stern 1995).[18] People with the same identity share targets of externalization (Volkan 1988) and high emotional salience is attached to

---

[17] Campbell (1975) proposes that cultural institutions such as religion have been important in extending cooperative behavior beyond small related kin groups to far larger social aggregates. One could compile a long list of cultural practices which have effectively built upon this propensity to form groups even among individuals who have no prior first-hand knowledge of one another.

[18] Modern psychoanalytic writing is particularly helpful for understanding identity development and the relationship between individual and ethnic identity (Ross 1995). Unlike older, drive-based theories of psychodynamic functioning, contemporary object relations theory with its emphasis on linking a person's inner and outer worlds focuses on the social development of attachment (Bowlby 1969; Greenberg and Mitchell 1982). This work sees early social relationships as providing a template for ones which develop later in life, and it is especially concerned with the parts of the outer world brought inside and with inner parts projected outward (Stern 1985; Volkan 1988).

group differences that are emphasized through in-group symbolic and ritual behaviors even when the differences are objectively small (Eller 1999).[19] Normal development involves developing progressively wider attachments to those in one's interpersonal world and building connections to larger, more abstract entities such as the nation or ethnic group (Ross 1995).[20]

While there is widespread recognition that attachment to social groups is a powerful dynamic, there are significant differences among the ways social scientists theorize this attachment. A key difference occurs around the extent to which identities are seen as mutable and contextual versus enduring and even primordial. My own view is that both extremes are caricatures in their denial of the other position. As Smith (1991) argues, while group definition is more socially constructed than popular images hold, it is not as easily altered in the short run as some constructivist accounts suggest (also see Horowitz 2002).[21] A second significant difference is the power of rational interest maximization versus affective

---

[19] Freud's expression "the narcissism of minor differences" is very apt here.

[20] Normal development, facilitated by what Winnicott (1965) calls the good-enough mother, encourages both the attachment of the individual to others and separation-individuation, as a person builds both a sense of self and connections to a progressively wider circle of attachment (Mahler, Pine, and Bergman 1975). Winnicott (1958) describes the importance of transitional objects – teddy bears, soft towels, and other treasured objects – that link a child's inner and outer worlds, and are infused with high emotional significance. It is easy to extend this linkage process to social, cultural, and political objects – significant symbols and rituals which are first encountered in safe, within-group contexts, often in childhood, revisited in adolescence when peer groups and wider social attachments are especially salient emotionally, and embedded in daily practices and their culturally specific sights, smells, and sounds. Finally, it is important to recognize that identity is not fixed early in life and unchanging. Quite the contrary, since identity is complicated by the fact that there is great range in the form and content of groups humans create. Identity involves the capacity to distinguish between people who are like oneself and those who are different in specific settings; and depending on the context the same people may be variously classified as alike or different as people manage multiple identities.

[21] A related question is how to explain the striking contrast between the mutable, contextual, and constructivist character of ethnicity – widely documented in recent social research (e.g., Cohen 1969; Eller and Coughlan 1993; Waters 1990) – and popular political discourse and ritual behavior that see ethnic groups as fixed, unchanging, and often biological entities which fight over "ancient hatreds" (e.g., Kaplan 1993). Why is it that social scientists are so ready to be, at least partial, constructivists, while popular conceptions are primordialist? Probably this gap between social scientific formulations about social identity and popular images tells us a lot that is useful about how people understand the social world, about our powerful need to see social categories as "real" and stable, and about the threats posed to individual identity by a constructivist view of the social universe.

which cultural expressions play a leading role. These events emphasize the role of symbol and ritual in claim making and group mobilization, especially around contested cultural expressions (Kertzer 1988). They are rarely fully resolved, but they are settled for a time when the conflict is redefined away from incompatible principles to the symbolic and ritual domain where disputants can emphasize shared concerns and super-ordinate goals. Psychocultural dramas offer an excellent analytic tool for examining cultural contestation and for understanding new possibilities for managing ethnic conflicts constructively, because they reveal core issues for the parties in conflict.

Culture, identity, and conflict mitigation

Polarization and escalation around contested cultural expressions is common in ethnic conflict. However, these are not the only possible outcomes. Groups in conflict also draw on culture to redefine long-standing conflicts in more constructive directions (Kriesberg 2003). While all groups are able to define outside enemies in cultural terms, all cultural traditions also contain core images of peace and peacemaking, which can serve deescalation and reconciliation (Gopin 2000). As a result, conflict articulated around cultural issues offers an opportunity to reduce the intense emotions associated with contested identities and can serve as a powerful mechanism to bring former opponents into new institutional arrangements. For example, in the American South, conflicts over the Confederate battle flag and civil war monuments have often been harsh and unyielding. However, there are states, such as South Carolina and Georgia, and local communities, such as Richmond, Virginia, in which dialogue between white and black southerners has produced new, partially shared, narratives of the suffering and experiences of people from all communities in the past (Chapter 10). As a result, people have developed constructive outcomes that have included new, redesigned, and relocated flags and monuments that are more inclusive, that acknowledge losses on all sides, and that reinforce inter-group understanding and tolerance.

Attending to cultural expressions is not a substitute for politics and negotiation, but it can be a valuable supplement to them. Signed agreements between long-standing opponents, such as Protestants and Catholics in Northern Ireland, are only one step in the peace process. From a cultural perspective, implementation of agreements obliges us to recognize interpretation and narrative as significant parts of peacemaking and peacebuilding either by developing new inclusive cultural expressions that link different communities or by redefining existing ones so they become less threatening and exclusive.

The new cultural expressions and narratives that develop in peace-making and peacebuilding processes begin with the parties' frames of reference, and their recognition, often implicit, that cognitive approaches aimed at persuading opponents to change their positions are almost always efforts that fail when used alone. A more productive approach must acknowledge the threats to identity that groups perceive and seek to diminish them and in so doing to create space to actively and jointly envision alternatives to ongoing confrontation. Conflict mitigation from this perspective occurs when there are explicit connections made between inclusive cultural images and metaphors, and events on the ground. This can be seen in changes found in verbal expressions and gestures, such as occurred when white South Africans began to see majority rule as coming soon and many worked to facilitate it (Sparks 1995). Mutual acknowledgment of prior loss through symbolic and ritual expression, when linked to a common future, can supplement interest-based bar-gaining or efforts at cognitive redefinition (Volkan 1988; 1997). Cultural expression of emotional and ritual acknowledgment does not mean abandoning one's position, but can provide room for creative reformu-lations that can result in new more complex, more inclusive symbolic landscape, and less directly opposed identities, for example the emergence of a European identity after World War II (Kelman 1999).[23]

What psychocultural analyses can and can't answer

Psychocultural analyses often tell us little about the specific interests that will emerge as critical in a conflict and why the parties define their identities around one set of concerns rather than another. While psy-chocultural analyses can offer plausible explanations for the definition of a conflict once it has emerged, the theory behind the approach is not yet powerful in suggesting why one form of expression will become so much more contested than another. A third problem is that psychocultural analyses focus on broad-gauged phenomena and can easily ignore the role

---

[23] In divided societies, there are few shared symbols and rituals and often those that are strongly positive to one group have a completely opposite meaning for the other side. When rituals, such as recast holidays and festivals, link previously disputing groups, they can support new narratives of coexistence and even reconciliation.

of proximate forces, including institutions, that direct a conflict in one direction or another. Fourth, while a psychocultural analysis may point to cultural expressions that arouse strong emotions, by itself it says relatively little about what a group will do in a given situation. When will arousal lead to collective action, and when is it associated with anger and displeasure?

Psychocultural examinations of ethnic conflict can inform us about the ways the parties understand unfolding events, the core issues that are at stake, and the way they express their fears. They offer evidence concerning the way the parties frame a conflict, its intensity, and what is at stake in it. These offer valuable clues to make sense of a conflict's dynamics and insights about matters that must be addressed for it to be managed constructively. The narratives surrounding a conflict are not just reflectors of the conflict but operate as well as exacerbaters and inhibiters of further conflict, and play a causal role in make certain courses of action more plausible and appealing than others. However, the fact that examining culture and cultural contestation can be helpful for examining ethnic conflict and identity doesn't mean that cultural analyses have no limitations or weaknesses. Quite the contrary. Ethnic conflict is not just about identities but also about tangible interests and power, constitutional arrangements and values (Ross 1993a; 1993b). Lastly, an exclusive focus on culture can mask underlying structural issues, homogenize groups, and essentialize differences (Avruch 2003).

Plan of the book

This book develops an approach to understanding identity conflicts, their escalation and mitigation. Central to the argument is the hypothesis that bridging incompatible identities in long-term ethnic conflicts is not simply a matter of finding a clever interest-based constitutional formula for sharing a limited pie. Rather, solutions must also address basic threats to identity and the intense sense of victimization expressed in cultural and political acts. This requires both institutional and informal procedures that promote the redefinition of conflicts, advance conflict mitigation, and facilitate reconciliation between long-standing opponents. To accomplish these goals, we need to better understand the role of culture and its enactment in specific ethnic conflict situations and its potential for conflict mitigation. The cases considered here are not a random sample of ethnic conflicts in the world but rather a selection of those in which cultural contestation is a prominent feature, and that exhibit significant variation in their intensity and violence. I selected the cases on the dependent variable because my goal was not to estimate how often identities were crucial in ethnic conflict but rather to examine in detail the role of psychocultural dynamics in ethnic conflict. I would, however, hypothesize that the longer a conflict continues and the more intense it becomes, the greater the likelihood that identities will be important.

Chapters 2 and 3 provide the tools of analysis with an emphasis on psychocultural narratives, rituals, and dramas that animate group identity with important political consequences. The argument is then articulated through the exploration of specific cases of cultural contestation; it is clear that once one begins to look for this phenomenon in deeply rooted conflicts, they are not hard to find. The specific issues of contentious cultural expression examined in Chapters 4–10 illustrate somewhat different features of this phenomenon as I analyze the role of cultural performance and memory in Loyal Order parades in Northern Ireland, language policy and regional identity in Spain, the holy sites in the Old City of Jerusalem, Muslim headscarves in French public schools, memory and memorialization in post-apartheid South Africa, and the display of the Confederate battle flag in the United States. In each of these conflicts, even as each conflict has taken different forms over time, fundamental identity issues raising deep fears about each of the parties' cultural and even physical existence are at stake. In these cases, cultural redefinitions have been central in shaping whether, and how, there has been conflict mitigation. The final chapter reflects on the findings of the cases and emphasizes the role of cultural expressions, narratives, and ritual acknowledgment in peacemaking and reconciliation.

2

The political psychology of competing narratives

Introduction

How do people make sense of complex, emotionally powerful events and why do different, seemingly contradictory, accounts of what seems to outsiders to be the same event so frequently coexist? A short answer is that the different accounts reflect the divergent socially and culturally rooted experiences of opposing groups. Each group expresses collective memories and perceptions through narratives that seek to make sense of its experiences and to explain events in terms of their interpretations of past and future actions. Shared narratives recount and reinforce emotionally significant events and experiences within a group, sometimes through dramatic rituals but also as they frame daily interactions and behaviors.

Psychocultural narratives offer an entry point to examining intergroup conflict. In focusing on narratives I am not dismissing the importance of the structural features of states or the international system, or the competing interests of different actors. However, structures and interests are not my focus here.[1] Narratives matter for at least four different reasons.[2] First, a narrative's metaphors and images can tell us a great deal about how individuals and groups understand the social and political worlds in which they live and explain the conflicts in which they are involved (Roy 1994). Second, they can reveal deep fears, perceived threats, and past grievances that drive a conflict. Third, narratives are important because they privilege certain actions over others. Fourth, recounting narratives,

---

[1] Exploring connections between cultural frames and interests, strategies and alliances is an important question that is recognized but not explored here.

[2] My interest here is solely in the narratives the parties in a conflict recount, not in the analytic narratives that academic or other analysts develop to explain the unfolding of events.

or storytelling, is part of the processes through which communities are constructed and strengthened (Roy 2004).

Narratives can be analyzed in several ways. On the surface level, narratives are stories about the unfolding of events. At a deeper level, they reveal the motivations and reactions of the parties, sometimes explicitly and sometimes indirectly, through the emotionally significant images and metaphors they invoke. Analysis of narratives at these different levels helps us understand what is motivating the parties in a conflict. Of great analytic significance is what a narrative includes and excludes. Opposing parties' narratives do not necessarily directly contradict each other. Rather, opponents draw on distinct metaphors, emphasize different actions, cite clashing motivations, and communicate different affects to such an extent that it is sometimes hard for a naïve observer to recognize that the narratives protagonists offer are describing the same conflict. We need to consider all of these factors to develop constructive solutions.

This chapter has four sections. The first discusses nine features of psychocultural narratives and their origin in deeply rooted collective memories, cultural worldviews, and group identity. Second, I explore the diverse, but not mutually exclusive, roles narratives play in intense conflicts: as reflectors, exacerbaters or inhibiters, and/or causes of conflict. Third, I consider how narratives are significant in developing constructive solutions that move a conflict toward settlement. Good settlements must meet the real interests of the protagonists, but they must also be framed to address the emotional fears and threats that drove the conflict in the first place. Central to this process is the development of new narratives, ones which do not directly challenge older ones, but which reframe them in more inclusive terms that deemphasize the emotional significance of differences between groups and identify shared goals and experiences. Finally, as one example I examine competing Israeli and Palestinian narratives to illustrate the general points made about narratives in the first three parts of the chapter. This part emphasizes the core events, personalities, and images in each group's account in an effort to show how the same events are understood so differently by each side and how they serve as significant barriers to peacemaking.

Psychocultural narratives

Psychocultural narratives are explanations for events – large and small – in the form of short, common sense accounts (stories) that often seem simple. However, the powerful images they contain, and the judgments they make about the motivations and actions of one's own group and opponents, are emotionally powerful. Narratives are not always internally consistent. For example, group narratives often alternate between portraying one's own group as especially strong and as especially vulnerable – and the same holds for the portrayal of the opponent (Kaufman 2001).[3]

Narratives meet a number of needs and people are especially likely to rely upon them when they are disoriented and struggling to make sense of events in situations of high uncertainty and high stress. In such contexts, group narratives with their familiar shared images provide reassurance and relieve anxiety while reinforcing within-group worldviews. Yet it would be foolish to suggest that within-group narratives are fully consistent or that there is no variation in how members of an in-group understand a narrative or the parts of it they emphasize. Rather, narratives are best understood as existing at different levels of generality, and as having elements that can be added, discarded, rearranged, emphasized, and deemphasized. All cultural traditions have access to multiple existing narratives that provide support for diverse actions in anxious times. Narratives, therefore, are not made from whole cloth, but are grounded in selectively remembered, interpreted experiences and projections from them that resonate widely in a group.

Psychocultural narratives have a number of features relevant for the analysis of group conflict. Here I describe nine of these to which I return throughout this book in the analysis of specific conflicts: past events as metaphors and lessons; narratives as collective memories; selectivity; fears and threats to identity; in-group conformity and externalization of responsibility; multiple within-group narratives; evolution of narratives; enactment of narratives; and ethnocentrism and moral superiority claims. These features are not mutually exclusive; many have overlapping elements, but the particular combinations and emphases vary in ways that are analytically useful.

Past events as metaphors and lessons

Emotionally meaningful narratives are rooted in shared culture and worldviews that are filled with deeply emotive images and meanings that

---

[3] The general argument is found in LeVine and Campbell (1972). A specific recent example is that although the US is by far the world's strongest military power, a recently published book on the US military is titled *America the Vulnerable* (Lehman and Sicherman 2002), a post 9/11 theme that is frequently echoed.

provide the psychocultural narrative's building blocks. Narratives invoke the past in response to contemporary needs. "By placing the present in the context of the past and of the community, the myth of descent interprets present social changes and collective endeavors in a manner that satisfies the drive for meaning" (Smith 1999: 62). At times narratives manipulate time sequences through what Delivré calls ascending and descending anachronisms (Bernbeck and Pollack 1998: S140). The ascending anachronism pushes an event back in time away from the present to confer legitimacy on it, while the descending anachronism reaches back in time, ignoring large gaps so that people in the present can claim it as their own. These processes serve political claim-making by linking a selectively remembered past to the contested present in defense of the in-group.

Narratives are normative accounts with heroes and villains and lessons about how life should be lived. They offer in-group versions of the past, including the origin and development of the group; they invoke past threats and conflicts and enemies; and they laud group survival. In some cases, there is a conscious effort to develop a narrative with an eye toward future political goals, as was the case in Israel during the Zionist period, in South Africa among Afrikaners following the Boer War, and again in South Africa as part of the peaceful transition to the post-apartheid present (Moodie 1975; Thompson 1985; Zerubavel 1995). In most situations, however, worldviews and the narratives to which they give rise are much more like patchwork quilts sewn and re-sewn over a long time period.

Harkening back to historical events, such as battles, that make up collective memories is one common way in which a shared community of experiences is communicated. Serbs emphasize the defeat of Prince Lazar in Kosovo in 1389, Québecers continue to mark the swift English victory over the French on the Plains of Abraham in 1759, and some French still remark that it was the English who burned Joan of Arc. These references offer a direct link between a shared identity in the present and one in the past that is constructed more to meet contemporary needs than to reflect historical reality via *descending* anachronisms that overrepresent continuity between past and present. Weber's (1976) masterful analysis of the transformation of identity in nineteenth-century France is very relevant to the argument that the past is often understood through the needs of the present via *ascending* anachronisms. The French today regard themselves as having a long national history and identity. However,

Weber argues that in the French countryside there was only a weak identification with the state and French culture as late as the mid nineteenth century and that elites in Paris saw their mission as one of bringing civilization to the primitive peasants. His detailed account shows how peasants were transformed into patriotic Frenchmen and women between 1870 and 1914 through improved transportation and communication networks, universal primary education in French, and military service. The development of a strong French identity produced a population ready to make sacrifices in World War I after which the sense of a much longer-standing national identity was further strengthened, in part, to explain the high cost and sacrifice the war entailed.

Narratives exist at different levels of specificity.[4] Some focus on general questions such as the origin of the group, while others are built around particular events such as a single battle or the fate of a past leader. Narratives rely on timeless images and metaphors, and this "time collapse" evokes the emotional rather than the chronological immediacy of the past (Volkan 1997). Significant dates in a group's emotional history are often centuries old. For Protestants in Northern Ireland it is William of Orange's victory in the Battle of the Boyne in 1690, for Catalans it is their loss of autonomy in 1714, while for Jews, it is the destruction of the Second Temple in AD 70, reinforced by the Holocaust. The significance of these long-ago events is their lessons and warnings about the present. It is misleading and too simple to regard people citing events from the past as either prisoners or exploiters of it. Rather, past events are significant because the lessons drawn from them are viewed as timeless truths relevant to each generation.

Narratives as collective memories

Ethnic groups commonly recount their narratives in a chronological fashion that blends key events, heroes, metaphors, and moral lessons (Kaufman 2001). These recountings can be usefully thought of as collective memories and products of social interaction and individual memory processes (Devine-Wright 2003: 11). Collective memories, as Halbwachs (1980) and others have pointed out, are selective and what is

---

[4] Some authors use the term "master narrative" for an account that is, for example, associated with a group's origin or its more general core values, to distinguish it from more specific narratives that recount specific events or the life of an important figure in the group's history. I prefer simply to say that some are more general than others.

emphasized is facilitated through socially produced mnemonic devices such as physical objects that become repositories of group memories. Social memory for Nora is at odds with history and "takes root in the concrete, in spaces, gestures, images and objects" (1989: 9).[5] For Connerton too, collective social memory is clearly different from the more specific activity of historical reconstruction, which is more dependent upon evidence than is social memory (1989: 13–14). He argues:

> We may say, more generally, that we all come to know each other by asking for accounts, by giving accounts, by believing or disbelieving stories about each other's pasts and identities ... We situate the agent's behavior with reference to its place in their life history; and we situate that behavior with references to its place in the history of the social settings to which they belong.
>
> (Connerton 1989: 21)

Groups, from this perspective, remember many of the same events, battles, and heroes that a historian might consider important. However, the explanations for them, and how the two modes of understanding interpret their significance are often highly divergent. In addition, while groups see collective memories as unchanging, objective accounts of a group's history, it is clear that not only are there often major changes in emphasis and the specific events or people included in group narratives over several generations but at any one time there is also variation in which memories are most salient across generations (Devine-Wright 2003: 13). Memories associated with historical events may often be far more recent and develop as political claim-making a good deal after the event took place. For example, the French did not celebrate Bastille Day until a century after 1789, the 1690 Battle of the Boyne in Northern Ireland only became significant in the nineteenth century (Roe and Cairns 2003: 174), the 1838 Battle of Blood River in South Africa was unmarked for several decades after it took place (Thompson 1985:164), and the emotional connections between Jewish and Muslim identity and the holy sites in the old city of Jerusalem have been dramatically strengthened in the past century. Thus particular events whose lessons and metaphors are emphasized can vary as collective memories evolve.

The objective manner in which collective memories are often recounted should not blind us to their emotional significance as links

---

[5] What Nora (1989) terms *lieux de mémoire* does not seem to be best understood as only physical sites of memory for they are not simply locations that hold memories but can be located in images and expressions as well.

between the individual and the group as well as the past and present. Otherwise how could we explain the strong reactions people have to totally non-utilitarian physical objects such as buildings, potsherds, and statues on the one hand and to household objects on the other?

Connerton (1989) asks how collective memories are conveyed and sustained. While he sees a role for unconscious dynamics, his emphasis is on social processes that make connections to the past that are useful in the present.

> We experience our present world in a context which is causally connected with past events and objects … [and] We may say that our experiences of the present largely depend upon our knowledge of the past, and that our images of the past commonly serve to legitimate a present social order.
>
> (Connerton 1989: 2–3)

For Connerton, the past matters because it shapes our present needs. My argument emphasizes the opposite relationship, namely that how we understand the past grows out of our present needs. The difference is parallel to the distinction between ascending and descending anachronisms. However, like Connerton, I emphasize the role that social participation and especially ritual commemoration play in conveying and sustaining knowledge about the past, a topic to which we turn in Chapter 3. For him, commemorative ceremonies and bodily practices are important because they are performative, and participation builds commitment to the group and to its core narrative. Like Halbwachs (1980), Connerton emphasizes that through group membership "individuals are able to acquire, to localize and to recall their memories" (1989: 36). Memories exist in relationships and because the group is interested in the memories they "provide individuals with frameworks within which their memories are localized and memories are localized by a kind of [group] mapping" (Connerton, 1989: 37).

Selectivity

Events in the present and the past and memories of them are used in complex ways as groups selectively focus on events, individuals, and how they are linked. For this reason, while group narratives refer to the past, they are different from a history of the group.[6] The selectivity arises for at least

---

[6] Nora (1989) explores the complex relationship between memory and history.

three reasons; first, the narrative's focus on emotionally significant events is central in prioritizing what is included and how central its role is; second, narratives are a form of naïve realism, offering an account of the unfolding events that, while presented as objective, makes no effort to understand an adversary's perspective; and third, an opponent generally receives little attention in the in-group narrative. Because present needs and challenges shape the narrative's relevance, specific events in it shift in importance, elaboration, and emotional significance over time.

As a result, it is sometimes the case that when faced with competing narratives of groups involved in a conflict, outsiders may believe that they refer to different places or the same place at different points in time. Even when it is clear that this is not the case, the shared images and explanations for events that opponents provide often seem to have little in common. Protestants and Catholics in Northern Ireland, for example, while agreeing that there has been significant violence in the past thirty-five years, generally offer highly divergent explanations of the events, just as whites and blacks in the United States provide differing narratives on race relations. What this says is that actions rarely speak for themselves and must be interpreted within a wider cultural narrative (Bates, Figueiredo, and Weingast 1998).

Fears and threats to identity

Narratives are central to understanding "who is a people," to spelling out what in their "imagined past" is shared, what dangers they face, and offering a dream for their future. These narratives articulate an ethnic conception of the nation and its past that emphasizes the group's community of birth and shared culture (Smith 1991). Even in minimal conflicts with no physical danger, individual and group self-esteem seems to be quickly invoked and defended, affecting judgments about worthiness and resource allocation (Brown 1986; Tajfel 1981). In bitter conflicts, among the strongest feelings people express are fears about physical attacks on their group, and about symbolic attacks on its identity. While the distinction between physical and symbolic attacks is not hard to make conceptually, it is much harder to separate the two in the heat of a real conflict. Both fears involve feelings of vulnerability, denigration, and humiliation that link past losses to present dangers. Fears can be about physical security and/or the extinction of the self, family, and the group and its culture, including its sacred icons and sites. For example, even where directly related deaths do not occur, Smith (1991) uses the term ethnocide to describe deliberate efforts to destroy a community's cultural icons. Recent examples of such attacks include the Hindu dismantling of the mosque at Ayodhya in Northern India in 1992, destruction of cultural treasures and mosques in Bosnia (Sells 1996), the Taliban's toppling the ancient huge Buddhist statues in Afghanistan in 2001, and government schools for Native American children in the early twentieth century that removed children from their families, prohibited them from speaking their language or wearing their traditional clothing, and even insisted on cutting their hair to resemble mainstream notions of civilization.

In-group conformity and externalization of responsibility

All groups exert conformity pressures on their members, and these are greatest in high-stress conflict situations when there is assumed high within-group agreement about the meaning of events, heightened in-group solidarity, an intensified sense of linked fate that inhibits social and political dissent, and blame for the conflict directed outside the group (LeVine and Campbell 1972: 21). As part of this dynamic, disagreement quickly becomes disloyalty, and often those holding dissenting views are careful not to express them publicly, and sometimes even in private. Within communities, high conformity pressures increase acceptance of the dominant elements in a narrative. This does not mean, however, that once a narrative emerges, it is unchangeable. Quite the opposite; as new events unfold, there can be questioning and conflict around, and change in, a narrative following the emergence of alternative versions of events. For example, in South Africa there was high consensus among Afrikaners about the justice of, and religious basis for, apartheid when the Nationalist Party first came to power in 1948, but by the 1980s there was widespread rejection of many of its core elements which meant the Afrikaner narrative no longer had the same broad emotional appeal. In this context, majority rule and the idea of Afrikaners as white Africans in a rainbow nation became more acceptable.

Political leaders know intuitively that building consensus around the key elements in a narrative can be crucial to mustering support for their actions, which are presented as "naturally" following from shared understandings. In short, building active public consensus around a narrative is a form of public opinion formation that both provides a strategy on the part of leaders to mobilize public support and helps individuals reduce their own anxiety. A good indicator of this dynamic is the greater homogeneity of publicly expressed opinions, greater public agreement on key parts of the dominant narrative, and externalization of responsibility for the conflict onto an out-group as a conflict heats up. For example, prior to the outbreak of the Gulf War in January 1991, American public opinion as expressed in surveys, newspaper editorials, and in Congress was quite divided on the question of the war with Iraq. Once the fighting began, however, public support for military action increased dramatically. This is seen at the level of political elites as well. Just a few days before the outbreak of fighting, the Senate narrowly voted in favor of action. Within a few days, however, few Senators publicly offered significant criticism of the war effort. Few surveys, however, clearly identify the extent to which people actually change their attitudes toward what they perceive as the dominant view in their society versus the extent to which they engage in what Kuran (1995) calls preference falsification to avoid ostracism or even persecution.[7]

Multiple within-group narratives

There are times when group consensus around a narrative increases, but there are others when within-group differences remain highly significant. Often our language implies that opposing parties in a conflict are internally unified, although the reality in most long-term conflicts is that there is considerable diversity *within* each community that reflects significant debates and disagreements. In Northern Ireland and the Middle East, for example, for a long time there have been strikingly different narratives *within* both the majority and minority communities over the use of violence and the conditions under which peace is possible. These disagreements reflect deep differences in the fears the conflict evokes and contrasting motives attributed to the other side, and different images of a desirable future. Within each group, there are some who view the other community as capable of living in relative peace and harmony with their own group, and others for whom any move toward peace is viewed with

---

[7] Noelle-Neumann (1993) describes a different dynamic as "the spiral of silence," arguing that for many people the fear of social isolation is more important than holding an unpopular belief. Consequently, people are quite attuned to public opinion in their society and not only are less likely to speak out when they perceive themselves in a minority but also change their opinions. Smith, Bruner, and White (1956) also identify social motives as significant in opinion formation especially for issues that are not crucial to people.

suspicion, heightened insecurity, and is perceived as a potential first step toward even greater demands. These competing interpretations sometimes reflect in-group differences in interests, but the emphasis here is on their very divergent emotional interpretations.

There is no simple relationship between culture and narratives, just as Eller (1999: 8) notes that there is no one-to-one correspondence between culture and ethnicity. The very flexibility of culture means that it can give rise to multiple narratives to cope with the same event or series of events. These narratives may compete, as in the Northern Ireland and Middle East examples in the previous paragraph, or they may coexist, providing complementary perspectives on the same experience. Linenthal (2001b) illustrates this idea particularly well in his examination of how Oklahoma City residents, in particular, and Americans more generally, came to understand the 1995 bombing of the Murrah Federal building, which killed 168 people. He describes three different, but not necessarily incompatible, narratives to explain the attack and responses to it. The *progressive narrative* emphasized renewal and recovery as people struggled to rebuild the city and their lives. The *redemptive narrative* put the horrific events in a religious context, emphasizing the struggle between good and evil and ultimate redemption. The *toxic narrative* stressed the ongoing disruption and insecurity in many lives after the bombing and the losses that could not be restored. Linenthal's analysis shows how each of these narratives is deeply rooted in American culture. They exist side by side, he argues, and many survivors and family members of victims could readily identify how each of the three reflected their own experiences and emotions at different times.[8]

Evolution of narratives

While a key feature of narratives is how they frame the past, it is often the case that the meaning of the past is contested and periodically redefined both within and between groups. For many years, American historians and educators have had bitter disagreements over what should be taught in social studies and history courses (Nash, Crabtree, and Dunn 2000).

---

[8] A fourth narrative Linenthal (2001b: 81–108) identifies is one that focuses on the role of trauma in the aftermath of the bombing. This account, he argues, dominated the response of health professionals and some government agencies. It was significant in medicalizing and individualizing responses to the events, and providing health care professionals with a standard, acceptable formula for treating those touched by them.

40

Conflicts over the control of historical narratives are fought out in decisions about museum presentations and battlefield and other memorials (Linenthal 1993; 2001; Linenthal and Engelhardt 1996). Contemporary conflict over the past is intense because it has implications for group identity in the present.

As conflicts evolve, contested cultural expressions and their significance shift. Eller (1999:141) notes how in Sri Lanka pre-existing differences were reinterpreted to emphasize antagonism and hostility rather than tolerance and exchange. New issues can emerge or ones that were latent for a long time can heat up quickly. For example, Jewish migration to Israel over the past 120 years increased the emotional significance of Jerusalem's holy sites for Muslims and in response raised the significance of places in the old city for Jews, an issue that is explored in Chapter 6. Similarly, after 1991, language issues emerged as significant foci of conflict in former Soviet Republics, often taking on an intensity that many had not expected a decade earlier (Laitin 1998).

Enactment of narratives

Powerful narratives are far more than simple verbal accounts. Music, drama, and art, often filled with richly powerful images, enact and reinforce psychocultural narratives. "We Shall Overcome," the anthem of the American Civil Rights Movement, still brings tears to the eyes of many participants and supporters, evoking not only memories of the struggle, but also of its goals. Collective memories are often symbolized through physical objects and sites that represent group identity and through rituals that enhance a narrative's persistence and emotional significance. Examples of this connection abound in group holidays and rituals that assert relationships between the present and past through sacred objects, holy sites, special foods, and prayers. Zerubavel (1995: chs. 5 and 8) describes the development of Masada in the Zionist period as a pilgrimage site for Israeli youth, and the powerful emotional role it came to play for them. The creation of, and visits to, the Vietnam War Memorial in Washington helped Americans to move past their pro- and anti-war positions of the 1960s and 1970s and to develop a new, more inclusive account of the period. It is not so much that past disagreements over the war changed, but that the events became less salient in comparison with the shared recognition of the large-scale loss and suffering for families and communities that resulted from bringing people together at the site where they shared common emotions. Flags, memorial sites, inaugural ceremonies, sacred holidays, and state funerals are ritual objects and events that reinforce in-group identity and the emotional power of the group's narratives.[9] Of course, the same symbols that unify a group can also be sources of intense conflict between groups.

Ethnocentrism and moral superiority claims

Group narratives are not morally neutral. Rather, they portray a group's experiences in a favorable light emphasizing moral qualities the group has displayed in overcoming enemies and threats to its existence over time. In recounting challenges and triumphs, groups invariably emphasize moral qualities as the most crucial resources to explain their survival. Even when the group has greater resources than their opponents, a group's persistence is often accounted for in terms of the group's hard work or dedication. What is notable here is the in-group ethnocentric bias in claims that both justify a group's collective actions and frame the group as the protector of the highest moral virtues. This ethnocentric pattern consisting of interrelated attitudes and behaviors fosters in-group solidarity and out-group hostility (LeVine and Campbell 1972: 7–21). While the concept of ethnocentrism posits that an in-group cannot exist without a real or imagined out-group, its intensity can vary cross-culturally and is a function of both out-group actions in long-standing conflicts, including particular moral superiority claims, and in-group responses to them.

Narratives as reflectors, exacerbaters or inhibiters, and causes of conflict

Psychocultural narratives matter because of the various roles they play as reflectors, exacerbaters or inhibiters, and causes of conflict. The way

---

[9] Smith is clearly talking about enactment when he writes, "These concepts – autonomy, identity, national genius, authenticity, unity and fraternity – form an interrelated language or discourse that has its expressive ceremonials and symbols. These symbols and ceremonies are so much part of the world we live in that we take them, for the most part, for granted. They include the obvious attributes of nations – flags, anthems, parades, coinage, capital cities, oaths, folk costumes, museums of folklore, war memorials, ceremonies of remembrance for the national dead, passports, frontiers – as well as more hidden aspects, such as national recreations, the countryside, popular heroes and heroines, fairy tales, forms of etiquette, styles of architecture, arts and crafts, modes of town planning, legal procedures, educational practices and military codes – all those distinctive customs, mores, styles and ways of acting and feeling that are shared by members of a community of historical culture" (Smith 1991: 77).

events are framed and motives are attributed shape behavior. In short, how people understand a conflict affects what they are likely to do about it. When, for example, an opponent is seen as untrustworthy and insatiable in its demands, conciliatory steps are much less likely to be contemplated or to receive public support.

As reflectors, narratives tell us how those involved in a conflict understand it. These reflections of their "real world" provide significant cues to in-group members and can make it clear that dissenting from a societal consensus is risky. For third parties, narratives can provide insights into what each side needs in order to move a conflict toward a constructive outcome. Political psychologist Vamik Volkan writes about emotional "hot spots" that are part of all intense conflicts. When narratives bring them to the surface (Volkan 1997), this not only promotes understanding of the deeper roots of complex conflicts, but also can identify barriers to change and opportunities for strategic intervention. Unless each party's central fears and concerns are addressed, settlement efforts are not likely to be successful. In many situations, one side in a conflict has an incomplete, or even inaccurate, understanding of what opponents need and how they frame the situation (Jervis 1976). Kelman argues that one of the significant benefits of the Israeli–Palestinian problem-solving workshops he has organized for over thirty years is that key people on each side acquired a more realistic sense of what the other side was thinking and what they required in a settlement. The narratives participants recounted in his workshops often surprised those on the other side, reflecting deep fears that were central to each group that had to be understood for movement to peace talks to occur (Kelman 1987; 1995). As a result, new understandings developed, new language and metaphors came into use, and each understood much more fully and realistically what a peace process and eventual settlement could look like. Sparks (1995) describes a similar pattern in the peace process involving the African National Congress (ANC) and the white South African government in the 1980s, prior to Nelson Mandela's release from prison and the legalization of the ANC in 1990. Meeting in a variety of places, often outside South Africa, each side developed a clearer picture of the other's positions and needs and concluded in this case that negotiations could be fruitful.

As exacerbaters or inhibiters of conflict, narratives emphasize differences or commonalities among the parties that variously support continuing hostility and escalation or moderation and deescalation in response to the opponent. Sometimes a dominant narrative leaves no room for negotiation as was the case of Franco's national narrative of a unified Spain that excluded all regional languages. However, following his death, the new government quickly endorsed a different way of thinking about being Spanish – that a person could have multiple identities, for example, as a Spanish citizen and as a member of the Catalan or Basque nation. Whereas the first narrative about Spanish identity exacerbated conflict between the central government and Spain's historic nationalities, the post-Franco narrative inhibited it, an issue further explored in Chapter 5.

Narratives play a causal role in conflict when they frame cognitions and emotions to structure and limit the actions individuals and groups consider as plausible (Bates, Figueiredo, and Weingast 1998). In this process, narratives shape what constitutes evidence and how it is to be used (Kaufman 2001). As Smith notes in writing about myths of ethnic descent, "By telling us who we are and whence we came, ethnic myths of descent direct our interests like Weber's 'switchmen' and order our actions toward circumscribed but exalted goals" (1999: 88). When narratives portray no possible common ground between opponents, a search for alternatives to fighting is unlikely. Thus there will be political pressures for leaders to pursue certain kinds of action, while other options will have been already eliminated. From this perspective, narratives do not force parties to take a particular action, if for example they lack the capabilities or support, but narratives may be crucial in limiting the range of choices that are considered. A good example of this is found in Holsti's (1967: 25–96) analysis of US Secretary of State John Foster Dulles' interpretation of the Soviet Union and its motivation in the 1950s. He argues that even when Khrushchev provided signals of a major shift in Soviet policy, after Stalin's death, Dulles continued to read these only as signs of weakness, and not as possible evidence of a change of motivation and behavior from the new leadership.

Narratives and peacemaking

Narratives are implicated in the onset, escalation, and maintenance of ethnic conflict. However, as we have noted already, it is important to recognize their potential in deescalation as well, because narratives can and do evolve over time. The role of narratives in deescalation is illustrated dramatically in the period following World War II, as new relationships among former enemies were built in Europe and between the US and Japan. Narratives are at play in more slowly changing relationships, such as the US and China since 1972, or US–Russian relations in the second half of the 1980s. Evolving narratives also play a role in peace processes in long-term conflicts, such as in South Africa, Northern Ireland, and even at times the Middle East, as groups on all sides come to believe that movement toward a settlement is possible, even with those who were previously viewed as "beyond the pale." In these situations, there is a significant shift in how each side describes the other (sometimes including the name by which they are called) and the gradual emergence of images of the benefits peaceful coexistence could bring. When the narratives begin to include more nuanced views of the other side, people can envision a future apart from the intense conflicts, and political leaders have newly opened space to move the peace process forward.[10] This occurred most dramatically in South Africa, but in Northern Ireland and the Middle East (prior to September 2000) the same shifts of public opinion and discourse also could be seen.

Narratives that promote peace processes arise when there are explicit connections made between culturally available references and events on the ground. These connections are seen in changes in discourse – for example, when white South Africans foresaw the inevitability of majority rule and many began to work toward its achievement. Changing the narrative frame can also facilitate deescalation when it helps people caught in conflict to envision alternatives to ongoing confrontation. In order for this to happen, each side must appreciate the perspective of the other, and learn that there is someone to talk to on the other side and something to talk about (Kelman 1987; 1995).

Because narratives contain and evoke emotionally meaningful images, we must examine their symbols and rituals. Some rituals involve very dramatic symbolic gestures, such as for example Egyptian President Anwar Sadat's 1977 trip to Jerusalem and his address to the Israeli Knesset, or Nelson Mandela donning a Springboks jersey after they won

---

[10] We have little good data on public opinion and its dynamics in conflict zones. However, surveys from Northern Ireland and the Middle East in recent years suggest that people are often "inconsistent" in that many express strong distrust of the other side and its leaders while supporting a peaceful settlement of the conflict. There is also some evidence that opinion is very volatile and there are strong reactions to recent events, such as movements toward peace or violent incidents, that can overwhelm long-held positions.

the 1995 World Cup.[11] Powerful narratives often include ritual behaviors such as reenactments of historical events, the construction of memorials, or sacred holidays when the narratives are retold and passed to succeeding generations. When rituals include previously disputing groups, they can serve to support new narratives of coexistence and even reconciliation. In Northern Ireland, for example, a Protestant cultural organization in Derry (the region's second-largest city) recently recast its annual cele-bratory parade in the context of a more inclusive city festival, which is open to Catholics as well as Protestants (discussed in Chapter 4). Both in South Africa and in southern US cities such as Richmond, Virginia, the sacred landscape that was once the exclusive province of one group is now more inclusive and offers both physical and emotional space for more inclusive narratives and politics (discussed in Chapters 8 through 10).[12]

Narratives can and do change, but not necessarily when they are directly confronted. Simply telling people that their version of events is wrong is rarely successful, because there is often great emotional attachment to an account, which is defended from such frontal assaults. It is the images and organization of narratives, not the facts alone, that give narratives their power. A strategy to develop more inclusive narratives needs to be part of an effort to address the causes of conflicts, but it has to be one in which the parties fully participate – not simply one imposed from outside. To develop inclusive narratives as part of the peace process, former foes need to incorporate new experiences and emotional con-nections that alter the salience of elements in the existing exclusive nar-ratives and invite new and/or revised linkages among their key elements. Given the iterative and interactive nature of narrative accounts, the development of more inclusive narratives is not a one-step process, and it can proceed only if events on the ground change as well. For example, when institutions and practices come to embody civic, as opposed to

[11] Springboks is a rugby team that for many epitomized white supremacy during the apartheid regime. Mandela's action, and the overwhelmingly positive response to it, clearly signaled a new relationship among all racial groups and especially blacks and whites.

[12] One strategy Volkan has developed for achieving greater acknowledgment is visiting "hot spots" – specific places where deep differences are evoked. In Estonia, for example, Estonians and Russians met at the site of a former Soviet nuclear submarine base, and the Estonians articulated how the Russian use of the base was humiliating to them (Neu and Volkan 1999). Montville (1993) developed a "walk though history" which involves members from different groups visiting contested places from the past and explaining to each other the emotional importance of the site and events that took place there for their community.

ethnic, nationalism, they, and the narratives associated with them, are more inclusive (Snyder 2000).

New narratives are not always sufficient even when they appear more inclusive. Several decades after the American Civil War there was significant reconciliation between Union and Confederate veterans that even included joint reunions. In this process, white northerners and southerners developed a shared narrative that the war was fought over constitutional differences and that the North had won because they possessed greater resources. What was missing from this narrative of reconciliation according to Blight (2001) and other historians is that it failed to address either the role of slavery as a cause of the war or the plight of African Americans after it. As a result, while the narrative was inclusive in terms of both northern and southern whites, there was very little acknowledgment of the probably 300,000 black soldiers in the war and the thousands of black deaths. When thousands of Civil War monuments were built in both parts of the country, prior to 1900 only three contained any images of black soldiers at all (Savage 1997). These white narratives permitted some healing between white northerners and southerners in the short term; but the price of a narrative that excluded the former slaves and successive generations is the racial divisions that remain far from resolved 150 years later.

The goal of peacemaking and peacebuilding is not to develop consensus around a single widely accepted narrative. This would be a denial of real differences found in all long-term conflicts. It would be naïve to think that differences in culture, historical experiences, and politics could be bridged so easily. The goal, rather, is to find sufficient common ground and tolerance to allow the groups not to feel threatened by differences in how they see the world. Paradoxically, doing this successfully often requires that these differences be acknowledged and explored rather than swept under the rug. In the Israeli–Palestinian conflict discussed in the following pages, there have been some moments when such acknowledgment and exploration have occurred and peacemaking has advanced, and others where the acknowledgment process has stalled and violence has increased. When acknowledgment occurs, more inclusive, less threatening, and partially overlapping narratives and identities can arise from mutual listening and acknowledgment, and a politics that emphasizes possible benefits arising from respect and cooperation develops. Reconciliation in this context includes ritual acknowledgment and behaviors that expand shared space, as has taken place in post-Franco Spain and post-apartheid South Africa.

Competing narratives in the Israeli–Palestinian conflict[13]

Hostile narratives do not directly cause the escalatory sequences in long-term conflicts. Narratives about long-standing conflicts contain the culturally rooted aspirations, challenges, and deepest fears of ethnic communities. One particularly poignant kind of narrative that is prominent in the Israeli–Palestinian conflict is what Volkan calls a "chosen trauma," referring to specific psychocultural experiences which symbolize a group's deepest perceived threats and fears and are filled with feelings of helplessness and victimization (Volkan 1988; 1997).

> [C]hosen trauma describe[s] the collective memory of a calamity that once befell a group's ancestors. It is, of course, more than a simple recollection; it is a shared mental representation of the event, which includes realistic information, fantasized expectations, intense feelings, and defenses against unacceptable thoughts.
>
> (Volkan 1997: 48)[14]

Volkan provides many examples of such events including the Turkish slaughter of Armenians, the Nazi holocaust, the experience of slavery and Jim Crow for African Americans, and the Serbian defeat at Kosovo by the Turks in 1389 (Volkan 1997).

When a group experiences traumatic, overwhelming losses, normal grief and mourning processes cannot take place, as the group feels too humiliated, angry, or helpless to fully mourn them. In these situations, Volkan argues, the group then incorporates the emotional meaning of the traumatic event into its identity, transmitting it from generation to generation. He suggests that in such situations complex memorial activities may occur for many years as each generation expects the succeeding one never to forget the unresolved humiliation and loss. Sometimes, however, in the face of overwhelming feelings people shut them out of their consciousness and engage in symbolic expressions that convey them indirectly or even in concealed ways. For example, Volkan (1997: 49) suggests present-day Mexican folk dances sometimes act out the defeat of the

---

[13] Although it is easiest to describe conflicts as involving two sides, complex conflicts include many more parties, each with its own distinct interests and interpretations of the situation (Raiffa 1982).

[14] Some have suggested that the word chosen is not necessarily appropriate here since a group does not choose to be victimized. Volkan argues, however, "that the word chosen fittingly reflects a large group's unconsciously defining its identity by the transgenerational transmission of injured selves infused with the memory of the ancestor's trauma" (1997: 48)

Spanish conquistadors. In this way, group traumas come to be associated with symbolic and ritual action.

In identity-rooted conflicts, group emotions link recent events to older, collective memories of unresolved losses in ways that make them difficult to settle. Vulnerability and fear mobilize followers and they can make groups especially wary of agreements. "Adopting a chosen trauma can enhance ethnic pride, reinforce a sense of victimization, and even spur a group to avenge its ancestors' hurts. The memory of the chosen trauma is used to justify ethnic aggression" (Volkan 1997: 78).[15] It is interesting how often disastrous defeats celebrated as heroic are also traumatic for many groups. Among the examples of this are Custer's defeat at Little Bighorn, the expulsion of Muslims and Jews from Spain in 1492, and Crusader massacres of Muslims in Constantinople and Jerusalem. While chosen traumas arise within groups, it is clear that their content and their salience at any one time is tied to the interpretation of their experiences with out-groups.

The flip side of the chosen trauma is the chosen glory in which a group celebrates triumph over an enemy in a way that brings honor and enhances a group's pride (Volkan 1997: 82–83). A common example is the celebration of national independence days. The Jews' escape from Egypt, a narrative of freedom and triumph, is a good example of a chosen glory that many groups have used as inspiration (Akenson 1992). Chosen glories include the stories of military victories and heroic figures, although the particular successes may be quite varied. In Uzbekistan, for example, Timur (Tamerlane) is venerated for his military conquests and the religious monuments he built, while his grandson Uleg Beg is celebrated as a wise ruler and outstanding mathematician and astronomer.

Israel–Palestine: an illustration

The Israeli–Palestinian conflict, further explored in Chapter 7, offers two competing psychocultural narratives which illustrate the nine features of competing narratives listed above. Each narrative is built around a chosen trauma that informs each side's understanding of the conflict. What is presented here are brief historical accounts that capture key images and

---

[15] The word "chosen" does not imply a conscious deliberate or manipulative decision people make but deeper emotional choices about which they are often unaware.

events in each side's narrative. No effort is made to mediate between the two or to judge which account of claims is more warranted; rather, I have sought to offer each narrative in its own voice. (To navigate the narratives, readers not familiar with the details about conflict might find Figure 6.3, page 171 helpful.) Reading the divergent Israeli and Palestinian narratives, it is not hard to see how each account presents its version of historical events, justifies its own motivations and actions while denigrating the other side's, and understands its own intra-group differences. Relating a narrative raises many terminological issues that illustrate the complexity of identity. "Israeli" and "Palestinian" are national identities that are also linked to, but not fully coterminous with, religious identities in that about 20 percent of Israeli's citizens are non-Jews and perhaps 5 percent of Palestinians are Christian, not Muslim. Furthermore, the term Arab refers to the indigenous people in the region and is also a political identity. In what follows, I employ these terms somewhat interchangeably, trying to take into account context, local usage, and the perspective of the people I describe.

The Israeli-Jewish narrative At the core of the Israeli-Jewish narrative is the desire of Jews to return to their homeland after almost 2000 years of exile, persecution, and the Nazi Holocaust. Independence in 1948 is a story of liberation, and the triumph of Zionist hard work and incredible determination. Exile, which began with the Roman destruction of the Jewish Temple in 70 CE, was, and is, a traumatic experience in Jewish collective memory, kept alive in part through persecution of European Jewry over the centuries culminating in the Holocaust. That Jews survived in such hostile settings is a miracle, and the establishment of their own state in their ancient homeland was a just reward for their patience, faith, and tenacity. Arab refusal to accept this state was, and is, an illegitimate denial of Jewish rights, which has resulted in years of unnecessary bloodshed, and prevented the economic flowering of the region.

Zionism, the political movement that spearheaded the creation of a modern Jewish state, encompassed a wide range of social, political, and religious views. The common ground across these viewpoints was the perceived "need to promote some form of revival of Jewish national life as experienced in Antiquity" (Zerubavel 1995: 14) with emphasis on the connections among Jews across time and space. Zionists advocating a return to the ancient Jewish homeland rejected the lifestyle and values represented by the long exile period. They called for a return to the land, the dignity of labor, self-reliance, and the development of the New Hebrew Man (Zerubavel 1995). Obtaining their own national state was the Zionist goal, and even secular Jews saw Ancient Israel of the First and Second Temple periods as a Golden Age and its leaders as heroes for their wisdom and for defending their people in a region filled with enemies. Zionist immigration to Palestine began in the 1880s and many Jews bought land and settled in small agricultural communities outside the cities, such as Jerusalem and Safed, where small numbers of religious Jews had lived for centuries.

Early twentieth-century Zionists drew inspiration and contemporary lessons from accounts of ancient Israel as well as from contemporary European nationalist movements (Zerubavel 1995). Physical links to the past such as the remains of buildings and archeological findings provided clear evidence of connections to the ancient struggles for self-rule and resistance that quickly made their way into narrative accounts, school texts, and holiday celebrations. Soon new myths and rituals merged with older ones, reinforcing notions of a seamless continuity across the centuries. The battle of Masada in 73 CE became enshrined as courageous resistance even though it ended in mass death. Celebrations of Chanukah emphasized the Macabee revolt against Syrian rule and downplayed the "miracle" of one day's oil burning for eight days, which had been the story's central lesson during the Exile period. Zerubavel (1995) adds that following the Nazi Holocaust, the lesson of "Never Again" further reinforced the meaning of ancient revolts of Bar Kokhba and Masada.

Zionism's call to bring together Jews from all parts of the world meant that immigrants arrived in Israel with little in common other than their religious/ethnic identity[16] and a belief that Israel was their ancient homeland, although for some people this was a religiously motivated understanding and for others it was far more political. Thus, the development of a common language (one that had disappeared as a lingua franca), shared institutions, and a national narrative became a

---

[16] At times, this has been contested and has produced conflicts over who is Jewish and who can decide this question. For many, the most dramatic conflict occurred over the status of Ethiopian immigrants. Although there was widespread agreement that they were Jews and thereby eligible to migrate to Israel under its law of return, orthodox religious authorities insisted that differences in their ritual practices required that they undergo conversion in Israel (including ritual male circumcision) before they could be fully accepted as Jewish citizens.

central part of the task of acquiring "a land without people for a people without a land."[17] A few made an effort to learn Arabic and build relationships with Arabs but most of these failed, and there was a growing self-reliance, a pride in new skills that Jewish settlers learned, and an emphasis on self-help as it became clear that the local Arab population viewed the Jews with hostility.

The small Jewish population of Palestine grew as Jewish migration, mainly from Europe, increased significantly after 1880, and in 1897 the World Zionist Congress was created to work for the establishment of a Jewish state. In 1917, toward the end of World War I, the British Cabinet approved the declaration by Foreign Secretary Lord Balfour, provided in a letter to Lord Walter Rothschild, that "the British viewed with favor the establishment in Palestine of a national home for the Jewish people" (Morris 2001: 75).[18] The Balfour Declaration along with the dissolution of the Ottoman Empire gave great hope to Jews (Kimmerling and Migdal 1993: 27). However, one result was that Arab verbal and physical attacks on Jews increased in the following two decades. Jerusalem's Grand Mufti, Amin al-Husseini, was particularly aggressive in his attacks, protesting against Jewish religious activity in and around the Western Wall, Judaism's holiest site, and rallying followers around the charge that Jews were planning to expel Muslims from the Temple Mount/Haram al-Sharif. In August 1929, there were rallying cries to protect the al-Aqsa Mosque, and Arab attacks on Jews in Jerusalem, Safad, Tiberias, and Hebron; in the latter sixty-four Jewish men, women, and children were killed. "The massacre of Hebron was a traumatic event in Arab-Jewish relations that exacerbated suspicions, mutual anxieties, and stereotypes" (Kimmerling and Migdal 1993: 87). Hostility continued to grow, and in 1936 a three-year Arab revolt against the British began, featuring many attacks against Jews, especially in isolated settlements where self-defense proved to be the best protection. When the British

---

[17] Note that this phrase reflected and reinforced a narrative which presumed that Palestine had been "empty" for 2000 years, and that the Arabs living there were mere visitors. The same image is one that the British used in describing East Africa when they first arrived and that Stalin used to characterize Central Asia.

[18] Morris adds that it is important to see the declaration as part of the British strategic interest in protecting the Suez canal, gaining control over the Arab population of the region, making sure American and Russian Jews did not support the Central powers during the war, and providing some cover for British imperial designs. Though the British position was not simply an ideological commitment to the idea of a Jewish state, the fact is that Zionist leaders were delighted with it (2001: 72–75).

proposed partition in the late 1930s, Jews were generally quite pleased even though some of the arrangements were not ideal.[19]

In Europe, Jews were increasingly vulnerable as the Nazis came to power in Germany. Despite the clarity of Nazi practices and intentions, few countries took concrete steps to protect Jews or to help them escape to safer lands. Following World War II and the Holocaust, the case for a Jewish state was stronger than ever but Jewish leaders had to fight the British to allow concentration camp survivors and war refugees to enter Palestine. As the British lost the will to retain control over the region, the United Nations endorsed a partition plan that Jews more or less accepted; the Arabs rejected it. War broke out and at first the Arabs seemed to have the upper hand, but after a few months, superior Jewish military organization proved dominant in the fighting and Arab civilians fled their homes. David Ben-Gurion announced Israel's independence in May 1948, and the 1949 armistice agreement gave the new Jewish state more territory than the UN partition plan had granted.

The surrounding Arab states allowed Israel no peace, and the only Arab leader who tried to make peace, Jordan's King Abdullah, was assassinated. Israel struggled to defend itself and to integrate new arrivals, including at least 750,000 from Arab countries. Arabs denied Israel's right to exist and a period of violence against Israel began that has continued on and off until the present. During the 1950s, the country's ability to quickly build new institutions and its economy was crucial to survival. First, Egypt supported guerrilla activity inside Israel in the 1950s. There followed a war with Egypt in 1956 in which Britain and France supported Israel. A decade later, in 1967, three neighboring states, Egypt, Jordan, and Syria, went to war with Israel and were quickly defeated in the Six Day War; Israel captured the Sinai, the West Bank including East Jerusalem and Gaza, and the Golan Heights. Jerusalem, which had been divided from 1948 to 1967, was reunited and became Israel's capitol. Israeli Minister of Defense Moshe Dayan, hoping for a long-term solution, moved quickly to allow the Muslim, Christian, and Jewish religious communities to control their own religious sites in the city, and the Jewish quarter that had been destroyed under Jordanian rule was rebuilt. Nevertheless, on Yom Kippur in 1973 the Arabs attacked Israel, crossing the Suez Canal

---

[19] Ben-Gurion and other Zionist leaders were willing to take what they could get at that point and they accepted the British proposal even though it would have given Jews only 20% of Palestine and did not include Jerusalem.

from Egypt in the south and attacking from Syria in the north. Although Israel was at first unprepared, it eventually prevailed in the fighting. In the aftermath of these wars Arab violence continued with the rise of the Palestine Liberation Organization, its increased use of terror tactics against Israelis, including civilians, and the bloody Black September attack at the 1972 Olympics.

After 1967 many Israelis talked about "land for peace," meaning that the areas captured in the war might be returned to the Arab countries in return for normalization of relations and acceptance of Israel's right to exist. At the same time, some advocated establishing Jewish settlements in the occupied territories to increase Arab incentives to make a deal. However, other Israelis spoke of the settlements in more religious terms, as part of the right of Jews to all the land of Ancient Israel and these differences remain at the heart of the strong tensions between religious and secular Israelis today. In the wake of the 1973 war US-brokered diplomatic efforts led to a disengagement agreement, and within a few years Egyptian President Anwar Sadat visited Israel. In 1978, the two countries, assisted by President Jimmy Carter and attracted by American aid, then negotiated the Camp David Agreement, and Egypt became the first Arab country to recognize Israel.

In the agreement, Israel agreed to return the Sinai lands captured in 1967 in return for formal Egyptian recognition, hoping that this outcome would be the foundation for a lasting peace. However, this did not lead either to more peace treaties with other Arab countries or to a settlement with the Palestinians. Rather, there were a number of dramatic PLO and other terrorist attacks that made strong Israeli responses necessary. In 1982, Israel, under attack from groups in southern Lebanon, invaded the country with the goal of removing PLO guerrillas in the south. Determined to deliver a knockout punch to the PLO, the army, supported by some Lebanese Christians, continued to Beirut where they routed the Palestinians. The PLO leadership then moved to Tunis.[20] In 1987, organized Palestinian resistance became rampant in the West Bank and Gaza as youths spearheaded the home-grown Intifada, or uprising. The result was many deaths on both sides and a crippling of the economy. Then, following the Gulf War, the US initiated another peace process beginning with a conference in Madrid in 1991, which was the first time

---

[20] The 1982 Lebanon war was highly controversial within Israel and the focus of many protests over the years. Israeli troops were not withdrawn from Lebanon until 2000.

Israel met officially with Arab states other than Egypt. Soon, secret negotiations between Israel and the Palestinians began in Norway, leading to the Oslo Agreement signed at the White House in September 1993 that brought great hope for peace to the region.

As part of the agreement, Israel allowed the PLO under Yasser Arafat to return from exile to the West Bank and Gaza, and they set up a provisional Palestinian Authority. Despite the good faith shown by the Israelis, negotiations between the two sides proceeded slowly and tensions mounted within and between both Israel and the Palestinians. Many Israelis felt that the PLO were not living up to the Oslo Agreement. In 1995 a Jewish extremist totally opposed to any peace agreement assassinated Prime Minister Yitzak Rabin; Hamas and other Palestinian groups resumed terror attacks; and right-wing Likud leader Benjamin Netanyahu returned to power.[21] Relations between the two sides worsened despite yet another summit held at Camp David under the auspices of Bill Clinton in 2000 with the goal of reaching a final status agreement. Palestinians had already signaled a possible return to violence, and a second Intifada erupted after Likud leader Ariel Sharon, accompanied by a large security contingent, visited the Temple Mount in September 2000. Palestinian suicide bombers attacked civilians inside Israel and settlers in the West Bank and Gaza. Israel responded by reoccupying these territories and began building a wall/fence to separate the Palestinian territories in the West Bank from Israel.[22] Negotiations ended despite several American led efforts to get the peace process back on track when it was clear that Arafat was not a partner for peace. With Yasser Arafat's death in November 2004, there were again hopes for a diplomatic initiative, but for this to occur, Israel insisted that the Palestinian Authority rein in terrorist groups. When this did not happen, Prime Minister Sharon moved to act more unilaterally and to disengage Israel and the Palestinians. In 2005 with strong public support for withdrawal, Israel withdrew from its settlements in Gaza. In early 2006 Hamas scored a victory in the

---

[21] A tit-for-tat pattern developed in which Israel would target Palestinian terrorists in Gaza or the West Bank and in response the group whose member was killed would launch a suicide attack against Israel. The cycle would continue with each side citing the latest incident by the other as the reason why it needed to respond.

[22] The wall, or fence, was controversial for several reasons. The main reason was that it often ranged far inside the west bank and expropriated significant amounts of Palestinian land. Earlier a fence was built separating Gaza and Israel and has proved to be an effective barrier against infiltration.

Palestinian elections and Israel said it would have nothing to do with the Palestinian Authority although it would continue to deal with Palestinian President Mahmoud Abbas.

The Palestinian narrative The trauma at the core of the Palestinian national narrative is 1948. Al-Nakba, the catastrophe, is seared in their collective memory as a time of exile, humiliation, and catastrophic loss when families, and even entire villages, were uprooted and lost the land and olive groves where they had lived for generations (Khalidi 1997; Sa'di 2002). To solve the consciences of the countries across the world who had mistreated the Jews, thousands of Palestinians became refugees in camps in Gaza, Jordan, Syria and Lebanon, although the Palestinian leaders and Arab governments promised that they would one day return to their homes.

Palestinians, both Muslim and Christian, see themselves as descendants of the Arab peoples, including the ancient Canaanites, who have lived in the region for centuries. They also recognize their common origin with Jews as descendants of Abraham, and their common history as victims of Christian oppression. Palestine's borders have often been unmarked, however its center in the Judean Mountains has always been clear (Kimmerling and Migdal 1993:3). Often nominally ruled by outsiders including the Jews, Romans, and Ottomans, the Palestinian population is descended from nomadic Bedouins and hill farmers. For most of this period, however, local groups were largely autonomous as political power and land ownership rested in the hands of local families. Palestinian society was rural and the few cities and towns in the region such as Nablus, Jaffa, and Jerusalem, were the centers of commerce and religious life with strong ties to the hinterlands. Palestinian political identity emerged as part of a larger process of political change and the emergence of states following World War I; it was not simply a response to Jewish immigration (Khalidi 1997: 20).

Zionist claims and Jewish immigration were, however, significant factors in strengthening Palestinian national identity. For many Palestinians, Zionist demands for a homeland and access to Jerusalem's holy sites recalled the Crusades and earlier European efforts to dominate the region. The increasing European interest in Palestine and the establishment of consulates toward the end of the Ottoman period reinforced their vulnerability, as they were increasingly made pawns in a much larger political game.[23] With the 1917 Balfour Declaration promising the Jews a homeland in Palestine, the continuing influx of immigrants, land sales, and the establishment of the British League of Nations mandate Palestinian fears rose rapidly.

In response to these threats, the Palestinians developed various forms of resistance that in the next three decades had two targets – the British rulers and the expanding Jewish community – as they sought to defend their villages, their land, their way of life, and their emotionally important sites such as Jerusalem.[24] Palestinian resistance focused on two forms of Zionist encroachment: on the Jewish acquisition of land, often from absentee landlords, and on Jerusalem (Kimmerling and Migdal 1993: 64–95). There was a significant Muslim campaign in the 1920s to restore the city's Muslim holy sites and to resist regular Jewish attempts to modify the Ottoman status quo regulations regarding Jewish prayer at the Western Wall, which represented a growing encroachment on their holiest site in Palestine. In 1928–29, when the Jews made changes including placing a divider to separate men and women who had come to pray and storing religious materials at the wall, Muslims rallied to forcefully defend the holy sites (Monk 2002). A British appointed Commission of Inquiry examined the situation; in these hearings Muslims made it clear that they faced an imminent danger in the form of Jewish plans not only to create a Jewish state in Palestine, but also to take over the Muslim holy sites and rebuild a temple in their place (Friedland and Hecht 1991, Monk, 2002).

By the late 1930s there was a courageous and broad-based Palestinian revolt against imperialist British rule and continuing Zionist land acquisition. The revolt was finally crushed through British military force that included a good deal of British–Zionist coordination. By its end, most of the Arab leaders were jailed, killed, or exiled. Although the heroic revolt ultimately failed, it generated widespread support and brought social changes in its wake. "[T]he violence was the sign of [a] steadily unfolding national movement and the unanimity among Palestinian Arabs about the

---

[23] Kimmerling and Migdal argue that the beginnings of Palestinian nationalism and resistance are rooted in the revolt against Egyptian control of the region starting in 1834 (1993: 5–20)

[24] In addition, however, there were significant internal divisions within Palestinian society: those among the large powerful families who had previously dominated the society, as well as economic tensions between the countryside and the towns and emerging cities (Khalidi 1997; Kimmerling and Migdal 1993).

Zionist threat" and a continuation of the anti-imperial struggle of 1929 (Kimmerling and Migdal 1993: 98). There were urban and rural actions, symbolic expressions of national unity, and a newer style of leader – less likely to come from the old noble families – rose to the fore. However, rather than responding to Palestinian concerns, the British used the events to propose partition, and Jews strengthened their own military position.

At the conclusion of World War II, as Jewish immigration of European refugees increased once again and it was clear that the British would soon leave the region, the Palestinians found themselves faced with a UN partition plan. When it was adopted and fighting broke out, the Palestinians first hoped to defeat the Jews militarily with the help of neighboring Arab states. However, by May 1948 the Palestinians found themselves defeated and displaced. Many were expelled from their homes or fled when faced with Jewish threats; by the end of the war, over 350 Arab villages had disappeared and the Arab populations of cities such as Jaffa or Haifa were a tiny fraction of what they had been just a few years earlier (Kimmerling and Migdal 1993: 127). Events such as the massacre of dozens of Arab inhabitants, including women and children, at Deir Yassin in early April 1948 served as warnings of the threats Arab villagers faced and as a symbol of Jewish injustice (Morris 2001: 207–09). Palestinian fear and the pace of exodus increased further as between a half and one million Palestinians became refugees living in squalid camps, as victims of a monumental injustice (Morris 1988; Kimmerling and Migdal 1993: 128–29).

Dislocated and disorganized, Palestinian resistance was slow to develop, and was often complicated by the efforts of the Arab states, who had been ineffective against Israel in 1948, to control it. Arabs who remained in Israel received Israeli citizenship but suffered from discrimination, while those living in the West Bank and Gaza were under Jordanian and Egyptian rule. In addition, there were thousands more Palestinians living in refugee camps in Jordan, Lebanon, and Syria. Israelis refused to acknowledge Palestinian identity; or to acknowledge Palestinian national aspirations as legitimate (Jamal 2000); in the words of former Israeli Prime Minister Golda Meir, "There is no such thing as a Palestinian people."

After 1967, Palestinians developed three different heroic images of national resistance (Kimmerling and Migdal 1993: 211–12). The first to emerge was that of the warrior who sacrificed for his community, associated with exile groups, the most prominent of which was Yasser Arafat's PLO (Kimmerling and Migdal 1993: 212). Within both Israel and the occupied territories, as Palestinians began to make political demands such as the complaints over never-ending Israeli land expropriation that Palestinians have marked annually from 1976 as Land Day, there emerged the heroic image of the steadfast survivor; this served as a reminder of pre-1948 Palestine. Lastly, from the first Intifada a third heroic image emerged – that of "the child of the stone," the young martyr confronting the occupation with his body and meager weapons (Kimmerling and Migdal 1993: 212).[25]

By the late 1980s, the PLO had moved toward recognizing Israel's right to exist. Following the PLO's decision to support Iraq in the Gulf War, international efforts to produce a peace agreement increased. The 1991 Madrid Conference provided a forum for public talks, although the PLO was not officially invited; the subsequent secret Oslo negotiations produced a preliminary agreement that Yasser Arafat and Prime Minister Rabin signed at the White House in 1993. It recognized Israel's right to exist, called for the establishment of a Palestinian Authority, a provisional government in the West Bank and Gaza, a return of the PLO from Tunis, and it provided a five-year window for the conclusion of a final status agreement that would address the toughest issues that were not settled in Oslo – those of an independent Palestinian state, final border arrangements, the status of Jerusalem, the return of refugees, and Israeli security concerns. By 1995, however, Palestinians felt that Israel was not fully abiding by the interim agreement and that they had received few tangible benefits from the end to terror and their political acceptance of Israel. When Rabin's assassination by an Ultra-Orthodox Jew removed the man who had shaken Arafat's hand at the White House, splits within the Palestinians increased and there was a return to violence. When right-wing leader Benjamin Netanyahu returned to power, tension increased; it was further inflamed when Israel, without consultation, decided to open an archeological tunnel running along the western wall of the Haram which Palestinians said would threaten the site's foundations.

Bill Clinton, with only six months left as president, spearheaded a final effort to reach an agreement, inviting Arafat and Prime Minister Ehud

---

[25] This image emphasized an Islamic discourse as "even the most secular and national figures appropriated cultural symbols that had strong Islamic resonances" (Kimmerling and Migdal 1993: 270). It also recalls the story of David and Goliath.

Barak to Camp David in July 2000. Palestinians discovered there was active collusion between Clinton and Barak and the meetings failed to achieve an agreement. Violence broke out two months later after opposition leader Ariel Sharon went to the Haram al-Sharif/Temple Mount, in a symbolic assertion of Israeli sovereignty. The violence escalated within Israel and the occupied territories. Although negotiations continued, Clinton offered a set of bridging proposals in his last month in office and Israeli and Palestinian negotiators came very close to an agreement in January 2001. However, by that time Ariel Sharon had been elected prime minister and was due to take office shortly (Agha and Malley 2001; Pressman 2003; Pundak 2001). Over the next six years, the violence on both sides increased and an agreement seemed further off than ever as trust between the parties reached its lowest point and there were no outside actors capable of providing an incentive to reach an agreement. Sharon and his American supporters refused to deal with Arafat and created impossible preconditions for the start of negotiations, strengthening the hand of Palestinians advocating violence. When President Mahmoud Abbas came into office in 2005, he was able to get Hamas and other Islamic organizations to agree to a ceasefire with Israel prior to the 2006 Palestinian elections. However, Israel continued to refuse to engage in serious negotiations and continued to take unilateral moves, building a fence that cut into the West Bank, and refusing to coordinate their withdrawal from Gaza with the PA. Palestinians feel they have made greater compromises than Israelis have to date and have little to show for it – not even sincere acceptance of their national aspirations (Jamal 2000).

Conclusion: competing narratives

The competing Israeli and Palestinian narratives offer different accounts of what seem to many people to be the same historical events. While there are a number of points of contact between them, the Israeli and Palestinian narratives differ in how they selectively emphasize and judge events, people, and motivations, and in the metaphors and images they draw upon. Jews stress the return to, and recovery of, their ancient homeland after centuries of exile and persecution. Palestinians see themselves as victims of a catastrophe not of their own making. However, "in the misery of the camps – in the permanence of temporariness – refugees developed a powerful new nationalism. Its fuel was longing and injustice, humiliation and degradation [and] ... at its heart was a vision of retuning to a Lost

Garden" (Kimmerling and Migdal 1993: 279). Thus, the core images and feelings are similar, but neither narrative acknowledges the pain felt by the other side. Each attributes great responsibility for the conflict to the other while offering little recognition of how its own actions, exclusive demands, and motivations have contributed to it. In these accounts, each focuses on its own fears and the threats the other poses as a reason for its own claims and actions. Through the externalization of responsibility, each side has come to demand in-group conformity and assert its moral superiority as the basis for its positions.

Each side draws very different lessons from their experiences – ones that are bolstered by the demonic image of the other that each has built. Palestinians focus on events such as Deir Yasin in 1948 and Jews point to the 1929 massacres in Hebron each seeing evidence for the notion that the other culture is murderous and uncompromising (Kimmerling and Migdal 1993: 152). It would be very wrong, however, to see these as examples of people "stuck in the past" or of "ancient hatreds" that drive conflict. Rather, these events come to represent eternal lessons which are perilous to ignore. As a result, mutual fear and anxiety feed expectations of future threats and produce behaviors consistent with each side's worst fears, making peace all the more remote.

For the most part, Palestinian and Israeli narratives have reinforced negative images of the other side and their motives, have exacerbated tensions, and have portrayed the situation in terms of zero-sum identities that have limited the ability of the opposing sides to search for, and agree to, arrangements that would allow for settlement of the conflict such as a two-state solution. While the narratives have not directly caused the conflict, their mutually exclusive representations, and their widespread acceptance within each group, have made the conflict's continuation easier and the task of peacemakers more difficult.

There have been several striking moments when the two narratives moved toward mutual acknowledgment. For Israel, the most dramatic shifts occurred relatively quickly around the Sadat visit to Jerusalem and the Camp David agreement in the late 1970s, and at the time of the Oslo accord in the 1990s. On both occasions, Israelis responded very positively to Arab acceptance and spoke of accommodation and coexistence with their neighbors. For Palestinians, the decade after the first Intifada saw a significant shift in public discourse moving from a refusal to recognize Israel's right to existence to partial acceptance and clear willingness to accept a viable two-state solution. There was disagreement among observers, however, about the extent to which this change represented a genuine change of position or was a tactical maneuver to legitimate the Palestinians in the eyes of the Europeans and other third parties.

Since 2000, the narratives on both sides have hardened once again into mutually exclusive positions as each side has engaged in increasing violence against the other. By 2002, Israel, with American backing, refused to deal with Arafat, insisting that he "was no longer a partner for peace" and imposed preconditions on the Palestinians that made negotiations virtually impossible. At the same time, few Palestinians thought there could be successful negotiations as long as Ariel Sharon headed the Israeli government; many began to see South Africa as an appropriate analogy for their situation, vowing that the appropriate strategy was one of patience until the day when they might achieve a democratic state in the land that historically was Palestine.

3

Narratives and performance: ritual enactment and psychocultural dramas in ethnic conflict

Introduction

Contested cultural expressions are frequently focal points in ethnic conflict. In these conflicts, psychocultural narratives and identities are invoked and reinforced through public actions. Participation in these expressions can be fleeting or prolonged, mundane or esoteric, active or passive, and easy or costly. Some actions are highly marked and occur only on particular days in special, sacred places while others are ordinary, everyday behaviors (Kertzer 1988). What are crucial to all of them, however, are the almost automatic affective connections people make between the symbolic expressions and the within-group bonds they strengthen.

Most public behaviors produce few strong reactions. The public contentious expressions that do spark strong and contrasting reactions organized around divergent social and political identities are those of particular interest here. These expressions provoke intense in-group feelings that we variously call patriotism, nationalism, ethnic pride, or group loyalty, as well as out-group fear and anger. At the same time, it is not the forms of expression themselves that do this; most parades, museum presentations, athletic contests, concerts, and religious ceremonies are just reassuring or entertaining. How is it, then, that the range of reactions to the same cultural expressions varies from reassuring to entertaining to threatening? The answer is that understanding cultural expressions and performances means considering not just the nature and content of the events but also how in-group and out-group audiences respond to them. A given parade, for example, can, at the same time, comfort, amuse, entertain, *and* threaten because divergent group psychocultural narratives interpret the same expressions or actions so differently.

Many of the expressions of interest here are highly ritualistic and are often mundane behaviors containing powerful symbols that evoke abstract images and strong feelings. For example, consider the difference between waving a piece of colored cloth versus a cloth designated as a national flag in front of a crowd. As physical acts these are indistinguishable, but the reactions to them are often highly divergent. It is this divergence in group reactions that characterizes cultural contestation and that leads many to conclude that the differences over them are irresolvable. Also important in evoking memories and emotions are sacred sites, places that have intense emotional significance for people because of their association with a group's identity. Sometimes these are religious sites but they can also be former battlefields, monuments, or memorials that are physical links to a group's sacred experiences, memories, and identity.[1] Other focal points of conflict are museums and other cultural expressions, such as those found in cultural festivals, which recount and legitimize important elements in a group's narrative. What joins these different specific cultural expressions is their significance for the construction and maintenance of the group, its identity, and its relationship with other groups.

While explicit conflict around cultural identities is common, con-testation and organization around cultural expressions can be more or less explicit depending upon how the parties – and particularly the weaker group – define their goals and actions. Anthropologist Abner Cohen draws our attention to contests, perhaps best described by his term "masquerade politics," in which ethnic and cultural organizations indir-ectly, and not necessarily consciously or explicitly, meet important poli-tical needs when explicit political organization around ethnic identity is either not possible or not strategically viable. Cohen has examined "politics articulated in terms of non-political cultural forms such as religion, kinship, and the arts" (Cohen 1993: ix) and he argues that in urban society it is common for economic and political power struggles to take place "in the form of a cultural movement" (Cohen 1993:1).

In his early work, Cohen studied the complex relationships between cultural and political organization in West African cities. In the 1960s he found that among Hausa traders in the Yoruba city of Ibadan affiliated with the Muslim Tijanyi brotherhood, their close religious connections served political communications, coordination, and identity needs (Cohen

---

[1] Volkan (1988) uses the term "linking objects" referring to objects or representations that mediate between the internal and external world.

1969). Similarly, he showed how among the Creoles of Sierra Leone, Free Masonry provided an organizational framework for members of the small, but well-placed minority to achieve political communication and coordination (Cohen 1981). In both situations, cultural organizations provided the mechanism for the pursuit of political goals. Cohen further developed his analysis of this same phenomenon in his study of the Notting Hill (London) Carnival. The yearly carnival in the heart of London "is essentially a cultural, artistic spectacle, saturated by music, dancing and drama; it is always political, intimately and dynamically related to the political order and to the struggle for power within it" (Cohen 1993: 4).

The linkage between cultural enactment and politics is the focus of this chapter, which has three sections. The first examines cultural expressions as performances and enactment – spelling out the dynamics of cultural contestation through a discussion of political rituals, chosen traumas and glories, pilgrimages, and festivals. The second section develops the concept of the psychocultural drama, derived from Victor Turner's (1957; 1974) notion of the social drama, as a tool to link cultural expressions and psychocultural narratives in order to analyze how the parties frame their own and others' goals and actions in conflict, and the important role that ritual plays in settling them. Placing ritual actions at the center of the analysis does not mean we should ignore real differences in interests; it does, however, make us aware of the role of ritual in escalation and settlement of conflict, as well as the need to find both ritual and substantive solutions to bridge the competing parties' differences. The third section argues that ritual acknowledgment through inclusive public speech, and action involving culturally rooted symbolic gestures, offers a mechanism for bridging emotional differences among groups, lowering the threats they feel, and achieving some degree of reconciliation in long-term conflicts.

Chapters 4–10 then go on to offer an analysis of specific cases of cultural contestation in which identity, collectively held worldviews, and within-group solidarity are mobilized. In these cases groups often find it necessary to establish and legitimate their collective past in order to make political claims. To do this, people readily turn to cultural evidence.[2]

---

[2] Today it is not generally acceptable to make simple biological or racial claims about the group. This was certainly not always the case. Nineteenth-century nationalist rhetoric was filled with biological assumptions. The language of self-determination following World War I was also built around the assumption that national groups were biological,

In this process, it is often the case that physical objects such as archeological evidence can have great significance when it provides material evidence that concretizes an abstract identity and political claims.[3] It hardly matters that potsherds, ancient jewelry, or building fragments rarely provide specific evidence for past political and social identity. Rather what is important is that people believe they do. As the present is read into the past, a descending anachronism, current identities are mapped onto ancient places and objects. As a result, intense conflicts occur over the social and political significance of ancient objects that embody group identity and are used to substantiate modern political claims.[4] Heritage from this perspective becomes sacred heritage, and issues of memory, voice, and control of the past assume central significance in contemporary political conflict.

Cultural expressions as performance

Ritual

Rituals are behaviors whose central elements and the contexts in which they take place are emotionally meaningful because of what they represent. In many rituals, people's actions are particularly mundane and the moods and motivations they elicit have to be seen through their connections to the social and political identities. In examining politically significant rituals, Geertz's distinction between rituals that are *models of* reality and those that are *models for* reality is valuable (Geertz 1973b). "In the first, what is stressed is the manipulation of symbol structures so as to bring them more or less closely into parallel with the pre-established nonsymbolic systems ... it is a model *of* 'reality'. In the second what is stressed is the manipulation of the nonsymbolic systems in terms of the relations expressed in the symbolic" (1973b: 93). He then adds, "Culture

---

not just cultural, entities. For elaboration of the underlying assumptions about kinship and family as the basis of ethnic communities, see Horowitz (1985: ch. 2). For a discussion and analysis of change in the twentieth century from biological to cultural explanations of groups and the differences among them in the United States in social science and popular thought, see Jacobson (1998).

[3] This is discussed at greater length in Chapter 6.

[4] During the nineteenth century European nationalism utilized archeological evidence to trace each nation's history, and archeology moved from an earlier focus on human evolution to one of recounting the story of specific nations (Kohl 1998; Kohl and Fawcett 1995).

patterns have an intrinsic double aspect: they give meaning, that is, objective conceptual form, to social and psychological reality both by shaping themselves to it and shaping it to themselves" (1993b: 93).

Cultural performances are expressions that communicate core parts of a group's self-understood identity and history. The cultural performances of particular interest here are those used to build or bolster political narratives and claims based on them. Normally we think of people as performers, but Kirshenblatt-Gimblett (1998) argues that objects in museums' presentations or public exhibitions, festivals, fairs, memorial and tourist sites perform as well. Performances, as she analyzes them, simultaneously reflect and produce plausible accounts of a group's past and present.[5]

Repetitive cultural rituals are a crucial way of creating and solidifying collective memories that are transmitted over time (Connerton 1989; Jarman 1997). Participation in a wide range of activities such as festivals and commemorative ceremonies are important in Connerton's analysis in which he emphasizes that rites are not merely expressive; rites are not merely formal; and rites are not limited in their effect to ritual occasions (1989: 44). Rituals commemorate continuity and in so doing shape communal memory (Connerton 1989: 48). Invented rituals often begin long after the events they mark, as we noted earlier. In addition, "Ritual is not only an alternative way of expressing certain beliefs, but that certain things can be expressed only in ritual" (Connerton 1989: 54). Ritual has its own performative, formalized language encoded in postures, gestures and movements (Connerton 1989: 58–59). He adds:

I approached ritual not as a type of symbolic representation but as a species of performative, and to this end contrasted myths, as reservoirs of possibility on which variations can be played, and rituals, on which no such variation is permissible ... In doing so I underlined the cultural pervasiveness of performances which explicitly re-enact other actions that are represented as prototypical; and to this end I itemized the rhetoric of that re-enactment, calendrical, verbal and gestural. What, then, is being remembered in commemorative ceremonies? Part of the answer is that a community is reminded of its identity as represented by and told in a master narrative ... Its master narrative is more than a story told and reflected on; it is a cult enacted. An image of the past, even in the form of a master narrative, is conveyed and sustained by ritual performances ... [To be effective for participants, they must not just be cognitively competent] they must be habituated to those performances.

(Connerton 1989: 70–71)

---

[5] This view of heritage also stresses its commodification.

States are keenly aware of the value of ritual performances that enhance their legitimacy and the political loyalty of their citizens, and all states have ceremonial occasions, which are moments of high ritual that assert the state's power and legitimacy. State rituals mark occasions such as political transitions, national holidays, military victories, the deaths of leaders, and the achievements of past and present heroes. State rituals take many forms and vary along a number of dimensions such as their size, degree of organization, key participants, and the emotions they evoke. Some of these celebrations are planned in advance and follow a calendric cycle, while others are a response to unfolding events. In both, the state invariably takes the lead in their organization and in determining the inclusion of national symbols and personalities intended to evoke strong affective response to the ceremonies. These large-scale rituals involve elaborate pomp and ceremony, and often large numbers of people.

To be effective, rituals require an audience that is physically present, although in the electronic era there is often large-scale participation in rituals through the media. Increasingly, such events, while requiring a live audience, are choreographed with the even larger number of worldwide live viewers in mind. Dayan and Katz (1992) use the term media events to describe televised historic events – many of which are state occasions – that transfix a nation or the world. Examples include royal weddings and funerals, coronations, Olympic games, funerals of world leaders, and international visits.[6] During these high holidays of mass communication, daily routines are suspended and community is emphasized, and settings such as homes or schools in which families, friends, and coworkers view the events are transformed into public spaces. Dayan and Katz (1992) identify three main themes in the scripts of media events: (1) rule-governed battles of champions that produce heroes; (2) conquest – giant leaps forward in which the hero reaches human limits; and (3) coronation, recognition, and glorification of the hero. Not all media events, they note, are pre-planned. Notable examples of media events include the 1963 Kennedy assassination and funeral, the 1994 O.J. Simpson car chase on the LA freeway, and coverage of the 9/11 attacks on the WTC and the Pentagon. As restorative events, Katz and Dayan argue that media events present an idealization of the past that reinforces dominant paradigms, while at the same time inventing traditions, sometimes quite

[6] We probably should add the live coverage of wars on 24 hour news stations such as CNN.

68

self-consciously.[7] Common themes in media events are their emphasis on communitas (the feeling of connections among people across time and space) and camaraderie, the personalization of power, and conferring status on persons and issues.

Rituals and symbols can generate powerful messages about a regime and its leaders and are routinely part of political mobilization and opposition. States are well aware of opponents' potential use of ritual and at times go to great lengths to limit, and even prohibit them.[8] When opposition is particularly aligned with a society's social and cultural cleavages, cultural institutions and practices, such of those of religious groups, are often a prominent part of an opposition's political actions. Examples of this phenomenon include the American Civil Rights Movement's reliance on southern black church congregations for organizational support and the expression of equality demands in broad religious terms, the use of religious appeals and the mosques to mobilize support for the Iranian revolution, and Gandhi's emphasis on Hindu symbols in his hunger strikes and other non-violent political actions.[9]

Alongside state-sponsored, or inspired, ceremonies are more low-key daily activities that involve ritualistic political actions that are rarely thought about self-consciously. Some of these include displaying symbols such as national flags and photos of present and past leaders, and playing a national anthem at sporting events and in movie theaters. One is sometimes aware of these only in periods of stress and conflict when group identities are contested. In visits to divided societies, the paucity of such unifying activities is often clear as there are few symbols and rituals which people in competing groups share. At Queens University in Belfast, "God Save the Queen" is no longer played at important ritual occasions such as commencement because perhaps half of the people in attendance see it as the recognition of a political claim they reject, the union of Northern Ireland and Britain into the United Kingdom. Rather than provoke two counter demonstrations at the graduation ceremonies, the university

---

[7] Princess Diana's funeral, watched by millions worldwide, offered an interesting combination of well-known rituals in sacred sites along with new, invented, emotionally significant components.

[8] States ban many sorts of events including religious ceremonies, political meetings, parades, anniversary celebrations, pilgrimages, and memorialization.

[9] It is not an accident that all three of these examples link religious symbols and political action. Religion is an especially rich source of cultural images and rituals as well as organizational resources.

simply leaves the anthem off the program, a decision that continues to anger many of the region's Protestants.

New, revolutionary regimes have a particularly acute problem in that having rejected the values and practices of the *ancien régime*, they need to develop new rituals and symbols that are not linked to the regime they displaced but still are emotionally meaningful to citizens. Following the destruction of royal and religious symbols during the French Revolution, the revolutionary regime self-consciously developed republican rituals and symbols such as new terms of address, a new calendar, new forms of dress, and new norms of interpersonal behavior (Soboul 1974). Large processions and festivals celebrating the revolution and its heroes marked newly established civic holidays (Lane 1981: 262–66).

A more recent example is that of the Soviet Union following the 1917 Revolution. As in the French case, the new Soviet rulers found little in the symbolic and ritual past from which they could draw (Lane 1981). To some extent, Marxist-Leninist ideology and the October Revolution itself provided a good deal of raw material that was integrated into state symbol and ritual. After several decades, however, there was a clear realization that the grand rituals of state were not the only ones the society needed. In the mid 1960s the Communist Party's Central Committee "singled out the introduction of new secular rituals as an important way to reduce religious involvement" and the Council of Ministers decreed a need for the elaboration and introduction of new civic rituals (Lane 1981: 46). The new rituals were intended to provide an emotional expression of the current way of life, the progressive ideals and communist morality, a synthesis of the logical and emotional, an atheist direction, inter-nationalism, and universality (Lane 1981: 47). The result was state-sponsored invention of ritual throughout the USSR's Republics that paid attention to many elements of the yearly cycles and life cycles of ordinary citizens.

Lane (1981) describes the wide range of rituals the Soviets developed, such as familial lifecycle rituals associated with birth, marriage, and death; rituals linking people to the collectivity including initiation into youth organizations and coming of age, labor rituals, calendrical cycle holidays, and patriotic and revolutionary holidays. Responses to the new rituals were mixed. There was widespread participation in some, while others languished and participation in them was low. Lane suggests that there was the greatest acceptance in areas where national churches or religions were weakest and economic development was greatest (Lane 1981: 242).

There was also variation across rituals, and she found there was much greater acceptance of lifecycle rituals such as those marking marriage and the birth of a child than for funerals. Similarly, participation in mass political holidays was far greater than participation in initiations into social and political collectivities (Lane 1981: 239–51).

Many ritual expressions that are of particular interest here are not state organized or sanctioned. Sometimes cultural performances that are meaningful to one group are simply ignored by others. At other times, however, public cultural performances become politicized (if they were not already) and provoke counter demonstrations and alternative rituals. In Israel, as was pointed out in Chapter 2, Jewish Israelis celebrate the anniversary of Israel's independence each May. In recent years, Palestinian Israelis publicly commemorate Al Nakba, the catastrophe, which places the same events in 1948 in an entirely different frame.

Chosen traumas and chosen glories, discussed in Chapter 2, often contain the core images for memorial celebrations and national holidays that recount a group's emotionally significant narrative. While there can be significant variation in the specifics of how they are recounted and marked, a common feature is that these celebrations are occasions for retelling a group's narrative in a participatory format. Participation in cultural celebrations is a crucial mechanism for maintaining powerful psychocultural narratives and the memories associated with them, although there is often great variation in the nature of participation, ranging from observing a performance that includes festive and solemn elements to taking part in one that requires months or even years of preparation and can involve high cost and risk to participants. Some are solemn, and controversial, acts such as the US government's decision to allow confederate veterans to be buried in Arlington National Cemetery or the creation of Martin Luther King, Jr.'s birthday as a national holiday. Others are lighter such as the presidential phone call to the Super Bowl winners and the obligatory visit to the White House in the following weeks. Through involvement in enactments, the emotional salience of events is often reinforced in ways that are more powerful than verbal accounts alone (Jarman 1997, Verba 1961). As a result, the narrative's key metaphors and lessons become accessible for everyday political discourse and, in periods of high stress, political leaders readily turn to its core images when they seek support for favored action strategies.

Cultural performances: festivals and pilgrimages

To illustrate the enactment of cultural expressions, I turn to two forms of performance – festivals and pilgrimages – neither of which is usually contested but which at times become a focal point in ethnic conflict. Festivals are commonly organized around calendrical, life cycle, and religious principles and can sometimes link and sometimes divide groups and individuals across geographic, kinship, generational, ethnic, and gender lines. Some culturally significant rituals are integrated into daily routines, such as the daily recitation of the Pledge of Allegiance in many American schools, in ways that render them almost invisible to in-group members while affirming the social order and distinguishing one group from another. Other rituals are highly visible, offering a distinctive break from the normal and routine in ways that render them emotionally powerful. This type of ritual is found where participation requires that people suspend normal daily activities and engage in special ones in locations where they might not otherwise go, associate with people whom they otherwise might not encounter, and behave in ways that they might not otherwise. While the distinction between routinely embedded and marked rituals is clear conceptually, it is appropriate to treat them as the endpoints of a continuum recognizing that many ritual activities combine elements of each.

Visible rituals vary widely in the degree of commitment required of participants. For example, in modern industrial societies, most holidays offer a break from daily routine and are distinctive, but participation in them is not very demanding. Many adults do not work at their jobs, children don't go to school, and families and friends get together for socializing and celebrating. Participation in visible rituals that involve high sacrifice or risk increases commitment among participants and emphasizes the boundary between the participants and outsiders. Ritual participation that entails at least moderate costs to participants can become contested in polarized conflicts as in the case of festivals (including cultural fairs and carnivals) and the phenomenon of pilgrimage, two forms of visible ritual participation.

Festivals

Festivals, carnivals, and fairs are large-scale organized activities that occur outside the routines of ongoing social routines. Festivals take diverse forms marking special days for a community and contain both sacred and secular as well as more private and more public elements. For example, Warner (1959) describes the combination of elements in the Memorial Day celebrations he observed in a small New England city in the middle of the last century. He identified four stages in the celebration that moved from diverse rituals separated in time and space to ones that bring members of the community's different ethnic and religious groups and social classes together. Each separate group organized and held their own activities including separate church services for each of the city's religious denominations during part of the day, while later the larger community came together for speeches and a city-wide parade to the cemeteries to honor the war dead.[10]

Sacred festivals, like national holidays, are often affirmations of the political order, although when the regime in power is contested, they can produce counter rituals and challenges to the order and the relationship among groups in it. As Cohen notes, "Generally speaking every major carnival is precariously posed between the affirmation of the established order and its rejection" (Cohen 1993: 3). A festival's interactions and activities provide a release from the constraints and pressures of the social order and "thus carnival connotes sensuousness, freedom, frivolity, expressivity, merrymaking and the development of the amity of what Turner calls 'communitas' as contrasted with structure" (Cohen 1993: 3).

London's Notting Hill Carnival has been since 1959 an on-going festival that at times has attracted over a million people; its changing dynamics illustrate the complex interplay between culture and politics (Cohen 1993). Cohen argues that the choices about music, instruments, competitions, house parties, and gala performances became a symbol of West Indians in Britain "as well as a mechanism for achieving corporate identity, unity and exclusiveness" (1993: 79) in a context where differences of island of origin, the decentralized British electoral system, and a strong distrust of formal organizations made West Indian unity difficult to achieve (1993: 80–83). Over the thirty years he studied the festival, Cohen found that points of contention and moments of unity were highly related to larger political issues in the British–West Indian relationship at

---

[10] An occasion such as Memorial Day in the USA is often marked differently across regions and can sometimes be the focus of conflict over what is and what is not appropriate for inclusion in activities such as a parade (Wagner 2000).

that time. When it began in the 1960s, the Carnival had a multiracial character. By the 1970s it became a black festival dominated by Trinidadian music and masquerading that came to include reggae music and Rastafarian symbols as well as confrontations between West Indian youth and the police. During this time it also emerged as an all West Indian institution (1993: 5). Then by the 1980s the Carnival was more "contained" and the state sought to co-opt and institutionalize it in ways that threatened West Indian identity and ownership of the festival.

Carnival was significant in building long-term primary social relationships among participants; these were particularly associated with musical presentations and masquerade bands. There were on-going contests among West Indians and between West Indians and the British over the production, distribution, and control over the pans, the steel drums central to West Indian music that showed the community's resistance to outside control. At the same time, Cohen makes it clear that the effort to develop communal forms of organization was not a direct and conscious one, and took the form of a search for common 'identity' and exclusive culture" (1993: 84). Carnival met both cultural and political needs, he says, and the revival of traditional forms it stimulated was not regression to the past, but served new purposes (1993: 89–90). Festival participation can represent a significant commitment as it does for the organizers and musicians in Notting Hill. For many attendees, however, participation is far more modest and represents perhaps half a day and a trip on public transportation.

Pilgrimage

Pilgrimage, travels to sacred sites where people participate in rituals and other activities, has a long history in virtually all religious traditions and generally involves a major commitment on the part of the pilgrim. Muslims may travel thousands of miles to go to Mecca and Medina, Catholics walk from the cathedral in Chartres near Paris to Santiago de Compostela in Spain. Hindus journey to the holy city of Varanasi. Mexicans travel in large numbers to see Our Lady of Guadeloupe. However, pilgrimages may also involve groups and sites that are not religious; for example, visits by veterans and others to battlefields or to a memorial such as the Vietnam War Memorial in Washington.

Pilgrimage can fuse culture and politics in particularly explosive ways as leaders manipulate it in pursuit of their own goals. Some of pilgrimages' crucial elements, including the frequent presence of religious symbolism, are easily adapted to political action. One dramatic example of this fusion, discussed in Chapter 8, took place in 1938 when Afrikaner nationalists set out from Cape Town in ox-drawn wagons to mark the 100th anniversary of the Great Trek from the coast to the interior. The reenactment created tremendous enthusiasm and built widespread support for Afrikaner nationalist goals and political leaders. Another example is from 2000 when Zapatista rebel leaders in Chiapas, Mexico, accepted President Vincente Fox's invitation to discuss their demands in Mexico City. However, instead of coming directly to the capitol, they organized a bus caravan that followed a circuitous route passing through and stopping at most major indigenous population centers, to bolster their claims that they were the defenders of the rights of Mexico's indigenous peoples. Traveling through the countryside is, of course, a well-known political campaign strategy and is seen in whistle-stop campaigning and trips such as the 1992 Bill Clinton–Al Gore bus tour in the American Midwest that generated great excitement and jump started their campaign.

Turner describes pilgrimage as a "total process," meaning it is the entire focus of the pilgrims' activity, in which "normative communitas constitutes the characteristic social bond among pilgrims and between pilgrims and those who offer them help and hospitality on their holy journey" (Turner 1974: 169–70). Normative communitas is a pattern of social organization, different from that of structured instrumental groups, that "began with a nonutilitarian experience of brotherhood and fellowship the form of which the resulting group tried to preserve" (Turner 1974: 169). Pilgrimage is often a matter of obligation but it is also a voluntary act involving a vow. "Even when there was obligation, it should be voluntarily undertaken, the obligation should be regarded as desirable" (Turner 1974: 174). Turner notes that pilgrimage shrines tend to be arranged in a hierarchy "with catchment areas of greater and lesser inclusiveness" (Turner 1974: 179). These areas spread across political boundaries as pilgrimage emphasizes universality.[11] Pilgrimage, for Turner, is an inclusive ritual in its organization of pilgrim centers and the relationships among the pilgrims themselves (Turner 1974: 186).

---

[11] Turner notes that "the paradox of the Middle Ages [is] that it was at once more cosmopolitan and more localized than either tribal or capitalist society" (Turner 1974: 183).

Pilgrimage can be viewed as both a religious and political activity. It is often a religious act that can deepen commitment and belief. However, it is also political in important ways. Most obvious is its role in connecting individuals to the larger community of believers. Pilgrimage is also a powerful mechanism for mobilizing sentiment and action in favor of specific political goals. While pilgrimage reinforces identification with existing communities it often offers the image of an ideal community that does not yet exist.

At its core, pilgrimage, like many ritual actions, is a simple, easily understood activity – traveling (often meaning walking) to a sacred place – which is well suited for political action. Often the mixture of religious and political elements captures popular imaginations in dramatic ways. Gandhi's march to the sea in 1930 to pressure the British government to rescind the salt tax mobilized local and world opinion against British colonial practices. Martin Luther King's 1965 Selma to Montgomery march brought national and international attention to American mistreatment of blacks in the South and mobilized support for the passage of the 1965 Voting Rights Act.[12]

Ayodhya

A pilgrimage that combined religious and political symbols in 1990 played an essential role in the dramatic transformation of Indian politics. Since the mid nineteenth century, Hindu nationalist voices in Ayodhya, an important Hindu pilgrimage center, claimed that the sixteenth-century Babi Masjid mosque stood on the spot that was the birthplace of the Hindu god Rama and an eleventh-century Hindu temple (van der Veer 1994: 2–11). Shortly after independence in 1947, a statue of Lord Rama was placed in the mosque one night. Following this incident, a court ruled that the statue could not be removed, effectively closing the mosque. Periodically, the conflict over the site became intense and violent as it did after 1990 when "the BJP [Bharatiya Janata Party] and its confederate, the Vishwa Hindu Parishad (VHP) . . . planned to retake the so-called *Ram janmabhoomi* (birthplace of Rama), to destroy the mosque, if necessary,

---

[12] One could analyze many parts of the American civil rights struggle in the 1960s in terms of its use of pilgrimage – meaning traveling to particular places that built commitment within the movement, mobilizing support from outside, and creating a series of crises that the country could no longer ignore. The Freedom Rides in 1960, various marches in the South, the march on Washington in 1963 all have many of the key elements of pilgrimage and communitas that Turner identifies.

and build a magnificent new temple to Rama to consecrate the sacred site" (Davis 1996: 28). A few years earlier, Indian state television aired an eighteen-month-long serial based on Rama's life and teachings that had come to be written down over the centuries (Rudolph and Rudolph 1993). It was the most successful Indian television program ever, attracting 100 million viewers, and priming Hindus for the subsequent appeals calling for Hindu mobilization in general and the call to rebuild the temple on what they believed to be Rama's birthplace in particular. Shortly after the series ended, in 1989, the VHP asked people throughout North India to make sacred bricks inscribed with Rama's name and to join processions bringing them to Ayodhya for the new temple. Many did so and their actions unleashed both riots and tremendous popular support including prominently exhibited bricks from the United States, Canada, the Caribbean, and South Africa (Davis 1996: 40–41; van der Veer 1994: 4).

The 1990 procession featuring Rama's chariot (a decorated Toyota van) and BJP leader Lal Krishan Advani began in Somnarth, the site of a famous episode of Muslim temple destruction in 1026,[13] and ended at Ayodhya, covering 10,000 kilometers through eight states in Northern India in thirty-five days. The circuitous route passed through a maximum number of north Indian states representing the Hindu heartland and the BJP electoral target. In its journey, the pilgrimage was able to call upon various symbols invoking a range of emotions that built great interest and support for the event and for its political goals.

Perhaps the most resonant icon the VHP disseminated, however, was the depiction of baby Rama, the cherubic child held prisoner in a Muslim religious institution at the very site of his birth. The imagery again drew on the family as an overarching metaphor and enlisted another type of devotional sentiment on behalf of the mobilization. If the aggressive young warrior Rama of the posters served as a militant role model for Hindus taking control of their homeland, the infant Rama called upon maternal devotion from those who would nurture the young reincarnation of Hindu nationhood.

(Davis 1996: 41)

Davis characterizes the procession's message as operating on two levels; "hard-core" militant, aggressive religious imagery coexisted alongside the more "soft-core" BJP anti-secularist (but not anti-Muslim) politics.

---

[13] The temple was rebuilt in 1950 "as a symbol of Indians' nationhood and Hindu dominance in Gujarat" (Davis 1996: 43).

When the pilgrimage procession finally arrived at Ayodhya and tried to reach the mosque, the police fired on the crowd and managed to turn it back. The VHP then campaigned against the police action and defined those who had died as martyrs, carrying their bones and ashes in special pots before immersing them in holy water. Tensions increased over the next two years and on December 6, 1992, the VHP and BJP organized a successful attack on the mosque that resulted in its complete demolition. Deadly riots followed in India, Pakistan, Bangladesh, and even Britain. The intensity of the violence shocked many and van der Veer suggests that "If we want to penetrate the very real passions and violence evoked by the temple-mosque controversy, we must understand how this controversy is related to fundamental orienting conceptions of the world and personhood" (van der Veer 1994: 8).

The 1990 procession created great popular support for the Hindu nationalist position in general, and in particular the BJP, which doubled its national vote in 1991 and moved from its position as a small fringe party to be the country's ruling party in a few short years. In their campaign, references to Ayodhya invoked a powerful narrative of Hindu humiliation resulting from Muslim conquest centuries before that served as a rallying cry for Hindu nationalists. The conflict over religious claims became, in part, transformed into one of personalities, pitting Rama, one of the most widely celebrated Hindu gods, against the Turko-Mogul Babur, who had invaded India and founded an alien Muslim empire (Varshney 2002: 81). The chosen trauma involving the conquest emphasizes Hindu humiliation and defeat and an essentialism in which fourteenth-century Muslim conquerors are equated with the country's present-day Muslim population, while ignoring the great heterogeneity within Hinduism itself (Davis 1996; Friedland and Hecht 1998; van der Veer 1994). "By transforming the mosque in Ayodhya from a local shrine into a symbol of the 'threatened' Hindu majority, the VHP has been instrumental in the homogenization of a 'national' Hinduism" (Ludden 1996: 8). In addition, Varshney argues:

Muslim leaders kept harping on the religious meaning of Ayodhya, refusing to encounter the nationalistic meaning. Worse, the various mosque action committees (and the secular historians) initially argued that Rama was a mythological figure, for there was no historical proof for either Rama's existence or his birthplace. This was a gratuitous argument. Core beliefs of many religions, after all, flourish without proof.

(Varshney 2002: 82)

These Muslim denials combined with a refusal to even discuss possibly moving the mosque enraged many Hindus and "gave the appearance of utter intransigence" (Varshney 2002: 82) leading Hindu nationalists to initiate independent action.[14]

In Ayodhya, the fusion of religious and political appeals, the performative elements of the pilgrimage, and the large-scale participation through activities such as making bricks for the new temple and turning out for the procession, all captured the popular imagination of many Hindus in Northern India. While Ayodhya had been a site of Hindu–Muslim conflict for almost 150 years, the VHP appeals and the Rama TV serial all heightened awareness around a specific humiliation, homogenizing Muslims and linking them across time and space, rendering the militant political actions more plausible. The personalization of the conflict pitting Rama as the defender of Hindu culture against the alien invader only further escalated emotions in an already tense situation.[15]

Psychocultural dramas

So far I have identified some of the forms that politically relevant cultural performance takes. Next I propose a general concept – the psychocultural drama – to describe and to examine cultural contestation that involves perceived threats to identity. Through the lens of psychocultural dramas, the multiple levels of these conflicts come into clearer view as both barriers to, and opportunities for, their constructive management are better understood. Psychocultural dramas sometimes reveal deep structure and vulnerable aspects of identity in a system that might otherwise remain hidden in a conflict (Turner 1974:34).

Psychocultural dramas are conflicts between groups over competing, and apparently irresolvable, claims that engage the central elements of each group's historical experience and contemporary identity. The manifest focus of a psychocultural drama can be over the allocation of material resources, or can involve differences about cultural questions such as language, religion, social practices, or music and popular culture

---

[14] Intransigence marked by humiliation, fear, and denials is also a feature of the conflict around Jerusalem's holy sites discussed in Chapter 6 (Friedland and Hecht 1991).

[15] When archeologists became involved, their results were used for making exclusive political claims built around pristine identities that were at odds with the complexity of peoples and religious fluidity of the area (Meskell 1998; Shaw 2000).

that are connected to a group's core identity. At a deeper level, psychocultural dramas are polarizing events about non-negotiable cultural claims, perceived threats, and/or rights connected to narratives and metaphors central to a group's identity. As psychocultural dramas unfold, they produce reactions which (a) are emotionally powerful; (b) clearly differentiate the parties in conflict; and (c) contain key elements of the larger conflict in which they are embedded. As psychocultural dramas unfold, their powerful emotional meanings link events across time and space, increasing in-group solidarity and out-group hostility (LeVine and Campbell 1972; Volkan 1997).[16]

The idea of the psychocultural drama is adapted from Victor Turner's (1957, 1974) concept of the social drama (Ross 2001). The term psychocultural, rather than social, emphasizes the deeply rooted identity dynamics in conflicts that link large-scale cultural processes through micro-level psychological mechanisms. Turner, particularly in his earlier work, showed little, if any interest, in the psychological dimensions of conflict or the concept of identity and focused exclusively on the level of social organization. Extending Turner's analysis in this manner is very useful for analyzing cultural contestation in ethnic conflict.

The social dramas Turner analyzed are conflicts that are not ever fully resolved, but they are settled for a time when the conflict is redefined away from incompatible principles to the symbolic and ritual domain where disputants can emphasize shared concerns and superordinate goals. The social dramas Turner described took place in a society with shared core values. Yet despite shared values, conflict regularly arises over serious breaches in the social order where there is disagreement over the relative importance of the competing principles that groups or individuals invoke to support their divergent positions in the absence of a jural mechanism to choose among the competing principles (Turner 1957: 89–90).

Turner defines four phases through which social dramas pass: *breach* of social relations or norms, mounting *crisis*, *redressive* action, and *reintegration* or *recognition of schism* (1957: 91–92; 1974: 38–42). "In a social drama it is not a crime [that constitutes the breach], though it may formally resemble one; it is in reality, a 'symbolic trigger of confrontation or encounter'" (1974: 38). As a social drama unfolds, tensions mount and the

---

[16] Not all conflicts are psychocultural dramas. I exclude disputes that do not meet these three criteria, meaning both those that fail to mobilize intense feelings and those which do not divide a community on group lines.

conflict escalates as each side works vigorously to strengthen its position and to draw in new allies. New issues are easily interjected into the conflict, including memories of past disputes and latent feelings of hostility that resurface as social dramas unfold. Social dramas that are especially difficult to resolve involve structural contradictions between norms that cannot be easily settled in the absence of centralized authorities able to render an authoritative and acceptable decision. In these cases, Turner emphasizes the importance of ritual mechanisms of redress, especially when jural mechanisms such as a judicial system, an administrative process, or legislative process that the parties accept as legitimate either do not exist, or are inadequate because none of the competing principles is clearly more important than any of the others. In these conflicts, the scope and intensity of disputes quickly escalates and the initial conflict grows into a crisis.

Movement between the phases is often uneven and some disputes remain mired at the crisis phase. Although Turner first developed his ideas while studying the Ndembu in Zambia, a society with little centralized authority, in divided societies such as Northern Ireland, Israel–Palestine, or Sri Lanka the inability to produce authoritative decisions that both majority and minority communities accept as legitimate produces a parallel impasse. Turner proposes that, at times, ritual can serve as a crucial mechanism to lower tension by emphasizing what the competing parties have in common, allowing the parties in conflict to continue to live together in a more or less peaceful manner without necessarily having resolved their differences.

Among the Ndembu, redressive action through ritual often focused on matters, such as fertility, which were manifestly unrelated to an ongoing crisis over village leadership selection that was a continuing source of tension. Mobilization of the wider community, including many who might have had little involvement in the original dispute, for the performance of reparatory rituals refocused peoples' emotional energy and situated the conflict in a context where disputants emphasized shared norms and goals. Because ritual activity linked disputants through affiliations such as ritual cults or age organizations, it cut across existing communities and lines of cleavage. As a result, it was not so much that the original conflict was resolved in any profound sense since the competing norms were still present. Rather, either the emotional significance of differences diminished sufficiently for people to find a "solution" that lowered tension so that they could return to their daily routines in relative harmony; or, there were outcomes such as the peaceful fission of a village into smaller ones. It is naïve to think that reintegration is immediate even following redressive action. "The reintegration of the disturbed social group or the social recognition and legitimation of irreparable schism between the contesting parties" frequently happened in Turner's cases only after several years (Turner 1974: 41).

Turner posits that ritual is likely to be especially important as a mechanism of conflict mitigation in situations where structural conditions regularly give rise to hard-to-resolve conflicts, a condition that is by no means limited to the specific communities he first studied. In many societies, for example, parties to such conflicts mark its termination with a ceremonial meal in which special foods are cooked and consumed toge-ther. In institutions such as courts or legislatures, decisions are taken and marked in a particular ritualistic fashion that separates the content of the outcome from the personalities of the parties. Power transitions are periods of high stress marked by significant ritual action designed to offer reassurance to people in a period of uncertainty. Central to ritual for Turner are communitas and liminality, conditions outside everyday life that emphasize root metaphors and conceptual archetypes associated with deeper shared meanings than those associated with everyday structure.

Turner's observation, that the intensity of social dramas can be diffused through the transformation of disputes over competing interests into ritual actions emphasizing what the parties share, has important general impli-cations for conflict mitigation in situations where it becomes possible for opponents to participate in mutual or joint ritual expression. Psycho-cultural dramas arise over competing claims that evoke deeply rooted images and cannot be settled by reference to more general rules or higher authority. This is, of course, what characterizes many ethnic conflicts, and what has to be addressed before politics and negotiations can occur. While psychocultural dramas have great political significance, they are not nar-rowly political events, particularly in their early stages. This is because the contending parties emphasize competing positions in such a way that negotiation, redefinition of goals, or compromise is not possible. For example, when a group believes it is fulfilling God's commands, com-promising its goals and modifying behavior become blasphemy.

Ritual acknowledgment and reconciliation

Cultural contestation in long-term conflicts is played out through psy-chocultural dramas in which the images and metaphors of the opposing sides' core narratives play a crucial role. As they develop, opponents frequently operate from such different frames that they misunderstand each other and fail to see how their own actions might be contributing to the escalatory spiral. As long as each side continues to simply reassert its positions, feelings harden and there is escalation and an attempt to defeat a threatening adversary. As violence emerges or increases, the chances of moving toward accommodation diminish. So how do cultural identity conflict cycles end? There are at least four answers to this question. One outcome is that in which one party prevails over the other militarily. Another is that change in external conditions can move one or more of the parties toward accommodation. A variation on this is that outsiders, regional neighbors, the UN, or a coalition of countries intervene to end the conflict. A third idea is that what Zartman (1986) calls the "hurting stalemate," one in which the parties find the cost of continuing the conflict greater than searching for a resolution of it. A fourth is that the parties come to see their own positions and those of an opponent as less incompatible than they had before and they move toward a negotiated settlement. It is possible, of course, for an outcome to combine elements of two or more of these possibilities.

It is the last possibility – the one in which the parties, with or without the assistance of outsiders, modify how they understand themselves and their opponents – that is my main focus. In this scenario psychocultural narratives and dramas play a major role. My argument so far is that when worldviews shift they make actions – including symbolic and ritual ones – possible that allow the opposing groups to respond constructively to each other. The next seven chapters will explore this dynamic and offer cases where the movement toward more inclusive framing of the parties' positions did and did not occur. Central to this dynamic is mutual acknowledgment of each other's perceptions and concerns; such acknowledgment is often implicit rather than explicit, and may not involve acceptance of the other's point of view. The question of how acknowledgment is communicated is important and it is only when we consider ritual and symbolic gestures that we can begin to make sense of this complicated matter.

In recent years, many of these processes have been discussed in the context of the concept of reconciliation as scholars and practitioners have focused on it as a critical aspect of peacemaking between long-term adversaries. Informed by the South African experience and the more than three dozen Truth and Reconciliation Commissions throughout the world, scholars need to ask how political reconciliation between large groups can be promoted through the development and expression of inclusive symbolic and ritual gestures.

As public expressions, more inclusive ritual communicates a change in relations, a notion of shared concerns, and a vision of a joint future. It can make the emotional barriers between the identity groups in conflict more permeable in ways that facilitate negotiations or the implementation of agreements. My argument recognizes that attending only to substantive interests in peace processes is incomplete, and that peace processes need to address the long-standing negative feelings and highly problematic relationships opponents have. As in the case of Nelson Mandela and F. W. de Klerk in South Africa, putting aside an awkward personal relationship to pursue a shared political agenda can in itself be very difficult. Much more challenging, however, is the need to persuade skeptical populations that a change in relations is not more threatening than continuing the conflict. Such persuasion requires that each side deal with two different audiences: the opposing group that has to agree to come to the table where substantive differences can be negotiated and an agreement can be implemented, and dissenting groups within its own community likely to argue that the group's interests are being sold out in any negotiation. The dilemma is like a two-level game in which the rewards for in-group political success are often antithetical to those that promote between-group cooperation.

Reconciliation in this sense is about changing the relationship between parties in conflict both instrumentally and emotionally in a more positive direction so that each can more easily envision a joint future. Reconciliation, from this perspective, is not just an outcome, but a process that is best thought of on a continuum, meaning that there can be degrees of reconciliation rather than just its presence or absence (Kriesberg 2003; Long and Brecke 2003). In the final chapter, I develop the connection between cultural contestation and reconciliation and the development of a vision of a shared future that does not deny, but integrates, memories of the past into a more inclusive narrative and symbolic landscape.

Symbolic and ritual action is integral to reconciliation processes for a number of reasons (Ross 2004): (1) direct apology is difficult, whereas symbolic action can be easier for former enemies to express; (2) words are seen as easy to utter, whereas symbolic actions may be viewed as more sincere; (3) verbal acknowledgments, including apologies, are more cognitive, whereas symbolic actions are affective. The argument is not that symbolic actions are more important than verbal ones but rather that because the two work differently, both words and actions can contribute to reconciliation processes. Symbolic actions are behaviors whose significance is less in the actions themselves than in the meanings individuals and groups accord to them. Symbolic actions, including verbal statements, take many forms and their significance lies in the capacity of symbols and rituals to evoke narratives about the past to make sense of the present (Buckley 1998: 9).

Use of symbolic action entails the development of inclusive rituals that link different communities, or redefinition of older rituals so they are no longer highly threatening and exclusive. Most commonly we think about the divisive role symbolic and ritual action takes in ethnic conflict. There is no doubt that ethnic entrepreneurs, political leaders interested in short-term gains, and even sincere patriots at times mobilize support through emotionally appealing symbolic appeals. It is easy to berate figures such as Ariel Sharon for further polarizing Jews and Palestinians with his visit to the Temple Mount/Noble Sanctuary in September 2000 or Slobodan Milosevic for his constant invocation of the Serb defeat in the battle of Kosovo in 1389 to mobilize support throughout the 1990s; however, the central issue is not about leaders' motives but about why followers respond as they do. The question is less about the "sellers," for it is obvious what they hope to gain from their action, than about the motivation of the "buyers," the followers who respond positively to them. The answer seems to lie in the dynamics of social identity in which individuals see their fate and self-esteem as intimately tied up to that of the group (Brown 1986; Tajfel 1981). Recent psychodynamicly informed theorizing gives a similar answer suggesting that leaders play on followers' need for attachment and on their vulnerability to assertions that the signs of their identity are at risk (Ross 1995; Volkan 1988; 1997). My analysis recognizes that these escalatory dynamics often occur and are common, but turns as well to the possibilities of mobilizing symbolic and ritual policies for bridging differences.

Conclusion

Good enough solutions to bitter conflicts are ones that set the parties on a more constructive course (Ross 2000b). Constructive conflict management does not involve the denial of divergent narratives, but makes space for them to coexist while redefining substantive issues in a way that permits the parties to feel there is something about which they could talk with an opponent (Kelman 1987). This is where symbolic and ritual expressions can come into play. Particularly in high anxiety situations, ritual is crucial in helping the parties reframe or redefine the symbolic and emotional aspects of the conflict so that the parties can move beyond signed agreements and develop the institutions and practices needed to avoid future confrontations.

Most fundamentally, ritual is a significant mechanism for communicating inclusion and exclusion. "Symbols instigate social action" (Turner 1974: 55) and when they are embedded in ritual, symbols "condense many references, uniting them in a single cognitive and affective field" (55). In some situations the result is a real transformation of social relationships.

> If communitas can be developed within a ritual pattern it can be carried over into secular life for a while and help to mitigate or assuage some of the abrasiveness of social conflicts rooted in conflicts of material interest or discrepancies in the ordering of social relations.
>
> (Turner 1974: 56)

While transformation is not necessarily common, the challenge of ethnic conflict mitigation is to enhance the likelihood of its taking place. Through this process rituals can build affective connections among wary opponents who begin to bridge their substantive differences. Of course effective rituals must be grounded in contextually meaningful symbols, and the greatest challenge, as we will see in the succeeding chapters, is the dearth of shared symbols that evoke similar reactions from opposing communities. Ritual is especially useful in conflict situations when it can enlarge a sense of participation and help redefine issues in less exclusive terms that reduce fear and threat.[17]

The discussion in the next seven chapters suggests that when it is possible for ritual and political action to go hand-in-hand, constructive settlement of psychocultural dramas becomes possible even in once bitter

---

[17] In this process cultural expressions can facilitate or inhibit what Zolberg and Woon (1999) call boundary crossing, boundary blurring, and boundary shifting through cultural confrontations. Analyzing similarities and differences between confrontations over religion in Europe and language in the US, they hypothesize that language conflicts are likely to produce assimilation and religious ones greater pluralism. My sense is that this hypothesis is more likely to be correct with regard to immigrant minorities than it is in the case of indigenous or territorially based groups, as Kymlicka (1998) argues in the case of language.

ethnic conflicts. Focusing on cultural disputes in ethnic conflicts is a device for understanding how this might be accomplished at propitious moments in some long-term, intense conflicts. The argument has a certain paradoxical side to it arising from the recognition that the cultural issues the groups fight about so bitterly, such as parades in Northern Ireland, the confederate flag in the United States, language in Canada, or even the holy sites in Jerusalem, are not really what the deeper conflict is about. Rather, they are surface manifestations that are significant because in the battles over these issues, the deepest feelings and fears of the parties on the deeper issues emerge. In the psychocultural dramas I examine, these polarizing fears produce conflict; at the same time the analysis suggests how ritual redress can, and must, be incorporated into any settlement for mitigation of the larger conflict within which they are embedded to occur.

4

Loyalist parades in Northern Ireland as recurring psychocultural dramas

Marches are not simple political demonstrations in Northern Ireland. Rather they are emotionally charged, historical re-enactments of communal triumphs and suffering. The insistence on being allowed to march through the other's neighborhood reveals the territorial and defensive nature of marching.

(Farren and Mulvihill 2000: 31)

Introduction

Protestant Loyal Order[1] parades in Northern Ireland (introduced in Chapter 1) are contentious cultural performances that evoke the core narratives, and the intense emotions associated with them, for large parts of the Protestant and Catholic communities. Parades in Northern Ireland are an idiom of contestation serving as a forum both for demand making and for communication in the region's on-going conflict. These cultural enactments are political statements – provocations and challenges, rights claims, assertions of power, and public acts of commitment. As public performances in which central elements of the Protestant narrative are presented, parades foster widespread mobilization among participants, spectators, and opponents. "Parades are rituals of both celebration and commemoration: they are regarded as a celebration of culture, a demonstration of faith and a commemoration of past sacrifices. They are also displays of collective strength, communal unity and of political power" (Jarman 2003: 93).

---

[1] The Loyal Orders are Protestant ritual groups who strongly support Northern Ireland's continued membership in the United Kingdom and express this through loyalty to the crown.

Widespread participation and engagement in parades reinforces the relevance of the Protestant narrative and the immediacy of the conflict it describes to the many people directly involved, and many more that follow the related events. One loyalist website in Northern Ireland claims, "The Annual [July] Twelfth celebration in Ulster is the largest cultural festival in Europe."[2] Perhaps, but size, however it is measured, is not the issue here. For my analysis the crucial point is that these parades engage people emotionally in ways that increase within-group solidarity and elicit strong out-group hostility, since the very same things that make Protestants proud evoke anger and threat and fear from Catholics.

Parade disputes are not fundamentally about parades; rather, they reveal each side's different understanding of the region's conflict and each side's basic fears and hopes that must be addressed in a successful settlement. Since the 1994 paramilitary ceasefires in Northern Ireland, conflicts over parades have increased in intensity as many "tensions and frustrations found their outlet in bitter disputes over commemorative parading" (Fraser 2000b: 1). In parade disputes, each side emphasizes issues of recognition, respect, and identity through carefully orchestrated symbolic and ritual expressions. Parade disputes reveal powerful feelings for both Protestants and Catholics because the parades, their imagery, and the rituals that surround them hearken back to the mutually exclusive narratives that have divided Protestants and Catholics in the region since the early seventeenth century. For Protestants, the parades evoke an idealized past of control and defense of the community as well as themes of siege, resistance, and self-reliance (Bryan 2000; Buckley 1998; Buckley and Kenney 1995). For Catholics, when Loyal Order parades pass through their communities they are humiliating reminders of no longer tolerable Protestant domination, discrimination, and triumphalism.

Protestant and Catholic worlds in Northern Ireland are socially distinct but politically interdependent as each side's political activity is rooted in the presence, and assumed hostility, of the other. This chapter analyzes this complicated relationship through parade conflicts as psychocultural dramas. First, I introduce some basic background to the Northern Ireland conflict, recognizing that any version of events about a divided society will almost by definition provoke some disagreement from

---

[2] http://www.the-twelfth.org.uk/.

into Scotland, Wales, and Ireland in the context of European emergence from the world of medieval feudalism. Although there had been English colonization in Ireland as early as the twelfth century, Ruane and Todd, like others, identify the early seventeenth century and the colonization accompanying it as the period of shift from efforts at conciliation and bringing the Irish into the framework of law and government to one of coercion and displacement (Ruane and Todd 1996: 19). Ireland, and especially the north, became a settler colony in which there was "the wholesale confiscation of Catholic lands, the expulsion of Catholics from the major towns and the banning of their priests and bishops" in Ulster (Ruane and Todd 1996: 20).

From the late eighteenth century, Irish nationalists struggled for self-rule but when the British finally agreed to home rule in 1912, the Protestants in Ulster objected fiercely and they organized the Ulster Defence Regiment who armed themselves and vowed to fight to remain part of the United Kingdom (Ruane and Todd 1996; Lustick 1993). At the end of World War I, the weary British decided to partition Ireland and in 1920, the southern twenty-six counties became the Irish Free State. Six of the nine counties in historic Ulster in the north, which were nearly two-thirds Protestant, remained part of the United Kingdom, and the Irish Republic, the successor to the Irish Free State in 1949[5] only accepted the division in 1998, when it approved the Good Friday Agreement in a referendum. Following partition, the British Parliament granted Ulster self-rule within the United Kingdom, and the Protestants dominated all aspects of its political and economic life and discriminated against Catholics in job hiring, political representation, the allocation of public housing, and higher education, and they used paramilitary units as police to control the Catholic population (Boyle and Hadden 1994; Darby 1983; Wichert 1991). Most Catholics refused to recognize the regime in the north as legitimate, and when the British suspended the Northern Ireland government in 1972, no Catholic had ever served as a government minister (Farren and Mulvihill 2000).

Civil rights protests in the North began in the late 1960s demanding an end to blatant anti-Catholic discrimination. The Rev. Ian Paisley, a fiery hard-line Protestant leader, advocated meeting every march with a counter

---

[5] The Republic of Ireland withdrew from the British Commonwealth of Nations. The Free State, as an expression of their hostility to the British, remained neutral during World War II.

Figure 4.1 Map of the United Kingdom and Ireland

march, and refused to denounce frequent Protestant violence by off-duty police – and sometimes ones on duty as well. In response, support for the newly reconstituted Provisional Irish Republican Army, the self-proclaimed defender of the Catholic community, increased. In 1970, the British sent in army troops to maintain order. First welcomed by the vulnerable Catholic community as protectors, the army lost Catholic support as it engaged in mass round-ups of suspects, internment without trial, and trials without

93

juries. As the Catholic IRA attacked Protestant militias and the British army, the region sunk into a spiral of violence. In 1972, the high point of the killing, the British suspended the Northern Irish government and imposed direct rule from London, which remained in place until the Good Friday Agreement in 1998. Violence continued throughout the period involving both Protestant and Catholic paramilitary groups, the police, and the British army, but remained at what John Darby has called a "tolerable" level, meaning that neither side felt sufficient pressure to seek a settlement (Darby 1986).

Protestants and Catholics oppose each other but are also internally divided.[6] These differences can be described in terms of general labels that are commonly applied and in terms of the political parties within each community. Unionists and Loyalists are overwhelmingly Protestant and these terms describe people who favor continuing the union of Northern Ireland and Great Britain in the United Kingdom. Unionist is the more general term focusing on political linkage while Loyalists are more focused on British, and especially Scottish, culture and identity in addition to their political support for the union. Loyalists often emphasize their connection to the British crown more than to the government. Politically Protestants are split between the mostly middle-class Ulster Unionist Party (UUP), and Paisley's more working-class Democratic Unionist Party (DUP). Among Catholics, Nationalists are those who continue to favor the reunification of Ireland, and Republicans, who while favoring a united Ireland, have been generally willing to endorse the use of violence and to support the IRA to achieve reunification. There are two major Catholic political parties, the more moderate and more middle-class Social Democratic and Labour Party (SDLP) that has long renounced violence as a legitimate political weapon, but not the goal of reunification of the island, and Sinn Féin (SF), the political wing of the IRA, headed by Gerry Adams.

In 1994, the IRA and the major Protestant paramilitary groups declared a ceasefire and since that time, political violence between the communities has almost ended.[7] The British army is no longer visible on the streets and

---

[6] At times there have been significant shifts in each side's emphasis and organization as well. Whyte (1990), for example, describes a gradual shift in both narratives from emphasizing an external opponent (the British or the Irish) to paying more attention to internal ones (Protestants and Catholics in the North). O'Malley (1983) offers a richly textured view of differences in narratives within and between both communities.

[7] There is some significant within-community violence especially among Protestant paramilitaries, increased criminal activities, punishment beatings in both Protestant and

most of the troops have been withdrawn from the region. In many places in Northern Ireland today, daily life is very ordinary for the first time in two generations. Negotiations involving all the major stakeholders, the political parties, the British and Irish governments, and even the US have replaced what had been an almost exclusive reliance on unilateral, self-help strategies. In 1998, there was a settlement, known variously as the Good Friday, or Belfast, Agreement, spelling out new power-sharing institutions, and shortly thereafter, majorities in both communities in the North supported it in a referendum (McGarry and O'Leary 2004).

Despite the fact that the new political arrangements provide incentives for all parties to share power, politicians in the region have been cautious in moving away from a politics of confrontation. Political competition still occurs only within each community since there is little cross-community trust, although the agreement does require a majority in each group to create a government. When it has operated, the executive included ministers from all four major parties but, twice since 1998, the British suspended it when the narrow Unionist majority disappeared over the issue of IRA weapons decommissioning. Elections in 2003 to try to break the deadlock failed to lead to a new government and the North is again ruled directly from London. At the same time, there has been no return to violence, as the different paramilitary groups know how unpopular this would make them in their own communities.

Because there are no politically significant cross-community appeals, the intense divisions within each community produce a strident political rhetoric emphasizing how individual leaders and their parties are defending their own community's interests. There is a great fear of appearing too weak in the face of out-group challenges, and a continuing distrust of the motives of the other side. Many have found that cultural expressions are one significant way they can express strong support for their community and its goals in a non-violent manner. As a result, polarizing issues such as Loyal Order parades are a continuing source of high inter-community distrust and vehicles for the expression of each side's anger.

Catholic narrative

At the core of the Catholic narrative is a focus on the injustice of colonization, displacement, discrimination, and the demand that the small

---

Catholic communities, and outbreaks of violence in some interface areas in north and east Belfast.

island of Ireland be reunited politically. Typically, the Catholic narrative begins with the twelfth-century Norman invasion of Ireland that marks the start of British displacement and oppression of the island's original inhabitants. However, the seventeenth-century Ulster Plantation draws the greatest ire from the Irish and marks the beginning of their struggle for self-rule. In this four-century struggle, Catholics have a long list of martyrs, including eighteenth, nineteenth, and twentieth-century Irish nationalist heroes, poets who wrote powerfully of their people's suffering, the leaders of the 1916 Easter uprising, and the IRA hunger strikers who died in the early 1980s (O'Malley 1990). Catholics grant little legitimacy to the Northern Ireland government that ruled from 1920 to 1972 since Protestant rule meant systematic discrimination against Catholics in politics, employment, and housing as well as denigration of their culture and attacks upon their religion.

While there had been resistance for centuries, Catholics believe that it was only when they began to organize and protest their treatment that matters came to a head. In the 1960s, the strategy of peaceful protest and dialogue seemed to be helpful as there were some sympathetic Protestant and British ears. However, it was soon clear that Protestant opposition had hardened and there was little belief that they would share power without being forced to do so. When quasi-state Protestant paramilitaries began attacking Civil Rights protesters and the Protestant-dominated police force did little to protect them, the moribund IRA began to revive to defend the community. The British sent the army into the region promising to protect Catholic areas that had become subject to beatings, fire bombings, and killings. However, Catholics soon felt that the British were siding with the Protestants, and the army became the target of Catholic violence. Catholic leaders demanded power sharing in the North and there were renewed cries for a united Ireland. There was a British-led effort to create a power-sharing government, but when a Protestant general strike brought it down in 1974, the British backed off and instituted direct rule of the region.

For a time various peacemaking initiatives got nowhere. Catholics attributed this to Protestant intransigence and to British support for them and as a result many saw the militarization of the conflict as inevitable. When IRA prisoners began hunger strikes to support their demands that they be recognized as political, and not criminal, prisoners, Margaret Thatcher's government simply said no and let ten of them die. Her action then turned Bobby Sands and his fellow strikers into martyrs whose funerals brought tens, and maybe even hundreds, of thousands of people into the streets, including many Catholics who were neither IRA supporters nor advocates of violence. Soon thereafter, the British government changed course when they acknowledged an Irish role in the North and the two governments negotiated the 1985 Anglo-Irish Agreement that provided the basis for the 1998 Agreement. In the 1980s Sinn Féin decided to participate in elections and achieved some successes although their vote totals were lower than those of the SDLP. The British inclusion of the Irish government as a partner, and talks between Sinn Féin and John Hume's Social Democratic and Labour Party, led to some Track 2 and back channel dialogues and a gradual reduction in IRA violence.[8] Negotiations were slow to get started, however, and it was only when the United States weighed into the process, with Bill Clinton's acceptance of Gerry Adams' renunciation of violence, and Senator George Mitchell's leadership of all-party negotiations, that an agreement was reached.

The problem for many Catholics is that the agreement has not been fully implemented because of what most see as Protestant foot dragging. In their view, Protestants have imposed arbitrary conditions on its implementation, have stalled on matters such as police reform, and have consistently failed to accord Catholics and their concerns the "parity of esteem" they committed to in the negotiations. One example of this is the refusal of many Protestant politicians to acknowledge the offensive nature of many Loyal Order parades and to take steps to curb those aspects most offensive to Catholics.

Protestant narrative

The Protestant narrative emphasizes the long struggle to maintain their religion and culture, their loyalty to the crown, and their membership in the United Kingdom against the threats of Catholic domination and violence.[9] Protestant settlement, especially in the north, began a period of development and early modernization in which the Protestants persevered despite the threats from the local population and dangers such as the counter-reformation. Three seventeenth-century dates are especially relevant in Protestant collective memories: 1641, 1689, and 1690. In

---

[8] By the 1990s more deaths in Northern Ireland were attributed to Protestant paramilitaries than to the IRA.
[9] For extensive treatment of Ulster's Protestants, see Akenson (1992), Bruce (1994), and McKay (2000).

1641, Catholics rose up and mounted attacks against the outnumbered and vulnerable Protestant settlers. In the next decade, under Cromwell, the Irish were subdued, and settler rule expanded. For Protestants, William of Orange breaking the siege of Derry in 1689 and his victory in the Battle of the Boyne the following year are central foundation myths.[10] The lessons of steadfastness and self-reliance are perhaps best summed up with the phrase "No Surrender," which Protestants evoke repeatedly.[11]

In 1912 when the British were about to grant the Irish self-rule, Protestants in Ulster created the Ulster Defence Regiment to prevent the change. For Protestants, their story is one of perseverance and survival in a hostile, threatening world where enemies forever challenge them. In this account, building a "Protestant state for a Protestant people" as William Craig, Northern Ireland's first prime minister put it, is viewed in heroic terms, and a united Ireland is a step backwards culturally, politically, and religiously. Protestants see it not only as a loss of control, but also a threat to the very existence of their community and their rights and liberties.[12]

The Protestant narrative portrays a world filled with dangers that can only be managed through vigilance and self-help. Protestants see themselves as a vulnerable small group emphasizing that while they may be a majority in Northern Ireland they are a minority on the island as a whole. Catholic use of violence and terror since the 1960s only reinforced this worldview. There is not only on-going anger against IRA terrorist activities, but disbelief at those who either expressed support for it, or failed to condemn it. For example, when the IRA hunger strikers were dying and there was a large public funeral for each man, Protestants expressed outrage that so many Catholics who claimed they rejected violence would participate in honoring people Protestants viewed as criminals.[13]

[10] Walker offers the interesting argument that emphasis on these seventeenth-century dates only became politically significant to Protestants in the 1880s when Unionist–Nationalist confrontations increased (1996: 5).

[11] Akenson (1992) describes Protestant culture in Northern Ireland as covenantal, referring to the Old Testament sacred covenant in the Exodus story in which God promises the Jews he will be their god if they promise to be his people. To do this they must obey his laws and follow an often difficult path.

[12] Protestant accounts emphasize the shrinking Protestant population of Ireland since 1920, the Catholic Church's influence over social legislation, and Catholic insistence that children of Protestant–Catholic marriages be raised as Catholics.

[13] Not only did Catholics hold a succession of public funerals, but Sinn Féin continued to elect a succession of the dying men, starting with Bobby Sands, to the House of Commons. The SDLP did not contest the seats not wanting to divide the Catholic vote in

Feelings of weakening British support, and condemnation of the British decision to accord the Irish Republic a role in Northern Ireland as treason, reinforce an historic Protestant sense of isolation and a turn to self-help as a survival strategy. For people such as Rev. Ian Paisley, the head of the largest party after the 2003 elections, resistance is the only course. The debate among Protestants is over the basic nature of Protestant cultural and political identity in a political environment that includes British and Irish membership in the European Community. In this context, the meaning of sovereignty, defensible borders, and cultural identity defined around loyalty to the sovereign and/or religious identity is increasingly problematic. Some Protestants seem fearful that if they fail to strengthen and defend the community culturally and politically their future is at risk, while others express a more strategic political view emphasizing instrumental concerns around power sharing and institutional development. Much of this anxiety, we will see, is played out through conflicts within and between each community about the meaning of traditions and especially those associated with Loyal Order parades.

Divergent narratives

Each side's account is highly selective and recognizes the other only as an oppressor or threat (as portrayed in Figure 4.2). Neither acknowledges the many shared themes in the two accounts (Nic Craith 2002). What the two narratives do share, however, is a sense of injustice and vulnerability, but the incidents that each recounts are either different, or described very differently. Each community stresses the need for internal unity and consensus while blaming the other for its problems. Differentiation means that there are distinct dates and events that each community finds significant and competing interpretations for those that both mark. For example, Protestants see the early seventeenth century as the time when they brought civilization and development to Ireland, while Catholics describe the same period as one of displacement and colonization. Protestants portray Catholic massacres in 1641, while Catholics remember Protestant retaliation in kind eight years later. The nineteenth and twentieth centuries are viewed equally differently for each community, with the Catholics focusing on the fight against British and Protestant

---

these elections and thereby reinforced the Protestant view that the Catholic leaders such as John Hume were insincere and duplicitous when they claimed they opposed violence.

Figure 4.2 *Selected divergence in Protestant and Catholic narratives*

EVENT	DATE	PROTESTANT INTERPRETATION	CATHOLIC INTERPRETATION
Celtic settlement	BCE		Establishment of Ireland's "original inhabitants"
Plantation – Scottish and English settlement	Early 1600s	Protestants bring civilization and development to Ireland	Period of displacement and colonization
Catholic massacres	1641	Vulnerability	
Protestant massacres	1649		Vulnerability
Protestants break the siege of Derry	1689	Necessity for self-reliance as a strategy for survival in a hostile world; "no surrender"; survival of Protestantism and democracy	
Protestant victory in the Battle of the Boyne	1690		
Movement for Home Rule	18th, 19th centuries	Catholic threats and the need for vigilance	Suffering of heroes and martyrs for the Irish people
Potato famine	1840s		Trauma, discrimination, and migration
Battle of the Somme; Easter uprising	1916	Protestant heroism and sacrifice	Heroes, martyrs sacrificing for their people
Total Protestant control of the Region	1920–72	"A Protestant State for a Protestant People"	Systematic discrimination and exclusion
"Troubles"	1969–94	Catholic terrorism	Protestant and British repression of people battling for self-determination
IRA prisoner hunger strikes	Early 1980s	Honoring killers	Honoring martyrs
Anglo-Irish Agreement	1985	British sell-out	Recognition of legitimate Irish role in Northern Ireland
Paramilitary ceasefires leading to Good Friday/ Belfast Agreement	1994–98	Insecurity and isolation as the British negotiate with Sinn Féin and the IRA	Turn to politics – "the war is over"
Stalemate – self-rule on and off	1998–2006	IRA resist real disarmament	Protestants unwilling to share power despite IRA renunciation of violence

oppression and control, and Protestants emphasizing their struggle for self-rule within the union. 1916 marks a common date for both that has strikingly different significance for each community. For Protestants it marks the death of thousands of soldiers from Northern Ireland in the Battle of the Somme, while Catholics commemorate the Easter Rising in Dublin and the British public hanging of its leaders.

In this context, it is not surprisingly that there is little shared symbolic space in the region. Murals, often with paramilitary images, flags, and painted curbstones mark off territory, warning outsiders they are not welcome. Few symbols and rituals are shared and the two communities differ even in the sports they are passionate about and the teams they support. Only rarely do the two communities share a common reaction to events or share a symbolic or ritual event together.[14] One interesting exception is an exhibit in the Derry City Museum that at one point, when describing events in the early twentieth century, asks visitors to look at one side of the exhibit to see key events for the Catholic community and at the other to learn what most concerned the Protestants. The exhibit graphically demonstrates how in 1916, for example, Catholics emphasize the Easter uprising in Dublin while Protestants emphasize the battle deaths of the Ulster Regiment at the Battle of the Somme. It does not try to mediate between the accounts, but makes it clear that both exist side by side (Figure 4.3).

Parades disputes as psychocultural dramas

Parading has deep roots in European guilds and religious celebrations (Fraser 2000b: 3). Parades can be commemorative and celebratory, a mechanism for supporting the existing political order, or can be used for protest and confrontation and for "powerful expressions of cultural identity especially when that culture seemed to be under threat" (Fraser 2000b: 3). Loyal Order parades in Northern Ireland have been all of these since they began over 200 years ago. The Loyal Orders – the Orange, Purple and Black Orders and the Apprentice Boys of Derry – are exclusively Protestant. The Orange Order is the largest of these and from 1920 to 1972, all government leaders in Northern Ireland were Orange Order members

---

[14] A few years ago, the *New York Times* reported on a professional ice hockey team in Belfast and described how team supporters met only at the arena where the games were played to avoid learning anything about each other's ethnic identity, for fear that such knowledge would threaten their shared rooting interest and friendship.

Figure 4.3 Two views of 1916: The exhibits in the City of Derry Museum include an explanation of how Northern Ireland's two narratives clashed early in the twentieth century as Catholics emphasized the need for independence while Protestants sought continued union within the United Kingdom; 1916 is especially striking as Catholics emphasize the Easter Uprising in Dublin and Protestants focus on the losses in the deadly World War I Battle of the Somme.

and Orange Order parades were ritual exercises in support of the state. Once the British instituted direct rule the parades became settings for protest politics, expressing increasingly strident anti-Catholic sentiment and support for paramilitary organizations. This pattern is hardly an exception and Wright (1992: 11–20) argues that majority groups often form cultural or fraternal organizations that express dominance and communal deterrence.

The Orange Order began in the late 1790s, although Protestant parading in Ireland is far older (Kelly 2000). The Apprentice Boys of Derry are older; Fraser reports that they have held commemorative parades since at least 1759 (2000b: 174). Loyal Order commemorations mark Protestant military victories and defeats that are significant in their narrative of struggle for freedom and democracy. For example Rev. W. Martin Smyth, former Grand Master of the Orange Order and a British MP, speaking about what a Protestant defeat at the 1690 Battle of the Boyne would have meant said, "I think it would have been a catastrophe for democracy and the Protestant cause" (McGeach

1990). During the Stormont period, 1920–72, parades emphasized the legitimacy of the state and were generally pro-government political rallies. No Protestant parades were banned during this time and only a few were ever halted (Jeffrey 2000: 82). Even after the imposition of direct rule in 1972, the Royal Ulster Constabulary (RUC), the Protestant dominated police force,[15] supervised parades and rarely intervened to reroute or halt them.

The marching season in Northern Ireland, when the vast majority of Loyal Order parades occur, is roughly from late spring to August. The over 2,500 Protestant parades each year take many forms. Some are church parades and include a religious service. There are small local parades as well as ones that grow larger as smaller feeder parades merge. Rural parades tend to be smaller and less strident while parades in the larger cities and towns are often louder, more provocative, and more contentious when they go on streets between the two communities, pass through Catholic neighborhoods, or march past a Catholic church. Furthermore, parades change in form and content over time – despite the images of timelessness that surround them – and should be seen as responses to contemporary political contexts (Jarman 1997; Bryan 2000).

The largest and most significant parades mark three sacred days, (July 1, July 12, and August 12) in the Protestant civil religious calendar: the Battle of the Somme in 1916 in which thousands troops from the 36th Ulster Division died,[16] the Battle of the Boyne in 1690 when William of Orange's Protestant forces defeated Catholic King James II, and the end of the siege of Derry in 1689 when William of Orange's forces reached the city and rescued it from the besieging Catholic army.[17] In practice, not all parades are as solemn as the occasions they mark.

---

[15] Estimates are that the force was over 90 percent Protestant at that time. Catholics had little incentive to serve and IRA threats to harm family members of Catholic police hardly encouraged recruitment.

[16] There were many Irish Catholics in the British army in World War I and a third of the deaths at the Somme were Catholics. However, only Protestants commemorate the losses in the battle. The 36th Ulster Division, made up of Northern Irish Protestants who in 1912 had vowed to oppose Irish Home Rule by force, if necessary, suffered especially high losses. For many years, hard-line Irish Nationalists believed that those Irish who served in the British forces were either traitors or dupes. I have been told about Irish families in which soldiers died in the war whose family accounts attribute their deaths to industrial accidents or disease.

[17] July 12 is the most important one and a public holiday. See Lucy and McClure (1997) for personal accounts of its emotional meaning in Northern Ireland for people in both communities.

Parades have a number of crucial elements besides the lodge members who walk in them and carry the lodge banners that contain images of King William and other Protestant icons. Individual lodges hire bands but band members generally are not lodge members, and certain instruments such as the fife and the large Lambeg drum are associated with these parades. Some bands are solemn while others, known as Blood and Thunder (or Kick the Pope) bands wear paramilitary insignias, are aggressive, and play blatantly anti-Catholic songs. Traditionally, larger parades often include political speeches from leading politicians although few spectators pay a great deal of attention to them. Lastly, the marchers and spectators consume a great deal of alcohol although parade organizers publicly frown on its use. As a result, a parade that is more or less orderly and well behaved early in the day might be one that is rowdy and aggressive seven or eight hours later.

Loyal Order parades have been contentious for years, and after the ceasefires in 1994, they became a major focus of intergroup tension, often as a function of political developments (Figure 4.4). Catholic residents groups with close links to Sinn Féin began to demand changes in what they saw as "triumphalist" and sectarian parades that went through their neighborhoods and they protested vigorously when the police (the RUC) either rejected, or refused to consider, their complaints. They demanded negotiations and argued that parades required community consent as a sign of respect. "No consent, no parade," and "No talk, no walk." In some cases, the government brought in heavily armed police, and sometimes the army, to ensure the marchers could walk their traditional routes. Parading served as a substitute for political discourse and "No observer of Irish affairs can afford to underestimate the seriousness of what was happening" (Fraser 2000b: 2). In 1996, the British government appointed an independent review panel to examine the deteriorating situation. Among its recommendations about how better to manage parades was one to create a Parades Commission to deal with contentious parades, which was made at least, in part, because the RUC was seen as too partisan and too vulnerable to political pressures (Jarman 2003).

The Parades Commission came into existence in 1997 and the next year began implementing review procedures that required groups wanting to hold parades to apply to the Commission in advance. The Commission then had the power to rule on their route, the size of the group, the time of day it would walk certain parts of their route, who would be included, the number and identity of bands in the parade, as well as what kind of music, would, and would not, be played.

Figure 4.4 *Timeline of political events and parading in Northern Ireland*

DATE	POLITICAL EVENTS	PARADE EVENTS	COMMENTARY
Early 1600s	Plantation – Scottish and English settlement		Much of the Irish population removed from Ulster; colonial rule provides few rights to Irish
1640s	Uprisings and reprisals		Tension as Catholics resist and Protestants assert control over Ireland
1750s		Apprentice Boys of Derry begin parades	
Late 1700s	1798 rebellion	Orange Order founded in County Armagh	Lines of division and discrimination are clear
1800–1920	Irish demand home rule	Ongoing parading	Continuing separation of Protestant and Catholic social and political worlds
1920–70	Irish Home Rule in the South and Protestant rule in the North	Loyal Order parades as state sponsored rituals	All government leaders in Northern Ireland are members of Orange Order; systematic discrimination against Catholics
1960s	O'Neill reform efforts; Civil Rights Movement emerges		Reform efforts stall and violence increases when Catholics demand equal rights and Protestant paramilitaries respond

Figure 4.4 (*Cont.*)

DATE	POLITICAL EVENTS	PARADE EVENTS		COMMENTARY
		Parades are sometimes occasions for violent confrontations		
		PORTADOWN	DERRY	
1969	"Troubles" begin			IRA organizes in response to Protestant paramilitaries; British sends in army troops
1969	British army troops sent to restore order		Battle of the Bogside	Catholics first welcome the troops as protectors; army's actions soon produce anger and violent opposition
1972			Bloody Sunday	British troops fire on protesters killing 13 in Derry
1972–94			City walls occupied by British troops; parades continue elsewhere	
1972	British suspend Northern Irish government and impose direct rule			Widespread internment and convictions without trials in response to the IRA bombing campaign
1985	Anglo-Irish Agreement			British and Irish governments acknowledge Irish role in the North

Year				
1985–86	Protestants protest the Anglo-Irish Agreement	Six major riots and violence when RUC changes parade routes		The Orange Order parade route was through a Catholic area; the RUC rerouted it to avoid incidents; Protestants violently protested the change
1994	IRA and Protestant paramilitary groups announce ceasefires		Some Apprentice Boys allowed to march on the walls; Catholic protests follow	Hope but uncertainly about whether the ceasefires will last
1995		Parades become increasingly contentious and violent; Psychocultural dramas begin in both Portadown and Derry		Fear that the situation will deteriorate and violence will return
	RUC first bans then allows Orange Order parade down Garvaghy Rd.; RUC removes Catholic protesters from the route; Trimble and Paisley lead the parade	Apprentice Boys seek to march on the city walls; BRG protests; negotiations fail; RUC removes protesters from walls; parade takes place; rioting erupts		High tension in both places as parade conflicts become ways to symbolically express opposing positions following the ceasefires; competing narratives – freedom of assembly versus freedom from intimidation; Protestants emphasize value of self-defense and self-reliance; Catholics express outrange at Protestant triumphalism

Figure 4.4 (*Cont.*)

DATE	POLITICAL EVENTS	PARADE EVENTS		COMMENTARY
1996		Pattern repeated; RUC first bans parade then reverses decision; police clash with Catholic protesters	Three nights of rioting in Derry following stand-off in Portadown; negotiations begin, but fail; Apprentice Boys parade on the walls in October	More of the same
1997			British appoint Independent Review panel	Proposes creation of Parades Commission that is quickly established
	Negotiations stall although election of Labour provides hope	Police and army secure the area; parade proceeds through Catholic neighborhood	Proximity negotiations begin; tensions ease	In Portadown tension and violence continue while in Derry shuttle diplomacy does not reach agreement but the parade is held in atmosphere of decreasing tension
1998	Good Friday/ Belfast Agreement	Parades Commission bans the part of parade on the Garvaghy Rd.; huge Protestant protests and violence, killing three children	Further negotiations between BRG and ABOD; peaceful march; parades take place with few incidents	The political agreement spells out power-sharing plan that is ratified in a referendum; Drumcree-related violence produces strong disapproval from some Protestants including many church leaders

Year			
1999	Last part of parade not permitted again; large army presence; peaceful protest/angry speeches	Agreement reached on the parade prior to December; Catholic dominated city council supports parade as part of city festival	Protests against the Parades Commission decisions in Portadown become more ritualized; significant movement in Derry towards redefinition of the parade as part of a more inclusive community ritual
2000–01	Pattern repeated	Continuing development of more inclusive ritual events	Parades Commission negotiates working agreements in many areas and its decisions are implemented
2002	Police reduce presence, but violence results		Widespread disapproval of Portadown violence; lower tension in Derry parades
2003–06	Protestants show some limited openness to negotiations; parades remain peaceful		Fewer parades-related violent incidents throughout Northern Ireland; Orange Order member agrees to join the Parades Commission

Most parades are not contentious and require no Commission ruling but about 60–100 each year require a decision. The Commission hoped many of these could be resolved through informal negotiations or with the help of Commission appointed officers. In many cases this has worked, although right from the start the Loyal Orders challenged the Commission's legitimacy and refused to participate in the Commission saying that the right to march their traditional routes was not a matter that civil servants should consider, let alone decide. In late 2005 the Orange Order changed their position and a former district master joined the reconstituted commission and the loyal orders issued a statement saying they "intended to engage with the government on the parades issue in the New Year" (BBC 2005).

Parade conflicts are psychocultural dramas in which each party's core narrative is played out and demands about the present are couched in terms of the past. The unfolding events invoke intense feelings of threat that produce a widespread need to defend the group's symbols and rituals (North 1997: 41–52). Each side's defensive moves are viewed as offensive ones by the other community, which then responds in kind – a classic escalatory spiral (Jervis 1976). As Bryan says, "Orange parades are ritual events and are cited by both those inside and outside the community as pivotal to local Protestant 'tradition', defining the ethnic boundary between Protestant and Catholic communities" (Bryan 1997: 375). "Much of their power comes from their ability to give identity and historical meaning to the world" (Bryan 1997: 392). Many Protestants contend that parades are simply expressions of faith and heritage while ignoring features of them that are so problematic to nationalists.[18] Catholics link Loyalist parades with powerful, negative, symbols associated with colonization, discrimination, and humiliation. As a result, confrontations are regarded in win-lose terms and a middle ground is hard to find as each side selectively emphasizes its own account while ignoring that of the other.

Parade conflicts can be examined as recurring psychocultural dramas that begin with a proposed parade to which Republicans object. Crises

---

[18] "Parades are very much part of the Orange tradition and heritage as two hundred years ago the founding fathers decided that parades were an appropriate medium to witness for their faith and to celebrate their cultural heritage . . . The Flags and Banners are full of religious, cultural and political symbolism showing biblical scenes, famous people or events in history and in themselves portray the rich cultural heritage of our people in colorful picture form" (www.grandorange.org.uk/parades/tradition_parades.html).

build as the authorities consider a contentious parade and escalate as each side makes its public case and mobilizes supporters. Appeals emphasize competing rights and the mutually exclusive rhetoric evokes powerful images of struggle, resistance, historical suffering, and identity from each group's core narratives.

In some cases, the Parades Commission makes a decision that the parties accept, at least tacitly, and a parade takes place but there is some form of symbolic, but non-violent, protest.[19] The weakness, or even absence, of a binding authority that the contending parties recognize as legitimate to resolve such disputes means that in highly contentious situations, redressive action requires symbolic and ritual steps as part of any successful outcome. However, Northern Ireland lacks shared institutions capable of producing mutually acceptable outcomes. For many years, the Nationalist community had no faith in the security forces – the police and the British army – to control the marchers' abusive behaviors, while the Orange Order refused to talk to residents' groups or deal with the Parades Commission since they believed it had no right to restrict the expression of their heritage. In this context, there are no settlements of differences, only imposed decisions, ritual repetition of stalemated confrontations, and all too infrequent outcomes that redefine parading in a way that is tolerable to both the Loyal Orders and nationalists.

Many psychocultural dramas arising from parades disputes do not effectively invoke redressive mechanisms, and remain stuck in the crisis stage; in Portadown, there is a yearly ritual replay of the stalemate. However, in Derry, wider community involvement, negotiations, and a creative leadership led to symbolic and ritual redress that moved the parties beyond confrontation and toward some change in the city's symbolic landscape.

Portadown: ritual stalemate

To explore parades disputes as recurring psychocultural dramas consider Portadown, a small town south of Belfast near where the Orange Order was founded, that has since the 1980s been the site of some of the region's most contentious parade disputes. In 1985 and 1986 there were six major

---

[19] Even non-violent protests around parades carry a threat of violence when angry crowds gather, in part because protest and parade organizers have incomplete control over them (Lee Smithey, personal communication).

riots and many violent incidents associated with the Orange Order parades when the RUC rerouted the July parades commemorating the Battle of the Somme away from a narrow road through a Catholic nationalist working-class area (Bryan 1997: 374–75).

Since 1995, there has been a series of yearly psychocultural dramas surrounding the Portadown parade. On the first Sunday of July, the Portadown Loyal Orange Order District No. 1 begins its Somme Commemoration parade around 10 a.m. at its Lodge on Carleton Street; it takes about an hour and fifteen minutes to reach the Drumcree Church a little less than 3 miles away, just outside the small town. At the church, there is a religious service and when it concludes shortly before 1 p.m., tradition calls for the marchers to proceed back to their Lodge on a route that includes the Garvaghy Road, once a country lane and now running next to a housing estate filled with Catholic residents.

This short stretch of road became the center of intense, sometimes violent, conflict that produced yearly psychocultural dramas. From 1995 to 1997, Catholics protested this part of the parade route, and the yearly crisis mounted as Protestants evoked images of earlier sieges they had endured. Each year there was escalation, protest, and violence as the RUC would first rule for the Catholics, and hard-line Orange Order members and their supporters burned businesses and cars, and clashed with police to defend what they saw as their inalienable right to "march the King's highway" following their service at Drumcree Church.[20] The police would then reverse their decision fearing more Protestant violence. Catholics would respond with their own protests and rioting when the police cleared protesters from the Garvaghy Road and allowed the Orangemen to walk the entire route. Catholics felt betrayed when the police reversed their decision and when, as in 1995, prominent Protestant politicians, including David Trimble and Ian Paisley, marched in the front of the procession, they again experienced Protestant triumphalism.

These outcomes were hardly effective conflict management. In 1998 following the Good Friday Agreement and its ratification, the newly created Parades Commission refused to let the Orange Order march on the Garvaghy Road unless they first engaged in dialogue with the

---

[20] On the Portadown Lodge's website Martin Luther King is quoted in defense of the right to freedom of assembly and speech. There is no quote from him, however, concerning the unacceptability of violence (http://www.portadowndistrictlolno1.co.uk/).

112

residents' association. Thousands of Orangemen and their allies gathered in Drumcree hoping, once again, they could force a reversal of the original decision. This time, however, when on the eve of the march the house of a Protestant man and his Catholic wife some miles away in Ballymoney was firebombed, killing her three children from a previous marriage, the fervor of the protesters dissipated and the ban stayed in place. Nevertheless, a hard core of protesters camped out next to Drumcree church, unwilling to call off their protest and vowing they would not leave until they could complete their march. The powerful yearly Drumcree psychocultural dramas gained the full attention of the region and beyond, evoking strong feelings from each community and displacing other concerns. In 1998, for example, the parade conflict clearly delayed, and distracted from, efforts to implement the recent Good Friday Agreement. In Portadown's psycho-cultural dramas, the movement from crisis to redressive mechanisms never occurred and the crisis rested unresolved in 2006 although its intensity had significantly diminished (Jarman 2003).

The Orange Order recognized that it would be held responsible if there were major violent incidents, and its protests became more and more ritualized after 1998. The Parades Commission did not alter its ruling on the Portadown Lodge's requests for its July 12 parades or those for any of the other dates when the proposed route included the Garvaghy Road. The Parades Commission made it clear that the Orange Order would first have to engage in dialogue and genuine communication with the local community. For years, in an almost scripted manner, the Orange Order continued to apply to the Parades Commission to return from Drumcree on the Garvaghy Road following the church service, and the Residents' Association protested that nothing had changed and that there had been no negotiations. Each July, the Commission banned the part of the march on the Garvaghy Road and the security forces braced for violence, erecting barbed wire barriers, flooding a local stream to turn it into a moat, and building a steel and concrete barrier.[21] The Orangemen responded with a symbolic handful of marchers who proceeded to the barrier, handed the police a letter of protest, and delivered angry speeches, after which they turned back. At the same time, there would be shouting, violent threats and shoving that marked these ritual events.

---

[21] The full text of the commission's rulings are found on their website (www.parades commission.com).

In the face of the on-going stalemate over the Portadown parade itself, there has been some change in the context and the conflict over parading. The violence from the Orange Order's supporters has been widely condemned and there has been increasing popular acceptance of the Parades Commission's insistence that there has to be dialogue between the parties. The Orange Order seems more isolated and weaker than ever (Bryan 2001; Jarman 2003). It is possible to view both Protestants' and Catholics' shock at the death of the three children, and the powerful, common reactions to the large car bomb planted by an IRA splinter group in the town of Omagh in August 1998, as a shared symbolic response that emphasized common values, especially the rejection of violence. Were these responses effective as redressive mechanisms? Not by themselves, but they were significant factors in changing the context of the conflict following the political agreement reached a few months before. It is reasonable to hypothesize that what the responses did was to isolate the perpetrators of violence on both sides more effectively than was possible in the past and underline values that had widespread cross-community support. Certainly since 1999 there were louder voices in the Protestant community calling for non-violent protest, including important church leaders insisting that Orangemen adhere to good behavior pledges in order to attend church services. Protestant church and political leaders realized that another violent confrontation would not serve their cause.

Despite numerous efforts of various third parties including politicians and professional mediators to facilitate dialogue, there has been no settlement in Portadown to date. Each party settled into a repetitive ritual with assigned roles that recreated the same stalemate each year. The Parades Commission and other third parties sought to change the situation through direct or indirect negotiations, making it clear that without genuine engagement between the disputants, there would be no marching on the Garvaghy Road. The Commission explicitly defined the elements of engagement as communication with no preconceived outcomes; listening to and trying to understand the other's concerns; showing respect to the other by taking their concerns seriously; being willing to communicate their own legitimate concerns clearly; focusing on issues that are capable of being addressed by the parties concerned; demonstrating a commitment to resolving the problem and addressing legitimate concerns, preferably within a target timetable; being represented by people with the authority to speak for the protagonists; and demonstrating a willingness to consider some form of third party intervention, such as mediation, if direct dialogue is not possible.[22]

In 2002 there was again violence when the police tried to deescalate the situation by decreasing their presence at the scene. However, following the march, after the chief security officer at the barrier was handed the "traditional" letter of protest, a group of protesting Orange Order members and their supporters forced open the gates and began throwing stones at the police. They were finally repulsed when the army brought in a larger barrier blocking the road and the police used water cannon to disperse the protesters. In the melee, two dozen police and several protesters were injured. Orange Order leaders condemned the violence, quickly realizing the public relations disaster it created, even among Protestants. As the Protestant *Belfast Telegraph* opined, "If the Drumcree stand-off has proved anything over the years, it is that nobody wins when peaceful protest degenerates into violence and disorder. Indeed one of the greatest casualties of the dispute has been the standing of the Order itself" (*Belfast Telegraph*, 2003).

Perhaps as a result, since 2003 the marching season has had an entirely different tone. In Portadown and elsewhere, there was significant deescalation in the rhetoric and provocation from all sides and the police presented a firm, but less overwhelming, presence; and many parades that had been the sites of confrontations in the past, including the Tour of the North in Belfast, and one in the Springfield Road area in West Belfast were relatively trouble free. The 2003 July 12 parades, in which perhaps 60,000 marchers and 800 bands participated in some 90 Orange district parades, were the most peaceful in a decade (Keenan 2003). The *Irish Times* reported a mood change in Portadown, "The local lodge with a membership of 1500 could only muster 600 marchers after it was joined by two other Orange lodges nearby" and the number of spectators was down as well (*Irish Times* 2003a). In addition, there was no paramilitary presence, security forces were, for the most part, at a discreet distance from the marchers, and Garvaghy Road residents did not gather.[23] At the police barrier, the Orangemen handed their usual letter of protest to the police, but unlike past years when they remained to engage in inflammatory speechmaking, this time they walked back up the hill where the deputy district master delivered a short address as the crowd dispersed. In

---

[22] Parades Commission Determination June 30, 2003: www.paradescommission.org/.

[23] It is not clear whether the Orange Order actively discouraged the paramilitaries and troublemakers from previous years or whether this resulted from uncertainties and the political dynamics within the paramilitaries themselves.

a press conference following the parade, the Portadown Lodge's spokesperson David Jones emphasized the Lodge's willingness to hold direct talks and suggested that some kind of civic forum might build trust in stages that could lead to a consensus. Leading Catholic politicians and Protestant church leaders, including Church of Ireland primate, Archbishop Robin Eames, welcomed the change in atmosphere, and expressed hope that the crisis might soon end.

What was especially apparent was that unlike the 1920–72 period when July 12 was the time to celebrate Protestant victories and to express Protestant unity, the day has been transformed into one of protest, opposition, and division, revealing severe differences with the British government and political differences within Unionism. The titular head of unionism in 2003, David Trimble, the head of the Ulster Unionist Party and an Orangeman, was nowhere to be seen and his party opponents Jeffrey Donaldson and Rev. Martin Smyth, a former head of the Orange Order, offered loud and critical assessments of the Belfast Agreement, British government policy, and Trimble's leadership.[24] A year later, the political situation had shifted, following the 2003 elections. Ian Paisley's DUP was now the dominant Protestant party and Sinn Féin the largest Catholic one. Despite their militant rhetoric, however, neither endorsed a return to violence.

For now, Orange parades continue to serve as a focus for Protestant political resistance. At the same time, there is a recognition that the order is losing members and public support and interest in its parades is diminishing. The close association with paramilitary symbols and certain bands makes some people more reluctant to attend parades and makes the events less of a family event than they were in the past. The changes in the parades and reactions to them after the violence in 1996 and 2002 suggests that there are times when the parade conflicts move independently of the political process and provide opportunities for new initiatives in deadlocked situations, as we see in the case of parade conflicts in Derry discussed below. The Portadown parades have been exacerbaters, not just reflectors, of conflict, emphasizing mutually exclusive positions and competing narratives. At the same time, the evolution of parades conflicts since 1998 has channeled the disagreements into a set of exchanges in which all sides have moved away from violent confrontation into a more ritualized

---

[24] On the Ulster Unionist Council 120 of the 860 or so seats are reserved for the Orange Order, and historically a far higher proportion of UUP elected officials are in the Order.

expression of differences. In the week prior to Drumcree each year, there have been press reports of a possible brokered agreement between the Residents' Association and the Orange Order that would allow the parade to pass on the Garvaghy Road. It is hard to say how genuine these offers have been, although it is clear that the atmosphere is now very different and the Orange Order recognizes at some level that if they ever want to parade on the Garvaghy Road again, some negotiation will have to take place. Perhaps the reconstituted Parades Commission that for the first time includes an Orange Order member is the breakthrough that will finally lead to a negotiated settlement in Portadown.

Derry/Londonderry: ritual redefinition

Interestingly, in Londonderry/Derry, Northern Ireland's second largest city, the psychocultural dramas arising from the parades disputes during the same period produced more effective redressive mechanisms that resulted in far more constructive outcomes than in Portadown (Jarman 2003; Kelly and Nan 1998:50–61). In Derry, there are Orange Order parades, but the most significant ones in the city are those that the Apprentice Boys of Derry hold on August 12 and in December to mark the beginning and the conclusion of the Siege of Derry in 1689; the siege ended when William of Orange's forces reached the city and liberated the Protestant population inside. For many years, a central element in their parade was a tour of the city's walls that included a portion overlooking the Catholic Bogside, then located at the base of the walls, where on occasion marchers would throw coins and other objects down into the area. In addition,

Mall Wall, where the parade assembled, overlooked the Bogside, particularly Naylor's Row, and the banners and music could be seen and heard by the area's inhabitants. It was not a spectacle they welcomed, and led to the tradition whereby Bogside residents set their chimneys on fire to incommode the marchers, relying on the prevailing wind to carry the smoke toward the parade on the walls.

(Fraser 2000c: 176)

The long history of parades in Derry includes both Protestant and Catholic parades. In the late 1960s the Northern Ireland Civil Rights Association (NICRA) organized marches in and around Derry to protest discrimination against Catholics and when the minister of home affairs prohibited a civil rights march and an Apprentice Boys parade in October 1968, rioting broke out and the "Troubles" began. The next spring police followed Catholic rioters into the Bogside and beat Samuel Devenney, a local resident, who died a few months later; perhaps 30,000 people participated in his funeral procession (Fraser, 2000c: 179). The July and August 1969 Loyal Order parades provided more occasions for sectarian confrontations and rioting that led to the "Battle of the Bogside" pitting the RUC against the Republicans. Perhaps the single best-known Derry parade was not a Loyal Order parade, but a civil rights protest on January 30, 1972 that ended with British paratroopers killing fourteen unarmed men in what became known as "Bloody Sunday." Apprentice Boys Relief of Derry parades continued in various forms over the next two decades although the parade could no longer walk the walls since the British army occupied them until 1994. Tension between the Republicans and the small Protestant community that remained within the old city remained high.[25]

With the IRA and Protestant paramilitary ceasefires in 1994, the RUC permitted some of the participants in the December 1994 Apprentice Boys Relief of Derry parade to march on a section of the walls for the first time since 1969. In 1995, the psychocultural drama over parades in Derry began when the Apprentice Boys petitioned that for their August 15 parade they be permitted to walk the entire circumference of the city's walls as they had done in the past. Tensions were still high, in part because of Drumcree a month earlier (Fraser 2000c: 185), and in 1995 and 1996 parades were often the key triggering mechanisms that provoked severe sectarian clashes. This was not terribly surprising given the history of violence in the city since the late 1960s. The Bogside Residents Group (BRG) strongly protested against the parades; there was rioting and, for a time, the conflict resembled Portadown. However, over the next few years, multiparty negotiations and redefinition of the August 15 parade within the context of a broader cultural festival in Derry provided important redressive mechanisms. How this occurred is worth describing in some detail.

---

[25] Derry, like Belfast, is more segregated than it was in 1969. Many Protestants moved from the areas in and around the old city across the River Foyle to the Waterside and only one small Protestant neighborhood, the Fountain, remains. In addition, it is worth noting that in Derry, as in Belfast, a visitor quickly learns how territory is marked. Republican and Loyalist murals have distinctly different themes that are easy to recognize. Curbstones are painted each year before the marching season with the different national colors. In 2002, another significant marker of territory and differentiation appeared in Derry as Palestinian flags flew in the Catholic Bogside, which encouraged Protestants to hang Israeli flags in the Fountain and Waterside.

BRG members occupied sections of the walls in the days before the August 1995 parade following unsuccessful negotiations, saying they were not prepared for a triumphalist march overlooking the Bogside (Fraser 2000c: 185). On the morning of the parade, the RUC removed the protesters forcefully and some of the Apprentice Boys paraded the full circuit of the walls. Demonstrators a few blocks away turned their backs in silent protest. However, later in the day there were confrontations in the city, and rioting broke out that continued for five hours (Fraser 2000b: 186; Kelly and Nan 1998: 50–51). The next year saw even more violence following the Drumcree standoff in July, when there were three nights of rioting in Derry. There was, however, hope of a breakthrough when civic leaders and local MP John Hume arranged for negotiations in which both the Apprentice Boys and the BRG took part. The sticking point was the BRG insistence that any agreement concerning Derry also contain limits to parading in other nationalist areas of Northern Ireland. Issues such as the time of the march on the walls, the number of marchers, who would march, bands accompanying the marchers, and the music they would play were discussed productively before the talks eventually collapsed. The government then banned any parades on the walls in August. The march was held in other parts of the city (Kelly and Nan, 1998: 55–56), and the head of the Apprentice Boys, Alistair Simpson, announced they would walk the walls "at a time of their own choosing," and while there was some rioting it was less severe than in July. In October, the Apprentice Boys marched the walls without incident with BRG leaders protesting. "After completing their circuit, the Apprentice Boys dispersed after singing 'God Save the Queen' while BRG head Donncha Mac Niallais made a speech denouncing the parade as sectarian and offensive" (Fraser 2000c: 188).

In 1997 the Apprentice Boys refused to enter into direct negotiations with the BRG but did agree to participate in "proximity talks" – a form of shuttle diplomacy in Derry City Hall. Once again, the situation was complicated by events in Portadown although cancellation of an Orange Order parade scheduled for Derry in July eased tensions considerably. Linkage to parades in other areas was still a sticking point, but the mayor, the head of the Chamber of Commerce and a member of the Parades Commission proved to be effective mediators and an agreement was eventually reached, and the parade took place without violence in 1997 and 1998. In 1999, relations in Derry were again tense, a reflection of the uncertain outcome of the political negotiations over the implementation of the 1998 Good Friday

Agreement. The BRG demanded face-to-face talks with the Apprentice Boys and again insisted that the negotiations include a discussion of feeder parades in other cities. Derry Catholics, the overwhelming majority in the city, were hardly united behind the hard-line protesters, however, and shortly after the August parade negotiations resumed and an agreement was reached around the important Apprentice Boys December march.[26]

The Catholic dominated City Council was important in the process that led to significant ritual redefinition of the issues in a way that facilitated an outcome most people in both communities could accept. It involved changes in the structure of the celebration including agreements regarding the time of day and the number of marchers on the walls, parade organization and routes, the music played, and control over the bands that accompany the march. Certainly some of the changes resulted from each side acknowledging the other's most basic concerns, although there is also pragmatic self-interest at work. At the symbolic level, the new arrangements are a form of mutual acknowledgment and a recognition that both communities could be able to share the city's sacred landscape.

Simpson and the Apprentice Boys in Derry have been far more pragmatic than Orange Order leaders in Portadown in seeking an outcome that would allow them to continue their parades. Their position, including their willingness to engage in negotiations, allowed them to gain significant support from nationalist politicians such as John Hume, and Catholic political and business leaders in Derry who early on endorsed the right to march. Perhaps because of this precedent, a few years later Derry's Orange Order leaders also engaged in negotiations and agreed that the July 12 South Derry parades would not be held inside the old city every year. An additional factor that seems to have contributed to tension reduction in Derry is the willingness of the Apprentice Boys to monitor the conduct of parade participants, especially band members in those parts of the parade route where explosive incidents are most likely. While observers suggest that some improvement is still possible, especially in connection with alcohol, their taking responsibility for owning the problem and training people to carry out the stewarding has helped gain significant support from Derry's Catholics for the

---

[26] The agreement included moving the parade to a date earlier in the month so that the downtown, mainly Catholic, merchants would not have to close on a Saturday right before Christmas.

right to march (Bryan and Jarman 2000; Jarman 2003). In 2003, Garvan O'Doherty, a Derry business leader, told the *Belfast Telegraph*, "Undoubtedly Derry produced a template that should be used across Northern Ireland. This year has seen a new maturity in thinking across the marching issue. It is no longer a doomsday dreaded by both communities each summer" (Brett 2003). The *Irish Times* rejoiced that 12,000 marchers participated in a peaceful parade three months later (Jackson 2003).

The negotiations in Derry are significant in that they allowed the Apprentice Boys with the support of the City Council to redefine their celebration as part of a broader, more inclusive cultural festival focusing on the city's history. This joint recognition of both Protestant and Catholic traditions in the city provided on-going space for a further easing of tensions, and since 2000 despite the political deadlock over political arrangements in Belfast, the August and December parades have taken place without significant problems. The festival, partially financed through municipal funds, has expanded to include an exhibition at City Hall, a bluegrass festival, talks on the city's history including one by a Catholic historian, contests involving both Protestant and Catholic schoolchildren, and a street fair. While there are still plenty of tensions and unresolved issues around the Apprentice Boys' parades, the lines of cleavage in the city have been blurred a bit and the deep threats to, or attacks upon, group identity associated with the marches have diminished as each side has clarified its needs and acknowledged those of the other side.

Conclusion

Signed agreements between long-standing opponents, such as Protestants and Catholics in Northern Ireland, Jews and Palestinians in the Middle East, or whites and blacks in South Africa are only one step in a peace process. Implementing agreements requires further negotiation around substantive interests, but it cannot neglect the importance of articulating more inclusive narratives and rituals emphasizing the parties' shared needs and common experiences.

Where cultural performances and celebrations have been central to building and strengthening within-group identity and boundaries, developing more inclusive narratives and ritual practices that lower perceived threat is not easy. Long-term hostile relationships emphasize incompatibilities that strengthen group boundaries and ignore, or even actively reject, what the communities have in common, and the symbolic landscape has little that is shared (Bryan and McIntosh 2005). In this context, modifying divergent worldviews is no simple matter. Differences often assume a moral quality and group members who fail to observe the accepted boundaries between their group and the opposition often become the objects of verbal or physical harassment.

Parade disputes in Northern Ireland show how closely intertwined cultural and political expressions can be. Loyal Order parades that were once powerful statements of support for the state have now become contexts for Loyalist political mobilization, protest against the redefined political order, and a source of Protestant division. The post-1994 transformation in the politics of parading is also associated with highly divergent between- and within-group messages and meanings. Externally, some Unionists use parading as a form of strident communication to assert a politics of opposition and protest to both Irish nationalists and the British government. At the same time, beneath their strident messages, there is often a weakness and vulnerability that makes dialogue and engagement with Republican residents' groups difficult. In asserting what the Loyal Orders consider their inalienable rights to assemble, there is actually a keen recognition that attaining this goal is dependent upon their ability to negotiate with the Parades Commission and the nationalist community, something that many Loyalists find humiliating. As a forum for expressing competing values and fissures within unionism, parades with their history of pageantry, symbolism, and political speechmaking offer a very public look into alternative unionist political narratives and perceived fears (Jarman 2003).

Unionists and Nationalists often describe parades as unchanging traditions. Yet the reality is that they have changed many times in response to new political contexts (Jarman, 1997; Bryan, 2000; Fraser, 2000a). These changes in ritual expressions reflect the external face of internal political relations within unionism and among Unionists, Nationalists, and the British and Irish governments. While professing unity, competing Protestant groups symbolically make claims about who is best suited to protect the community. The exclusive banners, uniforms, instruments, songs, and insignias visible in parades are threatening to Catholics and the cyclical tension between the two communities during the "marching season" puts politics on the back burner and threatens constructive dialogue around substantive issues. Despite a decline in participation among both marchers and spectators at a number of major parades (Bryan 2003; Edwards 2003), the electoral successes in 2003 and 2004 of Paisley's DUP with its emphasis on cultural unionism suggests that strong Loyalist appeals continue to resonate with many Protestants.

There is little inherent in the parades themselves that is necessarily provocative.[27] Rather, it is contextually defined meanings that the symbols and rituals evoke for Loyalists and Republicans that make them so powerful. Yet, even small markers of difference such as the colors orange and green are easily politicized during the marching season. At a 2003 July 12 parade, for example, an African vendor selling silver jewelry incurred the wrath of marchers because her wares included bracelets with green stones. "That Fenian junk shouldn't be sold here", she was told in no uncertain terms (*Irish Times* 2003b).[28]

As psychocultural dramas unfold, they reveal important fault lines among groups and identify both the specific interests around which ethnic conflicts are waged and the deeper identity dynamics at work that often make it so hard to find effective redressive mechanisms to settle these conflicts constructively. In addition, the expression of these differences in moralistic rights language means it is especially difficult to devise pragmatic solutions since rights are hard to compromise and hurting an opponent often becomes more important than minimizing one's own losses.

Turner's idea that effective redress of such conflicts requires performance of public ritual is fully consistent with what psychoculturally oriented theorists such as Kelman, Montville, and Volkan propose. Ritual enactment of narratives is often exclusive but when ritual becomes more inclusive it can connect people across groups and encourage the development of multiple identities as the parties sense that if an opponent gains something of value it necessarily means that their own side has lost. Redefinition of a conflict in ways that permit a group to understand that acknowledging another's identity does not mean denying their own is not easy to achieve. In Derry, this has occurred to some extent along with a

---

[27] Bryan (personal communication) has described the very different atmosphere at Orange Order parades in county Donegal, a county in the Irish Republic, just across the border from Northern Ireland.

[28] The significance of particular symbols is, of course, arbitrary and their significance is defined contextually. The Battle of the Boyne, for example, and even the Glorious Revolution of 1688, are not significant events for many people in England. However, in Northern Ireland, children learn their importance, and the symbols associated with them, early in life.

significant deescalation of tension and a decrease in violent incidents through an innovative, negotiated redesign of a ritual that helped the parties develop more or less mutually acceptable arrangements around parades that lowered mutual fears. The new ritual and revised narratives emphasize what groups, even those in conflict, share, and offer some reassurance that future relationships will be less threatening than past ones while pointing toward some common understandings, a sense of joint fate, and a partially shared symbolic landscape.

It is not completely clear to me why the Apprentice Boys of Derry were so much more willing, and able, to engage in negotiations than the Orange Order in Portadown. It is not the different histories of the two areas that account for the different outcomes, for while Portadown in County Armagh is close to where sectarian tensions have historically been high, the same can be said for Derry. In asking people in Northern Ireland to explain the difference in the two outcomes, I have received a variety of answers, all of which are plausible, but none of which is fully satisfying. Many suggest that the Apprentice Boys' leadership is more pragmatic and flexible than that of the Orange Order. Surely this is the case, but to me this is more of a description than an explanation. It also ignores the fact that while the Apprentice Boys have shown great flexibility over their Derry parades, in disputes over parades in Belfast their pragmatism is less apparent. Others have suggested that the differences result from the fact that in Derry, Protestants are a minority, while in Portadown they are still a dominant majority. However, it is not hard to find cases where minorities are completely uncompromising and majorities generous and flexible.

The explanation that is most plausible to me emphasizes that while Derry was a divided, tense city in the 1970s, in the past twenty-five years, political relationships in and around the city have evolved considerably creating conditions facilitating productive conflict mitigation. Particularly under John Hume's influence, there has been considerable cross-community dialogue and flexibility that has become institutionalized in Derry while Portadown has remained bitterly divided (Mulvihill and Ross 1999). Local Catholic and Protestant leaders in Derry found ways to talk to each other and the Derry City Council has engaged in power sharing for some time. In Derry, a good deal of civic involvement by business and other local leaders was manifest in their engagement as mediators in the negotiations that led the successful negotiations over the Apprentice Boys' parades

(Kelly and Nan 1998).[29] As a result, it was clear that there were many Catholics who supported the Apprentice Boys' right to march and who, at the same time, worked to address the concerns of the Bogside Residents' Association. There was also some significant flexibility from the Apprentice Boys, who were willing to enter into dialogue and to monitor unacceptable behavior in their parades, to ban the display of paramilitary insignias as well as the public consumption of alcohol (Jarman 2003).

This explanation is similar to Crain's (1968) effort to explain why some southern cities, such as Atlanta, in the United States, desegregated their schools with little overt conflict and violence while others, such as New Orleans, were the sites of bitter, and sometimes violent, conflict. He found that variables such as the proportion of blacks in the city had little predictive power. What did matter, however, was the engagement of civic leaders in the process – as was the case in Derry. In cities where business and other civic leaders played a significant role in working out desegregation plans, there was relatively little overt conflict, while in cities where these leaders were uninvolved, the management of the issue was far less constructive. This points to the importance of civil society NGO activities in creating space for dialogue and compromise that lowers tension and moves conflict toward a constructive outcome (Kriesberg 2003; Varshney 2002).

Jarman (2003) contends that the regularization of Parades Commission procedures and rulings available to assist negotiations at different levels provided another important mechanism of conflict mitigation. Although the Parades Commission has not always had an easy time, it has helped create new norms regarding violence and new ways to manage parading conflicts that provide alternatives to public standoffs and violence. The Parade Commission's participation as an authoritative third party has helped some disputing parties define common interests and get their most basic needs met – for the Loyal Orders this is the right to march, and for the Catholic communities the right to be free from humiliation and intimidation. To do this, the Parades Commission created ground rules that have altered expectations and behaviors on all sides to deescalate conflict and reduce violence. Jarman adds that part of the key to doing this

---

[29] This cross-community engagement also extended to civic groups such as the Peace and Reconciliation Group (PRG) in Derry that has long worked to increase effective communications and to lower tensions in the city (Mulvihill and Ross 1999).

effectively requires "acknowledging the importance of cultural, ritual, and symbolic events and processes within the construction and maintenance of ethnic identities" (Jarman 2003).

Although the outcome of the Portadown conflict is not yet clear, what we can say is that to be successful an outcome must include symbols and rituals that communicate some minimal level of respect and mutual acknowledgment to the parties which to date has been absent. However, to the extent that the Orange Order is concerned about its decline, they have a clear pragmatic motive for changing their position on negotiations with residents' groups and the Parades Commission. Repeating old offers through an approach to the British government in 2003 and 2004 might have been a public relations ploy or an initial step toward real talks. If the offer is sincere, it would put the burden on Republicans to take a reciprocal step, for it is clear that while the Parades Commission requires significant communication between the parties, it has, in a number of cases, refused Republicans a veto over parades they dislike.[30]

Because the issues in parade disputes are primarily symbolic expressions of the relations between the communities, any mutually acceptable outcome will have to attend to each community's powerful emotional concerns embedded in their narratives of the conflict. There is no single right way to accomplish this. Rather, while there are many possible formulas, those that are good enough are those that a significant portion of each community can accept. As the contrasting cases of Portadown and Derry demonstrate, cultural performances can harden positions or can be recast in ways that provide mutual acknowledgment and more inclusive expression that can diminish fears and reduce overt conflict.

---

[30] Republicans have been far more successful than Unionists at public relations on this issue. Given the indication that the Orange Order following the peaceful 2003 parades might be willing to engage in talks, Gerry Adams quickly emphasized the right of Orangemen to march and the "responsibility of Nationalists and Republicans to hear and understand the Orange perspective" (UTV 2003).

5

Where is Barcelona? Imagining the nation without a state

Introduction

Ethnic conflict is often framed around the most visible and mundane aspects of everyday life – customs such as food, clothing, and speech. These external manifestations of identity are readily contested when one group seeks to control the behavior of another. While the specific contentious behaviors that serve as focal points of contestation are rarely threatening in themselves, it is how they are interpreted that really matters, as each side understands action through psychocultural narratives replete with their version of the past and vision of the future.

In the contemporary world, language often marks the identity of the ethnic community or nation.[1] Consequently, we often hear strong views about the need for official national languages and the importance of citizens speaking a single language despite the existence of many bi- and multilingual people and states.[2] Why this is the case is a central question in this chapter. In considering the question of language use, we address how countries make decisions about what is to be their official language or languages; what is used in government institutions, educational systems, and public signs, and how these decisions are implemented. These issues can be, but are not necessarily, highly controversial. Even in

---

[1] The nation is made up of the people who share a cultural and political identity and the state is a governmental unit. In some cases nations and states are coterminous. Much more commonly states, or countries, consist of people with more than one national identity.

[2] Although neither the data nor the definition is precise several people (and web sites) have suggested to me that more than half of the people in the world are bi or multilingual.

places such as the United States where language issues seem relatively unproblematic to many, intense conflict can erupt over language questions as is seen in the widespread calls for "English Only" laws and attacks on bilingual education in recent years.

The question of official languages is a relatively recent one in the world for the simple reason that until 1800 few states cared or could enforce what language people living within its boundaries spoke. Since the French Revolution, however, the rise of states as representatives of the nation, democratic popularly elected governments, the spread of education, and the rise of mass media have radically changed the relationship between language and politics. Rulers, especially those who are elected, need to communicate with their constituents and it is obvious that this is easier when they all speak the same language. Likewise, mass-based public education became a responsibility of government which meant that it was also an opportunity not only to standardize what people learned but to use a single language as the medium of instruction as a way of building attachment to the state.

While we often assume that the present capacity of citizens in European states to understand their country's language is centuries old, this is seldom the case. As Eugen Weber points out in his classic study, *Peasants into Frenchmen*, as late as 1860 only about half of the people living in France spoke French as their first language and there were many who did not understand it (1976: 70). The development of universal primary education in France under the Third Republic changed the situation dramatically, so that by 1914, on the eve of World War I, French was close to being the universal first language of its citizens and the local languages that had been favored three generations earlier receded in importance. Weber argues that the low conflict over language in France during this time was due to the power of the centralized government and the incentives for learning French. This pattern is not uncommon and in many places the state emerged prior to the development of either a strong national consciousness or a shared culture and language. In the former Soviet Union, despite all the advantages that accrued to Russian speakers, Karklins (1986) reports that in the years just before its breakup only about half of the primary students in the country attended schools in which Russian was the language of instruction.

Upon attaining independence in the post World War II period, former Asian and African colonies needed to make choices concerning language for use. They could adopt the language of the former colonial ruler or choose a local language. The choice was often complicated. The colonial languages enhanced communication with outsiders and were the languages with which the bureaucracy and school systems were already familiar so that if it was maintained administrative procedures would need less rewriting and school curricula would be readily available. At the same time, symbolically there was great attraction in adopting a non-Western, indigenous language as the language of the independent state, an issue that was complicated in situations when there was more than one plausible choice and a decision to adopt one language over another would potentially exacerbate ethnic or regional tensions.

New states made a wide range of decisions in an effort to balance the needs for effective communication, education, and political unity. Decisions were often pragmatic and resulted in far more functional multilingualism than official state policies reveal. In North Africa, both Arabic and French are used; in East Africa, English and Swahili are pan-ethnic languages while specific regional (once called tribal) languages are also used. The case of India is particularly instructive. Both Hindi and English were India's official languages at independence in 1947 although they were used in quite different contexts and for very different purposes. During the 1950s there was great pressure to recognize regional languages and intense, sometimes violent, conflicts about these choices in multilingual regions. The result was a redrawing of regional (state) boundaries and the adoption of a regional language in each non-Hindi speaking state as a third official language in that state. As a result, Laitin reports that less than 3 percent of the Indian population has as its primary language one that is different from one of the official languages in their state and even in those cases minorities have the right to an education in their own language (Laitin 1997: 282–87). He suggests that a "3 plus or minus one outcome" might provide a model for language policy in Europe where in a few years citizens might well learn their country's language, a common language such as English, and a regional language (Laitin 1997).

Contemporary states generally have official language policies, but language adoption can be complicated and certain language choices, like other policies, are made and remade. Given the emotional salience of the question, these issues are not often settled easily and quickly. In addition, new political circumstances often reopen questions of language policy and practice in ways that can be highly conflictual. For example, consider the following recent cases:

- Some people find they cannot read or speak their country's official language after a sudden regime change. This occurred, for example, in the Baltic countries – Estonia, Latvia, and Lithuania – after they achieved independence in 1991. During the Soviet period, Russian speakers in these countries generally made little effort to learn the local language believing it was of little use to them. Yet to become citizens of the new state, in a place where they had lived for a long time, and might even have been born, they had to pass a test in the language they formerly eschewed (Laitin 1998).
- Laws are passed that prohibit merchants from posting public signs in any language other than the one approved by law. This sort of legislation has been passed in many places including Montreal; the Quebec government created a Commission for the Protection of the French language that decreed in 1983 that all commercial signs had to include French, with the French letters at least twice the size of those of any other language. For a time in Slovakia the law prohibited the Hungarian minority from posting street signs in Hungarian even in areas where Hungarian speakers were in the majority. Local governments in the US have passed similar "English only" laws regarding public signage.
- Language proficiency in a regional language becomes a job requirement so that civil servants (and some people in the private sector) who have held jobs for years, even if they are grandfathered in their positions, are likely to feel isolated, and people from other regions suddenly become unqualified to work in the region. This change in requirements and/or expectations is widespread and is found in such places as Quebec, Catalonia, many parts of Central Europe and the former Soviet Union, and parts of South Asia when regional languages become official or co-official (Woolard and Gahng 1990: 316)

Language use is often the most visible, but certainly not the only, marker of identity and one that readily becomes the focal point of tension and ethnic conflict. This should not surprise us, for language use, non-use, and misuse communicates a wide range of public and private, subtle and not so subtle messages regarding power, control, recognition, and legitimation as states adopt official languages and try to control what languages are spoken in public (and even private) contexts.

More often than not, language is a core aspect of identity and when identity is contested, language is a readily available weapon. It follows then that language conflicts will sometimes be very intense. For majority groups, the most apparent reason for pushing a particular language – typically their own – has to do with their desire to establish political control and the fear that cultural distinctiveness is evidence of a weak political commitment to the state. For minorities, centralized language policies readily increase their vulnerability and threaten their identity. Furthermore, if Kymlicka (1998) is correct in his hypothesis that cultural distinctiveness cannot be maintained without distinct governmental and other institutions in which a language is regularly used, abandoning minority or regional languages will, understandably, produce high resistance.

Sustaining a societal culture in the modern world is not a matter of holding ethnic festivals, or having a few classes taught in one's mother tongue as a child. It is a matter of creating and sustaining a set of public institutions that will enable a minority group to participate in the modern world in its own language.

(Kymlicka 1998: 34)

Unless commitment is high, such a task is not easy even given the existence of high resources, territorial contiguity, the skill needed to maintain a language, and favorable political conditions. At the same time, because language is easiest to control in formal public contexts, such as offices, schools, or public signage, government control is often incomplete and minorities can resist language standardization and use their own language to express political and cultural opposition and to mobilize collective action.

This chapter examines ethnic conflicts in which language use is a central focus and explores the importance of issues of recognition, legitimation and control underlying them. Identity conflicts over issues of linguistic and cultural autonomy can escalate into violence, as in the case of Sri Lanka where a conflict in which what initially seemed to some observers like a language conflict escalated into a much wider civil war. Not all language options come down to mutually exclusive choices. Multilingualism, which can take a variety of forms, is often an outcome that symbolically and practically meets the central needs of all the parties, as in Québec and Catalonia. In both there has been little or no violence in recent years, and they afford us a chance to examine culturally rooted conflicts that have been more or less constructively managed despite the participants' strong feelings. The next sections briefly explore the polarization that has escalated to on-going violence in Sri Lanka, and the polarization in Québec that has led to a good deal of ill-will and stalemate. The next one turns to Catalonia, first discussed in Chapter 1, where a number of substantive and ritual actions have produced a successful accommodation in the context of a highly decentralized post-Franco Spanish state. The conclusion suggests the importance of normalizing the narrative of linguistic minorities as small nations without a state so that they feel connected to other peoples in the same situation (Keating 2001).

Language, conflict escalation, and containment

It is easy for conflicts to escalate around questions of language policy when one group feels it confers unfair privilege on another. For example, in Sri Lanka, a bitter conflict in which over 60,000 people have died since 1984 first emerged as a political conflict over language in the mid 1950s. In the early years after independence from Britain in 1948, the country's Sinhalese majority felt that the minority Tamils had been relatively favored during colonial rule in terms of civil service and university positions and this continued in the first decade after independence. Although the Portuguese and Dutch colonized the island in the sixteenth century, it was under British colonial rule in the nineteenth century that Sinhalese national movements in the form of Sinhala revivalism first developed; there was little evidence of ethnic, religious, or linguistic antagonism or exclusion prior to that time (Little 1994; Tambiah 1992). During the 1957 elections, S. W. R. D. Bandaranaike ran a militant campaign promising passage of a "Sinhala only" language law aimed at reversing the situation. Language issues in the Sri Lanka conflict provided the spark that ignited deeper resentments reflecting the Sinhalese majority's long-standing sense of injustice that had been simmering for over a century (de Silva 1981; Kapferer 1988; Little 1994).

Language served as the focal point in the newly independent country (then called Ceylon), but it was clear that the conflict was about deep resentments over social privilege and political control. Bandaranaike came to power as a leader who appealed to Buddhist revivalist themes that once unleashed were hard to contain. A militant monk, believing that Bandaranaike had betrayed his people when he reached a compromise agreement with the Tamils, assassinated him in 1959, and militant organizations advocating extreme violence formed in both communities to fight not only the other side but also the more moderate forces in their own group (Little 1994). By the mid 1980s a massacre of Tamils in the capital Colombo with apparent government complicity set off a new round of fighting and demands for a Tamil homeland in the north and east of the country. At one point India invaded the country in an unsuccessful effort to restore peace. The continued escalation and long-term fighting has eclipsed the original language issues and the specific demands for affirmative action associated with them.

Not all language conflicts escalate the way the Sri Lanka conflict did. Two long-standing ethnic conflicts in which language played a prominent role that have been managed more successfully in recent years are those in Canada and Spain. Both countries are multicultural states, although Spain is not willing to publicly define itself this way. In Canada, French-speaking Québecers are a linguistically and territorially defined minority. In addition, there are native peoples throughout the country, and large groups of immigrants from dozens of other countries. Spain has struggled for centuries to control its territory and to impose a single culture within its borders. In the fifteenth and sixteenth centuries, Muslims and Jews were expelled and the expanding state exercised increasing control in parts of the north as well. Yet there are historic nations within northern Spain – Catalans, Basques, and Galicians and other groups that claim varying degrees of distinctiveness. Each of these still speaks their own language, as well as Castilian Spanish. At times in each of these regions there have been calls for independent statehood and the use of politics, and sometimes violence, to pursue it.

Both Québecers and Catalans identify themselves as a distinct people or nation with their own history and territory, but in both cases only a minority (in the case of Québec a large minority) has supported demands for independent statehood. At the same time, in both Canada and Spain today there is wide support for specific language and cultural rights, and a willingness to accord these regions the political autonomy to implement them effectively. The challenge involves specific administrative and resource demands as well as periodic conflicts that take the form of psychocultural dramas emphasizing identity and culture. Only when these dramas develop ritually inclusive expressions can the parties live together in a more or less constructive manner.[3] In both Québec and Catalonia this

---

[3] An obvious contrast is between the Catalans and the Basques. Although it is interesting, it is not my focus here (see Conversi 1997; Laitin 1995).

seems to have been achieved in the past thirty years, although there remain unresolved issues between the regions and the state in both cases. These cases are worth looking at because they are important examples of how cultural conflicts can be managed in non-violent ways while meeting many of the core needs of the small nations that exist within larger states and of the larger states as well.

Language and Québec nationalism

Canada is a large, sparsely populated country that cross-national data show to be one of the most stable and successful multicultural democracies. Nonetheless, it is a country that has experienced intense, but non-violent, conflicts over identity and inclusion/exclusion. While Canada was originally a French colony centered in Québec, the British gained control over it as a result of the Seven Years War (or what is called the French and Indian War in North America) that raged from 1756 to 1763. In 1759, the British captured Québec City in a brief battle on the Plains of Abraham that left the generals on both sides dead. Four years later, the 1763 Peace Treaty ceded French Canada to the British, a traumatic and still emotionally charged event Québecers call "The Conquest";[4] a psychological abandonment since the French chose to retain Guadalupe over Québec.[5] Québecers have struggled with how to refer to the past and Maclure describes the tension in their narrative as "melancholic nationalism" that recalls the pre-conquest period as a kind of Golden Age that was lost, the struggle to recover it in the repeated failures to refound the country, and an anti-nationalist, cosmopolitan narrative, often associated with former Canadian Prime Minister Pierre Elliot Trudeau that minimizes the impact of the Conquest and calls upon French Canadians to accept responsibility for their fate (Maclure 2004: 41).

Under the British, Québec maintained its language, Catholic religion and culture, and legal system. In the nineteenth century, there were various forms of resistance to British colonial rule and struggles to maintain French culture, language and political autonomy as the

---

[4] The loss in Volkan's terms is a chosen trauma, a humiliating defeat that cannot be worked through and is transmitted across generations. The film "The QuébeCanada Complex" portrays this in explicitly psychoanalytic terms (Wintonick and Tassinari 1998).

[5] Québec license plates contain the phrase "Je me souviens" (I remember). The question is what is remembered. When asked, some Québecers say it is trauma of the conquest, while others say they remember their language and culture.

proportion of French speakers in Canada decreased. The main strategies for cultural survival involved strong church control over society and institutions such as education and social services, a primarily rural society that had little contact with Anglophones, and collaboration between French and English speaking elites in Montreal. The twentieth-century decline of rural society and the emigration of young Québecers to the United States and other parts of Canada posed new challenges to cultural survival and by the 1960s the Francophones pushed for a more equal role, especially in the economy, and sought to become "masters in their own house" (*maîtres chez nous*) in what was dubbed "The Quiet Revolution."

However, as English Canada began to hear and meet francophone demands for parity and bilingualism, a more militant Québec nationalism arose that demanded either sovereignty in the form of an independent Québec or the replacement of the English language in public life in the region, creating a series of psychocultural dramas filled with high tension and anxiety for both English and French citizens (Waddell 1986). Language issues became the rallying point of the nationalist movement and its demands for political change but the cultural identity issues raised were much broader (Eller 1999: ch. 7). When the Parti Québécois (PQ) came to power in November 1976, street celebrations turned Montreal was into a veritable "collective effervescence that Durkheim imagined as central to the social order" (Handler 1988: 14).

Camille Laurin, the PQ Minister of State for Cultural Development, saw language as central to Québecer identity, and language policy as "collective psychotherapy" necessary to undo the effects of conquest and domination (Levine 1991: 113). The following year the new Québec government introduced Bill 1, "The Charter of the French Language" that included regulations mandating the use of French in government offices and large businesses along with fines for their violation, and emotionally provocative phrases such as "the French language is the language of the Québécois people." Opponents called it a violation of basic human rights and soon the government rewrote their proposal removing the more provocative language but keeping its substance intact. Bill 101 was passed making French the official language of the region. It required government offices and municipalities to conduct their business in French and made French the language of instruction in public schools. Access to English language schools was limited to those whose parents had attended English speaking schools themselves, thus excluding parental choice for the large number of immigrants in Québec. While the education provisions were the focus of much attention, the ones that required that public signs be in French were in some ways the most controversial. Over half the cases the Commission for the Protection of the French Language considered involved violations of its provisions (Levine 1991: 176). "Bill 101 culminated the push, begun during the Quiet Revolution, to assert Francophone hegemony in Montreal, and the laws quickly gained near-consensual support within the French-speaking community as the legal and symbolic cornerstone of the Francophone Reconquest" (Levine 1991: 119).

Many English speakers emigrated from Québec and in the next two decades there were two referenda on independence, the second of which in 1995 lost by only 1.2%.[6] Since then, however, issues of language and sovereignty are less charged and public support for independence has dropped a good deal. Some suggest that intergenerational change has made the younger adults who grew up in a fully francophone Québec, along with the emergence of a Québec literature, cinema, and music, more secure in their identity than earlier generations. English speakers have come to terms with the language law, and French speakers are in practice likely to be bilingual. Recently, an alternative narrative has emerged that views Québec as one of several small nations without states like Brittany, Wales, and Catalonia that have survived and prospered (Guibernau 1997; Keating 2001). This narrative connects Québec to other places from which it can obtain support and the reassurance that there are other minority cultures and identities that survive without their own state. One consequence is a diminished sense of isolation and vulnerability. As former separatist and Montreal mayor Pierre Bourque said, "Now that we have saved the culture, we don't need independence" (Krauss 2003).

"Language normalization" and identity in Catalonia

Catalonia, a region in northeast Spain, is a nation of about 6 million people which, like Québec, is larger in population than either Norway or Ireland (Figure 5.1). Catalans have a long history including periods of

---

[6] The narrow loss unleashed a diatribe on election night by Jacques Parizeau, the PQ leader, against Québec's immigrants who, he charged, did not have the same commitment to the nation as the "real" Québecers, meaning the descendants of the original French immigrants.

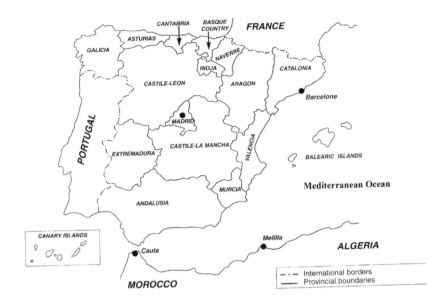

Figure 5.1 Spanish nationalities and regions

self-rule, a distinct language[7] and culture, emotionally powerful symbols and sacred sites, a clear identity, and a vibrant economy.[8] Once part of an independent kingdom of Catalonia-Aragon, Catalonia has been incorporated into the Spanish state for hundreds of years. Nonetheless, the nature of this relationship has regularly been contested and renegotiated, as has Spain's relationship with its other historic nations. Since the early eighteenth century language issues have frequently been a central point of contention between Catalonia and Madrid with the central government seeking to impose Castilian and many Catalans seeking linguistic autonomy.[9] Examining the Catalan and Spanish narratives reveals how the parties frame the key issues and what they see at stake with Madrid emphasizing that modern countries have a single language that expresses the nation's political unity and Catalonia saying it is a historic nation not willing to give up its language and culture. Since Franco's death in 1975, conflict has been

---

[7] Catalan is a romance language, most related to Provençal. It should not be considered a dialect of Castilian (Woolard 1989: 13).
[8] These features are typically those that are found among national groups making claims to an independent state (Laitin 1989).
[9] Laitin (1989) makes it clear that at various times Catalan elites were more than willing to be multilingual as they saw advantages to being part of a larger political and economic unit.

137

played out through political channels and civil society despite significant tension at times. How this was possible needs some explanation given the widely held view that ethnic conflicts escalate quickly and easily turn violent and the importance of studying conflict mitigation success rather than only just failures. The story is one of increasing inclusiveness; although change is not always even and there are moments of high conflict there has been little or no violence, as we see below in the account of identity representation in the 1992 Barcelona Olympic Games.

Catalans are a people with a strong national identity defined around language, culture, and a shared history with pre-modern roots, features that Smith (1999) finds in many national identities. Catalans trace their existence as a nation to the end of the tenth century when the Catalan Counts became independent from the Franks and created an empire that controlled a good deal of territory in the western Mediterranean between the twelfth and fourteenth centuries.[10] Catalans recount this period as one of a flourishing of culture and their experience as an early democracy. This Catalan Golden Age begins to decline with the Black Death in the fourteenth century, famines, and internal revolts. Catalonia became part of the Habsburg Empire through marriage, drawn into wars in the Iberian Peninsula, and finally absorbed into Spain under Felipe V when the Catalans supported the losing side in the War of the Spanish Succession. The defeat, on September 11, 1714, brought a "catastrophic loss of autonomy" and marks the most sacred day in the Catalan civil calendar.

Catalan elites were bilingual for a long time often speaking Catalan in domestic situations and using Castilian, the language of the Spanish administration in business and commerce (McDonogh 1986b). While Catalan declined as a literary language it always served as the *lingua franca* for the region. In decrees issued between 1768 and 1771, Carlos III ordered that schooling throughout Spain be in Castilian (Woolard 1989: 21). However, it was another 100 years before the Spanish state managed to create a school system and by then there had been a revival of Catalan

---

[10] The Catalan history museum in Barcelona and a 15 minute video they sell recounts a narrative that emphasizes the Neolithic and Roman origins of the Catalan people and the significance of their early history and culture. There is a good deal presented on the archeological evidence from the region and the history of Catalonia, with an emphasis on its cultural and political achievements. More recent developments, including much of the twentieth century, in contrast, are presented relatively briefly. Clearly, the message that a real nation has a long history is a crucial part of the museum's narrative.

national sentiments and an accompanying linguistic and cultural revival, the *Renaixença* (Renaissance). Language pride was an integral part of nineteenth and early twentieth-century Catalan nationalism, and political and cultural movements emerged that emphasized Catalonia as a distinct, historic nation. A number of writers describing Catalan political culture use the term "pactism," a view of life emphasizing free agents who bargain and negotiate among themselves, calling it "a useful way to understand the way conflict is managed in Catalonia down to the present day, the strategies that are adopted and the processes of accommodation that occur; and this is especially important when examining the way Catalan elites deal with each other and with the central powers" (Hargreaves 2000: 20–21).[11]

Twice in the first half of the twentieth century, a period of rapid industrialization and social movements, Catalonia gained significant autonomy from Madrid – first during the Mancumunitat (1913–1925) and then under the Second Republic in the 1930s – only to see it removed when direct rule from Madrid was reimposed. During these periods use of Catalan in the mass media, in cultural, and in educational settings expanded. When Franco came to power in 1939 after a bitter civil war, he was determined to smash regional nationalisms and build the strong state that had been the dream, but not the achievement, of Spanish rulers for centuries. Furthermore, Franco had little sympathy for Catalonia, a region that gave strong support to the Spanish Republicans during the Civil War, and he wanted to crush its separatist sentiments and leaders.

Initially Franco's rule in Catalonia was harsh and many intellectuals and political activists went into exile in France, Mexico and elsewhere.[12] Many less fortunate were imprisoned, where several hundred thousand died or were killed. Franco abolished the statute of autonomy, banned all Catalan political and cultural organizations and prohibited the use of the Catalan language. All Catalan language signs and notices were ordered removed, books were burned, Catalan culture was banned as a subject at the University of Barcelona and teachers suspected of nationalist sympathies were transferred outside the region and replaced by teachers from other parts of Spain. Even Catalan names were banned (McRoberts 2001: 40–41; Woolard 1989: 28–29). The attack on the language was ferocious

---

[11] Some writers link this to the importance of commerce and business in Catalonia and the pragmatism.

[12] There was a Catalan government in exile in France throughout the Franco period.

and citizens were exhorted to "Speak Catholic" (meaning Castilian) in signs and posters the Franco government posted throughout the region.

Following World War II, the regime became less harsh as it was more secure and at the same time it sought a place in the western, anti-Communist alliance. Although the Catalan language was still officially banned, there was some public reappearance of it beginning in the 1950s. The Catholic Church's decision to conduct some services in Catalan was emotionally and symbolically significant, as was the site they chose to first do this – the Abbey of Montserrat, a sacred site for Catalans, and Vatican II further encouraged Catalan priests to use the vernacular, meaning Catalan, in mass. The Franco regime tolerated some use of Catalan provided it did not directly challenge the regime as nationalists did in 1959 when they stood and sang the banned Catalan national anthem in the Barcelona Opera House one night when a number of Franco's officials were present.[13] For his role in organizing this and other protests, Jordi Pujol, who became the leader of the Catalan government in 1980, received a seven-year prison sentence of which he served two and a half years (Conversi 1997: 120). By Franco's death in 1975, Catalan was used much more freely in public but not in education or the media.

The fact that language is at the emotional core of Catalan identity (McDonogh 1986a: 11; Roller 2002) and the efforts of various regimes in Madrid to suppress it have only made Catalans more adamant about the language's emotional significance and the memories of the lost past it evokes. When Franco died in 1975 many expected disorder and violence, not the orderly political transition that King Juan Carlos, his designated successor, presided over with rapid movement toward democratic rule. All major political parties and civil society participated in the transition, including opponents of Franco who had returned from exile. Leaders negotiated a new democratic Constitution while the European Community made it clear that membership would be open to a democratic Spain. The king became a stronger than expected voice for democratization whose support was never doubted after his refusal to support a military coup in 1981.

As the transition began, it was clear to all that there would be significant Catalan demands for a return to regional autonomy and linguistic expression. Both were achieved within a few years and the 1979 autonomy

---

[13] Perhaps they were inspired after having seen Humphrey Bogart in *Casablanca*.

statute recognized Catalan as the official language of Catalonia, and Castilian as the official language of the Spanish state.[14] The Catalan desire for their language to be on a par with Castilian in the region was not the same thing as making it happen, however. To do that required both the development of linguistic competence in Catalan and the attainment of equal respect for it and for its speakers (Kymlicka 1998). At least two significant problems faced proponents: first, because of the suppression of Catalan during the Franco years, there were many people who could speak Catalan but who were not able to read or write it; second, because of the strong Catalan economy that Franco had encouraged, the region had attracted many immigrants from other parts of Spain who were monolingual Castilian speakers. It was not obvious they would have an interest in learning a regional language.

Both of these challenges have been overcome since 1980 with fewer problems than many anticipated so that the region is now functionally bilingual, although there are still moments of tension in interpersonal interactions and Castilian speakers sometimes suggest that Catalans can be overly strident in their demeanor. While schools in the region differ in how they use Catalan and Castilian as languages of instruction, in all cases students learn both to a high degree of proficiency. Woolard and Gahng describe the rapid increase in use of Catalan in schools, the spread of fluency, and the language's relatively high status among both Castilian and Catalan native speakers (1990: 321–22).[15] Data from the mid-1990s show that 95% of the people living in Catalonia understand Catalan, 75% speak it, and almost half can write it. The population is evenly split in terms of whether they use Castilian or Catalan as their first language at home and with close friends (McRoberts 2001: 8–9). Roller (2002: 285–87) sees greater tension over recent linguistic policy and argues that since 1997 Catalan nationalists are no longer interested in linguistic parity and that linguistic policy is increasingly exclusivist in its goals and practices.

Why language change or what the Catalans call, "language normalization" proved to be far less conflictual than many people had expected

---

[14] Once Catalonia, Galicia, and the Basque regions gained autonomy, the demands were made from other parts of the country for the same status. The country is now divided into seventeen Autonomous Regions. Despite its strong decentralization in practice, Spain does not refer to itself as a federation nor as a multicultural state.

[15] Woolard (1989) reports that by the mid-1980s 86% of the schools in the region used Catalan as the medium of instruction in at least some subjects and that 62% of elementary schools had primarily Catalan instructional programs. These numbers are surely higher today.

requires some explanation.[16] What is especially striking is the spread of Catalan among immigrants from other parts of Spain and the willingness of their children to learn and use the language. One simple explanation about why this has occurred is that Catalan is not difficult for Castilian speakers to learn. While this might be the case, by itself it is not very compelling since there are many cases of resistance to learning and using a language irrespective of how easy or hard it is to learn. More persuasive is the idea that immigrants see settling in Catalonia as relatively permanent and view language as central to their successful integration. Interestingly, where working-class immigrants might have been expected to oppose language normalization, one explanation of why this has not been the case is that they too had suffered during the Franco years and could easily identify with the Catalan experience. Both the Socialist and Communist parties who appealed to these people supported language normalization provided it did not hurt Castilian speakers.[17]

Certainly relevant as well is that as determined as Catalans were to change language policy following Franco, there was also keen awareness that it had to be done in a non-authoritarian manner that would protect the rights of Castilian speakers. Success, many understood, would depend upon good will and voluntary compliance, not heavy-handed tactics. This policy was facilitated in great part because immigrants and their children viewed Catalan as a high status language. Woolard and Gahng report that Catalans are positively disposed to Castilian speakers who learn and use Catalan. "It no longer matters so much to Catalans who speaks Catalan, but rather simply that it is spoken" (1990: 326). Laitin (1989) suggests

---

[16] In 1983 the Catalan government passed an Act for Linguistic Normalization that was replaced by the Act on Linguistic Policy of 1998. One of the aims of the Linguistic Normalization Act was to make Catalan a normal working language in public administration. Public officials and civil servants must have a knowledge of Catalan. However, each citizen has the right to use either Castilian or Catalan when dealing with the administration. Official documents are published in both languages. Catalan can be used in court, although this is often hampered by a lack of knowledge of the language among the judiciary. The 1983 Act stipulated that Catalan should be the normal language of education at all levels and by 1999–2000, 90% of the primary schools in the region taught students Catalan while 51% of the secondary schools taught all subjects in Catalan and employed a mixture of Catalan and Spanish for the remaining subjects. In Catalan universities any student or professor is entitled to use either Castilian or Catalan. In addition, there is also a large network of adult education in Catalan (Catalan Department of Education, 2002 Annual Report).

[17] For more details on the dynamics at work in the immediate post-Franco period see DiGiacomo (1986).

that tipping points are an important mechanism in linguistic change situations and that once language use reaches a certain level, it rapidly increases and that indeed this occurred in Catalonia during the 1980s.

Probably crucial too is the pragmatic and generally non-racial nature of contemporary Catalan identity – one that is inclusive and non-confrontational. Jordi Pujol, the head of the Catalan regional government for more than twenty years starting in 1980, was often quoted as saying that a Catalan is a person who lives and works in Catalonia and wants to be Catalan (Guibernau 1997). While for many this strongly implied that such a person also speaks Catalan, this means that immigrants from other regions and their children could become Catalans. There is no genealogical or racial test – no gatekeepers patrolling the boundary and turning away undesirables. Woolard and Gahng contend that Catalan is not an exclusive, ethnic language signaling identity, but a public one (1990: 327) although there are certainly some Castilian speakers whose perceptions of Catalans are more exclusive than they suggest. Their finding is, however, echoed in McRoberts' (2001: 171–75) data that shows that language attitudes are least politicized among young people. He suggests that the twenty-five years that have passed since Franco's death have significantly lowered the affect associated with linguistic choice in a bilingual society with many cross-cutting ties.

Non-Catalan-speaking immigrants and their children integrate relatively easily into Catalan society for the boundaries between Catalans and Castilians are relatively permeable and identity is defined in cultural, rather than racial, terms. The boundaries themselves, however, are not necessarily clear and distinctions are sometimes made between indigenous Catalans and newcomers even when they are fluent in Catalan. In addition, historically there were often class differences, with indigenous Catalans much more likely to be middle class and to have their own businesses (Hargreaves 2000: 35–37). Despite these differences, there were, and are, frequent intermarriage, mobility, and harmonious relations between people in part because the prestige of the language and region makes newcomers quite willing to learn it (Hargreaves 2000: 37).

Most Catalans do not particularly insist that people choose between their Spanish and Catalan identities. Numerous surveys have asked people whether they see themselves as Catalan or Spanish or both and regularly show that a sizeable, and increasing, majority answer both. People do not believe these are incompatible choices or that these identities are determined at birth. Hargreaves points out that "the criteria of membership are cultural, and cultural credentials, unlike race or ancestry, can, in principle, be acquired" (2000: 34). Keating makes a similar point, noting, "The language is seen as a crucial element in social solidarity and community values but not as an ascriptive marker. There is an emphasis on history and culture and on institutions, but with little concern with race or descent. This gives Catalan nationalism a strong civic, as opposed to ethnic, character" (Keating 1996: 133).[18]

Catalans have long seen themselves as the most European people in Spain. They draw attention to the long history of contact with France in particular and emphasize that the greater cosmopolitanism of Catalonia and its earlier modernization than other parts of Spain is due to its greater interaction with the New World and Europe. This is a source of pride for Catalans, and emphasizing links to Europe helps Catalans differentiate themselves from Madrid. But it is also a source of tensions, as when, for example, under Pujol, Catalans sought representation on European government bodies, signed formal agreements with regions in other countries, and were able to get the European Parliament to recognize Catalan as a European language (Keating 1996: 158).[19] Of course the substantive significance of these steps is far less clear than their emphasis on the importance of recognition and legitimacy for Catalans.

Finally, Conversi (1997) and Hargreaves (2000) among others, emphasize that elite openness and self-confidence affect the expression of political nationalism in Catalonia in ways that create room for people to be both Catalan and Spanish. This means that while there are tensions and differences, and sometimes simply living and working in Catalonia is not enough to make someone fully Catalan (Hargreaves 2000: 35), there is a pattern in which identity disputes remain manageable; there are ways for the parties, whether individuals in the region or the Catalan government and Madrid, to manage them more or less constructively and without violence. We see these mechanisms at work in the story of the symbolic expression of identity during the 1992 Barcelona Olympics.

---

[18] The distinction between civic and ethnic nationalism is widely used (Ignatieff 1993; Smith 1991), although some find it too neat and problematic in important ways (e.g., Shulman 2002; Yack 1996).

[19] Catalan is one of many minority languages in Europe. An interesting overview of them is found at the website of an NGO, the European Bureau of Lesser Used Languages (EBLUL, http://eblul.org) that "speaks on behalf of over 40 million EU citizens who speak a different language than the majority language of their State."

Where is Barcelona?

Catalan distinctiveness and the 1992 Barcelona Olympic Games: a psychocultural drama over symbolic displays

In the post-Franco period, the Catalan commitment to language and cultural autonomy within Spain caused many heated moments but no real crises. The Spanish constitution writing project was inclusive, emphasizing consensus building, and there was widespread recognition that the Franco policies of centralization and cultural suppression were inappropriate for a country seriously committed to democratization and desperately wanting admission to the European Community. For the most part, the transition was remarkably peaceful although there were many symbolic skirmishes and moments when hard-core nationalists in both Barcelona and Madrid protested against what was happening.

In many ways neither side fully recognize how successful it has been in achieving its goals and in preventing small irritating incidents that regularly occurred from escalating to the point where they became violent or unmanageable.[20] Yet there is some lingering uneasiness in the Catalan relationship with the Spanish government at times. The state regularly seeks more acknowledgment of how generous it has been in granting autonomy to Catalonia. It is also annoyed when Catalans emphasize their ties to Europe and deemphasize those to Madrid.[21] Catalans, for their part, feel vulnerable at times and seek reaffirmation of their national identity from the rest of Spain. This dynamic is revealed in a psychocultural drama surrounding the 1992 Olympic Games held in Barcelona.

In 1986 the International Olympic Committee (IOC) awarded Barcelona the 1992 Summer Games and the Spanish saw this as a terrific opportunity to present post-Franco Spain to the world. (Madrid was named the cultural capital of Europe, and Seville, in Andalusia, hosted a World's Fair in 1992 as well.) While the politics of the choice of Barcelona as a site is

---

[20] This pattern is very consistent with what Morton Deutsch (1973) calls benevolent misperception in which parties who regularly cooperate are able to not see as provocative the actions of others that under less positive conditions would lead to increased tension and escalation of conflict.

[21] For example, the video from the Catalan history museum ends with the following words which offer no explicit acknowledgment that Catalonia is part of Spain: "Catalonia has been, and is, a European country: pluralistic, with integration aims, creative, open to modernity, a country that maintains its symbols of identity as a nation. From a contemporary perspective, the new challenges are clear: the European unification, the establishment of a solid coexistence among the peoples of the Mediterranean, and a new world order."

probably quite interesting,[22] here I focus on the series of symbolic conflicts playing out Catalan and Spanish narratives in the years, and especially months, just before and during the games. Acrimonious conflicts over questions such as language, flags, anthems, order of marching, ceremonies surrounding the Olympic torch, uniforms, and the structure of the opening ceremony all drew attention to the latent tensions in the relationship between Catalonia and Madrid. As Hargreaves (2000) points out, however, in the end the fact that both the Spanish and the Catalans understood the limits beyond which they could not go produced a win-win outcome that solidified both Catalan autonomy and, paradoxically, their connection to the Spanish state, not their subservience to it. The emotionally powerful issues were managed without violence or a breakdown of relationships and both Catalans and Spaniards believed that the games were a huge success. The outcome is the sort of ritual resolution that Turner (1957; 1973) talks about – one that emphasizes what is shared even though not all the underlying differences between the parties are necessarily resolved.

Hargreaves examines the symbolic politics surrounding the games and provides great detail concerning "the war of the flags" and the other symbolic battles that he frames in terms of Catalanization versus Espanolization of the Olympics (2000: 59–95). Once Spain and Barcelona were awarded the games, the responsibility for organizing and financing them fell to the Spanish government, which paid the largest share, the Generalitat (the Catalan government controlled by Pujol's center-right party), the government of Barcelona and its Catalan socialist mayor, the Spanish Olympic Committee, and the European Community that contributed toward the infrastructural changes in the city. The competing agendas of these groups, as well as those of nationalist groups in Catalonia, made for a far tenser run-up to the games than what most of the world observed during the Olympics themselves. Each of the parties had an interest in the games' success but each had its own ideas about what success would look like. The Socialist government in Madrid wanted to give the world the message that Spain was indeed now a mature, modern democracy, a different country than during the Franco era. Barcelona sought support for urban renewal and modernization of its infrastructure. The Catalan government saw the games as an opportunity to enhance the prestige, economic

---

[22] It is very relevant that the International Olympic Committee president, Juan Antonio Samaranch, was Catalan.

development, and autonomy of the region. In addition, within Catalonia hard-line nationalists, Pujol and his ruling CiU Party, and Barcelona Mayor Pasqual Maragall, a Catalan socialist and head of the Barcelona Games Organization Committee, had competing electoral interests.

As a result, both contemporary political concerns and unresolved past issues provided more than enough material for the intense emotions that were played out in symbolic conflicts as the games approached. Describing them as symbolic, however, is not meant either to diminish their significance to those involved or to ignore the fact that there were several moments when it seemed that the confrontations could turn ugly and perhaps violent. Rather, it is more useful to understand the power of symbolic and ritual issues to capture fundamental differences in how different sides conceive of the appropriate relationship between Catalonia and Spain.

It would be a great mistake here to think that displaying the national flag, singing the national anthem, using the national language, putting on displays featuring national dance and national sports, and so on, was mere play-acting and posturing, or somehow a substitute for real action. The deployment of national symbols around the Games provided a direct link to the fundamental issue of Catalonia's autonomy and Spanish and Catalan identity.

(Hargreaves 2000: 162)

The Olympic Games officially opened on July 25, 1992 but for the previous five months there were skirmishes around every imaginable symbolic element of the games given the decision that the Games would reflect Catalan culture, although what this exactly meant was always vague. There were also Catalan protests against the games themselves and pro-tests against redevelopment that destroyed some working-class areas of Barcelona. Pressure to Catalanize the games came from a variety of nationalist groups and Pujol, at times, gave a good deal of support to them.[23] Even the question of the mascot became politicized, and nation-alists strongly criticized the one adopted as not even remotely Catalan. The Games' organizers realized that trouble was a real possibility when three years prior to the opening of the games at the inauguration of the

---

[23] One of the most persistent pressures came from the Catalan Olympic committee; headed by a former minister of the Catalan government and formed to oppose the Spanish Olympic Committee, it sought to gain recognition from the International Olympic Committee to have a separate team representing Catalonia participate in the games.

refurbished Olympic stadium, the king and the Spanish Olympic team were whistled at and jeered.[24]

Nationalist groups made a steady stream of escalating symbolic demands in the months prior to the games, sometimes fed by electoral and political pressures. Some nationalists drew a parallel between Catalonia and the newly independent states of the former Soviet Union and demanded that Catalan athletes march under the Olympic flag and display armbands with the flags of their nation. There were voices that called for the Catalan flag to be raised and their anthem to be played when Catalan athletes won a medal and those who suggested Catalan athletes march into the stadium together at the end of the opening ceremonies in recognition of Catalonia as the host nation. The Olympic Committee stuck with its earlier agreement to recognize Catalan as one of the four official languages of the Games, along with French, English, and Spanish, the use of Catalan flags (along with those of Spain, Barcelona, and the IOC) in all settings where the Games were held, and the inclusion of the Catalan patriotic song "El Cant de la Senyera" in the opening ceremonies. All of these were carried out, but not before there was additional acrimony and detailed negotiation to avoid overt conflict or aggressive displays during the Games that would have embarrassed the parties before a world audience.

The flag was the major focus of a number of incidents but virtually any symbolic expression was easily politicized. One group launched a "Freedom for Catalonia" campaign and widely distributed banners and T-shirts to be displayed in and around Olympic venues. Continual negotiation up until the last minute produced on-going adjustments in the plans, such as the addition of the Catalan national anthem, "El Segadors," with its anti-Spanish lyrics, and the decision to have a Catalan girl dressed in traditional costume present the medals to the winners. In mid June it was announced that both the Spanish and Catalan anthems would be played when the king entered the stadium and that both flags would be represented along with the Barcelona city flag. In addition, an agreement was reached between Spanish and Catalan TV to share coverage of the games. During the nine days prior to the Games when the Olympic torch passed through Catalonia the situation was especially tense as nationalists used the occasion to exclude and ridicule all that was

---

[24] The stadium was loaded with political significance. It was built originally in 1936 to host an alternative Olympic Games to those that Hitler and Nazi Germany held in Berlin. However, the outbreak of the Spanish Civil War made this impossible.

Spanish.[25] At one point, the central government and the governing Socialists were increasingly upset at the nationalist control of the agenda and emphasized that Catalan symbols represented Spain. Of course, it is probable that some nationalists were not happy until they provoked a reaction from the government which validated their efforts.

In early July, the Catalan government took out two-page advertisements in major newspapers around the world. On the first page was a blank map of Europe with only Barcelona marked on it with the question, "Where is Barcelona?" The second page provided the answer: "In Catalonia, of course." Needless to say, this created a furor in the rest of the country. Again the Socialists responded, stressing "the games belong to everyone" and they attacked the close ties between Pujol and some Catalan nationalists. At two dress rehearsals in the final week there was loud whistling when the Spanish flag appeared in the stadium and when the Spanish anthem was played.

Despite the apparent acrimony, none of the groups wanted to be responsible for the failure of the Olympics, and in the final days those threatening to disrupt the games declared they were satisfied with the arrangements and the Olympics took place without incident. The flags were potent expressions in a symbolic conflict that both asserted mutually exclusive political identities and promoted a redefinition of the Catalan–Madrid relationship. Hargreaves observes that "The conduct of the Games constituted the arena in which the compromise arrived at by the contending parties was put into practice, tested out, worked on and perfected" (Hargreaves 2000: 96). In the end, he says, the inclusive symbolic and multi-national presentations including both Catalanized and Espanolized elements met the basic needs of all sides.

The king, who was a potentially divisive symbol, turned out to be crucial in bridging the two identities much as he has done since 1975 in creating the political space and support for the democratic transition and alternation of power between left and right in the country. At the beginning of the opening ceremonies, the king and the royal family

---

[25] Hargreaves reports that the reception ceremony for the torch "was to be an almost completely Catalan cultural feast...[and] in marked contrast to the programmes for the opening and closing ceremonies... this was a relatively exclusive affair with the accent on high, rather than popular or mass culture" (Hargreaves 2000:79). There was little that was Spanish, as opposed to Catalan at the event, and when Spanish Minister of Education Javier Solana addressed the crowd he was drowned out in a chorus of whistling and shouting as soon as he opened his mouth.

entered the stadium to the music of the Catalan national anthem, "Els Segadors," making it impossible for the crowd to jeer and whistle, at the same time as the Spanish, Catalan, and Barcelona flags were paraded, according the Catalan and Spanish national symbols equal status. Later the king officially declared the Games open in Catalan, "*Benvinguts tots a Barcelona*" (Welcome Everyone to Barcelona), producing a reaction that Hargreaves characterizes as electric. "This single brief act seems to have won over the Catalan audience at the outset" (Hargreaves 2000: 101). His active involvement throughout the games, a highly Catalanized event, emphasized the connections, rather than the differences, between the two nations (Hargreaves 2000: 107).

During the Games the Catalan spectators were especially vocal in greeting, and celebrating, the victories of Catalan athletes, but Hargreaves reports that there was no animosity toward Spanish athletes.[26] Spanish medal winners circled the stadium with the Spanish flag but also with that of their autonomous community (region) after a Catalan had done this early in the games. The gesture put Catalan autonomy in a larger Spanish context, marking its distinctiveness but also recognizing Catalonia as one of a number of Spain's autonomous communities. Furthermore, the team uniforms – using the colors Spain and Catalonia share (red and yellow), the victory ceremonies, and the behavior of Spanish officials all were inclusive and recognized a clear Catalan role within Spain, not opposition to it.

Hargreaves concludes that the outcome was successful. Pactism worked and he attributes this in great part to an inclusive nationalism that gave a role to dual identity and flexibility (2000: 141–42). The public opinion data he presents on identity and perceptions of the Olympics show high agreement within Catalonia and Spain on the king's, and the royal family's positive role, the organizational success of the games (beating prior expectations), and the positive image of Spain, Catalonia, and Barcelona that was projected abroad. The data also show differences, however, between Catalonia and the rest of the country with respect to the issue of language and cultural symbols that are clearly sore points for many in the rest of Spain. When asked to evaluate the use of Catalan as one of the official languages of the games, there was a clear divergence. In Catalonia

---

[26] Interestingly, Hargreaves notes that there was an especially warm relationship toward the teams from small nations who had recently gained independence such as the Baltic states, Croatia and Bosnia (Hargreaves 2000:105). Perhaps Catalans readily identified with other small nations which they perceived to have experienced the same sorts of trials and tribulations that the Catalans have known.

84% said it was very good or good and only 4% said it was bad, while in the rest of Spain, the numbers were 29% and 40%. There were similar figures for the question about the use of the Catalan flag and national anthem together with those of Spain during the games; 82% of the people in Catalonia said it was very good or good and 4% bad or very bad, while for the rest of Spain the figures were 28% and 38% (Hargreaves 2000: 158).

In reading Hargreaves' account and the last minute accommodation that was achieved, a crucial question to ask is how disruption and even violence were avoided given the intensity of some nationalist sentiment. His analysis suggests four factors to explain the successful outcome: each major actor had an interest in avoiding disruption and each got enough of what it needed to accept a peaceful outcome; an inclusive nationalism did not force Catalans or Spaniards to view their identity narrowly and choose between them; there was no escalation of the conflict on the part of the Spanish government despite many small provocations; and the long Catalan tradition of hard bargaining and compromise (pactism) made it possible to accept an inclusive ritual resolution.

Conclusion

Catalonia's relationship with Spain has taken many forms over the centuries. However, one constant is that over time a significant number of Catalans have refused to abandon their language and national identity. At times this has provoked a strong response from Madrid and efforts to suppress expressions of Catalan identity; at other times, such as the period since 1975, there has been a good deal of accommodation and space within Spain for multiple identities and regional autonomy. In the post-Franco period, intense conflicts have occurred around identity issues, including prolonged violence involving the Basques, but the tensions related to Catalonia have not produced violence or strong support for independence. Most Catalans accept their status as a nation without a state and many point to the special role that Catalonia plays within Spain and Europe with pride and satisfaction.

Spain's successful democratic transition makes it clear that formal governmental arrangements and leadership matter (Linz, Stephan, and Gunther 1995). However, they are not all that matter, and as this chapter argues an additional dimension also played an important role in the process: the development of an inclusive narrative about Catalonia and its relationship to Spain that provided each side with basic reassurance so that when tensions rose, they did not turn into destructive conflict.[27] In addition, ritual expression of dual identity became acceptable in post-Franco Spain, as was demonstrated in the dispute over the symbolic landscape associated with the 1992 Olympics.[28]

In both Spain and Canada, restraint on the part of the state paid off in that neither of these conflicts turned violent despite moments when that certainly seemed possible. One important lesson is that tensions and differences aren't necessarily the problem – they exist in all relationships. The question is how parties manage them. In these cases, while the demands of the national minorities were often more than the state wanted to hear, they were not posed in terms of ultimatums or hard-line positions from which neither side could back down. In Spain, King Juan Carlos's inclusive actions, the acceptance of regional languages, and the existence of seventeen autonomous communities in the country have provided a framework in which Catalans feel that their core cultural concerns are more or less acknowledged and that they possess sufficient power and control in their region to protect their identity.

Part of the emerging national narrative in Catalonia and in Québec is that each sees itself as a small nation without a state and recognizes that there are other nations in the same situation. Small nations can be both regional and international actors, and while both Spain and Canada regularly express unease when Catalonia and Québec try to exercise an independent foreign policy, the external connections among small nations, and their connection to regional and international organizations clearly provide some significant emotional, economic and political support that eases tension between the region and the state. Finally, the existence of strong European institutions, Catalonia's ties to other regions within Europe, and widespread international and regional recognition of Catalonia as a small nation facilitates the Catalan–Madrid relationship and acts as a balancing mechanism that is crucial in accounting for the success of the current arrangements, increasing Catalan confidence that their autonomy is not at risk.

---

[27] If only the formal, constitutional arrangements mattered then one would predict that the relationship between Basque nationalism and Spain should have had a similar outcome to the Catalan one. This is clearly not the case, however, which means that the differences between Catalan and Basque identity in terms of inclusiveness and symbolic expressions are well worth considering (c.f. Conversi 1997, Laitin 1995).

[28] In the case of Québec too there have been many similar dynamics as Canada and Québec have worked to redefine their relationship in mutually satisfactory ways. Most observers would agree, however, that the situation in Québec is more uncertain and the mutual confidence the parties express weaker than in Catalonia and Spain.

Finally, while Catalan identity has existed for centuries, its content and emotional significance have ebbed and flowed over time. Whereas many in the Spanish Civil War generation and their children put a great deal of energy into maintaining Catalan language and culture, McRoberts' (2001) data suggest that their emotional salience may be diminishing among succeeding generations, which should not be surprising given the diminished threat to them in the contemporary political context. The point is that the core components of identity and their salience change over time and are tied to specific social and political contexts. On the other hand, following the years when José Maria Aznar's Popular Party ruled Spain, there was talk of clipping the wings of the country's regions and Catalans variously chafed and worried about their status. Following the 2004 elections when the a three-party coalition including Catalan separatists took power in the region and the Socialists defeated Aznar nationally, the Catalan legislature passed a revised autonomy statute that refers to Catalonia as a nation but there remains pressure to reframe their status as a nationality (Anderson 2006). The government in Madrid was once again careful not to escalate the tensions and it appeared that the parties would find a way to make the new arrangements work.

For small nations, such as Catalonia and Québec, there is always tension between the folkloric and the pragmatic-modernist sides of identity (Noyes 2003). Whereas the first emphasizes traditions and ritual expressions of culture, the latter links expressions of identity to the context of a globalized world. Of course the two are not always in opposition. Given the widespread interest in folk festivals, traditional music, regional cuisine, and local clothing crafts among tourists and others, there are many people who have very pragmatic, modern reasons to emphasize their heritage. For some people, this means moving between different, but partially overlapping, worlds daily, weekly, or seasonally, and these movements are not necessarily problematic or stressful. Furthermore, expression of regional cultures in many contexts is not necessarily threatening to modern states whose sovereignty is diffused upwards into cross-national and international organizations and downward to local governments and civil society. In places when identities are defined in cultural more than ethnic terms, inclusive political space can develop that allows for the expression of multiple identities and loyalties – in this case to the nation (Catalonia) and state (Spain) – in ways that do not produce tension and conflict that can be managed only through violence.

6

Digging up the past to contest the present: politics
and archeology in Jerusalem's Old City

Introduction

Metaphorically the holy sites in Jerusalem's old city are ground zero of
the Israeli–Palestinian conflict. The mutually exclusive claims Jews and
Muslims make concerning sovereignty, rights, and identity played out in
excruciating detail around contested above and below ground sacred
space parallel the emotionally intense differences about political existence found in the larger conflict of which Jerusalem is just one part.
While contestation in Jerusalem takes many forms and has many different foci, these always come back to questions of power, control,
vulnerability, and purity. The mutually exclusive claims each side regularly makes set off a spiral reaction from the other that leave little room
for the development of inclusive symbols and rituals that could define a
community that offers mutual recognition and shared spaces, and
where one group's existence is not necessarily a threat to another. The
competing narratives and psychocultural dramas over the Old City of
Jerusalem's holy sites occur because, "Sacred centers are not just
reflections or traces of political power: they are often instruments and
sources of political power" and intimately tied to the larger conflict
(Friedland and Hecht 1998: 147).

For the past 100 years or so, the most intense Muslim–Jewish conflict
in Jerusalem has been over the area on, under, and next to what Jews call
the Temple Mount (Har Habayit) and Muslims the Noble Sanctuary
(Haram al-Sharif) (Figure 6.1).[1] Jews believe that the ruins of their First
and Second Temples, including the Holiest of Holies, are beneath the

---

[1] Muslim–Jewish conflict in Jerusalem's Old City is often seen as coterminous with the
Israeli–Palestinian conflict in important ways although it is must be noted that 20% of

154

Figure 6.1 The Haram al Sharif with the Al-Aqsa Mosque and the Dome of the Rock and the Western Wall. The opening to the immediate left of the wall is the entrance to the controversial archeological tunnel that runs the length of the wall and exits on the Via Dolorosa.

present platform where the Dome of the Rock and the Al Aqsa Mosque are located. The Haram is Islam's third holiest place, after Mecca and Medina, and its Western Wall (Al Buraq in Arabic and Kotel Hamaaravi in Hebrew) is where Muslims believe Muhammad began his Night Journey to heaven. Jews consider the same Western Wall to be the only remaining visible section of their Second Temple which the Romans destroyed in 70 CE, although there are Muslims who say it is only a retaining wall from a Roman fortification. The wall is Judaism's holiest site and Jews believe that when the Messiah arrives, a third and final temple will be built on the Temple Mount that it supports. Thus, the Haram and the Kotel have come to represent the core of each group's religious and political identity. As Benvenisti writes, "Just as the Muslims had turned the Temple Mount into a focal point for nationalist activities, the Jews have transformed the Wall into a national site . . . the coexistence

---

Israeli citizens are Palestinians and that a minority of Palestinians are Christian, not Muslim.

of these two neighboring places of worship is not peaceful nor is the conflict over them merely religious" (Benvenisti 1996: 83).[2] Finally, many of each group's rules concerning access to, and behavior on, the site are mutually exclusive (Hassner 2005).

Consider just two conflicts that have developed into intense psychocultural dramas in the past decade. In 1996, soon after right-wing Prime Minister Benjamin Netanyahu took office, the Israeli government authorized the opening of an exit on the Via Dolorosa, in the city's Muslim quarter, to an archeological tunnel running the length of the long western side of the Haram (Figure 6.2). The tunnel had existed for a dozen years and visitors both entered and left through a small area at the northern end of the plaza next to the wall's prayer area. Palestinians and the Muslim religious authorities expressed outrage that the decision had been taken without consultation and claimed that Jews were attempting to tunnel under the Haram as they had done in the 1980s in search of the temple's remains, and that this threatened the foundations of the Haram itself and houses in the Muslim quarter. Rioting and fighting, some of which was clearly orchestrated, spread to the West Bank leaving eighty-six Palestinians and fifteen Israeli soldiers dead and many hundreds wounded the next week (Dumper 2002: 85). As Dumper notes:

For Palestinians, these confrontations with Israel were simply the latest manifestations of the struggle with Jews and the Israeli state over the control of the Haram compound in the Old City. Following the precedent set by the Western Wall incident in 1929, the demolition of the Magharib quarter, the expansion of the Jewish quarter, the penetration of settlers into the Muslim and Christian quarters of the Old City, the activities of the Temple Mount Faithful groups, and the Jewish underground to take over the Haram all were part of a broad strategy for their ultimate dispossession in the heart of Jerusalem.

(Dumper 2002: 85)

The archeological tunnel in question passes under the Muslim quarter and reveals the bedrock and portions of the underground walls of the Haram/Temple Mount. While it was obvious for some time that an exit at the northern end of the tunnel would provide for a more efficient flow of visitors to the tunnel, it was also clear that this would fan Muslim fears

---

[2] Just to make the situation more complicated there is the fundamentalist Christian belief that the Temple must be rebuilt to set off the battle for Armageddon that will presage "the end of days" (Gorenberg 2000).

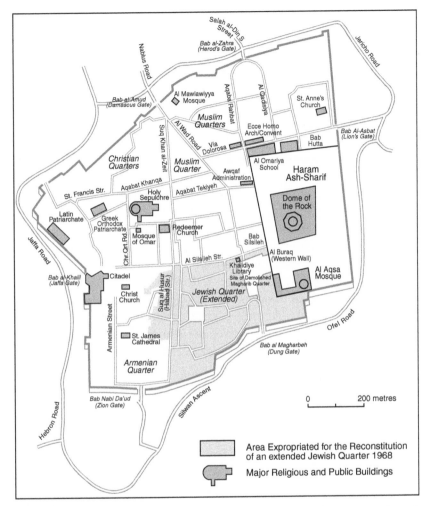

Figure 6.2 Map of Jerusalem's Old City showing key Christian, Jewish and Islamic holy sites

of Jewish encroachment. During the first years after the Oslo Agreement, therefore, nothing was done. Only when Benjamin Netanyahu, an opponent of the Oslo Agreement, was elected prime minister in 1996 after Yitzak Rabin's assassination, was opening the tunnel's new exit authorized.

The second psychocultural drama began several years later when some Israelis became infuriated by Palestinian building activity on top of, and beneath, the Haram. The conflict surfaced in 1999 and observers link it to

157

Palestinian anger over the 1996 tunnel opening after which the *Waqf*, the Islamic Religious Trust, stopped its informal pattern of cooperation with the Israeli government and the Israeli Antiquities Authority (Shragai 2000). But we should also connect Muslim actions in the recent conflict to Muslim vulnerability expressed in 1929 when they reacted to Jewish moves to alter the Ottoman status quo arrangements regarding Jewish access to, and prayer at, the wall, as described in Chapter 2. The project that provoked the strongest Israeli reaction was construction of a large new exit to the Marwani Mosque, an underground prayer hall on the Haram, in an area often called Solomon's Stables, that was built in the early Islamic period when Crusaders (not King Solomon) used it as a stable. While the Israeli authorities had authorized the exit, there was great surprise and anger at its size, the amount of earth – at least 6,000 tons – that was removed and scattered at various dumpsites, and the use of heavy machinery, including bulldozers.

Israeli opponents expressed outrage that the work was not carried out under archeological supervision and a group of archeologists and others from both the left and right formed The Committee for the Prevention of Destruction of Antiquities on the Temple Mount. They published photos of the excavation and building, conducted a survey of the tons of dirt filled with objects in the Kidron Valley next to a garbage dump, and lobbied the government to halt the project.[3] They charged that "this type of systematic destruction would be unthinkable at any similarly important site in the world, such as the Acropolis in Athens or the Forum in Rome" (Shragai 2000). *Waqf* authorities asserted that they needed no Israeli permission to undertake the work and that the Israeli presence is one of occupation. Most controversial is their argument that there was no evidence that the Jewish temples were actually on the site – a claim Yasser Arafat repeated at Camp David in 2000 – and the contention that the rubble was from the Islamic period (Arnold 1999). Others said that even if the material did contain objects from earlier periods, it was only located above Solomon's Stables because it had served as landfill there hundreds of years earlier and therefore was of no archeological significance.

Israeli politicians and archeologists asserted that "the remnants of Jewish history were being trampled on" (Arnold 1999), and the Jerusalem municipality released a statement saying that while the exit was needed,

---

[3] The detailed data and photos concerning the construction activity on the Temple Mount are presented in the group's website: www.har-habayt.org/

the action was "part of a political move intended to create a *fait accompli* toward the future management and control of the Temple Mount" (Sappir 1999). Gabriel Bar-Kay, an archeologist and member of the Committee for the Prevention of the Destruction of Antiquities on the Temple Mount, describes the area as "the Acropolis of ancient Judaism" that needed to be protected from politicians and activists. He described going to the dumpsites and finding objects he asserted were as old as the First Temple period, and charged the Muslim authorities with systematically "erasing evidence of Jewish presence" on the Temple Mount (personal interview). In many ways this is precisely the goal, driven by Muslim insecurity and fear that recognition of a historical Jewish presence will lead to Jewish appropriation of the Haram in much the same way as Arabs feel Jews have appropriated much of Palestine.

At the core of both these conflicts are the intense emotions the parties feel and express that parallel deep fears and suspicions embedded in the larger Israeli–Palestinian conflict. What is found in both the Jerusalem conflict and the larger conflict is that opponents view each other's actions as aggressive and make exclusive claims that negate the other's existence and identity (Sappir 1999). It is not hard to see that when Jews or Muslims assert exclusive rights to the holy sites while denying those of the other side, they are also making a claim concerning their larger political rights in the region. For example, for many years Israeli leaders, most famously former Prime Minister Golda Meir, denied that there was a distinct Palestinian identity, saying, "There is no such thing as a Palestinian people." If this was the case, then, Palestinians were hardly entitled to their own state and Jews were simply returning to their (empty) homeland after almost 2000 years of exile. In response, many Palestinians have articulated an alternative narrative, one that emphasizes the long-term existence of a Palestinian people within the Arab world and their continued presence in Palestine for millennia going back to the early Canaanites (Litvak 1994).

In each of these narratives religious and national claims are fused as Palestinians and Israelis see their own nation as the rightful heir to the land, and offer little acknowledgment of the possibility that both nations have legitimate rights. To bolster their own claims, each side appeals for support from its own citizens and outsiders. In this chapter, I focus on one that has a particularly strong appeal to multiple audiences – the use of historical and, especially archeological, evidence to put forth identity and sovereignty claims in ways that each side perceives as highly threatening to its own position. Archeological evidence is material and physical and, at the same time, problematic in many ways, most obviously because it is fragmentary and individual objects often reveal little or nothing about how people in the ancient past thought about their social and political identity. Nonetheless, both archeologists and popularizers often have little hesitation in drawing inferences from objects to identities. Especially relevant is that mass publics readily find these narratives emotionally and politically plausible and powerful.

Two dynamics come together here. The first is a tendency to essentialize groups and their identities and to minimize an opponent's within-group diversity. In this process, there is little acknowledgment of the social and political forces at play that create, manipulate, and alter identities over time. The second dynamic involves the ideological manipulation of time to meet political needs. Present identities are read backwards as in "Nos ancêtres les Gauls," and genealogical linkages are stressed in terms of contemporary political identities and group continuity (Horowitz 1985: ch. 2) while present-day beliefs and social practices are attributed to ancestors, providing emotional linkage across time. Essentializing and time manipulation serve political claim-making by connecting a selectively remembered past to the contested present to mobilize the defense of the in-group. Political use of archeological findings calls on both of these strategies to produce a seamless linkage between present peoples and ancient ones. Yet, archeological evidence, while having "scientific" and material credibility, is sufficiently incomplete and ambiguous to nurture mutually exclusive narratives that serve the interests of opposing political leaders and groups in conflict (Bernbeck and Pollack 1998: S140).

Psychocultural narratives and dramas around Jerusalem's holy sites are not new. Nor do they involve only Muslims and Jews. Because people believe that real nations have real histories, it is not surprising that groups put a good deal of energy into uncovering new, or reinterpreting existing, evidence to develop and support their claims. The narratives various actors then develop provide a rich testimony to the polarization resulting from exclusive claims, mutual denial, and deep existential fears. In Jerusalem, these fears are always close to the surface. Through symbolic and ritual actions and the use of real power the conflicting parties raise each other's anxiety levels in ways that reinforce the worldview that the only possible peace in the region will be one that is achieved by force. In this dynamic, symbolic and substantive actions are intertwined and take many forms, some as simple as throwing rocks from the Haram onto Jewish worshipers at the Western Wall below or Ariel Sharon proclaiming his right to walk on the Temple Mount and going there accompanied by hundreds of Israeli security forces as he did in September 2000. In each case, the actors are asserting their own group's sovereignty over the area and delivering the message in an aggressive, public manner whose meaning is hard to misunderstand.

This chapter uses the case of Jerusalem's holy sites to examine the role of archeology in the development of history and memory in the Israeli–Palestinian conflict. The next section explores the concept of sacred space and its political significance, emphasizing that sacred spaces are both powerful and vulnerable at the same time. The following one connects this to the use of archeological findings and the politics of mutual denial. Then I discuss psychocultural dramas and the Muslim–Jewish conflict over Jerusalem's holy sites, and the final section raises questions about reframing existing narratives and symbolic space, asking about the extent to which sacred sites can be redefined more inclusively, and even shared, to allow Muslims and Jews to live side by side more peacefully than they have in the past century, as part of managing the Palestinian–Israeli conflict.

Identity and sacred sites

One way to think about identity is to consider what it is that people with the same identity believe they share. Invariably, part of the answer is a shared past recounted in group narratives even though the content of that past is often partial and vague (Roy 1994).[4] From a psychocultural perspective and more important than the details about the past are emotionally salient reference points that elicit strong reactions and symbolize identity. These take a wide variety of forms, many of which are examined throughout this book. Some are highly abstract, such as religious beliefs and ceremonies, while others are focused on particular objects, people, and events. The focus in this chapter is on specific places, hallowed grounds that are physical locations imbued with a deep emotional significance that serve as "linking objects" to connect individuals to a group across time and space (Volkan 1997).

---

[4] It is, of course, an empirical question – what is actually shared versus what is perceived to be shared.

Chidester and Linenthal contend that sacred space is ritual space "set apart from or carved out of an 'ordinary' environment to provide an arena for the performance of controlled, 'extraordinary' patterns of action" (1995: 9). Hassner argues that a sacred site's power is defined by its centrality in a group's spiritual landscape and its exclusivity, which refers to the extent to which it is circumscribed, monitored, and sanctioned (2003: 7). In addition, a crucial feature of sacred spaces is their indivisibility, because they are cohesive, have unambiguous boundaries, and cannot be substituted or exchanged for another good (Hassner 2003:8). As a result, in conflicts involving competing claims over the same space, mutually satisfactory outcomes are hard to reach.

Because they "galvanize the deepest emotions and attachments, material and symbolic control over the most central sacred spaces are sources of enormous social power" (Friedland and Hecht 1991:23). This means, as Friedland and Hecht point out, that sacred sites are periodically contested. There can be conflicts to control them, over the objects presented on the sites, and/or around the narratives recounted about them. Battlefields, places where peace treaties have been signed, areas where heroic events occurred, and locations venerated for their religious significance are common sacred sites. Virtually every group has sacred sites and there are often special rituals associated with their preservation, rules for visitation, and sacred days when the sites are especially important and serve as the location for sacred secular and religious rituals. Sacred places, Chidester and Linenthal argue, inevitably produce "contests over the legitimate ownership of sacred symbols" that raise issues of power and purity (1995:15–20). This means that sacred sites are both powerful and vulnerable at the same time. Because their existence is testimony to a group's moral authority and legitimacy, sacred sites need to be protected against desecration and loss of control. Although they were not writing about Jerusalem's old city, Chidester and Linenthal could have been when they say:

Since no sacred space is merely "given" in the world, its ownership will always be at stake. In this respect, a sacred space is not merely discovered, or founded, or constructed; it is claimed, owned, and operated by people advancing specific interests.

(Chidester and Linenthal 1995:15)

The vulnerability of sacred sites means that groups go to great lengths to control and protect them, for an attack on the site is perceived as an attack on the group.[5] Friedland and Hecht argue that as a consequence "conflicts over the social order will ramify in its sacred center" (1998: 147).

It is interesting to ask why and how an abstract group identity comes to be embodied in specific mundane objects such as soil, stones, water, and trees to which groups attribute a sacred character. While identity is inherently non-material, it is nonetheless most powerfully expressed when it is linked to in physical locations or objects associated with specific people, places and events (Nora 1989). Once a physical site that represents the group is imbued with intense emotional significance, defense of the site and objects on it becomes necessary since their loss threatens the group's existence and legitimacy. Relics, ruins, and potsherds located in sacred spaces allow people to make the inferential leap from what they know through their senses to what they believe in their heart – although it is certainly the case that sometimes people make the connection in the other direction as well.

Christian, Jewish, and Muslim narratives all link present political claims to the city's historical, and even prehistorical, past in part by attaching great emotional significance to sacred sites in and around the old city of Jerusalem. Their intense attachment has often driven efforts to obtain exclusive control of the city, and in Jerusalem's history there have been only a few, short periods when the city's rulers provided fully open access for members of all faiths (Armstrong 1996). Armstrong (1996) recounts that early Christianity paid little attention to the city of Jerusalem and to the details of Jesus' life prior to Constantine's conversion in 313, after which he sent his mother Helena to Jerusalem to locate sacred sites and relics from Jesus' life (Armstrong 1996: 179–93).[6] Soon after her arrival in Jerusalem, Helena "discovered" the cave where Jesus' body was placed after his death and the "true cross" and ordered that the Church of the Holy Sepulcher be built on that site. In a short time, there was a dramatic shift among Christians toward an intense concern with holy sites and relics that had a tremendous ability to make the story of Jesus emotionally meaningful. The search for relics intensified, and the construction of shrines for them illustrates the power of a sacred landscape. "This act of holy archeology would lay bare the physical roots of their

---

[5] Chidester and Linenthal identify four strategies for contesting the production and control of sacred space: appropriation and exclusion are often used to dominate these sites, while inversion and hybridization are best suited for resistance to domination (1995: 19).

[6] "Constantine also knew that his Christian empire needed symbols and monuments to give it historical resonance" (Armstrong 1996: 179).

faith and enable them to build literally on these ancient foundations" (Armstrong 1996: 180). It was irresistible. Soon Christians became adamant about the holy nature of Jerusalem and the Crusades centuries later were an effort to wrest it from the infidels, to capture their shrines and holy places and to erect Christian ones in their stead. "The experience of living in Jerusalem had impelled the Christians to develop a full-blown sacred geography based on the kind of mythology they had once despised" (Armstrong 1996: 216).[7]

It must be pointed out that this phenomenon is hardly unique to Jerusalem. Similar dynamics linking specific sites and sacred past events are found in Muslim and Jewish narratives about Jerusalem, Hindu and Buddhist traditions in South Asia, and narratives emphasizing the sacred character of modern nation states. Connections between objects and collective identities are abstract and spiritual and at the same time intensely physical and literal, and are easily expressed through buildings, monuments, and fragments from the past.

Archeology, claim-making, and mutual denial

When it is useful for one side or another, archeological evidence can be part of the political legitimation of group claims and counter claims. In fact, archeological excavations are well suited for providing "hard evidence" to validate exclusive political claims and archeological work often gets strong government support when it provides objects and narratives supporting a group's long history and struggle for national identity as in Jerusalem (Abu El-Haj 2001; Kohl 1998; Kohl and Fawcett 1995; Meskell 1998; 2002; Shanks 1981; Shaw 2000; Smith 1999: 66). Throughout the world groups "dig for God and country" (Silberman 1982) and trace a nation's roots as far back as possible. Silberman suggests that the interpretative process and political needs often result in framing presentations of archeological sites such that:

the public's shared perceptions of the past is shaped by a wide range of presentational elements . . . and the explanations of tourist guides [that] combine to present the public with a composite historical "story" or narrative that is far more sweeping in its conclusions and implications than the specific archeological data on which it is ultimately based.

(Silberman 1997: 63)

---

[7] Christian archeological explorations in nineteenth-century Jerusalem exemplify this same phenomenon (Monk 2002).

As Abu El-Haj (2001) argues, there is a seamless movement from potsherds to peoplehood and the easy, but not necessarily correct, inference that contemporary identity groups are the linear descendants of past ones. Meskell warns that efforts to identify a literal match between artifacts, human remains, and modern people results in manipulation and misuse (2002: 290).[8] Central to this naïve position is the widespread belief that legitimation of present political claims is simply a matter of demonstrating who settled first in an area. In Northern Ireland, when Catholics cast their political claims in terms of ancient Celtic presence, some Protestants then developed archeological evidence to claim that a group of Cruthins from Scotland settled the island before the Celts arrived (Adamson 1974; Hall 1994). This is parallel to how Palestinians now describe their connection to the Canaanites who lived in the area before the arrival of Jews from Egypt to counter Jewish claims linking ancient and modern Israel.

In Jerusalem this past-oriented basis for legitimation claims is especially important for Jews and Christians, whose political claims to the city rest upon a linkage between the ancient past and the present, the notion of the ascending anachronism. In contrast, for Muslims their domination of the clearly visible landscape in recent centuries means that for them archeological evidence is less important to their claims. In fact, given the above-ground contemporary Islamic presence, there is real fear that subterranean findings might, if anything, be used to undermine their current exclusive *de facto* control over many sites, and especially the Haram. As a result, the greatest Muslim fears concern Jewish use (and what they see as misuse) of archeological evidence to legitimate their claim that Jerusalem is the eternal capital of Israel (Abu El-Haj 2001; Glock 1994). As the youngest of the three religions in the city, by definition Islamic artifacts will not be as old as Jewish or Christian ones. Yet Muslims, it should be noted, buy into the paradigm that older claims have precedence over newer ones. They seek to limit Jewish investigations on and under the Temple Mount by denying Jews access to potential evidence that might support their claims. Toward this end Muslims have built additional structures on the Haram and have declared the entire area a mosque making further excavations impossible.

---

[8] Nineteenth-century European nationalists used archeology in this way to bolster their political claims and to strengthen national identity (Kohl and Fawcett 1995; Kohl 1998). We can see the same pattern more recently in settings such as Sri Lanka and Central Asia and changing interpretation of sites in Southern Africa (Kuklick 1991).

It is in the context of competing narratives, worldviews, and political claims that we can understand the intensity in the arguments over archeological practice and evidence in Jerusalem. Archeologists uncover physical objects that in and of themselves often have little intrinsic interest or meaning to most people. Meaning comes from the accounts and theories that those who interpret the objects propose. Sometimes the meanings are self-evident but more often their emotional significance can be understood only if we ask several additional questions: why do certain objects become the focus of an excavation? What choices might other archeologists have made on the same site? For example, in a site that has been inhabited for thousands of years, which periods get the most (and sometimes exclusive) attention? How is the fragmentary physical evidence used to construct an account of the social and political worlds that are the focus of the popular reactions to archeological work? Without written evidence, how can contemporary scholars understand the nature of social relations and identities in older societies?[9]

In Palestine and Israel, nineteenth-century British and American biblical archeological projects and twentieth-century Jewish ones have focused on the ancient past and have paid relatively little attention to more recent periods, such as the Ottoman era. Abu El-Haj discusses the controversial use of bulldozers in the major Jerusalem digs after 1967 as Israeli archeologists intently sought evidence about the First and Second Temple periods in ancient Israel before the Jewish quarter was rebuilt. In contrast, Glock (1994) outlines what he considers an appropriate Palestinian archeology that would examine the social life of inhabitants of the region in a very different way. He argues that a Palestinian archeology would dig backwards starting with more recent periods and working back to earlier and earlier times. It would pay less attention to grand buildings and monuments and more to the social life of people living in villages and towns, asking how they lived, cultivated, and built.

Archeologists make important decisions that have an impact on how their work is used and on the narrative describing their results. Benvenisti illustrates the mutual denial in competing national narratives in the presentations in two sites in the old city. In the Museum of the City of Jerusalem located in a fortress called David's Citadel (which has nothing

---

[9] Abu El-Haj (2001) writes about these issues at length as do many of the other archeologists cited in this chapter.

to do with King David), he contends that periodization of Jerusalem's history affects our understanding of groups who have lived in the city. Israel is presented as spanning millennia, while the Arab presence is broken into much smaller, named periods that suggest little continuity between them (Benvenisti 1996: 4–9). One exhibit at the citadel offers the following Jewish narrative:

> Jerusalem is the capital of the Jewish people, where they established their kingdom and set up their capital 3,000 years ago. For 2000 years the city was subjected to the rule of foreign conquerors and the Jewish people were exiled from it. In recent generations they have returned to their capital, expelled the foreign invaders, and reestablished the capital of their sovereign state. Each of the conquerors left a mark, and billions of Muslim and Christian believers have embraced the sanctity of Jerusalem – an attachment they have appropriated from the Jewish people. No competing national claims to the city exist, since there is no national collective in Jerusalem aside from that of the Israelis.
>
> (Benvenisti 1996: 8)

Just as exclusively, the Palestinian narrative seen in the Museum of Islam on the Temple Mount, he says, presents no trace of the Jews and presents the Palestinian sacred history, heritage, and geography in ways that makes Israelis uneasy (Benvenisti 1996: 9).

Archeology is central to competing political claims in Jerusalem because it provides a framework for linking the past and present in an apparently scientific manner that provides an "objective" basis for group claims. Yet, it's not so simple. Nineteenth-century Christian archeologists sought to confirm biblical accounts. "Biblical names were understood to *belong to the land* itself and to be eminently present and identifiable therein once properly deciphered" (Abu El-Haj 2001: 35 – italics in original).[10] This set of practices and assumptions also fits the need of some early Zionists who found archeological evidence one of the most effective ways to demonstrate the connection between Ancient Israel and the hoped-for modern state (Silberman 1982; Zerubavel, 1995).[11] Digs became national

---

[10] Ironically, Arab inhabitants were needed to validate places and place names even though they were seen as people who arrived in a later period and had replaced the original inhabitants (Abu El-Haj 2001: 38).

[11] Secular Zionists are most interested in archeological evidence confirming Jewish presence in ancient Jerusalem, while for many religious Zionists their biblical understanding was sufficient although they often appreciated the "help" archeological evidence could provide (Alan Zuckerman personal communication). Many non-religions Israelis, in fact, joke that archeology is their secular religion.

events, providing sites for pilgrimage and emotional connections to an imagined community.

In the Israeli case, it is striking to note how much archeological finds helped create a seamless narrative linking ancient and modern Israel (Zerubavel 1995). "It was important, so the argument went, to uphold every archeological remnant that testified to the Jewish presence in the land, and confirmed the legitimacy of the Zionist claim" (Elon 1997: 34–35). "By digging up the hard ground they were retrieving memory – one is tempted to say – as though they were recovering checked baggage from a storage room" (Elon 1997: 36). Yet Silberman cautions that a wide variety of elements ranging from brochures, signposts, and guides "combine to present the public with a composite historical 'story' or narrative that is far more sweeping in its conclusions and implications than the specific archeological data on which it is ultimately based (Silberman 1997: 63). Narratives built from archeological findings can be understood as embedded not just in words but also in physical structures that communicate clear messages and visual images that offer "sequences of archetypal story elements, didactically arranged with clear beginnings, middles and ends [that] often address politically evocative themes" (Silberman 1995: 250).

Competing claims to Jerusalem's holy sites have been played out in formal negotiations, in violent confrontations, and in hotly contested arguments about what others are building or excavating in and around the old city. Because both the Haram and the Western Wall are sites of core memories for Muslims and Jews, intrusions or threatened loss of control of the sites are perceived as attacks on the group and reminders of their group's vulnerability. In such a setting, archeology serves as a double-edged sword providing "evidence" of a people's historical roots and bolstering their national narrative and its core political claims, while, at the same time, implicitly weakening those of the other side (Kohl 1998; Trigger 1984). When used to assert mutually exclusive claims, archeological evidence ignores the other and its narrative and as a consequence sets off a spiral of collective anxiety. Sometimes, of course, this denial is accompanied by actions to destroy a group's links to the past – what Smith (1991) calls ethnocide – such as the Taliban's destruction of the giant Buddha statues in central Afghanistan, and Hindu destruction of the Babri Mosque at Ayodhya along with the call for the construction of a Hindu Temple on the site, discussed in Chapter 3.[12]

---

[12] Throughout the war in Bosnia, Serbian ethnic cleansing included destruction of cultural sites such as mosques and bombing the National Museum in Sarajevo, containing objects

In Jerusalem both Jews and Muslims feel they have been victims of ethnocide. Muslims cite the destruction of houses, cemeteries, olive groves and entire villages, and eviction from Israel in 1948, as well as the destruction of the Maghribi quarter including religious structures and their eviction from the Jewish quarter of Jerusalem after 1967 (Abu El-Haj 2001: 165; Benvenisti 2000). At the same time, Jews have expressed outrage at limits to Jewish access to the Western Wall over centuries, the destruction of Jewish religious sites in the Old City between 1948 and 1967, and more recent threats to Jewish sacred sites in the West Bank. Each side's account is partial and in each denial of the other's perspective is notable.

Muslim–Jewish conflict over Jerusalem's holy sites

The history of the Old City of Jerusalem is replete with well-documented conflicts over its holy sites (Armstrong 1996; Benvenisti 1996; Dumper 2002; Friedland and Hecht 1991; Monk 2002). In its long history, there have been intense conflicts among Christians, Muslims, and Jews for control of the city and for control over sacred places within it. In addition to conflicts between religious communities, there have been times when the most significant differences were within each religious community. All this can be seen vividly in the complex arrangements regarding control over the Church of the Holy Sepulcher which is shared by no fewer than six different Christian denominations that have fought, sometimes literally, over the right to clean the church's floor, pillars, and steps knowing that "sweeping and other cleaning is considered ownership, since why would one sweep what is not one's own," and whose mutual distrust is so high that the key to the church is entrusted to a Muslim (Benvenisti 1996: 96; Cohen 2003; Wasserstein 2001).

Jerusalem is central in all three faiths and they each believe it was where God asked Abraham to sacrifice his son Isaac in the case of Jews and Christians, and Ishmael for Muslims. Jews built their most important ancient temples in the city, Jesus was crucified in Jerusalem, and Mohammed began his night journey from the city. However, my focus here is not on the history of religious conflict in Jerusalem, but on the contestation between Muslims and Jews in the past century over rival

---

that offered ample testimony to the historically multiethnic character of the region (Sells 1996).

claims to the Temple Mount/Haram al-Sharif and their relevance to the Israeli–Palestinian conflict as both an issue that divides the two sides and as a metaphor that reveals each side's deepest vulnerabilities. To discuss these, it is useful to briefly review the city's past.

Outside invaders have shaped Jerusalem and its politics for thousands of years. (Figure 6.3 offers a timeline of the Israeli–Palestinian conflict that might be useful for some readers.) The Bible says that Abraham, the patriarch of all three Middle Eastern faiths, lived in the Judean hills in about 2000 BCE. Due to severe drought and famine, his great grandson Joseph left the area for Egypt in 1910 BCE, and Jews remained there for over 400 years until Moses lead them out. Upon their return from Egypt, Jews settled in Judea and Samaria (the west bank of the Jordan River) building towns and cities, including Jerusalem where they constructed their first temple, often called Solomon's Temple, in about 950 BCE. In 587 BCE the Babylonians demolished it and sent the Jews into exile in Babylon for 160 years. Several centuries later King Herod undertook the restoration of the temple to its original splendor and traditional arrangement and in 70 CE the Romans destroyed it, sending the Jews into exile once again. Roman occupation ended several centuries later and Muslims conquered the city in 638.

Early in the next century, Muslims built the Dome of the Rock on the Haram. Crusaders conquered Jerusalem in 1099 slaughtering Muslims and Jews upon their arrival, and turned the Haram into a barracks and its mosques into churches. In the twelfth century Saladin retook the city peacefully and allowed the Jews to return. There was then continuous Islamic control of Jerusalem until 1917 with the defeat of the Ottomans and the start of the British Mandate. During most of the period of Islamic control, Jerusalem was a small walled city, about one square mile, with a relatively small number of Jews. By 1880, however, Jews constituted a majority of the old city's residents although they had little political power or voice in managing it and the city's population had spread beyond the old walled city. During the Ottoman and Mandate periods, parts of the Old City came to be named the Muslim, Christian, Jewish, and Armenian Quarters, and additional smaller geographic areas were also named although the actual population of each area was far more diverse than these names suggest (Dumper 2002). More important than geography were social networks that linked people across the neighborhoods and often across religious groups. "Participation in each other's religious festivals and ceremonies, including weddings and funerals, were ways in

Figure 6.3 *Israeli-Jewish and Palestinian narratives: selected key elements*

DATE	EVENT	JEWISH INTERPRETATION	PALESTINIAN INTERPRETATION
Third millennium BCE	Canaanite settlement		Earliest ancestors settle in the region and establish towns including Jericho
Thirteenth-century BCE	Exodus from Egypt and return to the region	Jews arrive in the Promised Land	Philistines who conquered the Canaanites resist the Israelites unsuccessfully
Eleventh-century BCE	Establishment of Ancient Israel	Jewish civilization prospers despite continued internecine fighting and outside enemies	
Tenth-century BCE	Reign of King Solomon; construction of the First Temple in Jerusalem	Golden Age of Jewish civilization	
586 BCE	Babylonian conquest	Defeat and exile	
Late sixth-century BCE	Jewish return and Second Temple built	Israel rebuilt	
70 CE	Second Temple destroyed	Roman destruction of the Temple ushers in exile and a long period of suffering	
638	Arab Muslims conquer the region ending Byzantine rule (the successor to Roman rule in the East); Mohammad begins his night journey to heaven from Jerusalem		Under Muslim control the region flourishes. Christians and Jews, as people of the book, are permitted to remain and to practice their religions

Figure 6.3. (*Cont.*)

DATE	EVENT	JEWISH INTERPRETATION	PALESTINIAN INTERPRETATION
685–705	Caliph Abdul Malik Ibn Marwan builds the Dome of the Rock and Walid Ibn Abdul Malik builds Al-Aqsa Mosque in Jerusalem		Golden age begins as Islam spreads throughout the region
1099–1187	Crusades	Jews in the region suffer along with Muslims	Humiliation under Christian occupation as they turn Islam's holy sites into army barracks and mosques into churches
1187–1917	Saladin liberates Jerusalem; period of Mamluk and Ottoman rule	Jews gain some rights and live in the region in small numbers under Ottoman rule	Muslims rule the area respecting the rights of Jews and Christians following Saladin's example
1880s	Jewish migration increases as First Alliyah begins	Symbolically the beginning of the return to the homeland	Concern about increasing European presence
1897	First Zionist Congress	World Zionist Congress provides a political voice and structure working for a Jewish homeland	Wariness about Jewish intentions and land purchases as Ottoman rule wanes
1917	Balfour Declaration	Jubilation among Zionist leaders	Palestinian despair over the British position that is reinforced as the British rule come to rule Palestine through the League of Nations Mandate

1920s	Continued migration and establishment of settlements and Jewish institutions	Development of agricultural settlements and social institutions; emphasis on breaking from the experiences and values of exile	Resentment against the British and with the growing Jewish population that continues to purchase Arab land
1928–29	Jews challenge the Ottoman era status quo agreement concerning access to Jerusalem's holy sites; Muslim riots result in many Jewish deaths	Anger and outrage following the outbursts of Arab killing that was especially intense in Jerusalem and Hebron	Strong fears that Jews want to destroy Islamic sites and to rebuild their temple
1936–39	Arab revolt against the British	Another example of Arab violence as Jews arm themselves and organize self-defense	Strong expression of Arab nationalism against the British; pride in the six-month general strike to protest land confiscation and Jewish immigration
1947–48	UN adopts partition plan; war begins	War of independence in which Jews battle both the British and the Arabs	Al-Nakba, the catastrophe, in which Palestinians are expelled from their homes and lands and become refugees
1950s	Sporadic guerrilla fighting; significant in-migration of Jews from Arab countries	Strengthening of the economy and political institutions as new waves of refugees are integrated; self-defense as critical in the face of ongoing Arab hostility	Bitter disappointment that Arab governments speak out against Israel but take few military steps to help Palestinians regain their land

Figure 6.3. (*Cont.*)

DATE	EVENT	JEWISH INTERPRETATION	PALESTINIAN INTERPRETATION
1956	War against Egypt	Swift defeat of Egypt builds confidence in the country's military and removal of Egypt as a threat to security	Israel, Britain and France attack to seize the Suez canal, recalling earlier colonial control
1958	PLO founded		Turn to self-reliance as Palestinians recognize that they cannot count on the support of Arab countries to liberate their land
1967	Six Day War	After months of increasing threats, Israel quickly defeats three neighboring states and occupies the Sinai, Golan Heights, and West Bank	Humiliation and despair
1972	Terrorist incidents increase; denial of Palestinian political identity	Incensed at increased violence including the Olympic attacks, Israel increases West Bank settlements and Golda Meir denies there is a Palestinian identity	Incensed by their expulsions from Jordan two years earlier, Palestinians turn to dramatic, violent attacks on Israel and Israelis to gain visibility and support
1973	Yom Kippur War	The country is not ready for the Arab attacks and there is great self-doubt after the war despite ultimate victory	Arab morale partially restored in the surprise attack on Israel despite ultimate defeat in the war

Year	Event		
1977–79	Sadat visit to Jerusalem; Camp David Agreement	Sadat welcomed; sense of Arab acceptance; Egypt recognizes Israel and Israel agrees to completely withdraw from the Sinai	Bitter feelings of being forgotten as united Arab front disappears and their central concerns are ignored
1982	Israel invades Lebanon; massacres in Palestinian camps in Beirut; PLO moves to Tunis	PLO is expelled from Lebanon but the war severely divides Israelis and there is great outrage following the massacres	Defeat, despair, helplessness, and vulnerability; Palestinians division between the PLO in Tunis and the emerging Palestinian leadership in the West Bank and Gaza
1987	First Intifada begins	Continued belief that all Palestinian violence is best met through strong force	Pride when homegrown resistance against Israeli occupation is expressed dramatically by young children hurling rocks against Israel's mighty military
1988	PLO recognizes Israel's right to exist	Israelis remain skeptical about PLO intentions	Palestinians see this as a first step toward statehood and international recognition
1991	Madrid conference	Israel and many Arab states meet together publicly to negotiate a settlement	PLO is not an official participant but Palestinians participate in the meetings indirectly – a first step towards Israeli recognition
1993	Oslo agreement creates the Palestinian authority holding out the prospect for a two-state settlement within five years	Elation at the prospect of a peace settlement; some protests from settlers and right-wing	Elation at the prospect of achieving statehood; joy as Arafat returns from exile and the Palestinian Authority established

Figure 6.3. (*Cont.*)

DATE	EVENT	JEWISH INTERPRETATION	PALESTINIAN INTERPRETATION
1995	Rabin assassination; increase in PLO violence; election of Netanyahu, an Oslo opponent	Outrage at the rise in Palestinian violence and increasing criticism of Arafat's rule; reassurance when Netanyahu promises security	Feelings that too few benefits have accrued from Oslo; loss of confidence in the peace process when Netanyahu takes office
2000	Camp David Summit	Barak offers the Palestinians "the most generous offer they ever received"	Palestinians feel manipulated by Israel and the US and are dissatisfied with the proposals on refugees and Jerusalem
2000–05	Al-Aqsa Intifada; high violence on both sides; Israeli reoccupation of Gaza and the West Bank; unilateral withdrawal from Gaza settlements; wall built	Loss of confidence in Barak and the peace process; Sharon elected in search of security; belief that Arafat is not a partner for peace; fence between Israel and the West Bank seen as necessary for security	Despair and feelings of powerlessness and increased support for violence as a political strategy; belief that Sharon is not a partner for peace; resentment over lands seized to build the wall; anger around lack of consultation over Gaza withdrawal
2005–06	Arafat dies; Hamas wins elections; Israel goes to war with Hezbollah in Lebanon	Israelis despair about the possibilities for peace and turn to using increased force against Hamas and Hezbollah	Increasing pessimism concerning possibilities for achieving statehood and peace as living conditions continue to deteriorate

which these solidarities were expressed" (Dumper 2002: 14). Although Muslims and Jews certainly had periods of high tension, it is probably fair to conclude that until the twentieth century their daily relations were hierarchically ordered and generally not tense. Each probably feared Christians much more than each other.

Under Muslim rule, Jews were generally granted some access to the city and its sacred sites but were not permitted to pray on the Temple Mount (Hassner 2005). In the early Islamic period, the cemetery on the Mount of Olives, outside the city walls, was the most significant site of Jewish worship. However, Armstrong reports that Suleiman the Magnificent, the Ottoman ruler who built the city walls in the sixteenth century, issued an official edict that allowed Jews to pray at the Western Wall and subsequent Ottoman rulers permitted this with some restrictions (1996: 327). For example, there were no special provisions for Jewish prayers and Jews were not allowed to store religious paraphernalia or to place any furniture on the site. During the British Mandate period from 1917 to 1948, there was a continuation of the Ottoman status quo arrangement regarding Christian as well as Jewish religious sites in Jerusalem dating from the nineteenth century. This guaranteed continued regular, though controlled, Jewish access to the wall. But there was also high conflict with Muslims following the 1917 Balfour Declaration in which the British supported the idea of a Jewish homeland. Coming at the end of the Ottoman Empire and the start of the British Mandate, Muslims perceived a direct political threat that was increasingly expressed in the next decade as a threat to the Haram and the buildings on it (Monk 2002). With increased Jewish immigration, tensions rose and Muslim loss of political control raised further fears concerning the vulnerability of their holy places. In the 1920s, the Muslim religious leadership under Jerusalem Mufti Amin el-Hussani aggressively opposed British rule as Jewish immigration and violent incidents continued to mount.

In 1928, Muslims charged that Jews had violated the status quo arrangements when they placed a screen at the wall to separate men and women during prayer and began to store religious materials in the area, and they viewed these moves as a serious threat (Friedland and Hecht 1991: 30–35). Rioting broke out and spread to other cities in Palestine – especially Hebron, where Muslims killed seventy-three Jews. Events of 1929 can be understood as an intense psychocultural drama that remained unresolved and has been repeated a number of times since. The problem of changes in the status of Palestine as well as the holy sites was complicated indeed since there was no mechanism in place for addressing political differences. The British response was to establish the Shaw Commission to look into the conflict around the holy sites, and it held months of hearings before issuing a report that reaffirmed the Jewish right of access to the wall and no change in the status quo arrangements. The process revealed little real understanding of the deep political and religious identity issues at stake and produced no direct dialogue between the parties.

Monk (2002) concludes that emotional testimony of the two sides was aimed at persuading the British, not each other, and it escalated tensions by simply restating their strident positions and bolstering them with pictures of dubious origin that further inflamed relations and mutual distrust.[13] Not surprisingly, there were more incidents and riots in the 1930s. The Arab revolt beginning in 1936 increased British and Jewish coordination and, in 1937, the British began drawing up plans for the partition of the country among the Jews and Arabs, a move the secular Zionist leaders strongly supported. They were clearly willing to accept a plan that would give the Arabs full control of the Old City, perhaps due to their own religious ambivalence as much as their desire to create even a minimal Jewish state in the belief that it could be expanded later.

Indeed, the Zionist response to the idea of a Zionist state without Zion was curiously complaisant. Their general view of the holy city had always had an undercurrent of hostility – particularly strong in the case of the dominant, secularizing socialist-Zionist movement. They saw Jerusalem as the fortress of the old yishuv', a symbol of all that it stood for by way of conservatism, unproductiveness and anti-Zionism . . . the Zionist leadership realized that, given international religious interests of Christians and Muslims in the old city of Jerusalem, there was no hope of its inclusion in a Jewish state. They therefore came to the realization that the only way to gain any foothold in Jerusalem was to urge that the city, like the country as a whole be partitioned.

(Wasserstein 2001: 110–12)

Lustick offers a somewhat different argument that emphasizes the pragmatism of the secular Zionist leadership headed by Ben-Gurion for "even without the Old City [Jerusalem] could be made politically and

---

[13] The Muslims presented a picture showing the Zionist flag atop the Dome of the Rock, and another picture that appeared in the New York Yiddish paper showing Theodore Herzl – from an old picture looking out from a balcony in Basel – but now watching Jews streaming into Jerusalem as evidence of Jewish designs on Islamic holy places (Monk 2002: 92–126).

emotionally satisfying as a symbolic evocation of Zionism's response to age-old Jewish yearnings for a return to 'Zion and Jerusalem'" (Lustick 2000: 10). In his view, "The crucial element, they argued, was to rule an area inhabited by many Jews which the Jewish state could portray to world Jewry and it itself as 'Yerushalayim'" (Lustick 2000:10). To do this, they proposed that Jewish Jerusalem be focused on West Jerusalem and its newer neighborhoods.

Following Israeli independence in 1948 and the ceasefire agreement with Jordan the next year, Jerusalem was divided and the Old City came under Jordanian rule. Jews could visit the Western Wall only if they traveled through Jordan (which was not an option for Israelis) and did not have an Israeli visa stamped in their passports. Jewish residents were evicted from the Old City, and there was significant destruction to their cemetery on the Mount of Olives, to the Jewish quarter, and to their synagogues in the Old City. In 1967, Israel captured the Old City in the Six Days War and Israel reunified Jerusalem, declaring it Israel's eternal capital and expanding its municipal boundaries (Wasserstein 2001: 205–38). Many Jews and others assumed that Muslims would be evacuated from the Temple Mount and some, including members of the Israeli army, expected the Dome of the Rock to be blown up. However, Moshe Dayan, Israel's defense minister, quickly negotiated an agreement with the Muslim religious authorities granting them continued *de facto* control over the Haram and its Islamic holy sites, and a ruling from Israel's chief rabbis that reinforced the prohibition on Jewish visits, prayer, or ritual on the Temple Mount, as it risked "violating the purity of this holy place" because the exact location of the Temple and the Holiest of Holies had been forgotten (Gorenberg 2000: 99–104; Hassner 2005; Shragai 2000).[14]

At the end of the war, Israel rejected the Ottoman era's status quo arrangements very quickly and authorized the bulldozing of the Maghribi quarter, a Palestinian neighborhood that included several Islamic sites, in front of the Western Wall, to build a large plaza (Figure 6.1) that would allow greater access to religious Jews and tourists (Dumper 2002; Abu el-Haj 2001; Benvenisti 1996).[15] Over the next ten years there were large-scale

[14] Hassner (2005) provides a detailed description of the process by which both the political and religious authorities came to hold the same position in 1967, explains the forces behind the widespread consensus, and examines why it has been under attack since the mid 1980s from Jewish fundamentalists and some rabbinical authorities.
[15] "Gush Emunim, and other Temple Mount aficionados, have often criticized the sanctification of the Western Wall – why make a big deal idolizing a retaining wall and

excavations in the Jewish quarter that was then rebuilt in such a way as to produce a visible link between the Jerusalem of 2000 years ago and the contemporary city. Establishing these linkages offered important "evidence" to bolster the Zionist narrative and its political claims (Abu El-Haj 2001). The most controversial excavations were in the old Jewish quarter and along the southern edge of the Haram and concerned the great emphasis of Jewish archeologists on the First and Second Temple periods (Abu El-Haj 1998; 2001).

Within a few years, Israel rebuilt a greatly expanded Jewish quarter, appropriating many Muslim properties in the process. The Western Wall became a pilgrimage site for Jews worldwide as well as a place of great significance for many of the state of Israel's civil religious memorial ceremonies such as Holocaust Memorial Day, the Memorial Day for Israeli's soldiers who died in war, Independence Day, and Jerusalem Day; some army units are sworn in there (Friedland and Hecht 1991: 38). In addition, in the past two decades a number of Jewish settlers – including Ariel Sharon – obtained control over properties in the Muslim and Christian quarters as part of an effort to change the character of the old city and increase the Jewish presence in it. Many of the small groups of settlers hope that their efforts will lead "to the reconstruction of Solomon's Temple on the site of the Dome of the Rock and the al-Aqsa Mosque" (Dumper 2002: 44).

For the most part, Dayan's arrangement that sought to separate religious and political questions functioned mainly because Muslims were unable to confront Israeli power directly and Jews focused their emotional energy on the Western Wall.[16] Tension is often close to the surface so it is not surprising that there have been periodic outbreaks of violence around the holy sites that have reinforced both Muslim and Jewish vulnerability and fears. Often these occur when Muslims claim that Jews are violating the agreed-upon arrangements, threatening their sites, as occurred in the 1996 tunnel opening and Ariel Sharon's 2002 visit to the Temple Mount surrounded by heavy Israeli security. Angry Muslim

---

yet refuse to build the Temple or insist on Jewish rights on that site" (Lustick personal communication).

[16] Shlomo Goren, the chief rabbi of the IDF in 1967 and later chief Ashkenazi rabbi of Israel, has been one of the loudest voices supporting Jewish prayer on the Temple Mount as long as it did not take place on a section where the Temple stood (Friedland and Hecht 1991: 37–45). Even Goren, however, did not publicly protest the ruling and did not publish his objections to it for twenty-five years (Hassner 2005).

crowds on the Haram throwing stones at people praying at the base of the wall below then set off Jewish anger and a response from Israeli security forces.[17] These periodic crises are unresolved psychocultural dramas involving mutual fears of pollution and encroachment evoking the need to defend sacred places from violation and attack.

Muslims have deep fears about what some Jews would do to the Haram and its sacred structures if they were given a chance.[18] As in many conflicts, each side cites the actions of extremists on the other side to show the enemy's "true intentions." Muslims pay great attention to fringe Jewish groups that advocate building the Third Temple on the Haram, and to the statements and actions of settler groups taking over properties in the Old City, especially those near the Haram. Palestinians greatly publicize the efforts of the Temple Mount Faithful, which each year on Tisha B'Av, the anniversary of the destruction of the temple in 70 CE, tries to visit the Temple Mount to pray and lay the cornerstone for the Third Temple (Dumper 2002).[19] Similarly, the demands of some Israelis, including Ehud Barak at Camp David in 2000, to build a small synagogue for Jewish prayer on the corner of the Temple Mount adds to Muslim fears.

In this dynamic of extreme distrust and vulnerability, provocative actions are consistent with a readily accessible narrative that makes their meaning almost self-evident. For many Muslims, the message is that Jews want to capture and destroy the Haram.[20] Since 1967, the more than two dozen attacks on the Haram and its buildings have reinforced the narrative of vulnerability. Among these were a deranged Australian Christian's attempt in 1969 to start a fire in the Al-Aqsa mosque (an act some

---

[17] Consistent with the argument we have made earlier that many symbolic conflicts involve a two-level game – one within each group and one between the group and outsiders – is Lustick's contention that a main motivation for Sharon's September 2000 visit to the Temple Mount was "to create a disturbance that would put his rival, Netanyahu, in an impossible political situation prior to the struggle of the two for the Likud nomination" (personal communication).

[18] By 2004 the situation deteriorated to the point where the Israeli internal security minister claimed that "extremist and fanatic Jewish elements" might use terror against the Temple Mount's mosques, and the Israeli press published articles discussing this possibility.

[19] There are also Jewish groups such as the Temple Institute, part of whose work is designing and making the clothing priests will wear and other ritual objects they can use at the third Temple when it is built (Gorenberg 2000: 173–78).

[20] One of the most widely available pictures in the Muslim world is that of the Dome of the Rock. This can be understood as both an affirmation of its existence and its vulnerability, and the need to defend it.

Muslims attributed to Jews) and an extremist Jewish plot in the 1980s, thwarted by the Israeli authorities, to blow up the Dome of the Rock. Muslims regularly charge that Jewish excavations outside the walls are damaging the Haram's foundations and that Israeli archeologists were tunneling beneath it to variously search for the ruins of the Second Temple or to build a prayer area.[21] The head of the *Waqf*, Adnan Husseini, said in 2000 "the Al-Aqsa Mosque has not faced so many challenges since the Crusades" (Atallah 2001).

Jewish fears are also easily evoked and are rooted in the narrative of the destruction of the Temple and exile, periods of exclusion from Jerusalem, and the bitter memories of European anti-Semitism and the Holocaust, all of which are central to Zionism and the state of Israel. More specific are moments of Arab–Jewish violence such as the 1929 and 1936 riots in and around the Western Wall. Since 1967 there have been incidents in which groups of Muslims standing on the Haram hurled rocks at Jewish worshipers gathered below. To guard against outbreaks of violence, there is a heavy Israeli security presence and periodic assertions of Israeli sovereignty such as selective admission of Muslims for Friday prayers, the opening of the Hasmoneoan Tunnel exit in 1996, and the Sharon visit in 2000.[22]

Exclusive claims and mutual denial

For Jews, the tense situation is aggravated by periodic Muslim and Palestinian denials that there is any evidence that the Second Temple was actually on the site or that the Western Wall was part of the Temple. This is extremely upsetting to Jews and the denial is seen as part of a broader Palestinian denial of Jewish history in Jerusalem and linked to the denial of the legitimacy of the present state of Israel. For example, an article on the Old City of Jerusalem posted on the Al Quds University website asserts that "the Al-Aqsa compound cannot possibly be in the

---

[21] The claim concerning Israeli subterranean excavations has some basis in reality (Meir Ben-Dov, personal interview; Gershom Gorenberg, personal interview). The claim that Israeli archeological excavations threatened the Haram's foundations is harder to evaluate.

[22] Some commentators have argued that Sharon's visit caused the Al Aqsa Intifada. While the incident clearly precipitated a violent response and escalation of violence on both sides, it is probably more accurate to view the provocative action as the precipitating incident in an already deteriorating situation.

same place as the first or second temple," [23] and that the Western Wall was probably the wall of a fortress built for Roman legions (also see Al-Ifrani 2001). It should be noted, however, that while the archeological record supports the claim that the Jewish temples were located on the Temple Mount, there is some disagreement over exactly *where* on the mount this was (Gorenberg 2000). The most widely shared view is that it was where the Dome of the Rock is today. However, there are some who place it on the Temple Mount but north of this spot while others argue forcefully that it was further to the south.[24]

Denials that Jewish temples were ever on the site rekindle Jewish fears that Palestinians aim to drive Jews out of Israel, in general, and Jerusalem, in particular, reinforcing the Israeli belief in strength, vigilance and incontrovertible evidence. From their perspective, archeological work in and around the old city provides this evidence of a Jewish past in Jerusalem that supports Israel's political legitimacy. At the same time, the absence of Jewish archeological activity on the Temple Mount, and specifically under it, hinders the search for evidence that they believe would make Jewish religious claims incontrovertible (Gorenberg 2000).

The strongest Jewish fears, other than the loss of access to the Western Wall, are that Muslim construction projects on or under the Haram will either destroy or render inaccessible specific details about the temples on the site. For example, an Israeli attorney general described *Waqf* building projects as an archeological crime "kicking the history of the Jewish people" (Shragai 2000), and one MK, a member of the National Religious Party, called for the arrest of members of the *Waqf* who were "desecrating antiquities at the [Temple Mount] in an effort to wipe out the traces of the Jewish nation from its most sacred site" (Shragai 2001). Often each community's emotionally intense cultural representations exclude any reference to, or recognition of, the other's historical presence. As Gorenberg says, "Anxious about the future, Muslims seek to erase the Temple from the site's past. In the work of radical rewriting, they are not alone" (2000: 72). In Jerusalem, history provides all groups with experiences in which the fears of physical destruction came to pass and these catastrophes are regularly invoked. Each group sees the other's refusal to recognize its history as a fundamental denial of their existence and a political threat. Mutual denials escalate and political distrust and polarization increase.

---

[23] www.alquds.edu/gen_info/index.php?page=jerusalem_history
[24] See www.templemount.org/theories.html.

Muslim denial of the temple's location is mirrored in the computer imagery found in a recently built Israeli visitor center just below the Haram that focuses on what the area might have looked like at the time of the Second Temple. Muslims were outraged when they realized that there were virtually no images in the center showing what the area looks like today and none with the Muslim holy sites on the Haram (Rubinstein 2001).[25] In this exhibit, the Muslim holy sites have ceased to exist, although if one were to just walk outside the front door and look up, it is clear that this is not the case. The same denial of Muslim presence is seen on T-shirts sold in the Old City's Jewish Quarter and in posters and books the Temple Institute has published that picture a newly built Third Temple astride the giant platform now holding the Dome of the Rock and Al-Aqsa.

In response, Muslims express the need for vigilance in light of alleged Israeli strategies to demolish Al-Aqsa through settlement, weakening the foundation through excavations, burning, blowing up the mosque, or by a manmade earthquake (Abdul-Ghafour 2002). Muslims experience denial in presentations of Jewish archeological excavations, tours in specific old city sites, and exhibits that emphasize the period of the Second Temple and its clear connection to the present (Abu El-Haj 2001; Benvenisti 1996). When it is suggested that the Muslim holy sites are merely an interlude to the coming of the Messiah and the construction of the Third Jewish Temple as in the picture seen on numerous web sites, and on posters such as the one in Figure 6.4, Muslim fears increase and the resolve to protect Al-Aqsa against the modern day Crusaders only grows.

Changing the landscape is a powerful form of denial and is something that both Israelis and Palestinians have done in ways that the other finds hurtful and threatening as "groups in both communities have chosen to desecrate the others' sacred space" (Friedland and Hecht 1991: 55). In and around the old city, each side works to emphasize its long-term presence and to remove or limit the other's visibility. This is mirrored in the country more widely – not just in Jerusalem – as both sides have engaged in this pattern of mutual denial though manipulation of the physical landscape, although it needs to be noted that as the more powerful party, the Israelis have done this to a greater degree. In a simple, but powerful, way this is done by changing place names, removing buildings,

---

[25] See www.archpark.org.il for the web presentation.

Figure 6.4 The Third Temple in Jerusalem astride the Temple Mount. An image from a poster in the old city of Jerusalem. Different versions are circulated by groups such as the Temple Institute (templeinstitute.org) or Temple Mount Faithful (templemountfaithful.org).

and displacing people who remember earlier living arrangements (Benvenisti 2000).

Conclusion: psychocultural dramas and holy sites

In this charged and distrustful setting of mutual denial, it is not surprising that psychocultural dramas have erupted in the past century focusing on the holy sites in Jerusalem. Typically these begin when there is a challenge or change in the status quo, a breach in the existing order. Examples include political protests, war, changes in religious practices, and, archeological and building activities that each side experiences as a direct assault on its own sacred spaces and historical claims. These crises intensify and easily move toward violence, which since 1967 is typically between Palestinian crowds and Israeli security forces who, for example, sometimes restrict access to the Haram for Friday prayers. Redressive action is difficult because there is no central authority whose legitimacy both sides accept. Instead of achieving any resolution, each side merely repeats its exclusive claims of sovereignty and the crises lose their intensity only when force is used to restore order. There is hardly ever any reintegration or ritual redefinition, so that after a time a new crisis erupts.

All of these elements are seen in the 1996 conflict over the decision to open the tunnel exit on the Via Dolorosa. As Gorenberg points out (2000), conflicts in the Old City about what each side is doing below ground are often even more charged than what is taking place above ground. The tunnel conflict's multiple levels contributes to its intensity and to the inability to resolve it. Viewed as a deep wound, this conflict reveals each side's most basic fears about their exclusive ownership of a sacred space. The psychocultural drama following the tunnel opening increased tension and drew international attention as the violence rose. When it had finally run its course, there was no settlement, but simply the stronger Israelis imposing their will on the Palestinians, and the tunnel remained open. For many Jews, the government's actions were an appropriate assertion of Israeli sovereignty. Jerusalem was their united and eternal capital and they accepted the surface explanation that the new exit changed nothing, simply making the flow of visitors more efficient. Israelis resented Palestinian charges that the moves were part of a larger effort to dig *under* the Haram and undermine its stability.

The tunnel has great significance for Jews who believe that sections of it are closer to the site of the ancient temples and their altars than any other location where Jews are permitted. The bedrock and ancient walls in the tunnel make many Jews feel especially close to their ancient religious sites. As Abu El-Haj points out, the tunnel is both an archeological *and* a religious site. The Ministry for Religious Affairs, not the Antiquities Authority, manages the tunnel, and religious services are conducted in parts of it. Reflecting this double meaning, the narratives the tour guides offer in the tunnel emphasize the origins and fragments and downplay more recent periods. "This is a museum dedicated to teaching a national heritage, and it is a place of prayer" (Abu El-Haj 2001: 224).[26]

For Palestinians, the tunnel exit opening was a reminder of their vulnerability and their long-term distrust of Jewish motives recalling earlier Jewish attempts to alter the status quo. Israeli authorities simply dismiss these assertions, while Palestinians distrust Israeli statements given Jewish settlement in the Muslim quarter and Israeli efforts to limit Palestinian housing and social services in the old city. Vulnerability is also evoked because Muslims see a clear parallel between conflict over the Ibrahimi

---

[26] Abu El-Haj took Hebrew and English speaking tours of the tunnel and reports significant differences in the language and images used in the one that is supposedly all-Jewish and the one that is not (2001: 314–15).

mosque in Hebron and the Haram. Hebron is where both Muslims and Jews believe that Abraham and his family are buried. After 1967, Jews gained some access to the site for prayer and gradually took more control over it and limited Muslim access to it (Friedland and Hecht: 1991: 50–51). But the solution is not a constructive one and, "the shrine in Hebron became the 'only house of worship anywhere with its own army commander'" (Hassner 2003: 25). What is not clear from this case alone, however, is the extent to which the extreme tension is a function of the indivisibility of the sacred site or of the fact that this site in Hebron reflects so completely the unresolved conflict in the region more generally.

As is the case with many cultural conflicts, the on-going conflict over Muslim and Jewish holy sites in the Old City of Jerusalem is a microcosm of many aspects of the larger conflict within which it is embedded. In each conflict, both sides present mutually exclusive claims, and there are great fears that acknowledging even part of the other side's narrative is a denial of one's own rights (Kelman 1987). Each emphasizes its own traumatic historical memories. Jews regularly recall the destruction of their First and Second Temples, the long period of exile, periods when they were variously banned from the city or denied access to the Western Wall and other sacred sites, and the Holocaust. Muslims remember the Crusades as a time when the Dome of the Rock and Al-Aqsa mosques were turned into churches and barracks for Christian troops and the more recent humiliations they experienced during British colonial rule and the Israeli occupation since 1967. Muslims also have strong feelings about the humiliating expulsions from Andalusia at the end of the fifteenth century. Each side's more poignant metaphors and images are about traumatic loss and making sense of them is central to understanding why Jews and Muslims are simultaneously vulnerable and aggressive in their view of, and relations with, each other.

While narratives draw on history, they are not most usefully under-stood as historical arguments as such (Nora 1989). Rather each narrative – as well as the internal differences in both sides' accounts – selectively utilizes historical references to bolster its position in building a non-linear argument. Time collapse is far more prominent than continuity – even at moments when one side or the other seems to be providing a chron-ological account. There are images that span centuries linking disparate events that are built from a selective recounting. Furthermore, they offer little acknowledgment of the other side's perspective, meaning its hopes, fears, and motivations, and it should not be surprising that in this context

Jews and Muslims interpret the same events very differently: 1929 for Palestinians is about defense of the Islamic holy sites; for Jews it is about denied access to their holy sites and unwarranted Muslim violence. The year 1948 for Jews is about independence and recreation of the state of Israel; for Palestinians it the "Nakba," or catastrophe of expulsion from their homeland (Sa'di 2002). Hebron for Palestinians recalls the erosion of sovereignty over the Ibrahimi mosque marking the Tomb of the Patriarchs since 1967 and the Goldstein massacre in 1994 in which 29 Muslims were killed and 125 injured, while for Jews it recalls access denied in the past and the 1929 massacres (Friedland and Hecht 1991). The Hasmoneoan tunnel is for Jews a concrete link to the Second Temple, while for Palestinians it is an Israeli threat to their holy sites. And so it goes. In Jerusalem there is little shared symbolic landscape or ritual activity at present. Differentiation and denial predominate as each side works to build an exclusive narrative that simply ignores or denies the other's existence and identity.

Considering the political dynamics of the intense threats both Jews and Muslims feel, it is obvious that no matter how archeologists view their work, their findings are easily used in service of contemporary political claims and mobilization. Evidence and assertions about the past are powerful because they speak to intensely felt fears and hopes. Yet we need to remember that at the same time the present shapes what part of the past is focused on and how it is understood. Archeological findings serve these goals and support political positions because their ambiguity with respect to social identity and prior meaning render them easy to use to bolster one side's claims and to denigrate those that opponents make.

Narratives about the holy sites in Jerusalem variously serve as reflectors of the deepest Muslim and Jewish fears and hopes, as exacerbaters of tensions when issues around the sites threaten each side, and as causes of conflict when they leave little room for negotiation or mutual recognition, encouraging unilateral actions that increase conflict. In this setting there is little benevolent perception of the opponent as Muslims view proposals to share the holy sites as a first step in an attempted Jewish takeover and Jews believe that if Palestinians had sovereignty over the Old City, or part of it, Jews would suffer the same mistreatment they had previously experienced under Muslim rule, such as limitations on religious practice at, or denial of access to, the Western Wall, destruction of the Jewish quarter, and the desecration of the Mount of Olives Cemetery between 1948 and 1967. Muslims quickly cite limitations they experienced under

Israeli occupation but also link their need for sovereignty to their humiliations at the hands of Christians during the Crusades and the expulsions from Andalusia.

When Yasser Arafat died in November 2004, Palestinians said he wanted to be buried in Jerusalem. Israel refused, although it did agree to a burial in Ramallah and it became clear that when, and if, there is a peace agreement Arafat's remains will be moved to Jerusalem, a step likely to provoke anger from some Israelis. Dead, as well as alive, Arafat will continue to be a divisive symbol tied to a powerful site for, as Verdery (1999) observes, some dead bodies, like live ones, have political meaning that unifies or variously divides groups in conflict. What we see is that the meaning of Jerusalem's sacred sites is central to both Israeli and Palestinian identities and to their national narratives, and that any proposed solution that fails to take these into account will be inadequate.

Finally, Jerusalem is not just a political conflict. As Shragai writes:

Jerusalem is also part of an intense religious conflict. Islam considers Israeli rule of the city as something that defiles the Muslim nature of the city. The religious Orthodox Jewish establishment also has halakhic reservations concerning the Arab presence in the city. The secular Arab leadership draws the legitimacy for its struggles over Jerusalem from Islam, and the Israeli leadership bases its arguments of the city on Jewish tradition.

(Shragai 2000)

So can Jerusalem's sacred sites be shared? While there have been a few periods of greater tolerance and inclusiveness, in the past century competing narratives about Jewish and Muslim holy sites have left little room for more inclusive framing that could allow both groups to share custody, use of, and access to the sites. Writing about Jerusalem, Friedland and Hecht (1991: 2005) conclude that sharing sacred sites is particularly difficult when control over the sacred center is at the core of a group's identity. Hassner (2003) says the indivisibility of sacred spaces rules out sharing within the context of current approaches to politics and policymaking. He rejects both pragmatic (Hobbesian) and cultural essentialist (Huntingtonian) approaches to resolving disputes over sacred places as unworkable.

However, Hassner (2005) suggests that bringing religious leaders and authorities into a process that creates and reshapes sacred space might be more fruitful. So do Gopin (2000) and Halevi (2002). Alpher (2005) points out that since religion cannot be removed from the conflict it has

189

to be part of any solution. Inclusion of religious voices in any political process could counter the pragmatism of Hobbesian approaches and the pessimism of Huntingtonian fatalism by utilizing "politics and agency to transform disputes over sacred space by introducing flexibility into the definition of that space" (Hassner 2003: 31). Because of their deeper understanding of the religious images and meanings surrounding the sites and the rules governing them, religious authorities could be in a position to find ways to redefine the present intransigent situation in constructive and more inclusive directions.

The emotional intensity of the conflicts in Jerusalem is found in the Israeli–Palestinian conflict more broadly. Metaphorically one side's heritage is merely the other's landfill. Settlement of differences over Jerusalem's holy sites is not likely outside of a broader political settlement of the Israeli–Palestinian conflict but as Hassner and Shragai point out, religious concerns must also be addressed and the intense fears about the holy sites will require special attention. To take these fears into account means providing each group with emotional, not just political, guarantees that the other side has sufficient incentives to adhere to an agreement. What form more inclusive symbolic reassurance would take is, of course, for the parties themselves to decide, for it must be one they feel capable of accepting, not one that an outsider thinks is good. What is clear, however, is that whatever the details, a good agreement must provide some mechanisms for substantively and symbolically acknowledging each other's claims and perhaps for providing some kind of inclusive arrangements that recognize the dual claims to the site rather than acknowledging only one or the other as legitimate (Alpher 2005; Ross 2004).[27] There have been proposals that God be declared the sovereign over Jerusalem's holy sites or that Jews consider that the Messiah will rebuild the Temple "in the twinkling of an eye," meaning the eye of the beholder (Waskow and Berman 1995). Such arrangements are most likely to be effective if they are part of a peace process that develops more inclusive shared narratives and symbolic expressions that address the deepest fears both Jews and Muslims feel, and redefines religious and political practices and understandings to produce some modicum of mutual reassurance and an overarching identity (Kelman 1999).

---

[27] The Geneva Accord that prominent Israelis and Palestinians, many of whom had participated in earlier negotiations, published in 2003 is one example of what an agreement aimed at achieving mutual reassurance might look like. The full text is available at http://www.mideastweb.org/geneva1.htm

7

Dressed to express: Islamic headscarves in French schools

Introduction

For two weeks in November 2005, pictures of crowds of young people throwing stones and burning cars in and around Paris and dozens of other French cities flashed across television screens around the world. The spark setting off the violence was an incident in Clichy-sous-Bois, a Paris suburb where two young Muslim boys died in an electrical sub-station while running from the police. In the course of a week more than 8000 cars, mainly in Muslim neighborhoods, were fire-bombed, mainly by young Muslims, and there were over 2500 arrests. Rage over Interior Minister Nicholas Sarkozy's racist comments that the scum would be flushed out and deported, and the government's use of tear gas in a local mosque combined with ongoing alienation over high unemployment, inadequate social services, and feelings of widespread discrimination, making the violence hard to contain. Knowledgeable observers suggested that the outbursts reflected tensions between the primarily Muslim immigrants and their children and the French that had built up over years (Bowen 2006; Cesari 2005; Silverstein and Tetreault 2005; Withol de Wenden 2005).

While there has been ethnic or racial violence at times in France, the most enduring conflict in recent decades has been mainly non-violent; it was a cultural conflict over the right of a small number of Muslim girls to wear headscarves to school (Ross 1993b). The first of many psychocultural dramas around this issue began in 1989 when a junior high school principal expelled three young girls who wore *foulards* (headscarves) to school in Creil, a town north of Paris (Figure 7.1). The principal told the girls and

191

their families that their attire violated the deeply rooted principle of secularism of the public schools (*la laïcité de l'école*). Within a month, the issue hit the press when one girl claimed the principal had struck her, and her family called in two Islamic "fundamentalist" organizations to talk to the principal. The action touched off a whirling controversy that quickly involved the nation's top political figures and raised a series of powerful issues at the core of French political life that cut across political lines and has continued to expand (Feldblum 1993; Ross 1993b; Scott 2005; Thomas 2000).

The country's highest administrative tribunal, the *Conseil d'Etat*, ruled that students could wear religious symbols, such as the headscarf or jewelry with a cross or star of David, but only if the symbols were not provocative or objects of propaganda, and were not used to pressure or to proselytize other students. However, the issue did not go away. Instead it expanded into other explosive questions about immigration, diversity, and terrorism until in 2004 the government passed legislation that banned all conspicuous religious signs such as headscarves, skull caps, and large crosses from public schools. What is the long-term conflict about and why does the headscarf engender so much anger, producing presidential commissions and national legislation? How, and why, are the young girls wearing them a threat to French society and the Republic? Not all are in agreement about the answer and as two skeptical observers noted, "Rather than address the real causes of minority exclusion, the state engaged in alarmist mobilizing around a cultural symbol" (Silverstein and Tetreault 2005).

At the core of this conflict are competing narratives. The French narratives about the French Republic and society can be aligned along a continuum I call hard to soft Republicanism – each having its own variations. There are also Muslim narratives about their struggle to be full French citizens while retaining their religion and identity. These issues all intersect with the historical French conflict over the relationship between the Catholic Church and the Republic.

A starting point is the French term *laïcité*, which is probably best translated as secularism or non-denominationalism and state neutrality with regards to religion; to some it also stands for rationality and liberty against obscurantism and religious authority (Thomas 2000: 170–71; 200b).[1] But

---

[1] For a good discussion of the development and changes in meaning of *laïcité* in France see Bauberot (1998; 2005).

Figure 7.1 Headscarf, a threat to the Republic? One of the three young girls originally expelled from school in France for wearing a headscarf in 1989

its meaning is far from straightforward and there are many ambiguities.[2] *Laïcité* does not imply that the French state has no relationship with

---

[2] Bowen (2004: 34–35) distinguishes between liberal and public *laïcité* which parallels my distinction between hard and soft Republicanism in many ways. The former emphasizes an individual's right to practice his or her religion and even allows students to draw on religion in reflecting on what they are learning in school while respecting openness and deliberative discussion. In contrast, public *laïcité* emphasizes limits to speech and behavior in public life and would more rigidly exclude religion from all public domains. Nordmann (2004) makes a similar distinction in considering the complexity of *laïcité* in France.

religious institutions. Napoleon secured a Concordat with the Vatican allowing the state to name Catholic bishops. In 1905 legislation following the Dreyfus Affair called for the separation of Church and state; yet when Pope John Paul II died in 2005, the French interior minister ordered flags on government buildings, including public schools, to be flown at half mast and told prefects "to 'attend services' conducted by the ecclesiastical authority in the memory of His Holiness, an order, essentially to go to church. He urged them to pay their condolences to local bishops" (Sciolino 2005). Historically, each religious community in France has designated authorities who deal with the state on matters of common interest and the state pays for the upkeep of older church buildings;[3] eight of France's eleven national holidays are Catholic in origin; and the 1905 law is not applied to the region of Alsace or the department of Moselle that were part of Germany at that time. In these parts of France, large crucifixes hang in some classrooms and nuns can teach wearing their habits; and the state supports Catholic, Jewish, and Muslim religious schools.

After 9/11, tensions in France rose when Muslims felt unfairly targeted as potential terrorists, and when there were protests and anti-Semitic violence connected to the Al-Aqsa Intifada. The success of the extremist National Front presidential candidate in 2002 made it clear to both the center-right and the left in France that neither could ignore the issues of integration and Islam in France. In 2003, Jack Lang, the former Socialist minister of culture, and other members of the National Assembly, introduced legislation to prohibit all religious symbols, including headscarves, in public schools. The center-right government indicated that while it considered this specific piece of legislation inopportune and perhaps unconstitutional given the 1989 ruling, it was considering new legislation that would reassert the secular character of the public schools in a period of communitarian (meaning Muslim) challenges that were increasingly common. Following the report of a presidential commission at the end of 2003, the government proposed legislation to ban conspicuous religious signs, including forms of dress, from school. The legislation was passed quickly and adopted into law in early 2004 to be implemented at the start of the next school year.[4] Despite about forty expulsions, the first and second school years were quiet, however, as people avoided escalatory,

---

[3] They are also now paying for construction and maintenance of mosques.
[4] Between the passage of the law and its implementation in 2004, the European Court of Human Rights ruled that Turkey had the right to ban headscarves from schools.

public confrontations, however, as the fall 2005 rioting showed, it would be foolish to think the underlying issues were resolved.

Since 1989, the *foulard*[5] and the emotions it triggers have been at the core of a series of French psychocultural dramas that involved administrative rulings, legislative actions, public protests, and electoral campaigns. These disputes divide those who see the *foulard* as a challenge to deeply held French Republican principles of secularism – the "hard" Republican position – from those who are more willing to entertain the notion of France as a partially multicultural society, and adopt a more pragmatic, "soft" Republican stance which seeks to create a middle ground by recognizing the reality of multiple identities (Kastoryano 1996; Nordmann 2004).

There is not a single Muslim community in France. Although the greatest number are people who emigrated from the Maghreb region of North Africa and their descendants, there are many Muslims in France from West Africa and Turkey as well. There is also significant diversity in how they view their future in French society, the images the French reaction elicited for them, and the role that Islam plays in their daily lives. In France only a minority of Muslim women wear headscarves, and in schools prior to the 2004 law banning them, the number was truly miniscule,[6] so it is reasonable to ask what the fuss is all about and why the issue won't go away. What different Muslim narratives agree on is that the French have treated them with little respect, that discrimination is widespread in housing, employment, and police practices, and that too many French assume both that devout Muslims necessarily support political violence and terrorism, and that behaviors such as wearing a headscarf or practicing their religion are statements of a rejection of French society's core values. At the same time, French Muslims are very diverse and often have friendship, job, and religious networks defined through their or their parents' countries of origin. Likewise, there is great variation in religious

---

[5] There has been a shift over time in how the scarves are described. The most common term in 1989 was *foulard*, or scarf; although sometimes the term *tchador*, referring to a full-length garment, or hijab, which is a general term for dressing modestly were used; in more recent years this been replaced by *voile*, which is best translated as veil and has much more of a religious connotation. In this chapter, I tend to use *foulard* in reference to the earlier period and *voile* for the later one. It is important to point out that there has always been a range of ways in which scarves are worn, and that the shift from *foulard* to *voile* is not basically about a shift in what is worn but in how it is described.

[6] In early 2004, Education Minister François Fillion suggested there were about ten cases a year that were hard to resolve (Madelin, 2004).

participation and the best estimates are that most, like the rest of French society, are not terribly observant (Nordmann 2004: 169).[7]

A highly charged symbol, the meaning of *le foulard* is in the eye of the beholder. It communicates piety and personal choice to some, and subjugation of women and religious fundamentalism to others (Silverstein 2004). It is a sign of religious identity that quickly and easily morphs into other issues large and small: immigration, discrimination, Islamic extremism, workplace attire, citizenship, cultural autonomy, unemployment, crime, and work ethics (Scott 2005). It triggers cultural battles that Jean Marie Le Pen and his neo-fascist National Front have used to their great political advantage in electoral campaigns, permitting them to define the political agenda around issues that have left the immigrants and their descendants with little voice and high alienation. As in conflicts examined in earlier chapters, the core issue is not over headscarves that young girls wear in school, but about the meaning of secularization, multiculturalism, and what it means to be French in a society that still has fault lines on these questions going back to the French Revolution and the nineteenth-century French nation-building project (Bauberot 2005).

France, of course, is not alone in its ambivalence toward immigration, immigrant communities, and how immigrant identities are expressed.[8] In recent decades high immigration has brought large numbers of newcomers to virtually all major industrial countries and with them have come increased social tension, economic and cultural demands, as well as political questions concerning participation, representation, and assimilation. However, the behavior of recent Muslim immigrants and their descendants is a particularly intense issue in France. The powerful psychocultural dramas over headscarves unleash strong emotions in which all the parties present their demands in a mutually exclusive manner while seeking validation of their core values and acknowledgment of their identity. As escalation has increased so has polarization as non-Muslims increasingly view "extremist groups" as typical of Islam as a whole, and as Muslims become more and more distrusting of French intentions.

---

[7] Instead of attentively listening to the diverse Muslim voices in France, recently there have been many articles emphasizing and picturing Muslims who have successfully integrated into French society (e.g., Khouri-Dagher 2006).

[8] There is a widespread literature on Islam and immigration in Europe. While my sole focus here is the French experience, a fascinating project would be to explain why the conflict between immigrants and the native peoples takes different forms across countries.

This chapter has three sections. The first discuses French nation-building, the development of the standard French national narrative, and challenges to it from regional identity groups and immigrants to France. The second looks at the troublesome disputes in France since 1989 around issues of immigration, integration, and identity as it became clear that many of the 5 million or so Muslims in France are not prepared to integrate into French society in the same way that earlier generations of Belgian, Italian, Polish, Spanish, and Portuguese immigrants did. While it is easy to describe the conflict as the French versus Muslims of North African origin, in fact much of the conflict has been over agenda control and issue definition among the non-Muslim majority (Lorcerie 2005). In this conflict, as in the others examined here, there are not two homogenous narratives or groups confronting each other. Rather, there are multiple issues and narratives on each side that make the ostensible issue slippery and hard to address. The concluding section explores the intense tension between two French narratives – the hard Republican one emphasizing the integration of migrants into French society that offers little space for hyphenated or multiple identities,[9] and the soft Republican one that recognizes the reality, and even partial benefit, in seeing France as a multicultural society. It also emphasizes the emerging Muslim voices in the debate and the complexity and diversity of France's Muslims whose voices have not been particularly sought or valued since the conflict first broke out in 1989, making any kind of conflict mitigation especially difficult.

Nation states, national narratives, and minorities

For reasons that are not hard to understand, contemporary nation-states emphasize their internal social and cultural homogeneity even when it is clearly at odds with their past and present diversity. States are about power and control; these are maximized when they convince their own citizens and others that the state is the appropriate (the older term was natural) unit to represent its population. This task becomes easier the more that states can point to shared historical experiences, a distinct identity, and cultural markers such as a common language or religion – in short, those very things that define a nation. As a result, although states are political units, their legitimacy is grounded in cultural beliefs about a shared past, as we saw in the previous chapters. Establishing internal

---

[9] There are "Italian Americans" but no "Italian French."

cultural unity is a particular problem of the modern state and only since the late eighteenth century did ideas begin to emerge concerning the state as the embodiment of a specific nation and the idea of citizenship as a particular form of membership in the state and nation. Nations from this perspective were natural units needing a state to make them complete and political movements in the nineteenth and twentieth centuries were more than willing to provide support for this notion.

There are at least four reasons why the correspondence between the nation and the state is often problematic. First, in many places peoples from more than one nation live cheek by jowl making it difficult in practical terms to line up identities and territories. However, without moving (and sometimes killing) large numbers of people – what is now called ethnic cleansing – the creation of several nation-states out of a larger entity will not necessarily produce homogenous units. Second, societal heterogeneity has increased with improved transportation, migration, the decline of small peasant agricultural economies, and war-created refugees. Third, ethnic groups and nations are not static entities but collectivities that form and re-form over time through interactions and in response to changing contexts. In some cases, smaller groups coalesce into larger ones, while in others larger groups dissolve into smaller ones (Horowitz 1985). Fourth, deciding what is an ethnic group or a nation and who is part of it is an untidy matter, and one that must be defined not only in terms of objective characteristics, such as shared cultural expressions like language, religion, cultural practices, physical characteristics, or ancestry but also on contextual and subjective factors.

It should not be surprising, then, given the complexity and changing nature of nations, that the idea of the nation as a social construction has received great attention in recent decades. Rather than thinking of the nation as a timeless natural unit, this work pays attention to how national traditions are invented, and recognizes how political the process of building nations is (Hobsbawm and Ranger 1983). What this brings into sharp focus is that states – sometimes residual empires and kingdoms, sometimes colonial constructions, and sometimes units created after wars – often come into being *prior* to the nation that modern ideologies contend they should represent. This is especially obvious in the case of countries, such as India, Indonesia, Nigeria, and Congo, that emerged from the end of colonial empires after World War II, the states of Central Asia that became independent after the fall of the Soviet Union in 1991, or Mexico and Brazil earlier. If we go back to the eighteenth and nineteenth centuries in Europe, we see the same pattern – the state *preceded* the nation. Countries, such as Britain, France, Spain, Italy, and Germany, emerged from older socially and culturally diverse kingdoms and empires; they then devoted great time and energy to establishing a narrative and culture of a shared past upon which to build the idea of a unified nation and legitimize the state.

It is indeed paradoxical that states work so hard to establish themselves as natural units when if this were actually the case, the matter should require little special attention. In Europe, states effectively used public schools to establish a common culture, transmit a shared narrative about the past, and spread the standardized national language. European intellectuals also played a key role in producing historically rooted narratives and used physical evidence such as objects from archeological excavations that took the present as the logical outcome of past events.

Weber (1976) offers a classic study of French nation-building. *Peasants into Frenchmen* (1976), provides a detailed description of how the French state mobilized its resources and influence to create a strong shared national identity. He begins with a portrait of early nineteenth-century France as a country separated into Paris and the hinterlands. The government in Paris had long controlled the vast countryside politically and militarily, but the people living in Auvergne, Alsace, the Alps, Provence, and Brittany hardly considered themselves French in any meaningful sense. As late as 1860, fewer than half of the country's population spoke French as their first language (Weber 1976: 70). Weber argues that people in the capital looked down on those in the provinces, most of whom lived in miserable conditions, as dirty, uncivilized, and backward in much the same way that Europeans saw Africa and Asia in the twentieth century.

Weber recounts how beginning with the Third Republic in 1870, Paris set out to control and "civilize" the countryside. By the start of World War I in 1914, the effort had been highly successful. A shared identity as French men and women emerged among the disparate Bretons, Alsatians, Avergnats, and Juracians who all learned in school that their ancestors were the Gauls and that as citizens they were the natural inheritors of the fruits of the French Revolution. French was now the first language of over 90% of the country's citizens. Participation in the state and its institutions increased and the French people were prepared, somewhat tragically, to die for their nation. How did this happen? Weber argues that the state was able to greatly improve the country's standard of living and develop a strong sense of national identity in three ways: through improvements in technology and transportation that brought peasants into the market economy; universal male military service that provided a common experience for all men through participation in a central state institution; and universal primary education with its standardized curriculum taught in French that narrated the story of the French nation.

In building a compelling vision of a shared present and future, states emphasize a common past with specific triumphs, defeats, sacred heroes and common purpose while downplaying long-standing conflict such as that between the church and state in France (Bauberot 2005). In this process, states develop ascending anachronisms in the form of metaphors, symbols, and rituals that interpret the past from the perspective of the present, and in so doing attribute contemporary perceptions and motives to past actors. This deft (though not necessarily conscious) maneuver provides people in the present with ancestors and a shared narrative of working toward the same timeless goal of building and maintaining the national community. From this perspective, Joan of Arc, Louis XIV, and Charles de Gaulle were partners in the same French national project even though they happened to live centuries apart. Just as psychoculturally plausible, though lighter, are the actions of Astérix le Gaulois, the renowned comic book hero, and his compatriot Obelix, who along with the other residents of their mythical village, resisted Roman conquest and paved the way for the proud French nation that emerged centuries later.

Weber's argument, and that of many others, is about how states make nations. Although there are significant scholarly disagreements about the specifics of this constructivist process, what is especially striking is how the larger argument is at odds with popular and political essentialist discourse that sees nations and ethnic groups as fixed, unchanging, and often biological entities that fight over "ancient hatreds" (e.g., Kaplan 1993). Whereas scholars now focus on the mutability and change over time of nationals and ethnic groups, people often see in-groups as enduring and unchanging.[10]

This discussion of the nation and national narratives with particular attention to France sets the stage for considering the conflict over the

[10] At the same time, we need to be careful not to go so far as to view all categories as arbitrary social constructions. As Smith (1991) argues, while group definition is more socially constructed than popular images hold, it is not as easily altered in the short run as some constructivist accounts suggest. Horowitz (2003) stresses problems with caricaturing primordialist arguments and also makes a good case for limits to constructivism and for taking seriously the primordialist claim that identities are enduring and hard to change.

Islamic headscarf in France since 1989. It locates the conflict in deep fears on all sides about identity and emphasizes ways that each side's efforts to assert its identity are seen as a direct challenge by the other. To a great extent, the issue is whether, and how, one can be French and Muslim at the same time, and many people have problems imagining how this is possible. The conflict pits competing narratives against each other and only sometimes includes Muslim voices as well. In the hard-core Republican narrative, the French emphasize the individual citizen's relationship to the unitary state that has historically rejected the relevance of intermediate group identities. It is the product of a centuries-long struggle to limit the power of the Catholic Church in the public domain. For its adherents, the secular state and its crown jewel, the public school, are not all that is at risk – so is French culture.[11]

The softer Republican narrative is not at odds with many parts of this account, but its adherents are generally more pragmatic and struggle to acknowledge the realities of contemporary migration and multi-culturalism in a world with weaker and weaker state borders.[12] One way to think about the difference between them is that while both hard and soft Republicans call for acculturation, meaning that immigrants learn French language and culture, hard Republicans also seek assimilation, meaning a rejection of any cultural identity other than being French, while soft Republicans show a greater flexibility in terms of family traditions, community habits, and the desire to foster inclusion (Safran 2004). Muslim societies, of course, have a very different cultural tradition without rigid boundaries between religion and politics and no conflict between local, clan, and national identities, each of which may be especially relevant at different times or contexts. Yet Muslims in France, as in other European countries, are not of one mind about the extent to which they wish to assimilate socially and culturally versus the degree to which they wish to maintain religious and cultural practices on a personal level and to live in culturally homogenous communities that will reinforce these.

[11] In early 2004 the *New York Times* reported a conflict in southern France between truffle hunters and local restaurateurs who began purchasing imported Chinese truffles for $25 a kilogram rather than paying the local price of $1250. Attacking the restaurants, Michel Tournayre, the president of the local truffle producers group declared, "They're killing French culture" (Smith 2004b). What is notable here is the ease with which a specific local matter in France can be perceived as a general threat to cultural survival.

[12] Almost all the voices endorse some version of Republicanism; few openly use the term multiculturalism.

norities versus immigrant minorities

(1998) in a very insightful discussion of multiculturalism in distinguishes between national and immigrant minorities. al groups are peoples who form an historical society, view them- s~ as nations, create movements to defend their language and collective autonomy, and whose territory has been incorporated into a larger country. Québecers, Catalans, and Basques in Spain are nations in this sense. Today in France there are regional cultural groups such as Bretons, Alsatians, Basques, and Corsicans that come closest to Kymlicka's definition of a nation although they do not have any real institutional autonomy or linguistic independence.

For a long time the French state vigorously opposed linguistic, or any other form of, autonomy for these regional groups. By the early 1980s, however, it was clear that with the exception of Corsica and perhaps the Basques, the demands of these small national groups for greater cultural recognition and autonomy were no longer any threat to the French state. Schools were allowed to teach regional languages, though there was no talk of using them as the language of instruction, and local folk festivals became more frequent (Safran 1985). Kymlicka's analysis makes it clear that the changes in France were essentially symbolic as the French realized that regional identities were not challenges to the state and there was no possibility of creating and sustaining a set of public institutions that would allow the regional groups to participate in the modern world in their own languages.

Immigrant minorities are very different from national minorities in several important ways (Kymlicka 1998). First, immigrant minorities are almost never territorially distinct even when immigrants live in cities or towns with relatively segregated neighborhoods and local businesses that cater to their needs. Second, although immigrant communities often have commercial, religious, financial, educational, and cultural institutions in which the immigrants and their children can speak their own language, they still must participate in the wider society's institutions and doing so requires learning the language and norms of the host society. Integration of immigrants is certainly the goal of most receiving societies,[13] and Kymlicka argues that Canada with its high level of immigration and explicit policy of

---

[13] This is not always the case however. In countries such as Germany or Japan that historically have defined citizenship in terms of genealogical ties, there is less interest in the integration of long-term immigrants than in countries such as France or Canada

202

multiculturalism has been highly successful in integrating immigrants in both English-speaking Canada and French-speaking Québec.

France has been a leading country of immigration for the past 200 years and during that period has received more immigrants than any other country in Europe (Noriel and Horowitz 1992). France, whose immigration rates since 1800 are very similar to the United States, is assimilationist and egalitarian, and in both countries it is relatively easy for legal immigrants to become citizens. At the same time, each has distinct ideas about the appropriate role of an immigrant's prior identity (Horowitz 1992). In France, there is an expectation that new citizens will discard their former identities, and intermediate institutions such as cultural identity based organizations are actively discouraged. In contrast, in the USA becoming American does not require immigrants to shed their former identities when they become citizens. In France, "the attainment of equality implied erasing blood privileges and therefore more generally erasing traces of origin" (Horowitz 1992: 18). For the French, Horowitz argues, there is a conflation of cultural and political unity and a belief that intermediate identities should not impinge on the direct relationship between the citizen and the state (Horowitz 1992: 19).

Since the French Revolution, immigrants have arrived in France from neighboring countries in response to economic opportunities. Until 1950 almost all were poor, white, and Catholic and they often filled jobs at the bottom of the economic ladder. Their children attended French schools and both the immigrants and their children learned French if it was not already their first language. Nonetheless, there were sometimes intense conflicts between the immigrants and the French and press accounts were filled with negative stereotypes and questions about their assimilability (Hargreaves 1995; Kastoryano 1996; Noiriel 1996). Since 1950, in addition to immigration from southern Europe, especially Portugal and Spain, France has received significant numbers of immigrants from former colonial countries including Vietnam, and those in West, Central, and North Africa. Over the past three decades, people of North African origin have become the largest and most visible minority in France – numbering perhaps 4 million – and have been the focus of sometimes intense political and social conflict. The North Africans – often called Maghrebians, referring to their region of origin, are almost exclusively Muslims, and

---

where citizenship is defined more in cultural terms, such as the ability to speak a national language, and residence (Brubaker 1992).

ⅼ in France probably now outnumber those who moved there and
ⅼalf of the total are French citizens (Freedman 2004: 8). Despite
ⅼzens, however, most experience various forms of discrimination.
ⅼrench feel that Muslims show little interest in integration and
hostⅼⅼⅼy between Muslims and non-Muslims has at times been high and
relations strained in and around many French cities. One focus of conflict
arises over the construction of mosques, including their location, size, and
design. There are also less dramatic sources of tension arising from work
and commercial relationships, interactions in offices, social service claims,
youth versus police interactions, the lack of jobs, and schools.

In the past twenty years, there have been a number of dramatic incidents
raising public fears about the non-assimilability of Muslims in France
despite indicators of their increasing integration. An anti-foreigner,
nationalist political movement has gained strength and its leader, Jean-
Marie Le Pen, received the second highest vote total in the first round of
the May 2002 presidential voting. The complicated relationship between
people of North African origin and French non-Muslims involves resource
and power issues and identity questions over the allocation of recognition
and prestige in French society. The most dramatic incidents have produced
drawn-out psychocultural dramas around religious symbols, and invoke
powerful French fears of Islamic fundamentalism and communalism. To
date few of these have had constructive outcomes.

Le Foulard, *everyday forms of resistance and identity*

Large numbers of people came from North Africa to France in the two
decades from the early 1950s to the early 1970s. There was real diversity
among those who arrived. They came from different countries – Tunisia,
Morocco, and Algeria – and among them were the French settlers and
administrators who left Algeria following an ugly colonial war, Arabs
known as Harkis who were loyal to the French during the fighting and
were afraid to remain, and other Arabs needing work. Most of the jobs the
Arabs found were on the lowest rungs of France's expanding economy.

In their analysis of Muslim social and political organization in France,
Withol de Wenden and Leveau (2001) argue that in the 1970s and early
1980s the community's leaders tended to be immigrants themselves and
their organizations were closely tied to unions and the political left. By
the mid 1980s a new generation of organizations and leaders had
emerged. In 1981, the French made it legal for foreigners to form

organizations and soon the *Beurs*, the children of immigrants, moved to the forefront of social and political action. *Le mouvement beur* organized several Marseille to Paris marches and demonstrations in Paris in the mid 1980s drawing attention to discrimination, problems of integration, and lack of participation opportunities in French society. They developed ties to the ruling Socialist Party and the left began to talk about multiculturalism and *la droit de la différence* (the right to be different). However, many of the movement's specific goals, such as obtaining the right for non-citizens to vote in local elections, were integrationist and unfulfilled and there was real disillusionment with their failure to produce significant integration and meaningful change in people's daily lives (Withol de Wenden and Leveau 2001: 43).

L'affaire du foulard: 1989[14]

The 1989 headscarf affair began in a context of other psychocultural dramas between Islam and the west – the death sentence for Salman Rushdie after he wrote and published *The Satanic Verses*, the rise of militant Islamic organizations in France, and the first Palestinian *Intifada*. As it unfolded, both the *Beurs* and the French left pulled back from their earlier efforts to build a close relationship and since the 1990s French Muslims have focused less on integration and citizenship than on social problems such as drugs, crime, and jobs in and around Paris and other large cities. Organizational efforts have become less public and political; they have turned to acquiring governmental and other support and assistance focused on the needs of their own communities, and the organized groups that have emerged are less integrationist and less middle class than those of the eighties, and are more Islamic culturally (Withol de Wenden and Leveau 2001). Their discourse emphasizes discrimination and exclusion and has turned to Islam as a refuge and as a tool for expressing their needs and demands (Chebel d'Apollonia 2002; Kastoryano 1996).

There have been ongoing skirmishes around cultural and religious expression but since 1989 none has attracted the intense emotion of the psychocultural dramas that have developed around the issue of Islamic headscarves in schools. The initial conflict's intensity surprised not only outside observers, but also many French politicians. Defining the issue as a simple separation of church and state, or young children manipulated by

---

[14] This section is adapted from Ross (1993b).

fundamentalist parents, struck a responsive chord for many people. It invoked the hard Republican narrative and historical challenges to it including the Dreyfus Affair and the wartime Pétain regime, and linked France's vulnerability to the outside threats that fundamentalist and extremist Islam posed. When Minister of Education Lionel Jospin was drawn into the conflict he first tried a low-key pragmatic approach declaring that responsibility rested with school authorities. Their job was to talk to the families involved to get them to understand the importance of secular public education and to abandon the open expression of religion in school.

However, he added, wearing a scarf is not sufficient grounds for exclusion, for the child's education must come first (Beriss 1990), and "French schools exist to educate, to integrate, not to reject" (Schemla 1989: 78). However, the image of "Islamic fundamentalism" in a French public school was far more powerful than Jospin's attempts at dialogue. On the political far right, the National Front talked about the evils of immigration, the problem of foreigners in France, and the threat they posed to French civilization. For many on the left the emotions were just as intense as they dramatically portrayed the deep threats to secular public schools, the key institution for the inculcation of democratic values. "The future will tell if the year of the bicentennial [of the French Revolution] will be seen as the Munich of the public school," declared five leading intellectual figures (Badinter 1989: 58). For many feminists the dispute was not about religious freedom or the secularity of the public school but the oppression of women in fundamentalist Islam (Moruzzi 1994). From the outset, the divisions on the headscarf issue created unusual alliances that did not follow traditional left–right lines.

Teachers throughout the country, feeling that their authority and the school's secular principles were under attack, spoke out against the *foulard*, bringing up cases where Muslim students refused to attend gym classes or where they objected to biology, philosophy, music, or art classes on religious grounds; some threatened to go on strike if the scarves were not banned. Soon Jospin realized that there wasn't much he could do to manage a conflict that increasingly invoked questions of the work habits of North Africans, housing, social services, illegal immigration, and integration. So Jospin kicked the matter upstairs to the *Conseil d'Etat*, the nation's top administrative tribunal. Their decision satisfied neither those who saw the issue as one of religious freedom nor those who wanted to ban the *foulard* from public schools. The *Conseil d'Etat* ruled that wearing religious signs was not necessarily incompatible with the idea of a secular public school if the signs were non-provocative, did not pressure other students, were not proselytizing, and were not objects of propaganda. Students, they ruled, could not refuse to attend certain classes, or threaten the liberty or security and safety of others.

Most teachers' organizations and administrators were not happy with the decision, but suggested that what was most critical was its implementation. Some students and their families, citing the case of Catholic students who wear crosses, saw the decision as favoring scarves and returned to school wearing a *foulard*. The headscarf conflict also expanded beyond school settings as in the case of a hospital in Dijon that refused to accept a young doctor when she told the authorities that she planned to wear a scarf while working. Soon the issue disappeared from the media and almost none of the specific decisions local authorities made received very much publicity. Two of the three girls in Creil whose actions started the whole controversy held out for the right to wear their scarves and acquiesced only when King Hassan II of Morocco intervened and asked them to go to classes without the *foulard* (Moruzzi 1994).

The 1989 dispute over the Islamic scarves in French schools was settled through the imposition of an administrative ruling, but the conflict was in no sense resolved. Instead, it was diffused and transformed into a broader concern with immigration and integration. No longer was there much talk of "the right to difference." Rather, French suspicions about, and anger toward, Muslims, whom they commonly described as immigrants even though many were born in France and were citizens, increased in intensity, while Muslims felt more vulnerable than ever and uncertain which, if any, of their basic rights the government would protect. While the government used administrative and judicial procedures to deal with the scarves, the deeper issues were far more divisive and raised important questions about what it means to be French and the limits to the public expressions of diversity that the French would tolerate.

The conflict over the young girls' scarves was marked by an intensity that is hard to imagine in a nation where dress codes have virtually disappeared, where public nudity is seen as a personal matter, and fashions shift quickly. The core positions were highly emotional and non-negotiable and they raised deep fears and threats for many people. Permitting scarves in school was returning the country to the cardinals for some and giving it to the ayatollah for others. For Muslims, despite the fact that surveys showed that more of them opposed wearing the *foulard* than supported it, the case provided more evidence of French racism and hypocrisy, eliciting intense feelings of vulnerability and rejection, and an increasing isolation from French society. Another emotionally powerful image for both Muslims and non-Muslims is rooted in French colonialism – especially the war in Algeria. There, the FLN (the Algerian Independence Movement) told women to don veils as a sign of opposition to the French, and many French believed that Muslim women were assisting the FLN and carrying under their clothing bombs and other weapons that were placed in French areas of the city. In 1958, "opponents of Algerian independence walked through the streets of Algiers ripping off women's veils in the name of the Republic" (Scott 2005: 120).

The intensity of feeling was seen in the rapid political fallout – the rise of the far right – an effect that has persisted since early December 1989, two months after the *foulard* crisis erupted, when the National Front received especially strong support in several local elections, particularly in the south, and won their first seat in the National Assembly. Both the socialist government and center-right opposition drew the lesson that the scarves had allowed the far right to focus attention on its overtly racist proposals for the exclusion of foreigners and a reduction of social services to them. Public opinion, in fact, showed that the issue of minorities in French society was potentially explosive. Large majorities opposed the right to wear the *foulard* in school; Muslims also opposed it, 45–30% (Sole and Tincq 1989: 15). Emotionally, many members of the French majority transformed the question of religious attire into a threat from fundamentalist Islam to the nation and its culture.

Take 2: 1990s

Following the *Conseil d'Etat*'s 1989 ruling, a small number of students began wearing headscarves. One estimate is that about 150 out of 5 million post-primary-school students did so between 1990 and 1992 (Kaci 2003). More students began to wear the scarves and there were new incidents in 1993 and 1994 that led François Bayrou, the minister of education, to issue two circulars that went beyond the 1989 ruling, one that referred to the "Islamic scarf" and a second that told schools to include in their internal rules ones that would prohibit students from wearing "ostentatious signs" of their identity.[15] More contentious cases

---

[15] The shift to a national directive concerning the headscarves meant that school officials now had to interpret terms such as ostentatious, conspicuous and non-provocative, and

arose, and in one parents in Strasbourg, whose daughters had been expelled from school for wearing the scarf, appealed on the grounds that the scarf is not in itself overly conspicuous, and won. However, the decision itself was denounced by Bayrou, and it did nothing to bridge the different positions. Simone Veil, the minister of social affairs, then named Hanifi Chérifi, a North African born scholar, as a mediator hoping she could reduce the tension. From 1994 to 1996, the number of contested cases, which had reached 2,400, dropped to 1,000.[16]

To provide a general framework for managing the issues surrounding Islam in France (not just the *foulard*), the High Council of Integration (HCI), a government appointed body, issued a long report entitled "Islam in the Republic" in 2000 (HCI 2000). In trying to mediate between the hard and soft Republican positions, it reminded the public that Islam is compatible with the Republic and that students should not be excluded simply because they wore scarves. The report emphasized the public school as the institutional setting where people learn to live together and said that identity-based incidents are amplified when they occur in schools. The HCI also recognized that headscarves were no longer the only area of contention in schools and identified three additional areas of conflict: school cafeterias where Islamic dietary restrictions are an issue; school calendars which conflict with Muslim religious holidays; and curriculum and activities (e.g., Arabic language instruction and mixed gym classes or swimming), and they offered proposals to find a middle ground. The report noted that when adolescent boys decide to grow a beard as a statement of their identity there is little problem.[17] However, the question of young girls wearing "a scarf around their face that covers their ears, neck and hair is a problem that is much more delicate" (HCI 2000: 3-3-2), because, they said, more than any other issue, it symbolized the tensions between Islam and the secular public school.

The report emphasized the limits to legal and administrative solutions to complex issues of culture and identity, and stressed the importance of

---

the motivations behind students' choice of clothing or other objects and their potential impact on others, to make a decision.

[16] Getting the numbers of cases is not simple. There are many simply settled at the school level relatively quickly. Others are dealt with in the school context but less rapidly, while there are some in which the outside mediator is involved, most of which were settled and a few that are not that lead to expulsion.

[17] The question of why female behavior and control over female bodies in cultural identity conflicts is often far more conflictual than that of males is potentially quite interesting to investigate comparatively (Paige and Paige 1981).

dialogue and mediation. Through dialogue there could be more room for the school authorities to better understand the diverse motives of the young girls who want to wear headscarves and an opportunity to raise with them the issue of the consequences of such a choice. However, in the end the HCI clearly spelled out its preferred outcome; they reiterated the view that the headscarf is an obstacle to integration with its emphasis on gender inequality, and that anyone who chooses to wear it would face significant employment difficulties. Employment in the public sector would not be possible since wearing the scarf violates "the neutrality of the state," and private sector work that involves contact with the public would be problematic for many employers.

In its conclusions, the HCI struggled with the tension between hard and soft Republican narratives and their underlying values: the reality of the country's diverse population and the secular public school as an institution for the integration of individuals – not groups – into French society. The message was mainly, but not entirely, one of soft Republicanism and creating space for Muslims in France, but without offering a full-blown multiculturalist position. This struggle recalls Turner's (1957) discussion of Ndembu social dramas considered in Chapter 3. In both situations, there was no simple procedure to settle conflict between two competing and equally important principles. In the end, the HCI report came down on the side of the importance of integration at the same time as emphasizing the inappropriateness of simply excluding students who wear scarves because it is incompatible with the goal of integration. The report also recognized, as Turner does, the inadequacy of treating value conflicts such as this one as strictly legal matters. At the same time, there was not a process of engagement of the unequal parties and the favored mode of conflict management was for the mediator to work with the families and students to try to persuade them to change their behavior. Finally, the report had a very fixed view of Islam in France and little appreciation was shown for its diversity and adaptations in France.

Renewed intensity: 2001–04

The HCI's call for low-key engagement rather than laws and rules had relatively little impact even though the number of incidents in schools requiring mediation had diminished dramatically since the mid 1990s. Much of this was probably due to school administrators having a clearer sense of how to handle the issue so that outsiders were called in less often. In some schools, students could wear bandanas[18] while in others students were permitted to wear headscarves in school if they agreed to place them on their shoulders in class. There were, however, continuing incidents often leading to court cases that attracted public attention. Even more important was that larger political events overwhelmed the chance that local, focused mediation and dialogue might succeed. In 2001, the September 11 attacks rekindled fears of Islamic fundamentalism, emphasizing the Taliban's oppression of women, and the threat of *jihad* to Western democratic societies. There were also an increasing number of anti-Semitic incidents invoking the Israeli–Palestinian conflict in French cities that were attributed to Muslims, and continuing high levels of crime and unemployment in suburban and urban areas with high Muslim populations. All this only strengthened the on-going French belief that Muslims wanted the benefits of residence in France but only on their own terms. This led many to suggest that compromise and dialogue with Islam was not possible and that the global dimensions of the conflict had overwhelmed the national ones.

The powerful narrative surrounding terrorism, fundamentalism, and immigration, combined with public disenchantment with politics and politicians in France following major scandals, propelled Jean-Marie Le Pen's xenophobic anti-foreigner party to be the second largest vote getter in the first round of the 2002 presidential election. While many took solace in the outpouring of anti-racist rhetoric and the beating Le Pen took in the second round, it is also the case that over the past two decades many of Le Pen's once marginal issue positions have become mainstays of French politics. Many politicians on both the right and left realized the threat many French perceive from the country's Islamic minority and in the year following the 2002 election there was a stream of proposals to address the social and political issues, aimed at undercutting the National Front's support. Among these was a renewed interest in headscarves in schools as a direct challenge, and threat, to the integrity of French culture and values.

There were several initiatives concerning Islam in France aimed at solidifying the government's position, and calls for change from the socialist left as well. Led by Interior Minister Nicholas Sarkozy, the

---

[18] The bandana, like the *foulard* and *voile*, covers the hair and ears. It is important to realize that there are many styles of how each is worn.

government moved to create a French Islamic Council, the *Conseil Française de Culte Musulman* (CFCM), parallel to one that exists for Protestants and Jews to facilitate communication and control. The government hoped the CFCM would reduce the influence of foreign-trained clerics, especially those whose views, such as promoting Islamic law in France, run counter to French values (Fernando 2005a; Sciolino 2003a: 16). However, in the April 2003 elections for the CFCM, there were more Islamists elected than expected and the Algerian-backed Paris mosque that Sarkozy supported did poorly.[19] Following the election, Sarkozy was quite explicit about his expectations. "It is precisely because we recognize the right of Islam to sit at the table of the republic that we will not accept any deviation. Any prayer leader whose views run contrary to the values of the republic will be expelled" (Sciolino 2003a: 16).[20] Within a year, tensions in the council grew between Muslims from different countries as well as between those who were foreign born and those who were second or third generation French (Fernando 2005a).

Sarkozy and others want "model Muslims" meaning Muslims who will integrate into French society and will separate religion and politics. "Model Muslim women would not wear headscarves in the workplace; model Muslim girls would not try to wear headscarves to school. Most

---

[19] The elections showed how factionalized Muslims are in France and how most groups have close ties to specific Muslim countries. The group that elected the most members on the council had close ties to the Moroccan government. There were also members elected with ties to Turkey.

[20] The rhetoric of many who have written or spoken out on Islam in France strikes an outsider like myself as inconsistent in many ways. Jean Daniel, long-time editor of the left-leaning *Nouvel Observateur*, has long opposed racism and anti-Semitism in France. At the same time he is capable of writing an editorial where he declared that the headscarf issue is a challenge to the Republic and its values and should be banned in schools, describing those who support the right to wear headscarves as provocative and threatening. He went on to say that he was "shocked, irritated, disconcerted that in their desire to wear the foulard, a yarmulke, or any other distinctive symbol, there is a desire to affirm a difference that is neither rooted in a Luddite eccentricity, nor an isolated challenge. It is an affirmation of collective difference and the existence of a community outside the nation. What is shocking, irritating, and disconcerting, is that the *guests* [italics added] of a state don't even have the politeness to respect the laws of their hosts and even battle against them. After all, it took a long struggle to obtain a public school that is Republican, secular, compulsory, and open to all. It is shocking that one brandishes religious freedom as a reason to deny equality before the law and fraternity among children" (Daniel 2003: 55). Thomas (2000: 178) reports that former President Valéry Giscard d'Estaing used the same guest-host image saying that the girls should remove their scarves in school as a sign of respect for their hosts the same way that he would remove his shoes before entering a mosque.

important, model Muslims would call themselves French first and Muslim second" (Sciolino 2003b). State efforts to shape official Islam are part of the effort since the 1990s to use financial power to direct and control local organizations in and around Paris that primarily serve Muslim populations. There is some criticism that these organizations, generally led by French born and educated somewhat secular elites, are a sort of colonial administration that does what the French bureaucracy cannot do directly (Withol de Wenden and Leveau 2001: 121–24).

With the debate over Islam in general, and the veil in particular, heating up, and with proposals for new legislation in the spring of 2003, French President Jacques Chirac appointed a Commission headed by former minister Bernard Stasi and consisting of twenty members drawn from diverse parts of French society (including six women, three Muslims, and three Jews) to examine "Non-Denominationalism in the Republic." He asked the Commission to engage in a wide-ranging constructive discussion, reminding them that secularism was a duty, not just a right, and that their object was to reconcile national unity and the neutrality of the Republic with the recognition of the religious diversity in France (AFP 2003).

Following testimony from 140 witnesses, the Commission's detailed report emphasized that "secularism is not negotiable" and they made twenty-six specific proposals including one for a law to ban students from wearing conspicuous religious signs – large crosses, skull caps, and veils – in school.[21] They emphasized how their five-month investigation and the testimony they heard persuaded them that the display of contentious religious symbols had become a matter that could no longer be handled adequately at the local level and required national legislation. The comprehensive report offered a vigorous defense of Republican principles and a plea for tolerance, emphasizing the importance of secular principles in the public domain while guaranteeing religious freedom to all. Its recommendations included proposals to add Yom Kippur and Aid as school holidays, to end school instruction in first languages of students in cases where it is not French, to increase the teaching of Arabic as an academic subject, and to make culturally appropriate meals available in school cafeterias, and encouraged the destruction of urban ghettos. To renew the national commitment to secular principles, the Commission called for

---

[21] The full text of the report is available at: www.ladocumentationfrancaise.fr/rapports-publics/034000725/index. shtml

the development and adoption of a "civil charter" (*charte de la laïcité*) that would reaffirm and renew the relevance of the principle of the separation of church and state. In sum, the Commission took a hard line on the headscarves while trying to expand the boundaries of what could be considered French.

A week after he received the report, President Chirac, aware of both public support and the upcoming local elections, announced his support for a law banning conspicuous religious signs, saying that if France succumbed to the demands of religious communities, "It would sacrifice its heritage; it would compromise its future; it would lose its soul" (Sciolino 2003c). However, students could still wear discrete signs such as small crosses, stars of David, or hands of Fatima. Six weeks later the legislative debate took place and the law banning religious signs starting the next school year was passed quickly. The outcome was never in doubt given Chirac's control of the legislature. Nonetheless, there was a vigorous debate that, like 1989, cut across traditional political divisions. Muslims were divided with the more militant voices strongly opposed but others such as Dalil Boubakeur, head of the Paris mosque, supportive of it, declaring, "We absolutely do not want any confrontations" (Sciolino 2004a). Catholic and Protestant groups opposed the law as did small numbers of people on the left and center, while most of the center-right governing coalition as well as the opposition socialists supported it. School teachers and officials generally supported it as they no longer wanted to deal with the contentious cases themselves at the local level.

During the debate, it became clear that the actual number of problem cases each year involving headscarves was small and hardly a good explanation of the need for the law. There were 1260 cases at the opening of school in 2003, 20 of which were difficult, meaning that a resolution was not found, and 4 exclusions (Lorcerie 2005: 22). At this time only about 100–150 students continued to wear the scarf in school, but this did not mean the issue had lost its emotional potency (Brizard 2003). Alain Madelin, a member of Chirac's coalition who opposed the law warned that if one symbol is banned, another will emerge. He asserted that the "national psychodrama" and the passage of this law might exorcise French fears of immigration, of the vitality of Islam, of communalism, and of the "other" but would hardly address the social problems in France's ghettos (Madelin 2004).

Following the law's passage, the administration began formulating specific rules for its implementation and Muslims opposed to it considered how to respond. One response was to turn to clothing, such as bandanas, which have no religious significance *per se*, rather than traditional scarves, that could permit girls to cover their hair, There was a certain amount of press discussion of how to define a bandana and when it might or might not be a fashion accessory rather than a religious garment.[22] One Muslim leader suggested the possibility of a student strike in defense of human rights if bandanas were banned and called for students to follow their conscience. For its part, the Education Ministry suggested that in some situations traditional clothing would be acceptable, which suggested further possibilities for accommodation.[23] Fillion also made it clear that specific decisions would be made inside schools – away from cameras and journalists. There would be a period of dialogue (but *no* negotiation)[24] before any hearing would be held that might lead to expulsion. Meanwhile, all of the Commission's other recommendations were ignored and Stasi himself said how he was sorry that only the headscarves proposal received any government attention (AFP 2004; Kramer 2004).

As schools were about to open in September, two French journalists in Iraq were kidnapped and their abductors announced that they would be killed unless France annulled the headscarf law. In response, French Muslims rallied behind the nation and called for the rapid release of the hostages; it was clear to them that this was not the moment to provoke a confrontation. The Ministry of Education reported that after the opening of the 2004–05 school year, of the 12 million students some 240 wore veils; a larger number wore them to school but removed them as they entered the buildings; 170 of them agreed to remove them in a short time, leaving 70 unresolved cases.[25] Most were in and around Strasbourg and involved Turkish, not North African, families, and Lille in the north.[26] The government interpreted the small number of cases, in comparison with

---

[22] To understand how contorted some of the discussion became, consider the view that some expressed that if it covered the forehead or was attached to other clothing, then it was no longer a fashion statement.

[23] It was not clear what traditional clothing might be included and some suggested this provision was made to prevent conflict in overseas territories such as Reunion and Martinique rather than with Muslims in France.

[24] Some have suggested that dialogue only meant that the more powerful school authorities would put pressure on the students, delivering the message that the law could not tolerate exceptions.

[25] The number shifted slightly over the next few weeks and was reported to be 101 late in September (Malingre 2004).

[26] There was only one case in Paris, and the student was reported to have removed her scarf within a few hours on the first day of school.

the 1200 students wearing veils at the opening of school the year before, as widespread acceptance of the law (Bronner and Malingre 2004). However, the chilling effect of the hostage taking certainly made a large difference too. A small number of Sikh students who refused to remove their turbans were caught in the battle over the headscarves as well. They argued that their practice was cultural, not religious, and some school officials sought a compromise that teachers, who feared a backlash if there were two standards, thwarted.

The schools moved slowly in the remaining cases in part because of the hostage situation that did not end until the two journalists were released just before Christmas. In late October, the first expulsions, two 12-year-old girls in Mulhouse, were announced. One father commented, "It feels like an Inquisition" (Laronche 2004a). By December there were forty-three expulsions under the law including three Sikhs. Forty-one students enrolled in correspondence programs and seventeen in private schools. There was continued bickering about whether, and when, a bandana is a veil and when it is a fashion accessory.[27]

Although the law was specifically about students, there were efforts to broaden its application. Some schools sought to prohibit mothers wearing head coverings from picking up their children at school although eventually the Education Ministry said such a prohibition was illegal. In late December the prefecture of Seine-Saint-Denis in the suburbs of Paris prohibited five women wearing veils from attending a naturalization ceremony in which three of them were to receive French citizenship; they were told that "for a ceremony as symbolic of their integration into the French national community where the Marseillaise is sung any conspicuous sign of community affiliation should be banned" (Coroller 2004). Although the women still got their citizenship papers, the daughter of one of them said she resented the exclusion and its accompanying humiliation (Bernard 2004). The next year, the same prefecture denied a Moroccan woman a residential visa because she was wearing a headscarf, a sign of Islamic fundamentalism. Only when the woman hired a lawyer to appeal the decision was it reversed (Coroller 2005b; 2005c).

---

[27] The Education Ministry got into this somewhat absurd situation when it attempted to distinguish between an ordinary bandana and one that has been turned into an Islamic scarf. It defines the second in terms of three defining criteria: "It must be worn all day without interruption, all the days of the week, and it totally hides the hair" (Laronche 2004b).

Conclusion: competing images of French identity

Psychocultural dramas surrounding the Islamic headscarf in France are recurring and unresolved and there remains a significant contradiction between the dominant narrative of the French nation and its Republican principles, and the multicultural reality of France today. The language of assimilation and acculturation that leaves little room for multiple identities is clearly at odds with the diversity of French reality and worldwide discourses concerning pluralism and multiple identities. While the French understanding of multiculturalism and the needs of Muslim citizens is far more sophisticated than a decade ago, the political situation is highly constrained as the public continues to express a visceral opposition to Islam and often perceives all Muslim religious expressions as signs of extremism and an unwillingness to integrate into French society. In this context, young girls and women wearing the *voile* are viewed as challenging the nation and the state; this perception keeps the conflict from moving toward deescalation and constructive dialogue. Absent are more nuanced and inclusive symbols and rituals that could emphasize how French and Muslim identities are compatible. "The headscarf law halted the fighting, but settled nothing" (Coroller 2005a).

Hanifi Chérifi, who has served on the HCI and on the Stasi commission, warned in 2001 that juridical solutions are inadequate by themselves, as Turner (1957) argued, although she backed the ban in the Commission report. More and more Muslim women are choosing to wear veils in public and Muslim women are speaking publicly on both sides of the issue more than they did earlier (Bouzar 2001; Bouzar and Kada 2003). The conflict which the headscarf has symbolized has clearly moved beyond the school in France particularly after the 2005 street violence. There are some like Chérifi who argue that the *voile* is a trap that marginalizes and isolates young girls who choose to wear it (Simon 2001). However, what she says is needed is not exclusion and rules but education and engagement, although it is not always clear what these entail. Chérifi emphasizes that there is a good deal of variation in Islamic practice, the headscarf is not worn at all in some Islamic countries, it is banned in others, and that in the Maghreb traditionally it was not worn by many women.

Central to the conflict are claims about the motives of the girls and women who wear the scarves. Yet, it is clear that wearing the headscarf, like other powerful symbols, does not have only one meaning or one motive (Coroller 2005a; des Deserts, Fohr, Monnin, and Vigoureux 2003). Opponents readily, and often aggressively, say that families or extremist religious groups obligate girls to wear the *foulard* and in some cases this is true. But there are other motives as well. Some girls and young women adopt it as a means of personal security, believing that when they wear it young men are less likely to harass them and make unwanted sexual advances in the tough suburbs where many live ("Ripostes" 2003).[28] Bouzar (2003), an anthropologist and a government appointed member of the CFCM, argues that the headscarf is a strategy for protection that expands opportunities for participating in French society rather than limiting them. It can communicate that the young woman wearing the *foulard* is pious, serious, and ready for marriage (des Deserts, Fohr, Monnin, and Vigoureux 2003) and can also provide social space for girls to move between their family and its culture and the French Republican traditions (Bouzar 2001; 2003). Wearing the scarf allows some women to do things they might not have otherwise imagined – going to university, having a career, getting involved with voluntary associations, and finding others like themselves (des Deserts, Fohr, Monnin, and Vigoureux 2003). It is indeed paradoxical, Bouzar says, that what she sees as signs of integration are widely perceived as a rejection of it (Millot 2003).

Fernando (2005b) and Bouzar and Kada (2003:12) emphasize the individualistic nature of the choice for many women. Bouzar (2003) says that the choice often pits younger women against their families. As a generational conflict, she argues that French-born Muslims wearing the veil are not rejecting integration but affirming it. The women feel sufficiently at home in France that they are willing to appear in public with it. For them, the *foulard* is about equality, respect, and authentic personal identity construction (Branine 2003). Freedman (2004) adds that for younger women it is often more a sign of self-identity than religiosity, while Chérifi too argues that for many of the girls Islam is "my culture, my identity" in great part as a response to stigmatization, hostility, and discrimination (Simon 2001).

What has been clear since 1989 is that the headscarf conflicts are hardly just about headscarves and that the many psychocultural dramas have failed to move the parties toward effective dialogue over the underlying identity issues. If anything, the 2004 law threatens to further

[28] Some Muslim women in the US make the same argument.

218

polarize the situation and invites challenges from which neither side will be able to easily back down, although none took place in the first two years after the law went into effect. Despite the fact that most voices from North African associations in France have sought more, not less, integration into French society, the political fallout from the affair since 1989 has had important consequences that have inhibited, not enhanced, integration. Public opinion has long been "persuaded that immigration – particularly from Islamic counties – represents a fundamental threat to the cultural cohesion of the nation" (Hargreaves 1995:85).[29] For many Muslims, the conflicts underlined their vulnerability in French society and their lack of public voice, and Muslim organizations in France came to pay less attention to integration and assimilation and focused more on their own community (Withol de Wenden and Leveau 2001). This then reinforced the dominant French view that these actions were evidence that Muslims were incapable of assimilation and their presence in France was a threat to the secular state.

In this, as in many, identity conflicts, the different parties have little appreciation of the others' sense of vulnerability. To the Muslims, the French express arrogance, condescension, and little respect for Islam as the country's second largest religion. At the same time, many French non-Muslims interpret Muslims as lazy and/or extremist and worry that they are incapable of developing the values and lifestyle needed to become truly French. Consequently, relations between the French mainstream and Muslims are characterized by high tension surrounding issues such as suburban violence and crime,[30] as well as spillover from conflicts in North Africa and the Middle East.[31]

[29] Concern for French cultural survival can be seen in the work of the Académie Française in defense of the French language, legislation restricting non-French language shows and films on French television, and French subsidies for francophone cultural projects throughout the world.

[30] Discussions of suburban crime or problems of suburban youth have increasingly become code words for anti-immigrant positions in French political discourse (Chebel d'Appollonia 2002) in the the same way that in the late 1960s the phrase "crime in the streets" was a code for referring to black crime in the US.

[31] One small moment when many tried to bridge the cultural divide came in 1998 when the multicultural and multiracial French soccer team won the World Cup before a delirious home audience. However, the lesson that the team was victorious because of cooperation among culturally diverse players did not generalize to widespread support for multiculturalism. In fact, many drew a somewhat different lesson: that the team's success was evidence of French non-racialism and the importance of shared goals and common understandings, reinforcing their prior pride in French assimilation and the integration of (deserving, model) immigrants.

There is a strong resistance to the use of ethnic or racial categories within the Republican framework that emphasizes state neutrality in matters of culture and religion, but little French self-awareness of how these cultural assumptions privilege the majority. Kastoryano (1996) and Chebel d'Apollonia (2001; 2002) argue that the way in which French political discourse approaches the problem and frames action is a significant barrier to deescalation and the analysis here supports their argument. One consequence of the French refusal to recognize ethnic or religious communities is that France collects no data on religion, ethnicity, or national origin, making it difficult to document the fate of immigrants over time and to address structural problems involving minorities, such as housing, segregation, and social services that were cited as primary causes of the 2005 riots. In addition, there is tremendous opposition to using terms such as ghetto or ghettoization because they are viewed as inconsistent with Republican ideology and symptomatic of (inadequate) American and British approaches to race (Chebel d'Apollonia 2002). An important consequence of French rejection of sub-national identities means that the government often dismisses underlying issues of discrimination out of hand which means that policies such as affirmative action (which the French call positive discrimination) are rarely even considered (Bleich 2001). As a result, to date despite the large size of the Muslim population, there are very few Muslims in visible public roles, as elected officials, top administrators, or television personalities, which only reinforces feelings of exclusion.

Hargreaves suggests that the non-Muslim French view of Muslims has overemphasized their homogeneity creating unnecessary fears of a unified, fundamentalism Islamic communitarianism in France, or obstacles to the very integration the French have called for:

if the French are often anxious over what is seen as the threat of ethno-cultural minorities, it is in part because they mistake the phantoms created by their own ethnicization of minority groups for the much more diffuse modes of ethnicity which characterize many peoples of immigrant origin.

(Hargreaves 1995: 37)

A related issue is that Muslims are decentralized politically and have not been integrated into the existing political structure since the failure of the *Beurs* and socialists to effectively work together in the 1980s. In the unfolding psychocultural dramas, it was often unclear who could speak for the Muslims. No members of the National Assembly are of North African origin and they are unrepresented in other elected bodies as well. In such a setting, Cohen's (1969) observations about how minorities use cultural organization to deal with political challenges offer a good way to understand French Muslim organizations as multifunctional and especially relevant for within-group communication. Furthermore, in Islamic societies religion is not compartmentalized from other domains as it is in France and other Western countries. French non-Muslims often view religious images and practices as expressions of blind faith and communitarianism, missing their function as a mechanism of social connectedness.

Because the French are uneasy about intermediate identity groups between the individual and the nation, when ethnic or religious communities undertake independent actions of any kind they easily see them as threats to the nation and its sovereignty, putting the two on a collision course. Kymlicka makes a strong case for the generalizability of Canada's multicultural policies to countries like France. He argues that multiculturalism is about the terms, not the idea, of integration. He examines a series of multicultural policies in Canada ranging from affirmative action to bilingual education and argues that they facilitate institutional integration in a way that "in itself is likely to generate a sense of psychological identification" (Kymlicka 1998: 53). The key, he says, is that multiculturalism has an important symbolic value in that it "makes explicit the principle that the interests and lifestyles of immigrants are as worthy of respect (and accommodation) as those of the people descended from the country's original colonists" (Kymlicka 1998: 56). Looking at France, a country far from adopting such a position, he adds that even if France rejects the term multiculturalism, it cannot avoid the need for multicultural policies in practice. Finally, Kymlicka agrees that multicultural policies cannot be a license for immigrant groups to do whatever they choose in the name of cultural autonomy. Instead, he argues that the norms of Canada's liberal democratic polity set limits on what behaviors and practices are acceptable. To make his case, he distinguishes between group rights that permit groups to control the behavior of their members and stifle internal dissent, and the rights of the group against the wider society to protect it from external pressures. He views the first, which he calls internal restrictions, negatively, while supporting the second, external protections, in terms of basic notions of individual rights.

The model of multiculturalism in Canada supports the ability of immigrants to choose for themselves whether to maintain their ethnic identity. There is no suggestion that ethnic groups should have the power to impose a conception of cultural tradition or cultural purity on their members, or to regulate the freedom of individual members to accept or reject their ethnic identity.[32]

(Kymlicka 1998: 65)

Certainly his suggestions are very much at odds with the hard Republican narrative as is the cultural diversity found in France and most of Europe today. Although the conflict over the *foulard* focuses on a symbolic object, one reason the conflict continues is the failure to identify new or existing inclusive symbols and rituals that might bridge some differences and emphasize shared experiences, values, and identities. Bouzar (2001) and Chérifi (Simon, 2001) point to a need for greater emphasis on what Islam and the French Republican tradition have in common than there has been to date, and my argument is that this might be most effective if it is communicated in an emotionally meaningful manner through inclusive symbolic expressions and ritual enactments.

For now, the existing narratives about diversity and integration appear far apart and the media emphasize their incompatible positions. While the narrative that one can be French and Muslim at the same time is more common than in 1989, Kastoryano argues that movement forward requires explicit recognition of communities and negotiation of their differences surrounding identity issues which has not yet taken place (1996). Bowen (2004: 35) points toward ways that Islamic scholars are exploring compatibilities between Islamic social norms and those held more widely in France.

Exactly how a softer Republicanism can replace hard-line positions is far from obvious. It is likely, however, that a successful outcome will take one of two forms: (1) the pragmatic position (soft Republicanism) will prevail and there will be some acceptance of intermediate identity groups and even multiculturalism in France in particular and Europe in general; and/or (2) behaviors and practices previously considered non-French will become incorporated into what it means to be French (as happened earlier with Protestants and Jews). This is similar to what Zolberg and Woon (1999:14) call "attenuated pluralism" to describe arrangements in many European settings, including France, referring to arrangements involving funding legal access and recognition, tolerance of differences in

---

[32] Here is where the discourse justifying the headscarf law as protecting young girls from fathers and community members who oblige them to wear them is relevant. What is absent, however, are good data on the extent to which this, in fact, happens.

marriage and family laws, provision of burial facilities, chaplaincy in public institutions such as the military and prisons, and sometimes recognizing differences in religious education in schools and holidays in ways that can produce boundary crossing, blurring, and shifting over time.

A good outcome cannot result only from formal negotiations; if the psychocultural dramas over headscarves are to decline in intensity the parties will have to engage cultural and affective concerns as well as substantive issues and practices. Just as a person from Brittany or Provence can maintain a national and regional identity, and the classrooms in Alsace can have crosses on their walls, there needs to be a cultural space for people to be both French and Muslim. To do that there has to be more real engagement characterized by respect even though complicated issues including ones rooted in the country's colonial past are sure to provoke some tough moments for all.

8

The politics of memory and memorialization in post-apartheid South Africa

How people understand the past matters, because it can tell us a lot about how they think about the present and future. As Connerton says, "Our experience of the present very largely depends upon our knowledge of the past. We experience our present world in a context which is causally connected with past events and objects" (1998: 2). This point of view focuses not on establishing objective facts about past events but on how present needs shape what people believe and emphasize about the past, and how this affects present beliefs and actions. Narratives rely on metaphors and images about the past, offering general, practical lessons about groups, their motives, opportunities, and dangers; worldviews make sense of the past in ways that can render present action alternatives more or less plausible, exacerbate or lower anxiety, and facilitate or make less likely the peaceful settlement of disputes.

From this perspective, the past is fluid in terms of what people emphasize, worry about, commemorate, and celebrate. Popular and scholarly accounts of the past shift as particular details are selectively remembered and forgotten and as the specific lessons that are drawn from past events are selectively emphasized. For example, in South Africa, the focus of this chapter and the next, historian Leslie Witz (2003) argues that Jan van Riebeeck, the founder of the first Dutch settlement at the Cape in 1652 and long a symbol of Afrikaner anti-British pride, was recast more broadly as a white hero during the 300th anniversary celebrations in 1952, four years after the Afrikaner-led Nationalist Party took power in the country. This recasting was part of an effort to build white solidarity following a long period of intense British Afrikaner conflict.

Societies have many ways of remembering the past, including emotionally significant narratives and rituals associated with key events, sacred places, holidays, and historical personalities. Preserving memory is complicated, of course, since there will be differences of opinion in any society concerning which memories are most important and how they should be remembered. Levinson describes the complex process in changing societies by which decisions are made concerning public art and the narratives it embodies. He points out that "Public power within a given society organize[s] public space to convey (and thus to teach the public) desired political lessons. . . [that] always promote privileged narratives of the national experience and thus attempt to form a particular kind of national consciousness" (1998: 10). As we have already seen, cultural institutions both reflect and create images of the past and are sometimes at the center of conflicts over how the past should be represented and who controls the narrative and images associated with it (Linenthal 2001a).

The physical presence of monuments proclaims a narrative's legitimacy while at the same time freezing an account that is often literally set in stone at one point in time. As Crampton says, monuments "focus on the use of public space in the production of national images. They are important sites at which national traditions are invented and situated symbolically on the landscape and in the popular imagination" (2001: 223). Any effort to alter a monument intimately associated with an emotionally powerful narrative is a potential source of controversy, as loss of control over a symbolic space and the symbolic landscape is easily perceived as a threat to a group. Yet over time, meanings are renegotiated, sacred sites and rituals are transformed, and changes in the narratives a site presents and represents occur. For example, Verdun, a World War I battlefield site in Northern France where about 420,000 French and German soldiers died and probably twice as many were wounded, evolved from a patriotic French memorial site to one that now marks mutual loss and celebrates the post-1945 peaceful relationship between the long-time former enemies. At the core of such transformation is the replacement of mutually exclusive accounts by more joint inclusive images and an acceptance of, if not necessarily support for, the symbolic presence of the former opponents on the site.[1]

[1] A space associated with one group may be redefined to include others. For example, in the early post-Civil War years, monuments at Gettysburg were built for northern soldiers. Only after a generation did southern states get permission to build ones to their dead there as well. Simultaneously, the role of slavery as a cause of the conflict was fast fading from the narrative shared by northern and southern whites.

Dominant groups find it particularly difficult to share symbolic space with subordinate groups when they feel that their dominant position is at risk. This is seen clearly in the case of Orange Order parades discussed in Chapter 4 where the intensity and expression of aggression has increased as Protestant dominance in Northern Ireland has declined (Bryan 2000). Almost always, initial requests or demands for transforming exclusive monuments, memorials, and other sacred sites into more inclusive spaces are rejected. At other times, symbolically important sites are controlled by the keepers of the faith for whom a change in their orthodox account is quickly experienced as an attack on their identity or a political risk they are unwilling to take. For example, in 1991 the US government and President George H. W. Bush rejected proposals for Japanese participation in the 50th anniversary ceremonies at Pearl Harbor on the grounds that the Japanese government had not yet apologized for the attack. Similarly, in 1995 at Washington's National Aeronautics and Space Museum a proposed exhibit on the end of World War II and the decision to drop the atomic bomb was radically scaled back when veterans' groups vociferously objected to questions the exhibit planned to raise about President Harry S Truman's decision (Linenthal 1996).

Memorial sites serve as key linkage mechanisms to the past (as we saw in the case of Jerusalem in Chapter 6), and even though the content and narratives associated with them change over time, visitors often experience them as timeless. Most ritual behavior is presented as timeless, even though often we can observe the use of current categories to explain past behaviors, and implicitly assume that present group goals are the same as past ones.

Two different dynamics of change in memorial sites and the narratives associated with them can be identified. The first is incremental change that accumulates over time as a result of intergenerational transformations, and new shifting contextual demands. One example is how holiday celebrations evolve. In the United States, Memorial Day was a sacred civil-religious holiday for as long as there were living Civil War veterans (Warner 1959). In the second half of the twentieth century, while parades continued in many places, the tone of the celebrants became more casual and the day provided an occasion for families and friends to enjoy the long weekend that marked the start of the summer. The second change dynamic is one that occurs when modification in the meaning and/or physical structure of a site occurs in direct response to demands reflecting changing political alignments. In the US, since the 1960s, prior exclusion of women and minorities from history museums and textbooks has produced protests that have led to major shifts in how American history is presented. While in this case the movement was toward greater inclusiveness, movement toward exclusiveness also occurs as it did in Québec and Jerusalem.

Linenthal (1993) offers an excellent description of the transformation of a sacred site in his analysis of the Little Bighorn battlefield site and the power of the symbolic conflicts pitting competing narratives – General George Custer as savior and Custer as oppressor. His accounts of Little Bighorn, and of the politics of memorialization at four other major American battlefields, are instructive in showing how groups contest whose narratives will be told on a site and in so doing can transform memorial sites in a more inclusive direction.

In June 1876 at Little Bighorn in South Dakota, Lakota Sioux, Cheyenne, and Arapaho warriors defeated Custer's Seventh Cavalry troops. The battle assumed mythic proportions and three years later the US government built a national cemetery named the Custer National Battlefield. For nearly 100 years the story of the heroic defeat came to symbolize the sacrifices those bringing civilization to the frontier made and for decades what was called the "massacre" was remembered as a model of enduring bravery and sacrificial death (Linenthal 1993: 130–32). Only in the 1970s did Native Americans begin to succeed in publicly challenging the presentation of the battle and their exclusion from the site and the surrounding symbolic landscape.

At the Little Bighorn, Native Americans have sought to resurrect their story from an alien patriotic landscape and an alien orthodoxy that excluded them for a century. Often the only form of power available to those who are excluded from the ownership of important cultural symbols is symbolic guerrilla warfare.

(Linenthal 1993:163)

At the centenary celebrations in 1976, Native Americans directly challenged Custer's symbolic dominance on the site, and the National Park Service, which manages it, recognized the site's very one-sided nature. Finding a middle ground was not easy, however, and there was strong resistance to the Native Americans' efforts to overturn a century of symbolic domination (Linenthal 1993:143). Native Americans began to hold their own ceremonies and presented the battle in a very different interpretive framework. While Native Americans emphasized Custer as a symbol of their mistreatment by the US government, supporters of the traditional narrative attacked the placement of a quote from Sioux Medicine Man Black Elk outside the visitor center that reads, "Know the Power that Is Peace" as the pollution of sacred ground (Linenthal 1993:148). There were virtually no symbols that did not produce opposing reactions from each side. In 1988 there was another powerful symbolic confrontation when members of the American Indian Movement (AIM) placed a plaque in a cement base next to a monument on a burial area for enlisted men of the Seventh Cavalry whose inscription read, "In honor of our Indian patriots who fought and defeated the US Calvary [sic]. In order to preserve our women and children from mass murder. In doing so, preserving rights to our Homelands, Treaties, and sovereignty" (Linenthal 1993: 159).

The Park Service's proposal to change the name of the site from the Custer National Battlefield to the Little Bighorn Battlefield National Monument unleashed another extended controversy. Finally, in 1991 Congress authorized the change as well as the construction of an Indian memorial on the site; it was not dedicated until 2003, due in great part to conflict among Indian groups (Linenthal, personal communication). Both the site and the narratives recounted there have greatly changed their meaning. The current focus on the clashing cultures deemphasizes Custer, and attention to Indian culture and life in the region provides a much broader and more inclusive narrative. Visitors are now offered tours of nearby Indian reservations and sites. While some diehards on each side remain unsatisfied, they seem to be a distinct minority.

When a site is constructed, it represents a particular constructed truth that the site's presence validates. Change can occur and often the dynamic involved is highly contentious because this means that contending groups are also renegotiating their relationship. This dynamic by which sites and their narratives change includes the specific locations that are defined as part of a site; the structures themselves; the location and content of objects such as plaques and statues; the written texts and videos; how tour guides describe past events; and the use of inclusive *versus* exclusive language.

Heritage sites and the South African transition

Collective memory that is institutionalized in public sites such as battlefields and monuments often serves a legitimating function for a regime, and for the same reason these sites are also likely to serve as focal points of political protest for those attacking a regime. When regimes change in radical ways, we can deepen our understanding of the escalation and mitigation of conflict by asking when and how previously important sites of memory and group identity are appropriated, accepted, destroyed, taken over, transformed, moved, or ignored. Levinson argues that when there is radical regime change, often one of the first tasks of the new rulers is the destruction of the old symbols (Levinson 1998: 12). Widely known images of regime change include those of statuary with its heads cut off after the French Revolution and monuments to Lenin and Stalin smashed with the fall of the Soviet Union. However, there are other possibilities, as Levinson (1998) points out, such as the Hungarian case where monuments from previous regimes were not destroyed but were removed to a park in Budapest where they are visible as historical, rather than contemporary, objects.

South Africa provides another striking example. The entrenched apartheid government perpetrated a racialized system of inequality and legal separation of the country's residents based on the government's constructed racial categories. Intense conflict went on for decades and politics seemed more and more stuck. Despite UN resolutions, diplomatic isolation, and economic boycotts, few foresaw the rapid negotiated transition in 1990–94 that led to universal elections and majority rule.[2] Furthermore, even given that change, few predicted the relatively non-violent manner of the transition after the elections, or the level of acceptance of the new government and its values that followed (Gibson and Gouws 2003). While the country continues to face huge challenges, its progress and stability to date make it a particularly interesting and important place to explore issues of symbolic representation and political transition. My attention in this chapter and the one that follows focuses on the transformation of an exclusive public, symbolic landscape into a more inclusive one in the post-apartheid period.

The vision of the new South Africa

The 1990–94 transition to majority rule in South Africa broke with the past in a number of dramatic and important ways, including the adoption of a new non-racial constitution that ended apartheid and instituted majority rule. The African National Congress (ANC) and the South

---

[2] Here I do not engage the important question of how a transition that few social scientists and other observers expected took place, although this fascinating question still remains mainly unaddressed and unanswered.

African Communist Party (SACP) had long emphasized how colonialism and capitalism constructed and employed racial and ethnic categories in their politics of domination. In addition, they had long emphasized the role that individuals from all groups had played in the anti-apartheid struggle. Nelson Mandela's statements and actions upon his release from prison had reaffirmed the commitment to build a non-racial society based on the equality of all people. South Africa's new leaders sought to avoid a vindictive and/or exclusive approach that would have been a political mirror image of the apartheid years, and therefore incompatible with the goal of reconciliation and the inclusive political vision that apartheid's opponents had articulated for decades. Thus, whites who wanted to remain in South Africa and participate in building a new "rainbow nation" would be fully accepted.[3]

Complementing its commitment to inclusion, the new government's decision to ensure widespread public testimony concerning the practices of the apartheid era and the many ways they had affected the country's citizens was of particular importance in the change process. Perhaps the most dramatic way this was carried out was through the Truth and Reconciliation Commission (TRC) that in 1995 was charged with examining gross human rights abuses committed during the apartheid era by both the government and liberation groups. It sought to make public the stories of victims and perpetrators in the belief that public recounting of people's experiences could be healing for individuals and the society (Minow 1998). Hearings were held throughout the country over many months and excerpts were televised daily. There is no doubt that the TRC process was incredibly powerful emotionally for many South Africans. Many whites who had dismissed stories of government atrocities as propaganda learned that they were real, while many blacks and some whites had their own experiences of victimization, or those of family members, validated (Hamber and Kibble n.d.; Krog 1999).

The TRC process clearly had an impact on South Africans in all racial groups. Gibson's (2004) data show that a large portion of the blacks, whites, coloured and Asians accept the TRC's core conclusions, and its work seems to have had some influence in creating a South African collective memory (Gibson 2004: 155). However, Gibson also finds that

---

[3] The image of the rainbow does not deny differences but emphasizes the way differences come together to produce a totality in which the parts combine such that the whole is more than the sum of its parts.

group identities filter how the past is understood and affect the extent to which acceptance of the TRC process and its findings are related to racial reconciliation and political tolerance. This collective mutual acknowledgment of pain and suffering appears to have mitigated some emotional barriers, and pressures for revenge, that might have made a vision of an inclusionary future impossible to share or to implement.

The "rainbow" vision of the new government, reinforced by the TRC process, has led to a great variety of efforts to recognize the country's multicultural past. Recognizing local and other identities will, it is felt, work toward building attachment to the country as a whole. For example, the country now has eleven official languages; and departments of "heritage" have been created in many of the country's universities to facilitate the study of South Africa's past in ways that go beyond official history. Narratives recounted to tourists in the disparate sites around the country emphasize its diversity and traditions, in ways that Rassool, Minkley and Witz (1996) call a narrative of "the world in one country," through a set of handy essentialisms, and snapshot histories that provide an exalted sense of knowing the whole. A past–present relationship is established through the gaze on human culture scripted as tradition and designed as authentic (Rassool and Witz 1996; Witz, Rassool, and Minkley 2001). These strategies raise concerns about the tension between focusing on acknowledging diversity that meets one set of needs, and the potential reification of colonial and apartheid-era racial and ethnic categories used in popular and tourist narratives that, once developed, become hard to modify (Witz, Rassool, and Minkley 2001).

Symbolizing the vision

The new government, highly conscious of the importance of symbolic presentations, appointed commissions that put a great deal of energy into the question of monuments, memorials, and museums. Other groups considered the issue of the flag, the national anthem, the coat of arms, public holidays, and languages (Wessels 1994). A widespread consensus soon evolved that the apartheid years and resistance to apartheid needed to be documented and memorialized in a variety of ways but that wholesale destruction of existing symbolic places or objects would not occur. However, the extent to which apartheid and post-apartheid era symbols and structures could coexist, and what forms they might take, was unclear at the outset. In 1999, Parliament created the South African Heritage Resource Agency (SAHRA) charged with implementing policies concerning heritage resources. SAHRA developed decisionmaking procedures for preserving older sites and buildings and for implementing a national heritage policy that would nurture a holistic celebration of the country's history with a particular eye toward healing and material and symbolic restitution.

Against this background, an obvious question regarding public symbolic space and regime change is what happened to the monuments, memorials, museums, and other sites representing the previous regime's core values and memories when the new South African government came to power. Many of the symbolic changes that some had thought likely did not occur. For example, there was no destruction of monuments and statues honoring the former white rulers and apartheid, although a few statues and portraits were moved out of prominent locations.[4] There was no construction of a new capitol. There was no closing of monuments, museums, and sacred Afrikaner sites. There was no wholesale renaming of cities, streets, and public parks.[5] Rather, it was widely accepted that whatever was done needed to take place within the ANC's long-stated non-racial framework with a focus toward building an inclusive society.

In examining memorials, monuments, and museums in South Africa, my goal here and in Chapter 9 is to explore the transformation of important parts of the symbolic landscape and the South African past, present, and future in the early post-apartheid years. To do this I look at memory sites and interpretations of the past at four heritage sites – the Voortrekker Monument outside Pretoria, Blood River and Ncome in KwaZulu Natal, and Robben Island and the District Six Museum in Cape Town – to examine how they recount the past and its lessons for the present and future. Underlying this analysis is the hypothesis that the narratives recounted in these and other significant symbolic sites can

---

[4] For example, the statue of Hendrick Verwoerd, the former prime minister who was widely recognized as apartheid's chief architect, was removed from the grounds of the Union Buildings in Pretoria, the seat of the country's executive branch.

[5] There have been some debates about names and some name changes, however. For example, beginning in 2003 there has been a vigorous and sometimes heated debate over renaming Pretoria, the country's capital that was named for Andreis Pretorius, the Boer Trekker leader at the Battle of Blood River in 1838. In 2005 the municipal council changed the name of the metropolitan area to Tshwane, after an African chief who ruled the regions prior to white arrival, while retaining Pretoria as the name for the central business district. The name Tshwane means "we are the same."

be crucial in articulating and reinforcing a new more inclusive narrative of the South African national experience (Gibson 2004).

In South Africa we can identify three strategies of transformation as part of post-conflict peacebuilding: *appropriation*, meaning associating the older holidays, symbolic places and buildings with the new regime's practices and institutions; *modification*, marking events and narratives that previously had received little or no public attention through physical alterations at an existing site, changing the story told on it, broadening the audience it is aimed at, and/or a shift in the objects exhibited; and in *addition*, creating new symbolic sites where the stories of previous oppression, struggle, and triumph are told. It should be noted, however, that while the analytic distinction between these three strategies is clear, they often occur in varying combinations at a given site.

Transformation of older symbolic spaces

While building new sacred locations of memory that acknowledge past injustices and horrific actions committed in the name of apartheid has been important in South Africa since 1994, the daunting challenge that I consider in this chapter involves the transformation through appropriation and modification of older sites intimately associated with the apartheid regime. Appropriation, which took a number of different forms, proved to be simpler than many had expected; modification has been slower and more complicated. Modification of a sacred site is never simple, as Linenthal's (1993) research tells us. Chapter 9 will focus on the strategy of addition.

Appropriation

The simplest, and in some ways most visible, forms of appropriation involved state institutions once associated with exclusive white rule, such as the Parliament in Cape Town and the Union Buildings in Pretoria. The new government and post-apartheid leaders simply took over these sites and used them to conduct business. For many, the image of Nelson Mandela taking the oath of office as president before hundreds of thousands of blacks, coloureds, Asians and whites in front of the Union Buildings evoked intense emotions and signaled the tremendous transformation that had taken place in the country. Likewise, the multiracial character of the new Parliament and the new voices heard within it had a

233

huge symbolic significance on the country as once outlawed and banned groups came to power in a peaceful, democratic election. The substitution of Nationalist Party apartheid-era officials with those from the ANC and other formerly banned groups including the South African Communist Party was symbolically dramatic. Most of the new leaders' faces were black ones and they included not only ex-prisoner Nelson Mandela but also the new defense minister, Joe Modise, who had headed the ANC's military wing while in exile, as well as other ANC and CP members reviled by many whites for years. Just as jarring was the appointment of whites such as Joe Slovo, the long exiled, one-time head of the South African Communist Party, as minister of housing, and Albie Sachs, a high-ranking exiled leader whom the South African Defense Forces had severely wounded in a car bomb attack, as head of the Constitutional Court.

Some sites were both appropriated and modified in dramatic ways. In Johannesburg, the Old Fort Prison which held political and other prisoners during the apartheid era was renovated and renamed Constitution Hill and now houses the country's Constitutional Court.

Many symbolic appropriations occurred in a comparatively short time, communicating both change and continuity. Continuity stressed a commitment to efficiency and sound fiscal management, a message that was particularly important to whites in general and the business community in particular. The change message emphasized the new values that would guide the ANC led government: an end to racially based allocation of resources, and a vigorous commitment to redressing past inequalities on social issues such as education and housing. The message of non-white inclusion was clear as public officials committed themselves to new programs and parts of the country that apartheid-era officials rarely visited.

Modification

Modification occurs when the group controlling a site alters some key elements in the site's meaning and presentation. There have been many such changes in South Africa – in the universities, in housing, employment, and government. Modification of a site's symbolic meaning differs from appropriation in that control over the site does not necessarily shift from one group to another. In South Africa, given that the new government's commitment to a multicultural society was central to its nation-building project, there have been no steps taken to appropriate non-governmental sites associated with the Afrikaners.

234

In thinking about the problem generally, Coombes points out the need to ask about the:

possibilities and impossibilities for rehabilitating . . . monument [s] with an explicit history as a foundational icon of the apartheid State . . . how far it is possible to disinvest such an icon of its Afrikaner nationalist associations and reinscribe it with new resonances which enable it to remain a highly public monument despite a new democratic government whose future is premised on the demise of everything it has always stood for.

(Coombes 2000: 173–74)

She also considers how monuments from the apartheid period are subject to public reinterpretation that can serve as "a staging post for self-fashioning for both black and white constituencies across the political spectrum" (2000: 175) through rich and varied examples of how the Voortrekker Monument served as a setting for identity redefinition in recent years.

The challenge to South Africa's apartheid-era sites at the emotional core of Afrikaner identity concerns their ability to now emphasize their role in the country's contemporary cultural diversity rather than in its political past. For decades, the narrative offered at the Voortrekker Monument just outside Pretoria, and at Blood River, a battle site in KwaZulu-Natal, provided a narrative of conquest that joined political and cultural images. The story of Afrikaner history recounted in the organization and images of each site was central to Afrikaner political identity and the Nationalist Party's political project. Given the emotional significance of these sites and their close association with white domination and apartheid, it was not evident what their role would be in the post-apartheid era. There was talk, for example, of tearing down the Voortrekker monument as a way of symbolizing the destruction of apartheid, as well as a suggestion to paint it pink and to turn it into a gay nightclub. Another, probably more serious, proposal was made to turn the lower level of the monument, which contains the cenotaph and the flame of civilization and which some consider the most sacred part of the monument, into an exhibition on the struggle against apartheid and the country's political transformation (Kruger 2002: 89). Similarly, there were many who wondered how the narrative at Blood River, which commemorates what some believe is the divinely inspired victory of a few hundred Boers who managed to kill 3,000 Zulu warriors in 1838, could continue to be recounted.

Forced modification of either site would surely have been perceived as an attack on the Afrikaners as a group and produced a strong counter-reaction that would have been very much at odds with the ANC's decision to emphasize reconciliation and tolerance. Because neither the Voortrekker Monument nor Blood River is now a government run or funded site,[6] and because the new government did not want to mandate specific changes in either, they offer important lessons in the dynamics of symbolic politics and the complex issues involved in transforming exclusive symbolic spaces into more inclusive ones. The stories of what has happened to date in both of these sites are not straightforward and in neither place can we say that there is a simple outcome that pleases everyone. In the rest of this chapter, I consider the case of the Voortrekker Monument, built to commemorate the migration of many Boers from the coast to the interior in the 1830s. Before discussing the monument, I offer an overview of the Afrikaner historical narrative, since it is central to the monument's design and images (Delmont 1993; Moodie 1975).

The Afrikaner historical narrative and the Voortrekker Monument

Afrikaner identity and cohesiveness emerged over several centuries, illustrating the interaction of identity construction and political context. Jan van Riebeeck, long celebrated by Afrikaners as the founder of the first settlement in Cape Town to provision ships sailing around Africa to Asia, is presented as the symbolic creator of white South Africa and the bearer of Christian civilization (Witz 2003). Settlement was primarily along the western coast where the Dutch met, and fought with, local black groups – the Hottentots and Khoi. Among the early settlers were Germans, Portuguese, French Huguenots, slaves from Madagascar, and so-called Malays (primarily from Indonesia). There is no evidence that the first settlers saw themselves as a cohesive group although they came to share a common language, Dutch, which later evolved into Afrikaans. Giliomee says that prior to 1850 Afrikaner identity was seldom invoked as a political claim (1989: 22).

---

[6] During and after the political transition, the status of these sites changed. The FAK, an Afrikaner cultural-nationalist organization purchased the Voortrekker monument in 1992 (Kruger 2002). However, as modification of their narratives has occurred, and the museum has become more inclusive, some government subsidies have been provided.

Afrikaner ethnic and political consciousness emerged in the nineteenth century in response to the arrival of the British in the late 1700s. After 1806, when the British took over the Cape, and especially after 1820 when British immigrants began to arrive, there was conflict with the earlier settlers, a significant number of whom moved eastward where they sometimes fought with local Xhosa groups. Unhappy with British rule, many Afrikaans speakers decided to move to the interior when in 1833 the British abolished slavery. Here is the explanation of the situation from the Voortrekker Monument's Guidebook:

At the beginning of the 19th century the Cape was conquered by Britain. For the pioneers at the eastern border this did not bring about any improvement in their living conditions, which in fact deteriorated because the Cape government did not show any understanding of their problems. Conditions at the eastern border became unbearable . . . They developed a strong feeling of independence and lamented the lack of self-government . . . A need arose among the pioneers to find a country that was beyond the reach of the Cape government where they would be able to live in peace and freedom.

(Heymans 1986: 5)

Over a half dozen years, many small groups set off in ox-drawn wagons with their household possessions, livestock, servants, and slaves to find a homeland in the interior, as part of a process later termed the Great Trek. Not all groups headed to the same place. Some moved far north into what became the Transvaal; others settled in the latter-day Orange Free State; and some tried to settle in what today is KwaZulu Natal (Figure 8.1). In all cases the journey itself was slow and difficult, testing the commitment and skills of the Boers. It was also dangerous, as there was at times significant conflict with local black groups. In some cases, they were able to negotiate alliances while in others there was fighting.[7]

In the Afrikaner foundation narrative the most significant conflict developed when a group of Trekkers, headed by Piet Retief, sought to negotiate the right to land from Dignane, the Zulu leader, in early 1838. In the Afrikaner narrative, after Dignane had agreed to accept the settlers, he invited them to a feast during which his warriors turned on the group and massacred them.[8] Later that same year, some 12,000 Zulu attacked a group of Afrikaners, now led by Andries Pretorius, at Ncome

[7] Some see strong parallels between the Trekker experience and that of Europeans settling the American west.
[8] This story is presented in a 1939 Hollywood film "Building a Nation" that is nothing short of pure Afrikaner propaganda.

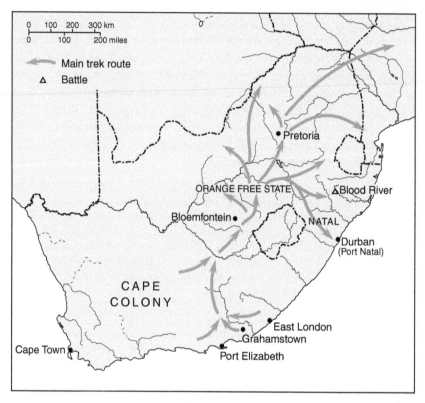

Figure 8.1 Map of South Africa with Trek routes

on December 16, 1838. It is said that the group of some 450 men had earlier vowed that if they survived they would declare a Sabbath day and build a church to honor God who delivered the victory. Sure enough, the Boer defenders who circled their sixty-four wagons into a defensive laager fought off the Zulu, killing some 3000 attackers, and forcing the remaining warriors to withdraw, while suffering only three injuries and no deaths to themselves.[9] The battle, named Blood River after the Zulu blood that supposedly turned the river red, was remembered as a testament to the Boers' religious faith and commemorated in Pretorius' church forty years later in Pietermaritzburg.

---

[9] There is good reason to be skeptical concerning the number of Zulu deaths because of the relatively primitive weapons the Afrikaners possessed, their inaccuracy, and the time needed to reload the guns after firing.

238

Thompson (1985: 154–68) says there was little contemporaneous evidence for key elements of the story concerning the covenant and that much of it comes from Saral Cilliers's 1871 deathbed statement focusing on the piety of the group and his own role as its religious leader. However, I am less concerned with the truth or falsity of the story's details than with their emotional power and relevance for the lessons Afrikaners drew from them a century later. As Akenson points out in his discussion of the significance of the memory of Blood River, "historical links do not have to be accurate in order for them to be real" (Akenson 1992: 68).

For Afrikaners, December 16 is the most sacred day in their civil-religious calendar. Akenson reports that it was first marked by a commemorative service on the site of the battle in 1864 and known until 1938 as Dugaan's Day (after the defeated Zulu leader); then it was called the Day of the Covenant, and subsequently renamed the Day of the Vow in 1980 (Akenson 1992: 66). Celebrations recount the Afrikaner struggle to escape the yoke of British colonialism and the miracle of the Afrikaner military victory.[10] Akenson (1992) suggests that analyzing the December 16 celebrations over time offers "a useful window" into the half-empirical, half-metaphorical Afrikaner self-understanding of their history. For him, the covenantal language drawn from the Exodus story with its "prediction of continued and wearying strife, and a prescription for how to deal with the ever-present enemies" is of particular significance (Akenson 1992: 67).[11]

The Afrikaners created two independent states, the Transvaal and Orange Free State, in the early 1850s, and fought a war (variously called the First Anglo-Boer War and the first War of Independence) in 1880–81 to defend their autonomy, rejecting British colonial rule. Paul Kruger, the president of the South African Republic (SAR) and a militant Afrikaner cultural nationalist, sought to guard the fledgling state's independence, but with the discovery of gold in and around Johannesburg in the 1880s and the influx of thousands of people, the British were intent on controlling the territory and its wealth. The result was the bloody Second

---

[10] During the apartheid era December 16 was a public holiday in South Africa marking the Afrikaner's perseverance, faith, and triumph. Since the transition, the day is still a public holiday, but to make it more inclusive it is now named The Day of Reconciliation. Many Afrikaners still celebrate it as the Day of the Vow although in a much more low key manner than during the apartheid period. Chapter 9 discusses the Afrikaner celebrations in recent years that mark the day at Blood River.

[11] Akenson (1992) emphasizes the power of the covenantal metaphor for Afrikaners but also for Protestants in Northern Ireland and Jews in Israel.

Anglo-Boer War of 1899–1902 in which for a time Boer forces used guerrilla tactics to thwart superior British numbers and resources. In response the British engaged in a scorched earth policy, and placed thousands of Afrikaner women and children in concentration camps where some 25,000 perished.[12] For many Afrikaners, this event constitutes their "chosen trauma," a significant loss that a group cannot fully mourn and integrate into the present. Asking about it today still evokes powerful emotions. Note, however, that in this trauma the enemy is not indigenous blacks, but the British.

The victorious British then created the Union of South Africa in 1910, bringing together the two former Afrikaner republics and the British Cape and Natal. While Afrikaner nationalists were defeated militarily, they refused to give up the vision of their own state. By the 1930s the Afrikaners were seriously split between those who were satisfied with the country's autonomy within the British Commonwealth and more anti-British, cultural nationalist Afrikaners who favored an independent republic. The pro-republicans had strong ties to the Afrikaner Broederbond founded in 1918, an elite secret brotherhood emphasizing ethnic consciousness, and the FAK, a federation of Afrikaner cultural organizations (Moodie 1975: 99–115; Delmont, 1993: 78–80). Both emphasized the ethnic component of culture, especially the need for the preservation of Afrikaner culture – particularly its language – and articulated a "Christian National" ideology that in some versions closely resembled German National Socialism. What was central to this civil religion was that it could be achieved only in a republic in which Afrikaners controlled the public sphere, mother-tongue education, and racial separation (Moodie 1975: 110–13).

The fortunes of the hard-line nationalists rose in the late 1930s when the centenary celebrations of the battle of Blood River crystallized nationalist fervor. As the anniversary approached, a number of plans were drawn up including the erection of monuments to the Trekkers in both Blood River and Pretoria. However, the most emotionally significant part of the celebration was a symbolic retracing of the steps of the Voortrekkers that Henning Klopper, who had earlier founded the Broederbond, organized through the ATKV (the Afrikaans Language and

---

[12] The government renamed the war the South African War in recognition that blacks as well as whites were involved and suffered, and museum displays in Pretoria as well as in small towns such as Ladysmith now acknowledge the involvement of all South Africans in the war.

Cultural Union of the South African Railways and Harbours) (Moodie 1975: 176–77). This quasi-religious political pilgrimage began in Cape Town at the foot of van Riebeeck's statue. Following a reading of the sacred vow, the pilgrimage wound its way to Pretoria in two replica ox-drawn wagons used one hundred years earlier. What started as a small-scale event continued to expand, capturing the imagination of many Afrikaners, and a certain number of English speakers as well. As it made its way north there were increasing demands for the wagons to visit small towns and villages where religious services were often held (Moodie 1975).

The sacred history was constituted and actualized as a general context of meaning for all Afrikanerdom in spontaneous liturgical re-enactment during the 1938 celebrations. Passionate enthusiasm seized Afrikaans-speaking South Africa. Men grew beards and women donned Voortrekker dress; street after street in hamlet after hamlet was renamed after one or another trek hero; babies were baptized in the shade of the wagons . . . and young couples were married in full trekker regalia on the village green before the wagons . . . At night folks would gather around the campfires of the trekkers in their hundreds and thousands to sing traditional Afrikaans [folksongs] and the old Dutch psalms, to watch scenes from the Voortrek enacted in pantomime, and to thrill to inspired sermons culled from the depths of civic faith. . . Wreaths were laid on the graves of all the Afrikaner heroes. . . Holy ground was thus resanctified by the visit of the wagons.

(Moodie 1975: 180–81)

Eventually, additional wagons were built and the celebrations reached their climax when nine wagons reached Pretoria where, on December 16 over 100,000 Afrikaners gathered for the celebration and the cornerstone was laid for the Voortrekker monument (Figure 8.2). Historians see the intense emotional outpourings linking Afrikaner cultural and political identity as central to the Nationalist Party's electoral victory a decade later in 1948. The following year on December 16, 1949, as part of an even larger four-day celebration with 250,000 celebrants, the Voortrekker Monument was dedicated.[13]

The monument is a massive stone construction atop a hill just outside Pretoria next to Schanskop Fort, one of four built to defend the city in the Anglo-Boer War, and in sight of the Union Buildings (Delmont 1993: 80). There is a granite laager of sixty-four wagons surrounding the building offering symbolic protection, and on the corners of the outside

---

[13] Although the cornerstone of the monument was laid on December 16, 1938, due to World War II it was not completed until 1949.

Figure 8.2 Voortrekker Monument, Pretoria. The Voortrekker Monument on the left and a statue of a Trekker mother and child on the right located near the entrance

of the monument are statues of three named Trekker leaders and one who is unknown. Close to the monument's entrance is a statue of a carved mother and child (Figure 8.2) that "symbolizes the culture and Christianity that were maintained and developed by the women during the Great Trek" (Heymans 1986: 6). Inside the monument are two significant symbolic spaces. The first is the twenty-seven friezes made from Italian marble that recount the story of the Trek from its beginnings in the 1830s to British recognition of the Transvaal Republic in 1852, filling the walls of the large dome-covered room on the entrance level (Figure 8.3).[14] The second is the monument's lower hall that contains two particularly significant objects that are visible from above: a niche against one wall holding an eternal flame that symbolizes civilization in South Africa, and at the center an empty cenotaph representing the symbolic resting place of Retief and his comrades and the Voortrekkers' spirit of sacrifice and suffering (Delmont 1993: 81). The cenotaph is laid out so that a ray of sunlight shines on the words, "We for thee South Africa" (in Afrikaans) carved on December 16.

---

[14] Delmont (1993) offers a detailed analysis of the individual panels and their significance in the Afrikaner narrative.

242

Figure 8.3 One of the 27 marble friezes in the Voortrekker monument showing "Battle against the Nbebelle at eGabeni/Kapain, 1837" one of the many attacks to which the Voortrekkers were subjected

The 1949 inaugural ceremony celebrated Afrikaner culture while laying out "a vision of society that legitimated the social ordering of South Africa under apartheid" (Crampton 2001: 224) and made up what Crampton characterizes as "the festival community." He analyzes the core themes at the Voortrekker Monument's inauguration that stressed the Afrikaners as an authentic nation that had tamed the African interior, bringing white, Christian civilization to it. There were calls for white unity, but it was clear that while the English could be accepted as partners in the nation-building project, it was the Afrikaners who would be the senior members of the team.

The opening of the monument just a short time after the Nationalists came to power and began to implement apartheid meant that the massive stone monument symbolized Afrikaner domination and power, and through its narrative the monument communicated, reflected, and justified Nationalist party leaders' vision of apartheid. Over time, however, key elements were challenged. By 1988, foreshadowing the changes de Klerk would make after his election, including the release of Mandela, the legalization of the ANC, and the negotiations to majority rule, the 150th celebration of the Great Trek at the monument revealed important

243

changes in the Afrikaner narrative. Speakers emphasized the forward-looking aspects of the pioneer Trekkers and stressed the need for a new political future requiring "sacrifices and compromises in an attempt to ensure their political survival" meaning power sharing (Grundlingh and Sapire 1989: 32). The new spirit "acknowledged the role of blacks, both in the original trek itself and in contemporary South African political, economic and social life" (Grundlingh and Sapire 1989: 32), and the FAK's public statement calling upon Afrikaners to "understand its role in the past without 'belittling' any other groups and to exercise reason rather than emotionalism in response to the celebrations, was a striking departure from the past as Afrikaners were urged to use the occasion to demonstrate that the enmities of Blood River had finally been buried" (Grundlingh and Sapire 1989: 32). Until 1992 when the FAK purchased the monument in anticipation of a new government (Coombes 2000), the government fully funded it, and during the transition period it was a site at which hard-line whites opposed to the negotiations held rallies.

Given the monument's close association with Afrikaner cultural nationalism and political domination, it was not clear that the building would survive the transition and remain part of the landscape in a new, non-racial South Africa. A psychocultural drama over its future began that escalated far less than many people expected. It is important for the analysis developed here to consider why this was the case.[15] For the Voortrekker Monument to operate as a cultural site would require an energetic effort to decouple Afrikaner culture from the politics of apartheid. Not an easy task. Indeed there were calls for its destruction, radical transformation, and appropriation, as noted above. The new government, however, did not compel any change in the monument. Nevertheless, as an independent cultural institution, it did not prosper in the early post-apartheid years.

The Monument's new leadership that was put in place in 2000 has worked to recast the Voortrekker Monument as a cultural, rather than political, institution. The challenge is how to do this while neither reviving divisive memories of apartheid among non-Afrikaners nor seeming to abandon the core Afrikaner values embedded in the monument. Working toward this goal has not been easy, however, for while the monument's

---

[15] In 1992 "History Workshop" held a Conference at which its future was discussed and a poster from the session shows the Voortrekker Monument teetering on its side possibly about to be pulled over.

contents make no explicit references to the apartheid era, the iconography and many of the objects in it were central images associated with white rule. In the twenty-seven marble friezes, for example, the overwhelming proportion of the images of blacks show them as fighting with, and often murdering or being murdered by the Voortrekkers, while presenting the Boers as courageous and inspiring.

The current leadership has taken some initial inclusive steps to emphasize the Voortrekker Monument as an Afrikaner cultural institution. One is its effort to attract black school children to the monument; they report that in some months there are three times more black school children than whites visiting.[16] A second is the development of a new museum-like exhibit in the lower floor of the monument that emphasizes cultural history rather than political images. It contains a presentation on the Great Trek that locates it in the context of human migrations more generally. There is also a good deal on Afrikaner heritage through material culture presented in displays of nineteenth-century tools, clothing, furniture, and farming that emphasize details about daily life; little in this exhibit evokes the most emotional parts of the political narrative.

A third strategy for inclusivity is emphasis on the parts of the site that go beyond the monument itself. These are Fort Schanskop, an amphitheater that can seat 20,000 people, a series of hiking, bike, and horse trails, a picnic area, an art gallery, ecology courses, and a planned campground. Many Afrikaners support the multiple uses of the site, and this is not surprising given Cohen's (1969) observations concerning the importance of cultural organizations when explicit political organization around identity is not likely to be productive. The site leadership is also developing a Garden of Remembrance, which will offer 6,500 niches holding individual last remains following cremation, and will address the "growing problems at traditional cemeteries . . . due to the general fall in standards and the high level of crime in the country" (press release 27/9/02).[17]

---

[16] It was suggested to me that black teachers are often more willing to bring students to the monument than white ones, who because of the monument's association with apartheid are either uninterested in visiting it or are embarrassed to do so.

[17] One motivation for this project arose from Afrikaner concerns about vandalization of their cemeteries. Obviously this is aimed at Afrikaners for it is not very likely that there will be many non-Afrikaners who seek "a dignified last resting place in a culturally sympathetic environment, in the shade of the Monument."

A fourth step toward inclusion has been an explicit effort to legitimize the monument by building bridges to the government agencies and political leaders. This has led to the return of, and then to recent increases in, government funding. In South Africa, there is nothing more valuable for a white cultural group seeking legitimation than a positive word from Nelson Mandela and he has spoken out in support of the site. In 2000 Mandela wrote to potential donors asking them to contribute to the monument's renewal projects. Then, in early 2002 he visited the Voortrekker Monument Heritage Site, delivered a speech, part of which was in Afrikaans, and laid a wreath beside the statue of Anglo-Boer (South African War) war hero Danie Theron. In his remarks Mandela stressed his esteem for the Afrikaner people and their resistance to imperial domination. He said he had learned a good deal from Afrikaner generals and "that shared experience of fighting for one's freedom binds us in a manner that is most profound."[18] He noted that Blacks and Afrikaners shared a common experience in struggling against British colonial rule. Finally, his inclusive comments acknowledged the role of Afrikaners in the country's development, noting that Theron's patriotism "would in the present circumstances have translated into a passion that we jointly build and develop this country for the common good of all."[19]

Conclusion

Transformation of sacred spaces is most likely to be rapid when it is imposed, as in the situations of appropriation following regime change. In pluralistic systems where there is a reluctance to forcing change in spaces or institutions associated with ethnic, religious, or regional communities, transformation can be slow and complicated, as is illustrated in the cases of Little Bighorn in the United States and the Voortrekker Monument in South Africa.

Guardians of sacred spaces such as religious sites, monuments, and battlefields frequently freeze a group's narrative at one point in time, think of it as recounting a literal, rather than metaphorical, truth, and see defending the narrative and the sacred spaces as defending their group. As a result, the guardians often see what appears to those outside the group

---

[18] www.theherald.co.za/herald/2002/03/07/news/theron.htm.
[19] www.theherald.co.za/herald/2002/03/07/news/theron.htm. The fact that some right-wing Afrikaner groups loudly protested Mandela's visit in 2002 only serves to further help the new administration separate itself from the apartheid-era policies.

as a modest request for change as an enormous and unrealistic demand. Furthermore, when the guardians do show some flexibility, there are frequently voices within their own community that accuse them of betrayal. This dynamic means that despite the language commonly used to describe ethnic conflict which emphasizes opposing ethnic communities as internally unified, the social and political reality is one of significant within-group differentiation. All large collectivities have diverse voices and there is within-group political competition as various factions claim to be the group's most legitimate representatives.

The Little Bighorn case reminds us of how slow and complicated the change process can be even when there is a third party – in this case the US National Park Service – as the manager of a site. The bitterness between the Custerphiles and Custerphobes made it difficult to mediate between the conflicting demands. In addition, significant differences among the Native American groups further complicated the process since they were not unified in their demands, reminding us how hard it sometimes is to alter a site once its meanings have literally been set in stone.

These lessons are certainly relevant to considering the possibilities for modifying the Voortrekker Monument and the psychocultural drama that did not escalate around its continued existence. To their credit, both the new managers of the site and the government worked to find some common ground and to avoid open conflict. General Opperman and his staff emphasize the changes they have achieved in reorienting the site as a cultural institution, and the government has recognized this through their increased funding. To an outsider, these changes feel modest; but those on the inside experience them as significant, a view that is reinforced each time there are attacks on the current site leadership from hard-line Afrikaner nationalists, such as those that occurred over Mandela's 2002 visit.

There is certainly some shift in the Monument's emphasis through the development of additional activities on the site, the addition of cultural exhibits in the new museum space, and the absence of any explicit link between the monument and exhibits in it and apartheid. However, given the strong political message the monument communicated in the past, separation of the connection probably requires that there eventually be bolder, explicit steps, not just implicit ones. When I visited in February 2003, the art gallery contained portraits of all the former heads of state and of the Transvaal government that had once hung in the union Buildings and Transvaal government offices. While there was explicit acknowledgment that these were not consistent with the Monument's current mission, the staff found themselves in a position where they felt that rejecting the portraits was not possible.[20] When asked if there was any thought about adding portraits of Mandela and President Thabo Mbeki to the group, the response was they were concerned about the reaction this would provoke from some Afrikaners.[21]

Separating the monument from apartheid and Nationalist Party rule is a daunting task indeed considering that its entire existence until 1994 was so intimately related to the NP rule and Afrikaner nationalism. It is not clear whether the modest steps toward this goal are sufficient in light of the very different experiences and perceptions among white and black South Africans. Because the dominant narrative links the monument and apartheid so strongly, explicit references are not needed to maintain it. For most blacks the Trek was a step toward political conquest and the creation of an Afrikaner dominated state. The connections are obvious and seamless and the challenge is how to *remove* an association that is so firmly established.[22]

Rather than demanding a change in the Monument itself, some Afrikaners and blacks have stressed modest points of convergence between the Afrikaner and black narratives, as in the 1988 anniversary celebrations and Mandela's 2002 speech at the Voortrekker Monument. As far back as the 1980s mainstream Afrikaner leaders began to acknowledge – and then emphasize – the role of blacks in the Trek and the Anglo-Boer war. In the 1988 150th anniversary celebrations at the monument, the FAK publications made it clear that they saw the occasion as a moment to demonstrate that the enmities of Blood River had finally been buried (Coombes 2003; Grundlingh and Sapire 1989). This is seen again in exhibits during and after the centenary of the South African war

---

[20] Increasingly, as the country's leading Afrikaner cultural institution, the Monument is receiving donations of old photos, newspaper clippings, artwork, and other objects. There is now a need to sift through these materials to decide how they should be managed and a potential need to develop storage facilites generally associated with museums.

[21] The question of the appropriate pace of change in the symbolic landscape is not easy to answer in the abstract. Those who think South Africa should move faster might reflect on the snail-like change in the United States following the Civil War that is considered in Chapter 10.

[22] To an American, it is obvious that the Afrikaner narrative shares much with accounts in the United States in its portrayal of the pioneers as freedom-seeking civilizing people intent on building a new life and in their reactions to the region's indigenous inhabitants.

that describe the joint suffering of both groups, not just that of the Afrikaners.

There are additional points of agreement in the discourse between parts of the Afrikaner and anti-apartheid narratives. Prolonged resistance and liberation are central to both accounts and efforts to memorialize them, and there is even agreement that there was a common oppressor against which each struggle for freedom was waged – British colonialism. Of course there are also important differences in the specifics, but their convergence around metaphors of resistance and liberation, and the identification of the same enemy has also made it possible for them to partially converge in some interesting ways following the country's political transition in 1994.[23]

The challenge of reversing or altering this association at the monument raises the issue of what bolder steps can be taken in the near future given the prominent positions of the marble friezes and other Afrikaner icons in it. These are set in stone, but the problem is not in the objects but in the values that they represented during apartheid and the need to offer a meaningful perspective on what they mean today. Ideas such as an exhibit presenting examples of black–Afrikaner cooperation in the pre-NP period (and perhaps after) or focusing on Afrikaners who opposed apartheid are currently seen as too controversial for the Afrikaner community. So is it possible for the Monument to maintain legitimacy among mainstream Afrikaners and acceptance among skeptical whites and blacks? The only images of blacks in the marble friezes are negative ones and there is no acknowledgment that many blacks saw the Afrikaners as conquerors. Perhaps this could be acknowledged textually and visually. There could be a brochure that acknowledges the competing perceptions of Afrikaner intentions suggesting that one reason some of the battles took place was a result of cross-cultural misunderstandings and communication problems.[24] Just as the brochures at Blood River now describe

---

[23] In many ways, there are two prominent narratives: an Afrikaner and a black one – with variations that reflect regional and ethnic differences (e.g., Xhosa vs. Zulu). In contrast, there is not a very prominent British narrative.

[24] A more fundamental question is what it meant to be an Afrikaner at the time. Such a question would problematize the standard narrative and invite additional questions such as Zulu and other black perceptions of events, the motives and actions of people such as Retief, and the story of the treaty he supposedly got Dignane to sign. These are not comfortable questions for a sacred site with its established narrative literally set in stone to pose and perhaps not appropriate for a site that sees itself primarily as a cultural institution and not a museum with an educational mission.

the presentation there as *one* version of the events on December 16, 1838, the Voortrekker Monument could also be presented in more historical, relativistic terms.[25] Another possibility is that a message the monument could offer to school children of all groups is "Never Again," emphasizing the country's racialized pay and how the images in the monument and the events it celebrates pay attention to only one group.

Another approach to modifying the Voortrekker Monument's symbolic prominence is being taken by the South African Heritage Resource Agency's Legacy Project through a decision to build Freedom Park a short distance from the Voortrekker Monument. This new heritage site will contain a museum that will serve to acknowledge, preserve, and present South Africa's pre-colonial, colonial, apartheid, and post-apartheid history and heritage. Freedom Park will emphasize the country's long history, from as far back as 3.6 billion years through the liberation struggle. It will also include a garden of remembrance where statues and sculptures will be located in honor of ordinary South Africans who contributed to the country's development in different fields. At the groundbreaking ceremony on the new site, South Africa's Minister of Culture Ben Ngubane emphasized the intention to make Freedom Park "a place of pilgrimage and inspiration." Recounting the stories of the struggles against colonialism and apartheid will, he said, "help us to develop a creative response to our past and promote the process of healing" that offers a model for other multicultural societies.[26]

Locating Freedom Park in the vicinity of the Voortrekker Monument will offer an alternative narrative of South African history without a direct confrontation. It will be interesting to see how the relationship between Freedom Park and the Voortrekker Monument develops and the extent to which visitors go to both sites. This strategy of building an additional site rather than either destroying or taking over an existing one is highly consistent with the South African policy of pluralism as the preferred method for giving voice to previously unheard people and events, and is spelled out more fully in Chapter 9.

[25] Coombes' (2000; 2003) analysis suggests that because of its significance, the monument will serve as a site for reinterpretations and deconstruction from many diverse groups in South Africa irrespective of the choices about the site its managers make.
[26] http://www.dac.gov.za/news/speeches/2002_06_16.htm.

9

Enlarging South Africa's symbolic landscape

Since 1994 the symbolic landscape in South Africa has been radically altered. As discussed in Chapter 8, transformations of older spaces such as universities, parks, public squares, beaches, and government buildings through appropriation and modification communicate new powerful messages. Any analysis would be incomplete, however, without consideration of new sites and cultural institutions such as monuments, memorials, and museums that recount and legitimate the experiences of the county's previously politically voiceless majority and those who actively struggled to rid the country of apartheid. The new monuments and memorials operate as "gestures of compensation" in an effort to mediate between the past and present and to acknowledge the events and experiences that went unmarked for so long (Marschall 2004).

Official and unofficial new sites throughout the country present a new and different symbolic landscape in a variety of ways. There are, however, certainly themes and images that are common across these new sites. For example, most include visual images and other references to Nelson Mandela, whose picture was banned from the country for almost thirty years, in telling the story of the ultimate triumph over apartheid. Accounts of the story of survival and the inclusive narrative of struggle and resistance are widespread, emphasizing that people from all groups were active in the fight against apartheid and that the previous regime's focus on race and racial differences was an explicit construction. There are some dramatic ways in which this is communicated. At the Apartheid Museum, located in Gold Reef City between Soweto and downtown Johannesburg, visitors receive entry tickets, randomly distributed, that oblige them to enter through a door marked "Whites" or "Non-Whites." Upon entering, there is an explanation of the arbitrary nature of apartheid's racial categories that sometimes resulted in members of the same family being classified differently, an explanation of the appeals process that could lead to reclassification, and the tests that government officials designed to place people in one of the four racial groups (black, colored, Asian, and white). Common too are accounts tying suffering and resistance to specific places of memory. For example, the Hector Pieterson Museum in Soweto (Figure 9.1) focuses its account around the 1976 uprising that began in that township when young schoolchildren protested the imposition of Afrikaans as the medium of instruction in local schools (Marschall n.d.).[1] The District Six Museum in Cape Town tells the story of forced removals under the Group Areas Act and uses a large map on which former residents are invited to mark the location of their former homes.

The focus of this chapter is on the strategy of addition – the construction of new sites of commemoration that are central to the production of public memory through the narratives that circulate about them (Doughty in press). A decision to give voice to previously unmarked events and silenced narratives is relatively easy to make; however, as Linenthal (1993; 2001a) has observed, the specific choices that are made about a new site's location, as well as the selection of objects for inclusion, the design and size of the structure, and the degree of government support it receives can all become points of contestation. My goal here is not to document the myriad of projects in South Africa. Rather I discuss three heritage sites to reflect the range of new narratives and to analyze some of the opportunities and complexities involved in changing the country's symbolic landscape.

The first, the Ncome memorial, is adjacent to the Blood River Battlefield Heritage site, which is a sacred location for Afrikaners, celebrated as the site of their "chosen glory" (Volkan 1997), the victory over the Zulu in 1838, discussed in Chapter 8. As in the case of the Voortrekker Monument, the issue of Blood River's place in the new South Africa was not easy given that the event celebrated there is intimately related to racial domination and oppression. However, the government did not propose specific changes at Blood River, but rather decided to build a memorial at Ncome, the Zulu name for the site, just across the small river, to facilitate

---

[1] Pieterson was a 13-year-old student killed the first day of the uprising, made famous in a *Life* magazine picture in which a running man is carrying the wounded boy in a manner resembling a pieta, while his sister runs alongside (Figure 9.1). The boy became a symbol of resistance to apartheid and the regime's brutality. This image appears widely in the country in accounts of resistance as well as in wall murals and in books.

Figure 9.1 The famous photograph of Hector Pieterson, the young student who had been shot at the outbreak of the Soweto uprising in 1976, as it appears in front of the Hector Pieterson Museum in Soweto.

reconciliation between the descendents of those who fought on opposite sides 160 years earlier, to acknowledge black suffering in the battle, and to offer a narrative of events that took place reflecting the Zulu and other black perspectives.[2] Coming to this decision, however, was problematic, according to Marschall:

Unbeknown to many, the government's initial plan was to have only one monument on this site, which would commemorate the battle and symbolize reconciliation. This might have entailed a replacement or inclusive modification of the existing monument(s) at Blood River – a thought that was completely unacceptable to Afrikaner representatives. For conservative Afrikaners, Blood River is hallowed ground, a sacred place, closely linked to their sense of identity and the foundation myth of the Afrikaner 'nation'.

(Marschall forthcoming)

The process of building Ncome offers insights into the complexity of constructing new memorials in close proximity to older ones whose narratives they are challenging (Dlamini 2003; Ehlers 2000; Girshick 2004).

The second site discussed is Robben Island, a barren 3 square miles in Table Bay, 7 miles from Cape Town. Robben Island has a long history as a site of banishment for those who opposed white rule in South Africa. Often compared to Alcatraz, Robben Island served for many decades as a detention center for criminals and political opponents and then as a hospital for the insane, lepers, and the sick poor (Deacon 1998: 162). However, its most recent notoriety came when the apartheid regime decided in the 1960s to use it as a maximum security prison to hold black, coloured, and Asian political prisoners (white political prisoners, although often subject to the same mistreatment as blacks, were held at different locations) (Buntman 2003). The island's most famous prisoner, Nelson Mandela, and all of ANC's top leadership not in exile were held there. In 1996, the government decided to convert Robben Island into a museum; a visit there is one of the most painful, as well as inspiring, ways to explore issues of memory and memorialization.

The third site considered is located in District Six, which was a large neighborhood near the center of Cape Town with some 60,000 racially diverse residents when in 1966 the South African government declared it a "Whites Only" area under the Group Areas Act and ordered it

---

[2] Building a site with an alternative narrative near Blood River is like the construction of Freedom Park virtually adjacent to the Voortrekker Monument described in Chapter 8.

destroyed.[3] There was great opposition to the decision and the last residents were not evicted until 1982. Although the neighborhood was bulldozed, most of the land remained vacant in the face of continuing organized resistance to its redevelopment. In 1988, there was strong support to build a museum that would tell the story of the forced removal. A District Six Museum Foundation was established and held a two-week exhibition that presented photographs from District Six in 1992 in the old Methodist church at the edge of the district. In late 1994, the new government's minister of justice and ex-District Sixer, Dullah Omar, opened a more ambitious exhibit, named "Streets: Retracing District Six." Although it was to be open only for a few weeks, Streets never closed due to the tremendous interest the museum generated in the issues of memory and community (Coombes 2003; Rassool and Prosalendis 2001: vii). Soon the museum expanded its presentations, and supported former residents and their descendants in their efforts in pursuit of land restitution claims in the courts.

Post-apartheid South Africa pushes us to consider the extent to which the symbolic landscape can present competing narratives in a multicultural society. Can the country allow space for the monuments and narratives that supported apartheid, while also constructing new sites that recount the trauma of the apartheid years, resistance to it, and its ultimate defeat?[4] The tentative answer a dozen years after the 1994 election is yes and to the extent that we can understand the underlying dynamics at work, there may be significant lessons for other post-conflict societies. At the same time, consideration of the symbolic landscape raises questions about the role that cultural enactments and expressions play as reflectors, exacerbaters or inhibiters, and causes of new relationships in the country.

All three sites discussed below challenge earlier exclusive, apartheid-era narratives and offer more inclusive, accessible images and accounts and new, more inclusive narratives. Although the museum at Ncome is

---

[3] District Six is only one of many areas in Cape Town and in other cities that were demolished under this legislation. In and around Cape Town, there were some forty areas where non-whites lived that were declared whites-only under apartheid. Fredericks (2003) and Angelini (2003) report that during the apartheid era over 4 million people suffered from forced removals as the government especially targeted mixed race neighborhoods.

[4] An important question is how to speak about the experiences of most South Africans whose daily goal was that of survival and who as a result never resisted or spoke out about apartheid. In addition, the structure of the economic and political system meant that many people both white and black engaged in activities that either directly or indirectly supported the regime.

small and the exhibits simple, its presence forces visitors to consider previously unasked and unanswered questions concerning the perceptions and actions of the Zulu and other blacks in the area at the time of the battle and today. No longer is the story of the battle only about the Voortrekkers' trials and tribulations; it is also about black reactions to the Trekkers' arrival and settlement. The addition of Robben Island as a heritage site appropriates a locale of banishment and transforms it into one with an entirely different meaning with lessons about the "survival of the human spirit" for the new nation. Here, not just the defeat of apartheid, but the detailed account of how the prisoners resisted daily humiliation and degradation, and the inner strength with which they emerged from Robben Island, are at the core of the new narrative (Buntman 2003). The District Six Museum provides a narrative built around the thousands of forced removals and destroyed communities that both recovers former residents' memories and provides a strategy of political empowerment and action. Its stories are not those of renowned national heroes, but rather those of ordinary people whose everyday experiences recreate the emotional community and connect former residents and first-time visitors to the daily suffering apartheid caused.

The South African strategies, and the outcome of these strategies to date, invites us to consider the hypothesis that under certain conditions cultural enactments and expressions are an effective vehicle for constructing widely shared, new narratives in societies emerging from trauma. The narratives articulate experiences that were previously absent from public consciousness and in so doing help people consider their own feelings of loss, shame, guilt and renewal. To the extent that new and modified sites activate personal experiences and emotions, they serve as focal points for grief and mourning, and contribute to the growth of new community self-images, new relationships, and new institutions in the post-conflict period. New narratives about the past can not only help people make emotional sense of what occurred, but also facilitate the creation of a political space that facilitates coexistence among former adversaries.

Strategies for linking memory and politics

Rassool describes two alternative strategies linking memory and politics in South Africa. The route that is most prominent, and featured in many of the SAHRA Legacy Project's initiatives, is biographical, using commemoration sites, plaques, and monuments that recount the accomplishments of leading figures in the resistance movement such as Nelson Mandela, Walter Sisulu, and Govan Mbeki who "achieved honor against great odds" (Rassool 2001: 4). As a result, "a biographic character was thus being given to the cultural landscape, with the life of leaders a central focus" (Rassool 2001: 6). It is not surprising that Mandela's life is especially important in celebrating the country's transition, and in the new master narrative; the message is both inspirational and didactic, using national heroes' lives – and especially Mandela's – to illustrate and teach lessons about nation building and reconciliation.[5]

There is no doubt that Nelson Mandela is particularly effective in communicating the meaning of sacrifice, humility, and reconciliation to South Africans and others. By any standards he is a true national hero who possesses a rare legitimacy and credibility and a capacity to communicate great sincerity and generosity to all groups. South Africans readily recount dozens of stories about Mandela's symbolic gestures that have become apocryphal tales filled with moral lessons for the nation.[6] His autobiography makes it clear, however, that Mandela's positions evolved over time. Many grew out of reflections during his prison years, and were not necessarily those that he held throughout his life. For example, for some time he was ambivalent about the role of whites in the liberation struggle and distrustful of their motives, before coming to the non-racial position with which he is now clearly associated (Mandela 1994).

It is not hard to find people, in South Africa and elsewhere, who give Mandela full credit for the democratic transition and South Africa's spirit of reconciliation and multiracialism. Without denying his incredible importance as a transformational, visionary leader, there is no good theory that permits us to argue that one person alone can transform a country solely through the force of his or her own personality.[7] We must

---

[5] A foreign visitor might expect even more reliance on Mandela's story than currently exists. Apparently both Mandela and the Nelson Mandela Foundation are concerned about this issue; and about the exploitation of Mandela for commercial gain. Nonetheless, he is the focus of important heritage projects such as "The Long Walk to Freedom: The Mandela Trail," which takes a visitor to significant places in his life including his homes, offices, and the sites of his trials, and the Statue of Freedom in Port Elizabeth.

[6] One of the most famous is when Mandela donned a jersey of the once all white and very Afrikaner Springboks Rugby team to congratulate them after they won the 1995 World Cup.

[7] One important influence on South African leaders is that of Gandhi and the mutual cross-fertilization of ideas around peaceful resistance that went on in Inanda near Durban

consider not just the role of the "seller" of ideas, but the reasons the listener "bought" his argument. To do this, it is important to consider the degree to which, and the way in which, Mandela's successful leadership grew from to his capacity to articulate incredibly effectively positions that resonated with long-standing widely held South African cultural values. My argument is that Mandela's style and ability to make explicit what resonated for many people built support for initiatives that became widely accepted positions of the ANC establishment, and were institutionalized in the norms and practices of the government following the transition.[8]

Whatever social science theory says about the role of an individual leader in change situations, it is evident that telling the story of the South African transition through Mandela is powerful and effective, meaning that large numbers of people accept the core message, adopt parts of it as their own positions, and make an effort to behave in ways that are consistent with it. Heritage sites such as Robben Island and other places where Mandela lived and worked are ideal for teaching the narrative of resistance and ultimate triumph to adults as well as children.

South Africa is investing a good deal in heritage sites, and one reason is the belief that their messages are crucial to the country's political transformation.[9] This emphasis on symbol and ritual is not especially distinctive. What is striking, however, is the extent to which discourse in South Africa is inclusive and has avoided simply replacing the language and images of the apartheid period with a new set of racially exclusive stories and rulers. It is also interesting that while Mandela's biography is central to many of the presentations, there is no cult of personality and there are many other people from all groups whose experiences are also featured in the narrative. In part, this is because Mandela was imprisoned

---

between Gandhi, Luthuli, Dube, and Shembe – all prominent leader figures associated with this fascinating place and perhaps inspired by his genius.

[8] If Mandela had said and done some of the things he did in Northern Ireland, Israel–Palestine, or Sri Lanka, it is not clear that he would have been a successful leader. Consider, for example, Martin Luther King and his organization's effectiveness in mobilizing protest in the American South versus his lack of success in Chicago. One hypothesis is that the problems were organizational; another is that even though many Chicago blacks came from the South in the previous one or two generations, his religious appeal and imagery were not as powerful with the urbanized population. This points to the great importance of the interaction between context and culture in explaining the dynamics of social change.

[9] Sometimes it is suggested that much of the presentation of the struggle in heritage sites also represents a need to compensate for the long years in which the opposition to apartheid had few successes.

for twenty-seven years and had no public role in many events in the country during this period. Another reason is that Mandela worked so hard to stress the collective and cooperative nature of resistance rather than emphasizing the bold actions of single individuals, including himself, as in themselves decisive.

The second, very different, and more complex path joining memory and politics that Rassool (2001) identifies is found in more grassroots projects emphasizing the rich diversity in the details of ordinary people's experiences. Heritage sites developed using this perspective work to uncover and explore the "archeology of memory" in communities, the impact of apartheid on daily lives and routines, and local forms of resistance. They draw attention to tension and diversity in local communities and sometimes question conventional, even romantic, ideas about the past while problematizing commonly used categories, such as those employed to discuss race and ethnicity. This approach to heritage emphasizes popular, publicly articulated memories to build local empowerment and engagement with on-going issues of justice and restitution for past mistreatment.

Grassroots approaches begin with the lives of ordinary people, using their mundane, everyday experiences to develop an account of survival and daily existence as they worked, raised their children, and engaged in cooperation and conflict with each other. These sites seek to offer an alternative discourse that "transcend[s] uncritical frameworks of triumphalism and celebration" (Rassool 2001) while recounting the complexity of experience and memory through the joys and tribulations that all people experience. As independent sites of engagement, they are works in progress that attempt to "reconstruct the material fabric and social landscape . . . in imaginative terms" (Rassool forthcoming), emphasizing heritage as an on-going participatory process, rather than one frozen in time, that rekindles community memories and mobilizes community action. Rassool emphasizes how such sites of memory can serve for recovering community and dignity while mobilizing legal and political demands to provide some redress to those who suffered. These sites, such as community museums, are interactive and political, challenged by the need to link what is presented and the discourse used to present it to the shifting needs and demands of the people it serves.

The three sites discussed below have taken on very different tasks and are quite different from one another. Yet each reveals particular ways in which South Africa's symbolic landscape has changed. Ncome is the most modest in terms of size, cost, and the ambitiousness of the project and yet, perhaps ironically, has had the greatest difficulties in expanding the narrative about the Battle of Blood River. In the effort to offer a broader perspective, it has raised the ire of Afrikaners as well as many black non-Zulu. Robben Island is without a doubt the leading site where the master narrative surrounding resistance to and triumph over apartheid is told in a compelling manner. The District Six Museum offers a very different story of resistance focusing on the countless people whose lives apartheid displaced and disrupted. Neither heroic nor grandiose in any conventional sense, the museum emerged on the margins of the national memory project to offer a powerful account of displacement that perhaps as many as 4 million South Africans experienced, to challenge the racialized order that dominated the country for so long, and to offer nuance and complexity rather than simple categories and answers.

South Africa's redefined and new symbolic spaces

Blood River/Ncome

For Afrikaners, the saga of the Battle of Blood River contains all of the key elements of their core narrative that was discussed in Chapter 8. Akenson (1992) describes it as an Old Testament Exodus narrative that includes suffering and subjugation, exile, the search for the Promised Land and freedom, the sacred covenant, and the miracle of redemption. For Afrikaners the 1838 battle site is sacred ground and each year prayer and ceremony mark December 16 as a special day (Girshick 2004).[10] For example, in 2002 the Blood River Heritage site (now managed by the Voortrekker Monument Trust), organized a four-day weekend program that included recreation, trips to historical sites in the area including Mgungundlovu, the place where Retief and his group were killed, and to Trekker leader Piet Uys' grave, as well as videos, singing, and religious services. On the morning of the 16th, there was a first light ceremony, a devotional service, a reaffirmation of the Covenant, and wreath laying, singing, a church service, a lecture on the history of Blood River, and finally a barbecue and a movie.[11]

[10] Ehlers (2000) describes contestation over the meaning of the day, its transformation into a sacred, religious day that met Afrikaner political needs, the weakening of this interpretation, and efforts within the Afrikaner community to transform December 16 into an inclusive Day of Reconciliation rather than a celebration of exclusive Afrikaner nationalism.

[11] Entrance of right-wing nationalists who caused problems in the past is now restricted.

Given the emotional significance of Blood River and its close association with white domination and apartheid (as with the Voortrekker Monument), it was not evident what would happen to Blood River in the post-apartheid era. Many asked openly how the monument at Blood River, which commemorates what some believe is the divinely inspired victory of a few hundred Boers who managed to kill 3,000 Zulu warriors in 1838, could continue to present the same account of the battle and its significance as it had earlier.

As is the case with many events that are now central to core narratives, the battle of Blood River was not marked in the years immediately after the battle took place.[12] Only in 1866, twenty-eight years later, did people come to Blood River in forty to fifty wagons to mark the battle site. They placed rocks in a cairn to mark the center of the 1838 laager and set commemorative plaques with words of the Covenant in Afrikaans and English on either side of it. The church that was promised in Sarel Cilliers' vow was built in Pietermaritzburg, miles from the battlefield (now part of the Voortrekker Museum). Yet several decades later the site and memories surrounding it were crucial for Afrikaners, and the 1938 centenary celebrations increased memorialization at Blood River. A large granite wagon, "a symbol of the Pioneer's (Voortrekker) home, stronghold and church" (Blood River Heritage Site, information guide) was built and placed along with the cairn that "stands as a beacon of the renewal of the Covenant." The wagon was moved to the site's entrance in 1971 when a full-sized bronze 64-wagon laager was built on the site of the original one (Figure 9.2).

The Afrikaner message at Blood River is one of struggle, courage, faith, and liberation, communicated through a detailed account of the battle.[13] Like the Little Bighorn narrative before recent changes, it offers the perspective of whites moving into the country's heartland with no attention to the perceptions of the Zulu and other blacks who are simply presented as the bloodthirsty enemy. In 1998, the government's Legacy Project launched an initiative to make noble the loss of Zulu life and extol Zulu bravery at the Battle of Ncome (the name of the river) (Dlamini 2001; Girshick 2004). Prior to the decision, a panel of academic historians was asked to consider ways to expand the interpretation of the battle. The

---

[12] Connerton (1989) notes that this is common. Bastille Day, he says, was not celebrated in France until the 1880s.
[13] Some suggest that there is good reason to doubt many of the heroic details in the standard account, including the number of Zulu killed that day.

Figure 9.2 The upper picture shows the shield covered outside wall in the new Ncome Museum located across the small stream from the Blood River Monument (below). Each is visible from the other, but the small footbridge linking the sites has yet to be built

report from the historians did not concern itself particularly with the details of the battle (Arts, Culture Science and Technology, n.d.). They did, however, focus on the Zulu interpretation of the battle and on events leading up to it and some of this material is incorporated into the new Ncome museum. The panel said that correcting the present imbalance required a presentation of the context in which King Dignane acted and argued that the "encroachment of the Boers into the Zulu kingdom . . . [and] the perceived treachery and greed of the Voortrekkers, whom the Zulus portrayed as landgrabbers" created the context in which the Zulu acted (Dlamini 2001: 130).[14] They suggested constructing a wall of remembrance that would include the names of Zulu warriors who died in the battle and building a footbridge over the river to link the two sites in a gesture of reconciliation. The government also decided to build a small museum that would present and interpret contemporary cultural activities (Figure 9.2).

A central goal of the state commemoration of the Battle of Ncome was to achieve some measure of inclusiveness and reconciliation between Zulu and Voortrekker descendants through various symbolic elements including mutual acknowledgment of sacrifice, and most obviously symbolized by the footbridge. The project was conceived to promote these principles and values, which included forgiving and reconciling and would represent congruence among citizens of the new state under construction. "The Battle of Ncome project was to serve a symbolic function in the promotion of these principles and values" (Dlamini 2003). In addition, it proposed that the new site be named the place of reconciliation.[15] The unveiling ceremony for Ncome was held on December 16, 1998 – with the footbridge connecting the two not yet built – and those present included Deputy President Thabo Mbeki and other top leaders of the country, among them a few Afrikaners who called for reconciliation (Ehlers 2000). However, not all Afrikaners were pleased. Hennie De Wet, executive director of the FAK, an Afrikaner cultural group, said, "we should also recognize that we are different and cannot commemorate this day together" (Dlamini 2003: 18). In addition, a group of right-wing Afrikaners in view of those assembled at Ncome laid a wreath in the middle of the Blood River *laager* while flying flags of the old Transvaal Republic and raising a banner proclaiming in Afrikaans "Apartheid is Holy" (Dlamini 2003: 18).

---

[14] The exhibit in the Ncome Museum that I saw and that is described in Dlamini (2001) and Girshick (2004) has since been modified.

[15] Since 1994 the Day of the Covenant has been kept as a national holiday in South Africa but is now called the Day of Reconciliation.

The Ncome project was also caught in the web of Zulu nationalism and the goals of the Inkata Freedom Party in the region. Dlamini (2001; 2003) reports that the panel charged with making suggestions for the site was asked to investigate the question of the participation of people other than the Zulu and Afrikaners in the battle; he concludes that Zulu nationalists shaped the museum and its exhibits in ways that ignored black participants other than the Zulus. As a result, he argues, the site presents an exclusive and essentialized view of Zulu ethnicity and ignores the role of other blacks in the political and military developments at the time, presenting Zulu culture as more unified than it was and even displaying objects in the museum that are not really of Zulu origin at all.[16] In the process it also "erases from the history of the battle 'other non-Zulu' Africans – the Tlokoa in the Nquthu District" (Dlamini 2001:135). "Clearly, reconciliation and nation-building cannot be served by this" (Dlamini 2001:135). Thus, Ncome provides a cautionary example reminding us that a "rainbow approach" may serve to essentialize rather than provide a path toward a non-racialized future.

Transformation of a site through addition is attractive but it can be difficult, as is seen here. The strategy of not seeking a direct change in Blood River but adding an additional memorial on the other side of the river at Ncome was probably a good one in this situation. However, the dual political problems of Afrikaner resistance and Zulu political needs reveal important limits to this strategy. While the Blood River site, now managed by the Voortrekker Monument, offers both a video and booklet saying the narrative of the battle presented at Blood River is one among several interpretations, meaningful transformation of the site has not yet occurred. SAHRA is still engaged in negotiations for constructing the small footbridge across the river. Perhaps the absence of the symbolic footbridge best symbolizes both the absence of connections and the absence of a more inclusive presentation of the events and the memories of them.

Robben Island

Throughout South Africa there are dozens of new heritage sites that mark the struggle and resistance against apartheid. While there is great

---

[16] "In its presentations of simplified polarized public history and in its exclusion of significant actors of the past . . . the Nquthu area is being 'Zulu-ized', and its past reordered in a revival of an exclusive ethnic nationalism" (Dlamini 2001: 137).

variation in what exactly is recounted and the way in which it is presented across sites in terms of Rassool's (2001) distinction between the biographic and the grassroots perspectives, it is not surprising that less than a decade after the transition, the majority of new heritage sites emphasize the actions and sacrifices of men (and an occasional woman) who actively opposed apartheid. In this emerging standard narrative, the heroes' lives are a powerful tool for communicating details about the struggle and for drawing lessons relevant to the country's present and future development.

Nowhere in the country is the story of the apartheid regime's inhumane treatment of opponents, Nelson Mandela's vision and wisdom, the ANC's coordination and control, and the triumph of the human spirit told more powerfully than in Robben Island. The barren island, once the symbol of the oppressive power of the apartheid regime, has been appropriated and radically transformed into a museum that recounts how the political prisoners refused to give up the hope that one day there would be majority rule in South Africa and that the ANC's non-racial vision for the country would prevail. Its future-oriented message communicates an inclusive optimism. "While we will not forget the brutality of apartheid, we will not want Robben Island to be a monument to our hardship and suffering. We would want Robben Island to be a monument . . . reflecting the triumph of the human spirit against the forces of evil. A triumph of non-racialism over bigotry and intolerance. A triumph of a new South Africa over the old" (Kathrada 1999).

To get to Robben Island a visitor departs from the new Nelson Mandela Gateway in the heart of Cape Town's spiffy refurbished Victoria and Alfred waterfront on a 30-minute ride in Table Bay. The boat arrives at the same wharf where thousands of prisoners once disembarked, and the two and a half-hour tour has two parts. In one, visitors board a bus and are driven around the small island where they see the house where Robert Sobukwe, the PAC leader who organized the Sharpeville protests in 1960, was held; the remains of the leper colony's cemetery; a church which is the only standing building from the leper colony era; the island's only school; the governor's house; blockhouses built to defend the harbor during World War II; and the limestone quarry where Mandela and other prisoners worked and were refused such amenities as sunglasses that would shield their eyes from the bright sun or masks to protect their lungs from the fine limestone dust they inhaled day after day.

On the tour a visitor hears an inspiring narrative of struggle and resistance. One is told how Sobukwe, who was prohibited from speaking

Figure 9.3 A cairn in the limestone quarry in Robben Island where prisoners worked. During a reunion there Nelson Mandela picked up a stone and placed it on the ground in an open space in the quarry. Other prisoners did the same as a way of marking their shared experiences there

to other prisoners, would pick up a handful of sand and slowly let it fall through his fingers as prisoners walked past – his only available means of greeting other prisoners. In the quarry, visitors are shown the small toilet facilities where prisoners exchanged written messages and could talk in private, and learn about the development of the secret Open University in which prisoners taught each other a range of subjects as they prepared themselves for their future leadership positions. In the center of the quarry there is now a cairn made of stones piled there during a 1995 reunion, when Mandela placed the first stone and was followed by many others (Figure 9.3). The message of the narrative is clear: no matter how oppressive the system and the guards, the prisoners clung to the belief that they would eventually prevail and become democratic South Africa's rulers. Finally, the narrative emphasizes the fundamentally non-racial character of the resistance and stresses that there were whites deeply involved in the struggle against apartheid and that there were blacks, such as prison guards, police and army officers, and black homeland leaders who profited from, and worked to maintain, apartheid.

The second part of the tour goes inside the prison where an ex-prisoner leads the visitors into his former cell and recounts his own treatment and experiences in ways that "authenticate" and increase the power of the narrative tremendously and shows visitors Mandela's small cell. The story one hears about torture, mistreatment, and daily degradation is not pretty. At the same time, the details of what the prisoners endured only make more poignant their inner strength and resistance that sustained their mutual support and shared vision. One also learns about their creative communication methods involving garbage cans and toilet seats, the painstaking translation, copying, and distribution of newspapers, and their commitment to focus on governing an non-racialized country, rather than to pursue racialized vengeance, when they gained power.

The Robben Island Museum and its affiliated Mayibuye Archives at the University of the Western Cape are centers for heritage activities. There are programs that highlight the importance of Robben Island, including school tours, and there are youth camps (also known as "nation building camps") that explore issues such as racism, xenophobia, education and training, sustainable development, sexism, and gangsterism. The Spring School is an annual event with a different theme each year that brings together participants from schools and museums for a seven-day program on heritage that includes educator and museum educator training. Lionel Davis, a 67-year-old ex-prisoner and well-known Cape Town artist who is involved with the education programs emphasized that blacks need heroes – including whites – who fought against the British, racism, and for human rights. A challenge he identified for the education programs is to emphasize the "equality of victimhood" and the need to build a country in which children develop self-esteem and respect for all (personal interview).

Because many South Africans cannot get to Robben Island, there is now a "Robben Island on the Move" program that brings its message to other parts of the country. Colloquially called the "Apple box" program, it was designed by the 1998 Spring School participants. The colorful name comes from the fact that released prisoners carried their personal possessions out in the boxes growers used in transporting apples to stores and markets. The program goes to small places in remote regions and explains the history of the prison at different periods with an emphasis on the recent past. The presentation is also linked with dramatic performances that engage young people and offer an opening for heritage educators to discuss apartheid and the rise of resistance to it.

The museum's Reference Group program conducts four-day workshops that bring together former prisoners and their families to talk about specific aspects of their Robben Island experiences including the trauma resulting from them. One task the program has undertaken is to connect the families of former prisoners with one another, and for a time there was a widely praised exhibit at the Mandela Gateway on the impact of imprisonment on the prisoners' wives and children, who in many ways were often more isolated from support than the prisoners who were so close to one another.

Finally, Robben Island has a training program that seeks to fast-track the transformation of the country's heritage sector by helping staff working in museums across the country to move from lower positions in museum hierarchies to middle and top management. To this end, the museum has formed a partnership with the University of the Western Cape, Robben Island Museum, and the University of Cape Town to create a post-graduate program in Museum and Heritage Studies.

Although Robben Island is not readily accessible physically to many South Africans – it is not centrally located in the country and requires a boat ride from Cape Town – it is very available emotionally and is easily South Africa's most prominent heritage site. It has been declared a World Heritage Site and this further enhances its symbolic significance and the universal message it communicates. The transformation in the island and its meaning from a repressive prison to one of sacrifice and triumph over evil is dramatic and easy to comprehend. Emphasis on the details of the personal experiences of Mandela and other political prisoners is emotionally engaging and compelling. The ex-prisoners who conduct the visits to their former cells and describe their treatment and the details of prison life have real credibility. The basic narrative of triumph and liberation following decades of struggle is an incredibly optimistic one that even includes accounts of present-day friendships between ex-prisoners and their guards to which many people in all groups can connect. Finally, the Robben Island narrative's optimism is inclusive, recognizing the role that people from all groups in South Africa played in opposing apartheid, and inviting people from all groups to participate in nation-building.

District Six Museum

Under apartheid, South Africa's non-whites had few rights, and power inequalities made effective resistance especially difficult. Although protest groups continued to resist the government's racialization of daily life, the differential treatment of whites, coloreds, Indians, and blacks (and economic and cultural differentiation within each of these categories) meant that South Africa by the 1960s had constructed the world's most self-consciously institutionalized racial society. Through the establishment of rural homelands and urban townships, non-whites were marginalized from cities and industrial centers physically, economically, socially, and politically. Despite the overwhelming power that the government did not hesitate to employ, there was intense conflict and resistance to its policies as many non-whites and a good number of whites refused to accept apartheid as morally or politically just. Nevertheless, many whites refused to believe the accounts of government and police practices used to maintain the regime.

The TRC documented thousands of cases of physical, emotional, and psychological abuse under apartheid. What people elsewhere consider normal in daily life was unknown in South Africa; for many years all social interactions and privileges were organized and distributed through a racial filter. In the past dozen years, South Africans have worked hard to find ways to express and understand what happened during centuries of white domination that extend back far before the apartheid period and to employ these insights as building blocks in the construction of a more inclusive and more just society.

Robben Island tells the story of resistance and triumph in South Africa through the lives of national heroes; the District Six Museum joins memory and politics in a very different way through its grassroots exploration of the community's "archeology of memory" (Rassool 2001: 6). Through an emphasis on the daily lives of the area's 60,000 residents before they were shattered through forced removal, and their varied forms of resistance to apartheid and exclusive white rule, memories and a sense of dignity are recovered. Here memory is not just a mechanism for a nostalgic view of the past, it is mobilized for the restoration of the district's unjustly appropriated and still undeveloped land. As a result, since its establishment the museum has pursued two goals: to tell the story of District Six and other forced removals, and "to mobilize the masses of ex-residents and their descendants into a movement of land restitution, community development and political consciousness" (Rassool and Prosalendis 2001: viii). In the view of the directors, process is key to the museum and its presentations should reflect changing present needs and interests, not a static view of the past.

District Six is an old Cape Town neighborhood not far from the city's downtown port, where there had been forced removals going back to the arrival of the first Dutch settlers in the mid seventeenth century. Although

269

there were a number of white residents in District Six in the early part of the twentieth century when many Eastern European Jews lived there, by the mid 1960s District Six's more than 60,000 residents were primarily coloured (mixed race in South African parlance) although there were also blacks, Indians and Malays as well. District Six's prime location made it an obvious target for appropriation and in 1966 it was declared a White Group Area under the apartheid government's Group Areas Act. Removal of residents to more remote colored and black townships in Cape Flats took until 1982, by which time virtually the only buildings remaining were the District's schools, churches, and mosques. The religious institutions refused to sell or deconsecrate their buildings and many former residents continued to travel back to District Six for religious services. Protests and legal challenges made redevelopment much more difficult than anticipated and only the Cape Technikon (a technical college) and a small number of apartments for whites were ever built in the area. Most of District Six is still vacant and traces of former buildings and streets are still clearly visible.

District Six had long been a site of resistance to apartheid and there was strong opposition to the forced removals and to subsequent proposals to develop the areas for whites (Smith and Rassool 2001). Religious and community leaders formed the "Friends of District Six" and the "District Six Rent, Rates and Residents' Association" in 1979. Other protest groups followed, including Organizations United Against Traitors (OUT), and Hands Off District Six (HODS), although these two did not include the active involvement of former residents (Layne and Rassool 2001: 146). In 1988 HODS held a conference that called for the establishment of a museum for District Six; soon after, the District Six Foundation was created and began working on the project.

The foundation held a two-week photographic exhibition in 1992 and planned another two-week exhibit for late 1994 entitled Streets: Retracing District Six, which generated so much enthusiasm and excitement that it became the basis of a permanent museum. Housed in the since renovated Wesleyan Methodist church (a church that had previously served as a center for resistance activities) on Buitenkant Street, the exhibit was built out of materials from the District Six site (Delport 2001: 34). Three features are the central emotional points for the exhibit and the present expanded museum. One is the old enamel street signs from District Six that a white foreman who worked on the demolition crew managed to save in his attic despite having been instructed to dump everything from

District Six into Table Bay (Figure 9.4). The signs were hung in three vertical columns and catch a visitors' eye immediately upon entering the building. To many, their reappearance almost magically signaled the return of the streets and houses they marked.

Second is a large canvas on which a map of the district had been painted (Figure 9.5). It covers most of the central floor space, and former residents and their descendants were invited to write their names on the spot of their former homes and to indicate the names of shops and other places of importance in their daily lives. The map proved to be of particular emotional significance in several ways (McEachern 1998). In her thoughtful analysis, McEachern (1998) notes that invariably former residents visiting the museum first locate their own house on the map and that it is at the center of the personal stories they tell one another or their children or grandchildren.[17] She argues that walking across the map is an active process of recovering what is lost and this helps build popular narratives and "makes *visible* the people in contrast to apartheid making them disappear into Cape Flats. . . The map works as a mnemonic, allowing the recall of the place. . . [and] in the revaluing of the District, the walkers achieve distinction and value themselves" (1998: 58). Story telling, McEachern argues, is about meaning making and the stories are both models of District Six and models for South Africa and the future.[18]

A third device that the museum employs to turn visitors into active participants is a memory cloth on which people are asked to write comments which are later hand embroidered (Figure 9.6). From the outset, people were interested in writing their own memories and comments on the cloth and the tremendous response is perhaps best measured by the fact that in eight years it grew to more than a kilometer long. Those who write on it are both former residents and visitors.

Since its renovation in 2000, the museum has added an exhibit entitled Digging Deeper that focuses on the district's more private and interior spaces. "The approach in the new exhibition is to avoid taking a single,

---

[17] McEachern (1998: 55–56) considers the many reactions to, and uses of, the map for eliciting deep memories, and notes that for some people their visit to the museum provided their first occasion for talking to their children or grandchildren about District Six. This is not surprising, and is consistent with reports from many places around the world that people who have experienced trauma often have great trouble talking about it with family and friends.

[18] Bar-on (2002) makes a similar point about the value of story-telling as part of healing in his work on the Israeli–Palestinian conflict. It is also consistent with Geertz's (1973a) view that culture is about the construction of shared meanings.

Figure 9.4 The street signs from District Six on display, District Six Museum

Figure 9.5 The large map of District Six that covers the main floor in the District Six Museum

Figure 9.6 A section of the memory cloth that has been embroidered, District Six Museum

safe narrative and sets out consciously to disrupt and unsettle certain conventions about District Six's past" (Rassool 2001: 8). It contains a timeline that goes back to the seventeenth century offering a District Six based view of events rather than the more standard white history narrative.[19] It encourages people to consider District Six's diversity and

---

[19] The timeline can be seen at www.districtsix.co.za/frames.htm.

the varied experiences of residents over time, the earlier expulsions going back to the seventeenth century, and epidemics. It reports on tensions and changes in the community, consciously aiming to avoid romanticizing the era and its inhabitants. The exhibit contains a room that faithfully reconstructs the inside of a woman's home; the Sound Archive has recordings of music from the district, and oral histories of former residents that can be heard in the reconstructed barber shop (Layne and Rassool 2001: 146–53).

While the museum offers a special place to former residents, its message is far from exclusive and Bohlin contends that "the category of 'we' is broadened to encompass all who suffered under apartheid" (1998: 181). In fact there is a great deal of emotional room for outsiders, including foreign visitors, as witnesses and learners as they both identify with former residents and see the process of recovering memories and community in post-apartheid South Africa. In the museum's symbolic reappropriation of the land and community that was destroyed, "the memories of the events in District Six are construed as belonging collectively to all South Africans, regardless of race, economic status and political affiliation" (Bohlin 1998: 184).

The widely acclaimed museum has done a terrific job in making visible and personalizing the story of forced removals under apartheid and in making "the object of conservation [that which] has already been destroyed" (Angelini 2003: 17). Just as important to its founders is the role that it has played in the movement for land restitution, community development, and political consciousness. For years, the museum hosted meetings to mobilize support for restitution and informed people of their legal rights. The District Six Beneficiary Trust representing some 2200 families demanded restitution under the 1994 Land Restitution Act and in 1998 reached an understanding with the governments of Cape Town and Province of the Western Cape that was signed at a public meeting in the museum. Under the agreement, there would be a participative and consultative redevelopment process. For the Beneficiary Trust it was important that there was no distinction made between previous landowners and tenants and that land would be restored to the community that would then assign it to individuals.[20] The process of working out a specific agreement

---

[20] Among the reasons for this is that blacks could not own land in the district although Malays, white, and coloreds could.

was slow however and only in March 2003 did the government agree to begin construction of the first twenty-four houses in the district.

Conclusion

Large-scale regime change provokes many challenges resulting from social role transformations. In South Africa perhaps the most immediate was the need to recount and publicly acknowledge the tremendous injuries inflicted by apartheid. This took place in many ways including the publication of books and articles, media interviews, and testimony before the Truth and Reconciliation Commission. This chapter has focused on the role of museum exhibitions as another tool for understanding the past in a period of transformation.

Through their presentations cultural institutions both reflect and create popular, accessible accounts about a society and its core values. Of course, their accounts vary in specificity and focus so that often, but not always, differences in apparent content can mask more basic agreement in their underlying themes. In long-established countries, where there is high consensus around issues such as the founding of the state and the legitimacy of its institutions, national heroes, and core values, this material is often barely noticed by citizens who have internalized the messages since childhood. In new, or transformed, states great effort and resources are often put into addressing these matters. Israel, as Zerubavel (1995) shows, developed a powerful and rich symbol-laden narrative linking the modern state to the biblical one.

In South Africa since 1990, there has been interest in expressing openly and publicly ideas that previously were explored only in private or protected settings. In particular, there has been a widely felt and intense need to have state institutions and the media address the past and to legitimate the experiences of the previously marginalized and powerless. The three museums discussed in this chapter all express the commitment to give voice to the past; however, they show great variation in their styles and specific messages as each offers a narrative that reframes the past in ways that are politically relevant for the present and locates them in a specific historical and spatial context.

There are many common elements of the new national narrative recounted in heritage sites throughout the country. What these sites share is a long historical perspective, identification of the abuses and brutality of the apartheid regime, description of the forms resistance took, and the faith in the inevitability of a successful outcome, meaning the end of apartheid and exclusive white rule. To those who, like me, are foreigners, the accounts are dramatic and inspiring, forcing one to ask how a negotiated transition to a non-racial society could come out of a system filled with so much racialized violence and oppression. The accounts reinforce the view of Mandela as an extraordinary figure and the strength of so many people in South Africa who rejected the path of revenge and bitterness. In Ncome we see how complicated it can be to make room for additional complexity and how local and national political concerns can intersect with these efforts. In Robben Island, Mandela's creative, long-term responses to his treatment there are used as a model for the South African future, and meet a widespread, basic need to have a coherent explanation for the transition from apartheid, a rationale for reconciliation (and non-vengeance), and an optimistic vision for the future, offering the country inspiring heroes and moral principles.

Robben Island and sites such as the Hector Pieterson or Apartheid Museums raise difficult questions that may be especially relevant for audiences such as school children or jobless South Africans living in inadequate housing with few, if any, amenities and social services. The narrative has a paternalistic side that emphasizes the role of amazing people triumphing over incredible odds – and somehow, from the start, having a vision that in the end they would prevail. How, one might ask, might a child or young adult process this story? While it is intended to communicate efficacy and hope, might he or she not see this as something no ordinary person like himself or herself could possibly do? There is little in these exhibitions that actively engages viewers as democratic citizens or in fact suggests what democratic participation entails. It is a narrative of triumph over adversity indeed, but one that offers few specifics about the future other than the reassurance that the same leadership that defeated apartheid will lead the country and build a more just South Africa and empower its citizens.

In contrast, the District Six Museum's narrative offers a different perspective although it too contains many of the same elements found in other heritage sites. It uses a narrative built from the stories of District Six's residents' daily lives showing how they both paid the price for apartheid and managed at times to create spaces in which they could insulate themselves from its oppressive presence. The museum's founders and board clearly believe that recovered complex truth is needed to reddress past injustice and to do this, political consciousness must be built and action strategies developed. What is so compelling in the District Six story told through the street signs, the map with thousands of names, the memory cloth, the sights, sounds (and almost the smells) of daily life is how reasonable, even necessary, land restitution is.

The South African experience offers an important case where one can examine the hypothesis that long-term conflicts must address psycho-cultural issues as well as conflicting interests. In comparison with Northern Ireland, for example, where attention on constitutional con-cerns and interests has dominated peacemaking efforts, South Africa's transition has paid significant attention to the trauma citizens experi-enced during apartheid as a step in building an inclusive society. From a psychocultural perspective, the Truth and Reconciliation Commission was a crucial aspect of the effort to provide a public record of past abuses and possible models for building a shared future (Gibson 2004; Hayner 2002; Krog 1999). Cultural institutions and expressions such as those considered here are another mechanism the country has devel-oped. It would be naïve to believe that there is one best strategy for dealing with past injustices for all citizens or that any one method will be equally effective for everyone. There are many unresolved issues in the aftermath of long-term conflict: issues of silence and shame; issues of mourning, including loss of victim status; justice and restitution; making sense of what happened at different levels; and questions of access and institution building in a multicultural society. There will no doubt be ongoing psychocultural conflicts and dramas as South Africans continue to address issues of recognition and inclusion. In fact, the presence of such conflict and drama is probably far healthier than not dealing with these matters in a society that was so recently severely divided. These challenges will not go away over night. Rather, the question is how the society will deal with them. There will be ongoing demands for recognition and rectification of injustice and surely there will also be challenges to the new narrative of struggle and resistance that will raise the issues of new emerging voices that confront those in power and those who control the narrative of transformation at present.

At the same time, there are significant dilemmas given the continuing inequalities between groups. Moving too quickly to rectify them threatens to disrupt the country's economic stability, while acting too slowly will produce political disillusionment and protest. The South African transition and the country's success in the first years of majority rule offer great hope that even the most racially divided societies can find ways to heal past wounds and build a shared future. As Gibson (2004) concludes in his study of public reactions to the TRC process, the answer is a clear "maybe they can." In this day and age of ethnic hatred and clashes of civilization perhaps this is not such a pessimistic conclusion.

The emphasis here has been on the effort in post-apartheid South Africa to enlarge the country's symbolic landscape, and to develop an inclusive narrative and set of symbolic attachments with which a majority of all of South Africa's racial and ethnic groups can identify. The analysis in the past two chapters emphasizes the content of these narratives and images but offers no evidence concerning the extent to which they have had an impact on how ordinary people understand the past and imagine the future. Although he did not study the country's heritage sites, Gibson's (2004) analysis of the Truth and Reconciliation Commission's findings suggests that there is a good deal of support in South Africa for a common national identity and a broad acceptance of the TRC's findings about the abuses of the apartheid era. His results are certainly consistent with the hypothesis offered here that narratives found in the country's heritage sites not only reinforce the new national narrative but transmit it in ways that change how many people think about social and political relationships and open possibilities for a continuing inclusive, democratic political life in the country.

10

Flags, heroes, and statues: inclusive versus
exclusive identity markers in the American South

A theme running through the previous chapters is that in symbolic conflicts the specific objects of contention are the surface manifestations of deeper issues of identity, recognition, inclusion-exclusion, and respect. As Bryan (personal communication) noted in the case of Loyal Order parades in Northern Ireland, "Parades conflicts aren't about parades." They are about the threatened identities of Protestants and Catholics and each group's mutually experienced lack of respect. In this chapter, I examine how flags and monuments can be the surface manifestation of conflict over issues of race and power (Leib 2002: 306).

In previous chapters, the substantive cases have all come from societies other than my own, although I have also lived in France a good deal on and off over the past thirty-five years. Here I apply the tools and insights from the cases I have already considered to show their relevance for understanding race in the United States. The Lost Cause narrative is a powerful example of a socially constructed narrative that played a politically significant role in the effort to come to terms with the legacy of the Civil War and slavery in the US. It framed white American understandings of race in both the North and South for decades and was not seriously challenged politically until 100 years after the Civil War. The narrative not only reflected existing views on race, but at times exacerbated differences, and shaped behavior, as it made some actions more or less socially and politically plausible than others.

In doing the research on conflicts over the Confederate battle flag, there were times when I realized once again that it is often harder to examine narratives from my own society than from those in which I had never lived for extended periods, as my own experiences and political views framed how I processed and reacted to the different positions. At

280

the same time, I hope that my engagement in the most enduring conflict in American history, while painful at times, also offers an opportunity to understand why and how taking people's narratives seriously is a crucial starting point for constructive conflict management (Roy 1994). A goal here is to examine a conflict, on which I admittedly have my own strong views, to explore what is needed to encourage mutual acknowledgment and recognition that could lead to more constructive race relations.

The starting point for this chapter is the conflict over the display of the Confederate battle flag in official settings in the American South.[1] Once one asks about the display of the battle flag, such as over Alabama's or South Carolina's capitol or as part of Georgia's or Mississippi's state flag, it is easy to identify related symbolic conflicts in the United States (North and South), which are ostensibly about the meaning of slavery, the Civil War, and past constitutional conflicts but whose emotional intensity alerts us to their contemporary relevance for understanding the politics of race. While the Civil War ended legal slavery, the war's aftermath hardly provided meaningful social or political equality for former slaves and their descendants, and certainly did not eliminate the importance of race as a social and political issue in American society. Rather, as Blight (2001), Linenthal (1993), and others have argued, regional reconciliation in the two generations after the war required the construction of a narrative from which questions of slavery and race were omitted to permit white Northerners and Southerners to come back together. An important cost of the only partially inclusive reconciliation narrative is that Americans are still grappling with the legacy of slavery and the civil war in current contestation around race.

First articulated in the South in the years immediately following the Civil War, the "Lost Cause" narrative argued that the war was about different constitutional principles and ways of life, not slavery, which Jefferson Davis said was just an "incident" (Blight 2001). Slaves, in this account, were well treated and content with their position. Whites provided economic security, health care, Christianity, and civilization for which slaves were grateful. "No argument in the Lost Cause formula became more an article of faith than the disclaimer against slavery as the cause of the war. In reunion speeches, committee reports, and memories, it is remarkable to note the energy Southerners spent denying slavery's centrality to the war" (Blight 2001: 282). It emphasized that the war was

---

[1] Actually the controversial flag is just one of the battle flags Confederate troops used (Coski 2000; 2005).

lost because of superior Northern numbers and resources – not for the lack of Southern commitment and bravery. Blight identifies five central aspects of the Lost Cause narrative:

First, veterans (and their supporters) continued to glorify the valor of Southern soldiers and to defend their honor as defensive warriors who were never truly beaten in battle. Second, Lost Cause advocates of the 1890s especially promoted the Confederate past as a bulwark against the social and political disorder of that tumultuous decade. Third, the UCV (United Confederate Veterans) and the UDC (United Daughters of the Confederacy) established history committees that guarded the Confederate past against all its real and imagined enemies. Fourth, contrary to the norm in Blue-Gray fraternalism, many Lost Cause writers and activists during the reconciliationist era were not at all shy of arguing about the *causes* of the war. Fifth, and most strikingly, a nostalgic Lost Cause reinvigorated white supremacy by borrowing heavily from the plantation school of literature in promoting reminiscences of the *faithful slave* as a central figure in the Confederate war. Together, these arguments reinforced Southern pride, nationalized the Lost Cause and racialized Civil War memory for the postwar generations

(Blight 2001: 273–74).

The Lost Cause narrative that argued that slavery, was an "incident" but not cause of the Civil War is certainly at odds with the dominant view of historians over the past half century (McPherson 1997; Dew 2001). However, the substantive question for this chapter is not establishing whose account of the origin of the war is most correct, but reflecting on the intensity with which competing narratives about it are held and their relevance for contemporary understanding of American race relations. The powerful Lost Cause narrative is a particularly good example of how a psychocultural narrative did more than just reflect existing beliefs, but also shaped behaviors over decades and limited the possibility of effective black–white dialogue in the North and South.

The Lost Cause narrative achieved hegemonic status among whites in the North as well as the South by the turn of the twentieth century and its core assumptions about black inferiority gained wide acceptance, appearing in political rhetoric, popular literature, and war memories. There was little white recognition of African American perspectives which were sharply at odds with the romantic vision of Southern ante-bellum life, perhaps best captured in *Gone with the Wind*, and these got little attention until the civil rights era. For 100 years after the war, most whites had little knowledge of what African Americans felt, not because their views were not available, but because, for the most part, blacks were considered uninformed and/or ignorant, and were treated as socially

[handwritten margin note: correctness isn't the goal, but reflecting on competing narratives.]

invisible. Whites readily accepted the views of the few blacks who said what they wanted to hear, and systematically ignored dissonant views that challenged their own strongly defended positions. When civil rights protests began in the 1950s, more than a few southern whites responded with anger, but also with hurt, a sense of betrayal, that blacks whom they thought they knew well had deceived them. Most whites, North and South, engaged in little self-reflection about how their own intimidation and discrimination might have contributed to the situation. While there was some change once the civil rights movement began, for the most part there was little sustained white engagement in matters of race. By the 1970s, after the Johnson era civil rights legislation was passed, whites grew increasingly impatient with continuing black demands, rejecting the idea that blacks were doing enough for themselves and showed diminished support for social programs and for affirmative action which they saw as unfair.

Race, in both the North and South, remains a topic about which constructive dialogue is all too rare. There is still very modest socializing across racial lines and there is little trust that cross-racial discussions around race can be honest and not hurtful. Much of this is related to the very different experiences and beliefs of blacks and whites and the very different narratives about American life they recount (Hacker 1992). For example, black–white differences in interpretation were especially visible in the reactions to the O. J. Simpson verdict in 1994. The jury's decision was announced on television during the workday and throughout the country people in dormitories, schools, offices, and factories gathered around television sets or radios to hear it. Many of these settings had both whites and blacks who reacted emotionally to the announcement that the jury found Simpson not guilty. Whites were overwhelmingly incredulous and dismayed, while many blacks responded joyfully. Each looked at the other in disbelief and anger. Two competing narratives drove these divergent reactions as whites focused on what they considered the overwhelmingly persuasive prosecution evidence, while blacks – including many who thought Simpson was, in fact, guilty – were delighted because of the jury's refusal to convict a black man on the testimony of a lying racist white cop. For whites the question was about Simpson's innocence or guilt; for African Americans it was about the justice system and their long experience with racist police practices, trumped up evidence, and lack of equal justice. Their joy at the verdict was not for Simpson, but for the validation that a white racist cop had lied in court once again but this time his testimony was rejected.

Interestingly, black and white Americans in different settings – both public and private – could have used the decision to talk about the very different spontaneous reactions each had to the verdict. But that didn't happen for the most part as many remained either too puzzled, angry, or hurt to talk about what had happened. Few whites and blacks are comfortable engaging each other and they often move either toward hyperpoliteness or bluntness, rather than to genuine exchange in an effort to comprehend why each understands political and social events so differently.

Conflicts over flags, statues, and murals in the South have, ironically, promoted some constructive exchanges that have increased the complexity with which blacks and whites view each other's worldviews. While surveys show that most people tired of these issues over time, there is evidence as well that conflicts over them forced increased engagement with the most basic concerns of the other side, a constructive reframing of positions, and outcomes that while not fully satisfactory to almost anyone were good enough for many.

To explore conflicts over the South's symbolic landscape, this chapter focuses on two specific conflicts from the past decade to better understand contemporary racially structured narratives in the United States. First, I look at the Confederate battle flag controversy in South Carolina and Georgia, and second, I consider on-going symbolic skirmishes in Richmond, the capitol of the former Confederacy, over statues and murals representing the city's history. These conflicts are marked by the intense emotions they evoke that are paradoxically both polarizing and opportunities for reframing competing narratives. The hegemonic status of the Lost Cause narrative affected black–white relationships in many basic ways. By the 1990s, however, the psychocultural dramas described in this chapter challenged many of its core elements, and the movement toward dialogue in South Carolina, Georgia, and Virginia that is described here suggests that the dramas that were played out in these states moved race relations in a more constructive direction. All sides seem to have done a better job of listening to each other than in the past and this has helped all parties to explore jointly their core needs and to articulate a somewhat more inclusive narrative about a shared past and present.

Flags and emblems as sources of division and conflict

Flags are the focal point of intense emotions in many settings (Prince 2004). As condensation symbols, flags and other emblems represent a collectivity to its members and outsiders so that an attack upon the flag is viewed as an attack upon the group itself. This is seen in countless times and places as, for example, when soldiers in battle protect their flags at great risk to themselves. Displaying the flag is a statement of attachment and political commitment for all to see, as we saw in the discussion of the 1992 Olympics in Barcelona. Many have remarked at how millions of Americans expressed their grief after the September 11 attacks by hanging a flag in front of their houses or businesses or putting flag decals on their cars.

Desecration of a flag such as by burning it publicly is often viewed as a crime act and sometimes enraged crowds attack the perpetrators of such acts.[2] During a Vietnam era protest, I well remember when a group of normally mild mannered faculty secretaries at Northwestern University attacked a group of protesters who displayed the American flag upside down, the naval sign of distress. Marvin and Ingle (1999) who write engagingly about the psychocultural and political significance of flags recount that one year Marvin began her class on the subject by burning an American flag to get the students to reflect on its emotional power and significance.

Most political communities are very careful about the design of their flag and the messages it communicates to citizens and outsiders. For example, in 1993 as part of the transition process, South Africa appointed a commission to consider the issue of flags and other symbols and the result was a series of proposals that emphasized inclusion of all groups in the country. The new national anthem, for example, includes two verses of *Nkosi Sikelel' iAfrika*, the unofficial anthem apartheid's opponents sang for many years, and a verse of the Afrikaans anthem, *Die Stem* or The Call of South Africa. In 1994 at Nelson Mandela's inauguration the new South African flag was flown for the first time "not as a symbol of a political party, nor of a government, but as a possession of the people – the one thing that is literally and figuratively above all else, our flag" (Beckett 2002).[3] The new

---

[2] Most countries have rules about how to dispose of a tattered, no longer usable, flag. Generally this should be done in a "dignified" manner such as burning so that remaining pieces are not used in an inappropriate way such as cleaning rags. What this reveals is that it is not the burning *per se* that is the problem but it is who is doing it and the context in which it is done that matters.

[3] The quote comes from the introduction to *Flying with Pride: The Story of the South African Flag*, a coffee table book "derived from the incredible variety of ways in which this unique cloth has become woven into the fabric of South African society" (http://www.safrica.info/ ess_info/sa_glance/history/flag.htm).

flag's design and color represented an explicit, conscious effort to link all groups in the country in an inclusive symbol.

Northern Ireland has had its share of controversies over flags and emblems – as we would expect in such a divided society (Bryson and McCartney 1994). Because Northern Ireland is part of the United Kingdom, the Union Jack is its official flag and Protestant support for the union is aggressively reinforced though red, white, and blue emblems, flags and painted curbstones – especially during the summer marching season. However, it is the Irish Tricolor that is the emotionally salient flag for the region's Catholic population who regularly display it in areas where they are dominant. Following the Belfast Agreement in 1998, there was some attention to developing new, non-sectarian symbols in Northern Ireland "such that symbols and emblems are used in a manner which promotes mutual respect rather than division" (Bryan and Gillespie 2005). This has, however, proven difficult to do in practice.[4]

Confederate battle flag controversies

The flag known as the Confederate flag is today a racially charged symbol to many black and white Americans (Coski 2005). It consists of the St. Andrew's cross and three red and white bars (Figure 10.1). Its significance, like that of many powerful symbols, has changed over time and much of its power derives from the different and strong uses and connotations it has. For many southern whites, the flag is associated with southern culture and community – what many call heritage – while for most blacks and some whites it evokes slavery, Ku Klux Klan violence, Jim Crow era segregation, and present-day discrimination.

It was actually never the official flag of the Confederacy but has become that in popular parlance over time. The first of three official flags of the Confederacy, commonly called the Stars and Bars, consisted of a rectangular field with a corner square and a circle of stars to represent the seven states which originally seceded, and three alternating red and white bars (Figure 10.2). The flag featuring the St. Andrew's Cross was first used as a battle flag by Robert E. Lee's Army of Northern Virginia in part because the official Confederate flag so resembled the US flag that soldiers in battle sometimes confused the two. Its use spread to other units during

---

[4] The Irish and British flags are not the only ones that are controversial in Northern Ireland. So are sectarian paramilitary flags that are often displayed.

Figure 10.1 Square and rectangular Confederate battle flags. The square flag is a captured flag from Lee's Army of Northern Virginia and the rectangular one is originally the Confederate naval flag

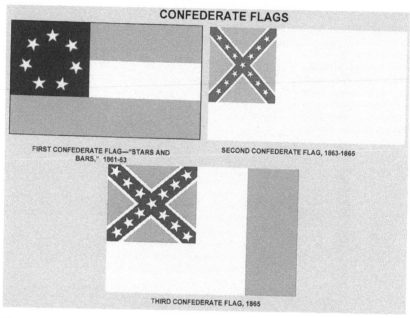

Figure 10.2 The three different official flags of the Confederate States of America

the war even as it took different shapes and forms but it was at no time either the only flag that Confederate soldiers used in battle or the official flag. The second and third Confederate national flags incorporated the St. Andrew's cross into the upper-left-hand corner replacing the blue field with stars. In the decades following the Civil War, it was the battle flag (which in its rectangular form was known as the Confederate naval jack) that most often appeared at Confederate Memorial Day commemorations and it was more and more referred to as simply the Confederate flag (and even the Stars and Bars) in common parlance (Coski 2000; 2005).

Coski (2005) points out that for many years the flag was widely displayed in the South, and sometimes in the North, and carried by American troops in battle, but was not necessarily politically contentious despite its association with the Confederacy. He contends that while the flag was always problematic for some northerners and many blacks, it only became an especially contentious political symbol in 1948 when it was used widely at political rallies during South Carolina Governor Strom Thurmond's Dixiecrat presidential campaign. The rallying theme of Thurmond's campaign and rhetoric was his defense of segregation, so it is not surprising that the flag soon became a widely used symbol of southern resistance to civil rights in general and school desegregation in particular. In the 1950s and 1960s segregationist politicians prominently displayed it at campaign appearances and public speeches while anti-black political groups including the Ku Klux Klan and other extremist organizations used it widely as well.[5] Before 1956 Georgia's flag resembled the "Confederate Stars and Bars" with the state seal in place of the stars; in 1956 the state changed it, substituting the Confederate battle flag for the state seal (Figure 10.3). Alabama (1963) and South Carolina (1962) hung the battle flag atop their state capitols in what were widely interpreted as statements of resistance to integration. Mississippi's state flag, adopted in 1894, also incorporates the Confederate battle flag in its design. Defenders of the flag do not agree that its display is anti-black, saying that the flag is a statement of remembrance for Confederate soldiers who died in battle. Opponents argue that the timing of these gestures makes the argument suspect.

During the 1970s and 1980s southern blacks began to protest the state-sanctioned displays of the Confederate battle flag and called for their removal from the capitols in the cases of South Carolina and Alabama and the flags' redesign in Georgia and Mississippi.[6] White heritage groups such as the Sons of Confederate Veterans (SCV), the Southern Heritage Association (SHA), and many Republican politicians vigorously opposed any change and charged that the flag opponents were attacking their heritage and the honor of Confederate soldiers who had fought for their nation's liberty. Clearly, the competing narratives differ in many ways and over the next two decades the flag conflicts regularly returned to legislative dockets and political campaigns. In Alabama, after a decade of political wrangling, Governor Guy Hunt, following a court decision, ordered in 1993 that the flag no longer be raised over the capitol (Coski 2005: 237–44). In contrast, in South Carolina and Georgia, the conflicts were long and drawn out but eventually white and black coalitions developed to build widely supported compromise outcomes.

---

[5] Coski (2005) argues that older heritage groups such as the Daughters of the Confederacy and sometimes the Sons of the Confederacy often voiced concerns that the popularization of the flag as a cultural symbol and its use in political campaigns threatened its solemn meaning and objected to its use in these ways. He also says that the Ku Klux Klan displayed the US flag even more than the Confederate one.

[6] Coski (2005) discusses many disputes over the display of the flag involving public schools and universities as well.

Georgia State Flag 1956-2001

Georgia State Flag Since 2003

Figure 10.3 Georgia state flags

As in many other cultural conflicts, there is nothing especially complicated about the surface issues in these flag controversies. At the core is not the flag but two entirely different interpretations of its significance, so that where it was displayed could not be separated from what it meant. As a result, each side repeatedly rearticulated its intensely held position, and for the parties modifying their position on the flag issue raised deep identity-rooted fears. In the end, only a public that grew tired of the issue, a mobilized business community worried about the economic consequences if the disputes continued, and politicians who feared the consequences of inaction more than action finally cobbled together the compromises.

The outcomes that were reached were not especially new or clever. They were fairly obvious and had been discussed as possible solutions for a long time. Here, as in other psychocultural conflicts, the issue was not how to invent a better outcome, but to create a process that would permit one of the many competing proposals to gain sufficient support from the diverse parties; that proved to be no mean feat. In a context of distrust and strong feelings of vulnerability – both of which were present – solutions that one side strongly supports often result in the ire of the other. An acceptable outcome requires a dialogue around difficult issues of race that in itself is a constructive process. As an editorial in South Carolina's leading newspaper said in 1997, "The victory for all South Carolinians would not lie in the physical act of moving the banner itself but rather in the *process* of agreeing to do so" (Prince 2004: 5; italics added).

South Carolina

In South Carolina the psychocultural drama began in the early 1970s and was especially acrimonious and it was not until 2001 that a compromise was reached that while receiving significant black and white support also left some blacks (including the state and national NAACP) and the white heritage groups dissatisfied (Coski 2005; Prince 2004). The compromise was one that had originally drawn significant white and black support seven years earlier when a group of hardcore pro-flag senators and seven of the state's eight African American senators negotiated a plan called the 1994 Heritage Act. It proposed moving the rectangular battle flag from the dome and placing a *square* battle flag, the one originally associated with the Army of Northern Virginia (ANV), next to the Confederate Soldiers Monument, and putting the first Confederate national flag (the

Stars and Bars) next to the Confederate Women's memorial on the state house grounds. They agreed that there would be an explicit statement "placed in the legislative record saying that the flags were being flown solely for the purpose of honoring South Carolinians who had fought and sacrificed in the Civil War (and that no racial or segregationist sentiment of any kind should be inferred from the display)" (Prince 2004: 162–63). In addition, the bill would have preserved existing Confederate monuments in the state and the group committed themselves to work toward the creation of a monument to honor African American achievements and contributions in South Carolina. The bill passed the South Carolina Senate but not the House, and it would take another seven years before a deal could be struck, one that was modeled on the 1994 proposal (Coski 2005: 244–252).

In the intervening years, a number of proposals were introduced and at one point there were up to twenty different ones under active consideration. Some involved moving the flag to a new location but then there was disagreement over which location was best. Flag supporters favored the Confederate Soldiers Monument while opponents either wanted it in a less prominent place on the state house grounds or inside the state's Confederate Relic Room and Museum. There were proposals to leave the flag but to put up additional ones with it such as a black nationalist flag; suggestions to put it in a display with all the flags that had been used in the state. Others advocated holding a referendum which would take responsibility for making a decision away from politicians wary over the potential fallout.[7] There were those who suggested that the flag fly over the capitol only a few days a year, such as on Robert E. Lee's birthday and Confederate Memorial Day. Even the height of the flagpole that would be used if it was moved next to the Confederate Soldiers Monument was a source of contention.

There was constructive dialogue in public settings and the press as well as some fanciful cultural exploration of the underlying issues. For example, two young clothing designers in Charleston formed a company

[7] The referendum strategy was used in Mississippi. In that state, in 2000, the Mississippi Supreme Court ruled that the state technically had no flag because the 1894 design had been accidentally omitted when the state code was updated in 1906. The legislature then appointed a commission to design a new flag and asked the voters to pick between the old and new designs. The old one that included the battle flag won easily, getting two-thirds of the vote. In addition, it is worth noting that even though voters were clearly split on racial lines, one survey showed that about one third of blacks favored keeping the old flag (Sack 2001; Smythe 2001).

called NuSouth that sought to promote discussion by designing clothes that used the battle flag, but changed its colors to those of the black liberation movement – black, green, and red – to represent unity (Prince 2004: 117–24). Sherman Evans, one of the company's founders, said that the new emblem was forward looking and proclaimed, "I am proud to be an African American and I am proud to live in the South. We transformed the symbol that oppressed us, we took away the power it had over us and eliminated the hatred it represented" (Prince 2004:119).

The flag conflict expanded beyond the state. National media covered the story which seemed more and more like the movie Groundhog Day as it came up in the legislature each year in more or less the same way. Politicians wanted the dispute to end and were afraid of political fallout from it, especially after Governor David Beasley went down to defeat in 1998 after having tried to work for a compromise. Presidential candidates running in the South Carolina primaries were pushed to take a position on the flag and did their best to say whatever they thought would not hurt them with their core constituencies. The most sustained outside involvement came from the NAACP which called for a tourist boycott of the state that gradually gathered momentum. While the economic losses were modest, the boycott brought more attention and embarrassment to South Carolina and strengthened the voices both inside and outside the legislature calling for a solution.

By 2000, it was increasingly clear that the flag would come down from the capitol as there was a strong consensus developing that only flags representing sovereign governmental entities should fly over the State House.[8] With many proposals floating around by early 2001, it was not obvious how to build an effective consensus. There were proposals regularly made to include Martin Luther King Day and Confederate Memorial Day as official state holidays as part of any solution. Flag proponents were fearful that removing the flag would just be the first step in what Senator Glenn McConnell called "cultural genocide." Opponents were always uneasy with any official state recognition of the battle flag given its past associations. Many blacks found it particularly hard to accept the argument that the flag simply represented cultural heritage and was "just a soldier's flag."

---

[8] Prince reports that as the eventual removal of the flag became more and more certain, sales of souvenir flags that had hung over the capitol – even for only a few minutes – skyrocketed (2004).

The New York Times reported that "profound mistrust and animosity between the two sides kept any plan from mustering a majority" (Firestone 2001). In the end, the Senate compromise built around the 1994 Heritage Act proposal was a product of personal trust among members of the body and "flag fatigue." Prince (2004) suggests that the fact that the NAACP's continuing opposition to the compromise proposal because the battle flag (albeit the square ANV version) would still be on the state house grounds and in too prominent a place for them probably made it easier for proponents to vote to remove the flag from the capitol building.[9]

Georgia

In Georgia, the psychocultural drama went on even longer. The compromise that was finally adopted in 2003 provided for a return to the pre-1956 state flag. The difference between the two is that the earlier Georgia flag incorporated the Stars and Bars, the first Confederate national flag, while the post-1956 flag had substituted the battle flag for the national flag (Figure 10.3). While both evoked memories of the Confederacy, the battle flag's explicit connection to racial violence and segregation meant that it was totally unacceptable to blacks and their white supporters. When South Carolina adopted its compromise, pressure increased to end the Georgia controversy. In 2001 Governor Roy Barnes proposed a new flag, one that had five former Georgia flags on it – each one quite small – including the 1956 one with the battle flag on it. The legislature passed his proposal but Barnes was defeated in the next election and a major issue his opponent Republican Sonny Perdue raised was that he never submitted the new design to the voters in a referendum. This position won Perdue the strong backing of flag supporters.

Perdue, however, lost control of the issue two years later when the legislature voted for the state's third flag in three years, this one based on Georgia's state flag from 1879 to 1956 and modeled on the first Confederate national flag, the Stars and Bars. The governor had supported the new design, but proposed a two-stage referendum process. The first vote would have asked voters to approve or disapprove the new design and if it failed there would be a second one asking voters to choose between the

---

[9] There were significant disagreements within, and just between, the groups. Whites were split, but so were blacks. In South Carolina, while all but one African American senator backed the compromise only three of twenty-six black house members did.

pre-1956 flag featuring the Stars and Bars, and the 1956 one with the battle flag. Black legislators balked at the two-stage proposal, opposing any vote involving the battle flag.

The coalition supporting the pre-1956 design and a one-stage referendum barely got through the legislature as politics finally prevailed over ideology. Republicans, a good number of whom supported the rebel flag, wanted the issue behind them as did business groups worried about a possible boycott of the state, a number of black legislators, and some white Democrats. Black Caucus head Senator Ed Harbison said the pre-1956 flag based on the Stars and Bars was one he could live with. "It has never been used by neo-Nazis and the Klan to intimidate and really deprive people of their freedom of speech and right to do what they want to do . . . I will call it a reasonable compromise" (Halbfinger 2003). The following year, 2004, voters overwhelmingly supported the new flag in a non-binding referendum by a 3–1 margin, and it passed in each of the state's 159 counties.

Toward greater inclusivity

Why were these conflicts so prolonged and hard to settle? The problem was that the opposing sides while ostensibly talking about flags and their placement were in fact disagreeing over more basic emotional issues such as respect, acknowledgment, recognition, identity, and the meaning of the past, while renegotiating their relationship in the present. The hurt and loss each experienced was compounded when there were explicit denials of the validity of their long-held beliefs. Only when some mutual acknowledgment occurred could the parties work to invent an acceptable compromise solution.

Although the flag disputes dragged on endlessly in the eyes of many of those involved, they did provide a public context in which each of the core narratives was articulated and at times – but not always – the disputants acknowledged each other's positions in ways that created more common ground than had previously existed. In Georgia, long-time flag supporter and former SCV member Bobby Franklin, who helped design the new flag, said his action resulted in part from the fact that hate groups and white racists had hijacked the battle flag and that they had never been publicly repudiated (Halbfinger 2003). In South Carolina, Senator Glenn McConnell, a long time prominent pro-flag spokesman, said he backed the compromise because he realized how keeping it on the capitol offended many South Carolinians. In the end, some blacks acknowledged the distinction between heritage and racism in both states. In South Carolina, they did this by accepting the square version of the flag that had been first associated with the ANV but not the more familiar rectangular one connected to the Klan and other racist and segregationist groups. In Georgia, although some found it ironic, blacks supported the design based on the first official Confederate national flag. Georgia historian James Cobb said that that was because the Stars and Bars was not associated with the Lost Cause, was not the flag the Klan waves, and was not the one that Strom Thurmond carried when he campaigned as a segregationist (Smith 2004a). An acceptable outcome required that each side develop a more differentiated view of the other and its positions. For blacks, this meant acknowledging that not all elements or proponents of white heritage were equally racist, while among flag supporters it required recognizing how for many African Americans the battle flag was a symbol of intimidation and racial domination.

Monuments: Lincoln in Richmond

As groups renegotiate their relationship, contestation frequently arises over public and official symbols since the weaker group is invariably un- or underrepresented in the symbolic landscape. Certainly this is true of race in the United States – especially in the American South. Richmond, Virginia, the capital of the Confederacy is a good example of this phenomenon. Historically, Richmond's public buildings, museums, and monuments all have been intimately associated with white rule and it is the Confederacy that is honored while the city's large African American population and its heritage is hardly visible. The city has a long history, but it is only the white parts which are renowned and celebrated.

Richmond was first settled shortly after Jamestown in the early seventeenth century and there are important colonial and revolutionary sites in and around Richmond, such as the church in which Patrick Henry delivered his, "Give me liberty or give me death" speech. The city served as the Confederate capital, and the Confederate White House where Jefferson Davis resided throughout the war is one of the Richmond's prime tourist attractions. In and around Richmond are dozens of major battlefield sites, the city's Hollywood cemetery is the burial place of Davis and other Confederate leaders, and Monument Avenue (sometimes grandiosely referred to as the Champs Elysée of the South) is home of the large statues of five Confederate heroes: Robert E. Lee, Stonewall Jackson, Jefferson Davis, Jeb Stuart, and Matthew Morey.

It should be no surprise that dominant groups control a region's symbolic landscape and that when there is pressure to broaden representation the majority feels threatened and the minority is impatient. As in the South African case, public monuments focus on the past, yet, as Savage reminds us, "in defining the past we define the present" (1997: 4). In the United States, that present has overwhelmingly been about white rule. From the country's earliest days, there has been a notable absence of African American images in spaces that define the nation's public symbols. "Before 1860 there are no known images whatsoever of African-Americans slave or free, in marble or bronze" (Savage 1997: 16). Following the Civil War there were several waves of monument construction as Americans sought to come to terms with the four years of death and destruction. Northern memorialization began in battlefields such as Gettysburg (Linenthal 1993) and in public squares and parks. By the 1880s southern monuments began to appear as well, led by local committees often spearheaded by the United Daughters of the Confederacy. The southern wave of monument building reached its crescendo over the next few decades. By 1920 there were thousands of monuments and memorials to the war in both the North and South.

The first wave of monuments featured heroic figures such as Lee or Lincoln. While there was a great deal of discussion about how to represent both slavery and emancipation in post-war monuments, few that do so were actually built, and even in those that were completed, such as the Freedman's Memorial in Washington, DC, paid for by freed blacks, they are portrayed in a subservient position.

Thus the juxtaposition of standing Lincoln and kneeling slave was probably meant to suggest a narrative of uplift from slavery rather than continuing dependence after slavery. The problem with this argument is that it takes no account of the genre of commemorative sculpture in which this image would be created and read.

(Savage 1997: 75)

Savage argues that as a result such monuments were less about emancipation than domination and that "the nation's most ambitious proposal for a monument to emancipation collapsed, we can argue, because it was dedicated to a new order that it did not comprehend and could not visualize" (Savage 1997: 113)

By the end of the nineteenth century, common-soldier monuments were more and more frequent. The soldier figure was supposed to be universal in its reference – yet it was invariably white (Savage 1997: 162) as "the marginalization of African Americans went hand in hand with the reconstruction of white America" (Savage 1997: 19). Despite the hundreds of thousands of African Americans who served in the war as soldiers and the 36,847 who died, "only three monuments in the nineteenth century depicted blacks in military service, all appearing in the last decade of the century and none of them generic war memorials" (Savage 1997: 192).[10] Savage concludes, "At the most basic level the monuments were white because the American polity itself was structured as white" (Savage 1997: 191).

Like flags, monuments and memorials following a war or other intense traumas serve two important functions as reflectors and as shapers of narratives.

To be erected, monuments usually had to mesh with the beliefs and aspirations of the majority, even when those were so deeply seated that they were unspoken. And once monuments were erected, they reshaped those beliefs and aspirations simply by giving them a concrete form in public space.

(Savage 1997: 210)

Historical memorialization emphasized white rule freed from the morally questionable institution of slavery (Savage 1997: 157). In the early phases, Confederate heroes, especially Lee, were symbolic figures of white domination and the wide acceptance of them and the lifestyle they were protecting paved the way for representations such as a monument to faithful slaves in South Carolina as "white Southerners came to see slavery as peculiarly suited to commemoration, a kind of golden age of race relations, built on intimate bonds between blacks and whites" (Savage 1997: 157).

One hundred years later, these representations are historical to some, and offensive to others. The question of what to do with monuments and other public representations of an earlier and politically problematic regime or era is not easy to decide. As we saw in South Africa, there is an effort to enlarge symbolic space to be more inclusive than in the past

---

[10] The best known is certainly the Shaw Memorial on the Boston Common honoring the 54th Massachusetts regiment, the first black regiment, organized in the North, made famous in the film *Glory*, and led by Colonel Robert Gould Shaw, a wealthy white Bostonian.

rather than to eliminate existing monuments. These issues also have arisen in the American South and some states have passed or considered legislation barring the removal of Confederate monuments or renaming of parks, roads, or towns named after Confederate leaders (Levinson 1998; Martinez *et al*. 2000). Levinson discusses various options of what to do with Confederate monuments in ways that are far more nuanced than the simple choice between doing nothing and removing them, including building additional ones close by, changing the text presented with them, or including them in a museum that offers different viewpoints on the war (Levinson 1998: 109–129). It is against this background of symbolization that recent conflicts in Richmond are best understood.

Arthur Ashe statue

Several proposals to alter the symbolic landscape have set off recent psychocultural dramas in this now black-majority city. The first one discussed here arose in 1993 when Richmond-born tennis star and human rights activist Arthur Ashe died, and it was proposed that the city erect a statue in his honor (Leib 2002). First, it was to be placed outside a youth sports complex, but then the city council decided to locate it on Monument Avenue. The proposal for the first prominent statue of an African American in Richmond unleashed a torrent of controversy that was often embarrassing for the city. However, Richmond went ahead with its plans and the statue was unveiled three years later (Black and Varley 2003; Levinson 1998). Both whites and blacks on the city council supported the statue's placement but it should be noted that there were different reasons for this; some blacks opposed this location to express opposition to honoring Monument Avenue because of its association with Confederate heroes whose statues are there (Leib 2002).

The Lee mural controversy

In 1999 Richmond was again embroiled in a psychocultural drama when Richmond's Historic Riverfront Foundation hung thirteen murals with twenty-nine different images on the city's floodwall along a newly built canal path. The murals focused on important personalities and events in Richmond's history including Robert E. Lee in his Confederate uniform which turned out to be controversial. Immediately City Councilman Sa'ad El-Amin met with the foundation and threatened a boycott if the

Lee portrait remained. The foundation's response was to put together a committee to assess the images on the floodwall. Former black Governor L. Douglas Wilder spoke out saying there was a place for Lee on the wall and surveys showed public support – much higher among whites than blacks – for maintaining Lee's image. The committee recommended that Lee's image be included but as a civilian after the war rather than in uniform.

After an intense debate, the council voted 6–3 in favor of a resolution to place the murals, including the one with Lee's image as a civilian, on the floodwall. A few days later it was revealed that several black organizations were shunning the two black city council members who voted for the resolution supporting an inclusive compromise. Both black and white public opinion, however, supported Lee's inclusion. Several months later – in November – the murals were completed and hung including the one with the new image of Lee. On January 17, 2000 the Lee mural was firebombed during the night. An interracial group restored the damaged mural and it was rehung within a month.

Bridge renaming

Richmond is filled with monuments, memorials, and streets named for white Confederate heroes and the city's Hollywood Cemetery is another place where they are honored. There are still a Robert E. Lee bridge over the James River and a Jefferson Davis Highway. In 1987 there was controversy when the Jefferson Davis Bridge was renamed the Manchester Bridge. Following on the heels of the Lee mural controversy, the City Council voted to rename the J. E. B. Stuart Memorial Bridge and the Stonewall Jackson Memorial Bridge (commonly known as the First and Fifth street bridges) after two local civil rights leaders, Samuel Tucker and Curtis Holt. It was claimed that the Confederate generals had no significant ties to the neighborhoods adjoining the two bridges, but this explanation really avoids the more basic motivation which was that blacks in Richmond have long felt they were unrecognized in public places despite their long-term presence and contribution to the city's culture and economy.

The issue of street, school, and bridge names is far from dead in Virginia and future skirmishes are likely. In 2004, the Virginia Senate unanimously passed a bill that would prohibit the renaming, relocation, or removal of Virginia's historic monuments, streets, and bridges but it died in the House. What this could do is set the state on a course more like South Africa where there is addition and modification rather than removal in the symbolic landscape. This, however, would require resources whose allocation may set off additional controversies. Tied to this issue is the recurring debate about whether to designate April as Confederate History and Heritage Month. Black legislators call it offensive and repugnant. One said it would be akin to proclaiming January as "Third Reich History and Heritage Month. . . . Confederate history is nothing more than exultation of one of the most shameful episodes in this country's history" (Bellantoni 2004).

Lincoln's second visit to Richmond

Perhaps the most vituperative recent psychocultural drama in Richmond arose in late 2002 when the United States Historical Society, a Richmond-based non-profit organization, donated a small statue of Abraham Lincoln and his son Todd to the National Park Service to be placed outside the Tredegar Richmond National Battlefield visitor center (Figure 10.4). Lincoln had visited Richmond only once – less than two days after the Confederate army and government fled at the very end of the war and a few days before his assassination. The statue is reported to be the only Lincoln statue in the former Confederacy. It shows Lincoln sitting on a bench with his arm around the 12-year-old Todd who was in the city with him that day. Behind the bench is a wall with the inscription, "To bind up the nation's wounds." It is hardly triumphalist, but that is not the point. Opponents who included vocal members of the Sons of Confederate Veterans denounced the move to the press and wrote furious letters to local papers (Ferguson 2003).

Brag Bowling, the SCV Virginia commander described the statue as a "slap in the face of brave men and women who went through four years of unbelievable hell fighting an invasion of Virginia led by President Lincoln," and comparisons were made between placing this statue in Richmond and the placement of a statue of Osama bin Laden in New York, of Hitler in Tel Aviv, or of Tojo at the USS *Arizona* memorial in Pearl Harbor (Williams 2002). The opposition was vocal but there is little indication that it was very widespread. Editorials from Virginia newspapers and the *Washington Post* supported the placement of the statue and the Richmond City Council backed the project, contributing $45,000 and calling it a symbol of unity and reconciliation. In a letter written

Figure 10.4 The first, and only, statue of Abraham Lincoln in any of the former Confederate states. He is shown sitting with his son. Behind him are the words "To bind up the nation's wounds." It is located in Richmond, Virginia since 2003.

by a descendant of a Confederate soldier to the Richmond *Times-Dispatch*, the author said he was "saddened and embarrassed by those who would be so ignorant as to see the statue of Abraham Lincoln as being anything more than a symbol of liberty, equality and unity" (Richmond *Times-Dispatch*, January 24, 2003). The mayor said the money for the project was the "best 45K this city ever spent." Deputy Mayor Dolores L. McQuinn said, "Lincoln is just the beginning . . . you haven't seen anything yet. I am going to go out of my way to try and diversify the statues [in Richmond]" (Redmon 2003). Some hard-core opponents, somewhat ironically, claimed that Lincoln was a segregationist and should not be honored, and they even sponsored a conference, "Lincoln Reconsidered" featuring a series of Lincoln bashers that emphasized that Lincoln had no real affection for blacks and was an inattentive father who told bawdy stories.[11]

The Lincoln statue conflict escalated quickly but also ended abruptly once the statue was dedicated. The dedication went off with a few dozen SCV protestors outside the park but there was no violence. Former Governor Linwood Holton delivered the keynote address and there were a number of distinguished people in attendance. The next afternoon there was a walk in downtown Richmond to retrace a possible route Lincoln had taken in 1865. The SCV sponsored an alternative "weekend for those who hold their heritage high" holding a rally at Hollywood cemetery and a parade along Monument Avenue, announcing, "It's all part of Confederate history and heritage month" (Jones 2003). While the open controversy ended, the underlying issues were hardly resolved.

These disputes over Richmond's symbolic landscape could suggest that the city is paralyzed around racial issues. The reality is more complicated, and more hopeful. As each of these controversies developed there has been significant black and white cooperation that has worked toward inclusive solutions – as was the case in the Ashe statue, the Lee mural, and Lincoln statue conflicts. In addition, there are a number of other examples of how public symbolic space in Richmond has been defined more inclusively with respect to race in recent years.

Contrary to what many visitors must expect, the Museum of the Confederacy is not simply one that offers either an unvarnished version of

---

[11] Many of the hard-core opponents were highly inflammatory. One example is the blurb about a story on the http://southerncaucus.com website: "The Jefferson Davis Memorial Site is Reopening Again to the Public – This is great news. Now if they would just close down the Lincoln Memorial and reopen it as a memorial to the Lincoln Holocaust."

the Lost Cause narrative to visitors or advocacy for the Confederate cause, as some would like. While the museum and Confederate White House are built around Civil War era Confederate and Southern artifacts, they have presented exhibits that offer a more complex view of the war and the region's politics that has not always pleased hard-core neo-Confederates.[12] A decade ago the museum presented an NEH funded exhibit on "Before Freedom" which addressed many of the core issues involving slavery head on. Slavery is not skirted in its permanent collection either and it includes panels that show slavery's role in the succession and there is at least one that specifically challenges the Lost Cause's emphasis on contented slaves. However, the Confederate artifact-based exhibits offer insights into only one of the narratives framing the period.

Another emerging effort in Richmond that shows great promise for building a more inclusive narrative around the past is a newly opened museum, the American Civil War Museum at Tredegar, at the site of the former Tredegar Iron Works along the James River, the factory that produced about half of the Confederate army's heavy artillery.[13] The project's executive director, Alex Wise, explained that the museum juxtaposes Confederate, Union, and black narratives about the war, its causes, and effects, in one site. The project has an impressive range of board members including distinguished scholars, local representatives, and diverse voices that helped articulate the three narratives. In addition, it displays a significant number of African American, Confederate, and Union objects from the period that either are part of its collection or available through loans from other museums to facilitate reflection and dialogue over alternative perspectives on the past and present.

A third promising initiative is spearheaded by Hope in the Cities, a national organization that has its headquarters in Richmond. For more than a decade it has worked to use the past to address present-day racial issues in Richmond. One of its most interesting innovation projects is built around Montville's (1993) idea of "Walking Though History," in which participants visit historically significant sites to talk about past events and their present relevance. Hope in the Cities built a 1993 Walk

---

[12] The dilemma, as at the Voortrekker monument, is the issue of what the hard core wants and needs and how this is to be balanced against the professional judgments of the staff. As a result, some of the hard core feel that their views are marginalized.

[13] Today part of the site is a visitor center for the federally run Richmond National Battlefield.

around Richmond's history as a center of the slave trade. The city had one of the most active slave markets in the country and served as the port for sending slaves from the east coast to Gulf coast cities such as New Orleans. The walk began at the church where Patrick Henry delivered his impassioned call for liberty, wove its way through historically important African American sites in the old city including those where slave auctions were once held, and ended at the docks along the river where slaves were shipped out. The group reflected on what these experiences might have been like, and at the conclusion tossed flowers into the river in memory of those who had gone through these experiences. Since then, among its other activities, Hope in the Cities in conjunction with the city has developed a mile-long Slave Trail to mark the route slaves probably took to the docks; it is now included along with other ante-bellum sites on tours of historical Richmond.

Conclusion: moving toward inclusivity

Memorialization and memories about the past change over time in many ways. In the American South, for example, immediately after the Civil War Confederate Memorial Days were marked in ceremonies in cemeteries (Savage 1997). On these occasions, the battle flag was often displayed as "a soldier's flag," not a political symbol. Two decades later memorialization began to take new forms and moved into other settings. While as early as the 1870s, there was elaboration of the Lost Cause narrative and popular literature glorifying the ante-bellum South, it was not until the end of the next decade that veterans' groups and the United Daughters of the Confederacy began to organize. The former sponsored reunions, and by 1900 there were often joint events with Union veterans' groups, while the UDC focused its efforts on memorial construction in small towns and cities. Soon Confederate battle flags captured during the war were returned to the South, Confederate dead were reburied in Arlington National Cemetery, there were monuments to the dead from both sides at Gettysburg and other battlefields, and the Spanish American war and World War I brought together soldiers from both regions in ways that symbolized reunion and reconciliation. In World War II the Confederate battle flag occasionally appeared among American troops, but it was not seen as a divisive symbol – at least by white soldiers.

The symbolic and political context changed in 1948 with the push for civil rights and southern resistance crystallizing around Thurmond's presidential campaign, and then opposition to the 1954 Brown *vs.* Board of Education decision ruling that segregated schools were inherently unequal (Coski 2005). Blacks still had few rights in the South and white politicians used the race card to build support and organize resistance to change. During this time Confederate iconography and the Lost Cause narrative became key political symbols and provided a readily available narrative around which to organize resistance. Groups such as the UDC and SCV played key roles in many ways in the campaign against civil rights legislation although they were uneasy with and often opposed the political and pop cultural display of the flag (Coski 2005).

Another burst of interest in the Civil War and its meaning followed Ken Burns' incredibly successful PBS documentary series in the 1980s. Visits to battlefields and battle reenactments shot up (Horwitz 1999). Heritage groups continued to prosper, regularly participating in reenactments, holding local meetings, and political and ritual celebrations. In Richmond, members of these heritage groups were involved in all three of the controversies outlined in this chapter. Both the SCV and the UDC have a regular ritual calendar and a high point for these groups is marking Jefferson Davis' birthday each June. Clearly, conflict has moved toward contestation over symbolic and ritual representation and is elaborated in reenactment rituals that limit direct confrontation. The SCV holds a yearly memorial service and rededication of the Davis Circle at his grave site in Richmond's Hollywood Cemetery combining civil, religious, and political expressions. Throughout the one I attended in 2004 there was little talk of slavery or race, although there were a few references to blacks who fought for the South, and the focus was on the cause and states rights. In the afternoon of the same day, the United Daughters of the Confederacy hold their Annual Massing of the Flags, an elaborate ritual in which the flags of eighteen states in the Confederacy or sympathetic to it in one way or another are presented to the audience one at a time by a man dressed in a Confederate uniform and a woman often, but not always, wearing a period dress who process from the back to the front of the auditorium while a song associated with each state is sung and the flag unfurled for presentation to the audience.

The elaborate expression of political positions through ceremony and ritual is surely not unique to the South. Rather, as Cohen (1974; 1993) suggests, it is through cultural organizations that emphasize ritual and symbols that groups often mobilize to articulate and work for political goals that might be otherwise unachievable through direct action.

Southern heritage groups have worked hard to articulate and defend their interests in recent years and their activity reveals two different motives: explicitly political ones often associated with race, and cultural ones more connected to identity and recognition needs. The more clearly the latter are expressed, as they have been at times in the conflicts that are the focus of this chapter, the more it becomes possible to identify ways that the core needs of whites and blacks can be met.[14]

What might a constructive dialogue look like around issues of race and the Civil War? In the South, the hurts of both blacks and whites would probably be at its core. For blacks it is the pain and humiliation of slavery, Jim Crow, segregation, and discrimination. Slavery was earliest and most profound; it was accompanied by lack of control over the most basic relationships – families that could be split up at the whim of an owner, rape of women, selling of children, and treating people as property. It doesn't matter if they were treated well or not on a daily basis. Slavery was just plain wrong and horrible. The post-war freedom was a significant, but not sufficient, change, since the next 100 years continued a presumption of inferiority, and introduced legal segregation, overt discrimination, and physical intimidation that included lynching.

For whites, the Civil War produced losses and humiliations too. Here too there was destruction of families, deaths, maiming, and defeat. There had to have been considerable depression and anger – not just stoicism – after the war. Anger got turned against Lincoln, Sherman, Grant, and the North but also against former slaves for their perceived disloyalty. The sequences no doubt were complicated, but when during reconstruction blacks moved into authority positions they became a particular focus of wrath. The Lost Cause narrative, as Blight (2001) argues, built on this anger through nostalgia for what people wished had existed before the war and it took root in both the North and South among the many people seeking white reconciliation and reunion. Mourning the loss and change was far from complete and explains, in part, the American inability to turn the page.

This analysis suggests that both African American and Confederate narratives are about loss, suffering, and humiliation. In the one case, it is rooted in slavery and power relationships; in the other, it can be argued

---

[14] There have been a good many dialogues between SCV members and those taking different positions on issues such as the Confederate flag and other symbolic disputes in Richmond.

that whites did it to themselves. They did not have to continue the system of slavery; they did not have to go to war. But this is beside the point. What is common to both is the suffering each experienced; the humiliation each felt; and the lack of acknowledgment of these feelings and experiences. An effective narrative of reconciliation does not necessarily have to address cause and responsibility so much as recognize the deep vulnerabilities, humiliations, and losses all have had, and their implication for the present and future.

In interviews, John Coski and Alex Wise both discussed possible bridging narratives for Richmond. Coski said that many white southerners have problems around the issue of slavery as a cause of the Civil War for it often feels to whites that to say slavery was a motive for the war is a moral condemnation of their ancestors. What they need is a space in which judgments about slavery are separated from the motives and moral character of those who fought for the Confederacy. If this distinction could be made more publicly, whites might more easily recognize the role that slavery played and contextualize, rather than deny, it. Wise suggested that many whites seek black acknowledgment that whites delivered blacks from darkest Africa, giving them a higher standard of living and Christianity. I don't believe that this is an easy starting point for African Americans unless it is also accompanied by acknowledgment of the evils of slavery, Jim Crow, post-war segregation, and physical intimidation. Is this possible? Perhaps for some people, some of the time, especially if African Americans also acknowledged white family disruption and suffering in the war.[15]

The aftermath of the Civil War raises the important issue of a too-limited reconciliation. As Blight (2001) makes clear, the story of reunion is one of North–South white reconciliation. It brought together both sides to rebuild a stronger union and was concretized in a number of ways including joint reunions of former soldiers from both sides at Gettysburg

---

[15] It should also be remembered that while this discussion emphasizes black and white differences, each group is not homogeneous in its actions and beliefs. In each of the conflicts examined in this chapter, there were coalitions of whites and blacks who worked together for the settlements that were achieved. Many whites have supported real change in the South, opposing the use of the battle flag as an instrument of intimidation, and recognizing its history and meaning to blacks. Those who resist change are a small hard core of heritage militants. Two strategies are possible for dealing with them. One is to simply ignore and try to isolate them and their claims. The other is to reach out; engage in dialogue and deescalate public rhetoric through mutual acknowledgment and effective communication.

and elsewhere, the return of captured flags to Southern units, and reburial of Confederate dead in Arlington National Cemetery. But in the process, black experiences, needs, and a very different narrative of exclusion, discrimination, intimidation, and unfulfilled promises of full participation was suppressed, as Fredrick Douglass, Booker T. Washington, and W.E.B. DuBois pointed out at the time. The legacy of the white North–South reconciliation is the sorry story of American race relations in the twentieth century; one that excludes blacks from American public life and then blames them for their failure to be engaged. Southern practices and policies of intimidation, segregation, and unequal resource allocation get a heap of responsibility here. But northern whites were complicit in excluding blacks in ways that were just as significant, and in doing little or nothing to push the South, where most blacks continued to live until 1960, to change.

What this raises is the question of what is a "good enough" narrative following a conflict? When is reconciliation a mechanism for avoiding a hard issue that few want to touch, as occurred in the United States following the Civil War when black voices were absent from American public life? While the focus has been on race issues in the South, the more I have worked on this chapter, the clearer it became that the same issues of denial were very present in the North as well. Race is hardly just a southern problem in the US, but an American one, as Tocqueville, Myrdal, and many foreign observers have pointed out. In the North, as well as in the South, issues about slavery and black–white relations are hard for Americans to confront.

Philadelphia, the city in which I live, has recently had a controversy around the newly built Liberty Bell Pavilion in Independence National Park. Excavations of the site, part of which contained the house in which George Washington lived and worked as president from 1790 to 1797, turned up evidence that during these years Washington, a native of Virginia, had slaves who lived and worked there. Also, on this site he signed the Fugitive Slave Act in 1793 that strengthened the rights of slave owners to recapture escaped slaves from other states (Mires 2002). Although he was not the only person who had slaves in this house or in Philadelphia, the revelations set off a controversy about northern practices in the country's early years and the question of how the story would be marked, and perhaps incorporated into the new building that would hold the country's sacred icon (Nash 2003).

Led by African Americans, a group called Avenging the Ancestors Coalition (ATAC) was formed demanding that the National Park Service which had spent $300 million on the project that would be located across from a new National Constitution Center also mark the location; in an appropriate manner as one in which slavery existed. They charged that ignoring the presence of slavery in the nation's first White House was hypocritical (Hughes 2004). Historians also organized and demanded that the site engage the contradictions between the notational narrative of liberty and the reality of slavery on the site. There were public hearings and discussions and slowly the Park Service agreed that they needed to do more than simply put up a plaque noting the history of the spot and that Washington quartered his slaves there while he was president. Plans emerged for a more significant presentation on the site of Washington's home and offices and an emphasis on slavery in Philadelphia at that time.[16]

Those pushing the Park Service argued that the power of place needed to be utilized to communicate the complex and braided history of the country's founding on a location that most people associate only with liberty (Mires 2005). Achieving this raised complicated issues, however, since archeological remains and archival records about the property are sketchy. It is not completely clear to all exactly where the slaves were quartered, and how they interacted with indentured and other servants. We do know that two of them escaped and gained their freedom and that despite the fact that there were slave-owners in Philadelphia at the time, there was also a free African American community and some of its leaders lived nearby. By 2004, following a Congressional directive to design an adequate presentation on the site, there was movement toward a specific design that would make use of the site to raise important issues about race and the country's founding that had literally been kept underground for decades (Salisbury 2005; Waters 2005).

New York is another northern state where many people view race conflicts as primarily a southern problem. They have had little awareness that during the eighteenth century New York city was a center of the slave trade and that the number of slaves in New York was second only to Charleston, South Carolina (Berlin and Harris 2005).[17] Slaves were

---

[16] A recent report on developments in the controversy is reported at www.ushistory.org/presidentshouse/news/index.htm.

[17] In 2005, the New York Historical Society presented a widely publicized exhibit on slavery in New York providing detailed descriptions, maps, and teaching materials (www.slaveryinnewyork.org/gallery_2.htm).

critical in building the early city, and during the eigh
many as 43 percent of New York families owned slaves
much as 20 percent of the city's population, and slavery
in New York until 1828, far later than in most neighbo
the foundations were dug for a federal office building in
in 1991, workers uncovered a forgotten colonial-era c
20,000 Africans were buried outside the city walls. Research revealed a
great deal about the individuals and their lives in the city (Blakey 2001). In
2003 the excavated remains were reburied in a commemorative ceremony
that included caskets made in West Africa expressly for this purpose,
processions through cities on the east coast, and a well attended memorial
service. The site is now being considered as a National Monument. A
crucial question is why so little was known about the extent of slavery in
New York and its role in the city's economy over two centuries. How did
such a large part of the population and their experiences become so
invisible in the city's historical memory and symbolic landscape? Why
and how does it matter that some stories about the past are told and retold
and others are ignored?

Culture's central role in ethnic conflict

Introduction

Unlike most political analyses of ethnic conflict, the one offered here has not emphasized the detailed history of specific disputes, all the substantive issues separating the parties, or the institutional arrangements that often dominate such discussions. This is not because these elements do not matter; rather, it is because they are not all that matters. Political analyses tend to ignore, dismiss, or under-theorize the role that identity and emotional framing play in long-term conflicts. In order to address this imbalance, I focus here on the role of cultural expression and enactment and link them to conflict expansion and settlement. This is not a rejection of structural and institutional analyses, but an effort to expand a what is considered relevant.

Early in 2005 the news was filled with stories of conflict involving emotionally powerful cultural enactments and expressions intertwined with substantive issues. There were Chinese demonstrations against Japan protesting changes in Japanese school textbooks that seemed to downplay Japanese World War II atrocities, including the 1937 Rape of Nanking. Analysts linked the current protests to Japan's push for a permanent seat on the UN Security Council and economic competition in East Asia. Following the mounting protests, Japan expressed "deep remorse" for the tremendous damage and deep suffering it caused during the war. However, this was not sufficient and Chinese President Hu Jintao held a meeting with Japanese Prime Minister Junichiro Koizumi in which Jintao said Koizumi's controversial visits to Tokyo's Yasukuni shrine honoring war criminals are the "crux" of the problem in Sino-Japanese ties and had prevented state visits by either leader to the other's country for the past three years.

312

Concurrently, in South Africa, there was on-going controversy over whether or not to change the name of Pretoria, which serves as South Africa's administrative capital. The Metropolitan Council voted to change the name of the region to Tshwane, the name of a former Ndebele chief and the river in the region which means "we are the same," rather than keeping the name of the Trekker who led the Afrikaners at the battle of Blood River; however, the Council agreed to keep the name of the central city itself as Pretoria. Various opposition parties and Afrikaner groups said that name change threatened to increase Afrikaner alienation at a sensitive time, while some blacks insist they should not have to continue to live with place names that honor former colonial conquerors or those that include derogatory terms.

In France, the conflict between Muslims and non-Muslims continued to simmer; in addition, and when Pope John Paul II died, there was a series of controversies over how France with its militant ideology of state secularism should mark the occasion. The Interior Ministry announced that the French flag would fly at half staff over all public buildings, including schools, for 24 hours and on the day of the funeral and told all prefects to attend services to mark the death and pay their condolences to local bishops. Some mayors, mainly on the right, complied; others, mostly on the left, did not. A national parents' organization protested, saying, "How can the young understand this secularism at two speeds that then forbids the wearing of the veil but authorizes political and media excesses following the death of the Pope?" (Sciolino 2005). Supporters of the government's move and of President Chirac's decision to attend the funeral said it was in recognition of the death of a head of state who enjoyed privileged relations with France, not an expression of religion.

In Jerusalem, Israeli security services reported that they had thwarted a planned Jewish extremist attack on Islamic holy sites including the Al-Aqsa mosque, while Israel's Islamic Movement called upon Israeli Arab Muslims to flock to Jerusalem to protect the mosque from Jewish extremists (Harel and Lis 2005). The police closed the Temple Mount/ Haram al-Sharif to Jews for a period when a right-wing extremist group called Revava planned a mass rally there in an effort to disrupt the government's Gaza disengagement plan, perhaps provoking a Muslim led attack on Israel.

The BBC reported plans in India to build the world's first Hindu theme park that would be the "world's biggest ever mythological theme park" and honor gods such as Rama, Hanuman, and Krishna (McCaul 2005).

The planned park is part of the Hindu nationalist effort to emphasize India as a Hindu nation and is tied to the conflict discussed in Chapter 3 over the disputed mosque/temple at Ayodhya and other religious sites in the northern part of the country. The organizer of the Gangadham theme park project, which will be located in the pilgrimage town of Haridwar on the Ganges River, is Shiv Sagar, the grandson of the man who produced and directed the immensely popular TV serial "Ramayan" that aired throughout the country in the 1980s and mobilized Hindu nationalist sentiments (Rudolph and Rudolph 1993). Although not planned as an expression of anti-Muslim sentiment, the theme park, through its emphasis on past Hindu heroes, will offer an exclusive view of Indian identity that emphasizes the country's Muslims as outsiders.

Nine months later as I was completing the final revisions for this book, a conflict over the publication in a small Danish newspaper, *Jyllands-Posten*, in September 2005 of twelve cartoons depicting Mohammed erupted into protests and violence. Muslims in Denmark had quickly protested the publication of the cartoons and Muslim ambassadors complained to the government. The conflict then simmered for a time as news of the cartoons spread through the Muslim world from clerics in Denmark. In late January, Saudi Arabia recalled its ambassador and gunmen seized the EU office in Gaza demanding an apology. The next day, papers in France, Germany, Italy, and Spain as well as many websites reprinted the cartoons asserting the right to free speech; this was followed by attacks on the Danish Embassies in Syria and Lebanon and public protests in other countries. Additional pictures offensive to Muslims were circulated and web sites offered more and more unrestrained visual and verbal attacks on Islam. Most Western governments were especially uneasy and issued statements condemning the specific images, noting that freedom of speech must be accompanied by responsibility, and calling for an end to the violence.

As the conflict escalated and new voices were added, it became clear that the conflict was only in part about the cartoons themselves. At a deeper level, it engaged two starkly competing narratives: what Muslims see as on-going unfair attacks on their religion and its symbols, as opposed to the position of many Europeans that free speech and freedom of the press are at risk from Islamic intimidation and violence. As long as the confrontation emphasized these competing, non-negotiable principles, any kind of constructive deescalation remained unlikely. Again, Turner's (1957) observation that conflicts over competing principles, or rights, are likely to deescalate only when they are reframed and when new symbols and rituals redirect the disputants' attention is on target here. How this might occur, and whether it can overcome the efforts of conflict entrepreneurs exploiting the controversy for their own reasons, remains to be seen.

All of these examples emphasize the close connection between cultural expressions and political action, and the need to take seriously the accounts that participants in a conflict offer, not because they are necessarily correct in any absolute sense, but because these psychocultural narratives are a valuable tool for understanding how participants frame their identities and threats to them (Roy, 1994). Changes in narratives are one reason why ethnic conflicts such as the ones I have examined are rarely simple and straightforward. Over time there are changes in goals, perceived interests, participants, strategies and tactics, and how both the disputants and outsiders understand the conflict. They are central in the dynamic by which parties make decisions about what or what not to do and say based on what others do and say, which means that the study of conflict at the micro-level requires an examination of interaction sequences and reciprocal changes in attitudes, behaviors, and group narratives.

This concluding chapter has three sections. First, I reiterate my core argument about how and why cultural contestation is central in many ethnic conflicts and conflict mitigation. Second, I examine some dilemmas surrounding the concept of greater inclusiveness in cultural expressions. One route to greater inclusiveness and changed group relations is that of reconciliation, often most usefully expressed through cultural expressions and enactments that signify a new relationship between formerly hostile groups. Third, the conclusion raises the issue of how cultural enactments and expressions can be leveraged to contribute to conflict mitigation that changes a society's institutions and practices in a constructive direction.

Reiteration of the main argument

Psychocultural dynamics are central to how culture frames interests, structures demand-making, and shapes the extent to which opponents can find common ground to produce constructive outcomes to long-term disputes. Narratives are not simply just-so stories people recount to justify their own actions. Narratives matter because they are the lenses through which groups and individuals view themselves and their opponents. They structure expectations and provide readily available interpretations for the meaning of action and the motives of different actors.

Narratives define interests, often in mutually exclusive terms, and in so doing limit and direct the action possibilities that parties consider to achieve their goals. Narratives are not simply recounted in a straight-forward and low-key manner; rather, in emotionally significant situations they are expressed and enacted in ways that heighten the salience of group differences, facilitate mobilization of people to action, and polarize the parties. Performance and passionate expression of a narrative provide political support for exclusive positions that diminish the common ground between the parties and their willingness to engage in cooperative actions. In these ways, cultural expression and performance are strategic political acts, although not necessarily always conscious ones, that reiterate each party's positions, assert group interests, and promote selective demand-making and political action. Framing interests and demands around culturally significant accessible images and metaphors heightens each party's emotional commitments, enhances within-group communication and coordination, and strengthens group boundaries.

Attending to the metaphors and analogies that frame a group's analyses of ethnic conflict is crucial to making sense of them. They serve as reflectors of a group's core assumptions about a conflict and what it needs to make a good-enough agreement with an adversary; in addition, cultural expressions play an exacerbating, inhibiting, or causal role in conflict when they heighten or diminish tensions and make certain action possi-bilities more plausible, and hence more probable, than others. Psycho-cultural dramas join past and present issues and emotions, as we see so clearly in the China–Japan dispute over the textbooks, the World War II shrine, and Security Council membership, and in the other conflicts discussed throughout this book. In exchanges between the disputing parties, the strong emotions unleashed fuel a strong sense of cruciality and drive confrontations in which at least some of the participants come to believe that the group's honor, and even existence, are at stake.

When groups play out culturally salient conflicts through intense psychocultural dramas, where they take the parties is rarely obvious at the outset. In some cases, such as the Israeli–Palestinian conflict, each psy-chocultural drama appears to morph into the next one as the parties are unable to find sufficient shared ground to negotiate their interest differ-ences, to define structural arrangements to manage their differences, or to acknowledge the core elements in each other's national narrative as a step toward tension reduction. In the absence of either significant formal or informal agreement among the parties or an externally imposed arrangement that addresses the differences among the parties, new issues regularly arise that threaten to spin out of control.

On-going escalation is not, however, the only possible outcome to intense psychocultural dramas. Conflict mitigation occurs and new more inclusive narratives and ritual expressions and enactments can be a crucial part of deescalating conflict and solidifying partial or comprehensive settlements. All cultures have images of peace and peacemaking and drawing on these can help opponents see each other in a new light, and to explore shared concerns and mutually beneficial arrangements. For such beliefs to be politically effective, however, the parties must express them in emotionally evocative ways through images and rituals consistent with more inclusive narratives which, at the same time, define interests and positions in less absolute, strident terms.

Attending to cultural expressions is not a substitute for politics, negotiation, and institution building, but a valuable supplement before, during, and after the development of new structural arrangements. Parties in conflict need to negotiate, but negotiations by themselves are not enough. In long-term conflicts, opponents also need to face the past, redefine their incompatible identities, and engage in rituals that express their new relationship. Conflict mitigation through the development of explicit connections between culturally available images and metaphors and events on the ground goes hand in hand with attention to interest differences and institutional arrangements. Attention to psychocultural dynamics as a part of conflict mitigation requires emotional and ritual redefinition in order for more complex, and less directly opposed, identities to develop, such as the emergence of a European identity after World War II. The new narratives and enactments that develop in peacemaking and peacebuilding processes must alter the parties' frames of reference; exclusively cognitive efforts to convince adversaries to change their attitudes and behaviors are almost always efforts that fail. Conflict mitigation must include the recognition and acceptance of a group, and its narratives can create possibilities for cooperation linking identity to new metaphors, rearranging the content of old ones in culturally acceptable ways, and creating space to actively envision alternatives to ongoing confrontation, as we saw in the case of the new festival in Derry and changes in the symbolic landscape in South Africa.

The challenge of inclusiveness in ethnic conflict management

I have argued that cultural expressions and enactments must be part of the analysis of any long-term ethnic conflict and are integral to any strategy for their constructive management. In this section, I want to highlight ways to enhance our understanding of the dynamics of conflict and strategies for ethnic conflict mitigation through more explicit consideration of narratives and the deeper meanings cultural contestation makes visible. All the conflicts I considered were long-term ones, not single disputes that flared up and then rapidly disappeared. They did, however, range in terms of their intensity, use of violence, and the degree to which they have escalated in dangerous ways. While I focused on cultural contestation in each conflict, I want to reiterate for one last time that I have not argued that cultural differences by themselves cause ethnic conflicts. Rather, while groups and individuals often employ these differences to make claims, mobilize supporters, and seek positions and power, people, battle over real interests, and identities and culture is one of the resources they mobilize to do this. Yet because of the ambiguous and emotionally charged nature of many cultural enactments and expressions, they are too easily assumed to be the cause of conflict rather than the vehicle through which it is played out.

The paradox of inclusiveness

Central to my argument is the contention that a shift from exclusive to more inclusive cultural expressions and enactments helps the disputing parties move from conflict to coexistence to cooperation. At the same time, this can sound like the argument that if we just get one (or both) sides to give up their identity then conflict will diminish or disappear. While there is empirical support for such a proposition under certain conditions, there are both theoretical and political problems with such a strategy because the concept of inclusiveness is paradoxical in important ways: namely, that inclusiveness must be balanced with differentiation. Theoretically, it is clear that while humans have a strong propensity for group attachment (Tajfel 1981; Brown 1986; Bowlby 1969), people also exhibit a clear need to differentiate themselves from others on the group and individual levels and use a variety of psychological and social strategies to do this. As a result, Brewer describes the social self in terms of a need to be "the same and different at the same time" (Brewer 1991).

What this means is that either extreme separation or merger of individuals and groups induces strong fears; it is not something that can simply be mandated, and is politically unproductive when that is tried.

The tension between attachment and differentiation is highly relevant to understanding some constraints on inclusiveness in cultural enactments and expressions as a conflict reduction strategy. It means that while drawing attention to what people from diverse backgrounds and traditions share, at the same time there must also be appreciation of their need for differentiation. Probably the best way to mediate these apparently contradictory tendencies is to begin with the realization that because people possess multiple identities, changing or adopting one identity does not require discarding or abandoning another. Making space for multiple identities is likely to be more productive than simply promoting a new one and extinguishing an existing one. European identities are instructive here for in recent decades we can see that while people have maintained attachments to the states in which they are citizens, in many cases they have also increasingly identified themselves as Europeans and in many cases as members of regional cultural groups. As the Catalan case shows, the opportunity to be part of Europe paradoxically facilitated the Catalan national identity as inclusive and compatible with Spanish citizenship.

A political reason to be cognizant of the paradox of inclusiveness is that it is rarely the case in divided societies that people are willing to give up their group-based identities. If people are told that the price of peace is that they must abandon their identity, then ending identity conflicts will be even harder than it now is. Although I have seen no systematic evidence on this question, many studies point to a desire among minorities for pluralistic political arrangements such as autonomy, decentralization, and other measures that permit, or guarantee, the right to maintain local cultural traditions and institutions. Of course, not all groups need or want the same things. For example, indigenous minorities are often geographically clustered and identify with territorial homelands, and their demands emphasize autonomy, while immigrant minorities who are more dispersed often are more concerned politically about access to resources and integration. Finally, we must recognize that in many cases majority groups are not keen on the assimilation of minorities.

When inclusiveness requires relinquishing highly valued behaviors, beliefs, traditions, or institutions, it often dooms such efforts to failure. A good example of this phenomenon is the persistence of languages which have only a modest number of speakers despite the pressures to adopt a more widely spoken language. Why in Europe, for example, are there more than two dozen lesser used languages and at least 40 million EU citizens who regularly speak a language other than the official language of the state in which they live? Forcing people to abandon their languages, as Franco's Spain tried to do with the Catalans and Basques, is not likely to be politically effective unless the incentives for doing so are upfront and desirable (Laitin, Sole, and Kalyvas 1994; Laitin 1989).

A common identity or narrative that is widely accepted by groups in a long-term conflict will not emerge from, nor should it be the goal of, good conflict management. It would be naïve to think that differences in culture, historical experiences, and political disagreement could be bridged so simply. When there are strong differences in how two parties see the world, it is important that these differences be acknowledged and explored and that emphasis must be on shared experiences, hopes, and aspirations without denial of separate identities. To achieve greater complexity, a narrative needs to be nuanced and one way this is achieved is to invoke or strengthen images of cross-cutting identities and experiences in a way that inhibits the power of any single polarizing dimension. Rather than one joint narrative, complexity can support multiple, nuanced narratives that lower polarization, hostility, and distrust to promote, or at least permit, interaction and mutual adjustment.

Politically, more inclusive identities are not necessarily an end in themselves. They are significant, however, when they establish, or strengthen, practices, rules, and institutions in societies coming out of conflict. A sense of greater inclusiveness gives formerly excluded groups a stake in public institutions that can limit the pressures on possibly weak institutions to deliver goods and services to the public. Inclusiveness can also build support for turn taking, reciprocity, and tolerance.

Using inclusiveness to facilitate and express reconciliation

Reconciliation is about changing the relationship between contending parties instrumentally and emotionally so that each can more easily envision a joint future (Kriesberg 2004; Long and Brecke 2003; Ross 2004). Reconciliation can be a complex process understood as involving degrees of change in attitudes, behaviors, institutional practices, and/or symbolic expressions (Kriesberg 2003). In large group conflicts, acknowledgment is often communicated through symbolic and ritual action – exactly the sorts of cultural enactments and expressions that have been described throughout the earlier chapters. Such acknowledgment may be especially important in situations where explicit verbal apology, forgiveness, and reparations – central features of reconciliation for some – may not be possible or even desirable. Emphasizing the symbolic and ritual aspects of intergroup reconciliation means that acknowledgment involves a two-part game, the first between leaders and the public in each community and the second between the two societies.

Symbolic and ritual action can be significant in reconciliation processes for a number of reasons (MacGinty 2003). Direct apology is difficult; symbolic action can be easier for former enemies to offer. Words are sometimes perceived as easy to utter; symbolic actions can be viewed as more sincere. Verbal apologies are more cognitive; symbolic actions are more affective. Ritual helps build new narratives and can strengthen weaker existing ones (Jarman 1997). The argument is not that ritual and symbolic actions are more important than verbal ones but rather that because the two work differently, they make distinctive contributions to reconciliation.

One practical problem is that the need (and timing) of reconciliation is often not the same for all parties. While this is not surprising it means when one party reaches out to the other and feels rebuffed, anger and rage are sometimes the response, again raising tensions.[1] In situations of great inequality in power and economic resources, for example, a central question asked by the weaker party – and this is often a key test of the sincerity of the desire of the more powerful party for reconciliation – is the willingness of the more powerful to redistribute resources. In South Africa, Israel–Palestine, and black–white relations in the United States, reconciliation for weaker parties is much more intimately connected to questions of inequality than it is for the majority – a reminder of how the needs of different parties are not necessarily reciprocal.

It is easy to conjure up images of dramatic reconciliatory gestures such as President Bill Clinton reviewing Vietnamese troops in Hanoi, Willy Brandt kneeling at the site of the Warsaw Ghetto, and King Hussein of Jordan on his knees with the families of Israeli children killed by a deranged Jordanian soldier. What these images communicate is

---

[1] Both Gulliver (1979: 81–120) and Volkan (1988: 146) point out that conflict management can be fruitfully understood as a cyclical rather than a linear process. As the parties move closer together there can be either new issues that once again divide them or fear of having come too close that then drives then to separate, in what Volkan calls "the accordion effect."

acknowledgment of a past and the image of a different future. They establish, or strengthen, a connection among previously divided people. They are, however, single actions and to have enduring effects they need to be generalized and institutionalized as part of altering and enlarging the symbolic and ritual landscape in ways that diminish threats and change relationships. Three of the forms such expressions can take, that were discussed at length in the earlier chapters, are language, holidays and ceremonies, and a society's symbolic landscape. A concluding thought on each of these might be helpful.

Language Language serves as an obvious symbolic and ritual expression of group differences, and can be a focal point for bitter ethnic conflict when groups make demands that their language should be the state's official language or have a privileged status in the public domain. Language is one of the easiest ways to associate the state with a particular group and can readily be linked to issues of economic power and political control as contestation increases. In Québec and Catalonia language is the basis on which regional (and cultural) autonomy demands are justified but the claims are much broader than language rights. In many third world countries and recently independent states in eastern and central Europe recognition of language rights is seen as central to issues of group recognition (Laitin 1998).

In central and eastern Europe, bitter conflicts over language policy after 1990 in Slovakia, Moldova, Estonia, and elsewhere unleashed violence at times and pitted hard-core nationalists against regional minorities in the newly independent states. In Slovakia the conflict focused on Hungarian speakers in the southern part of the country and demands that they show their loyalty by learning Slovak and removing public signs in Hungarian. While the ethnic tension seems to have eased following the 1998 elections, there is no reason to think the conflict has been settled yet. Estonia and Moldova are two newly independent states with large Russian minorities. In Estonia the conflict turned around the question of citizenship. Estonians passed legislation that granted citizenship to Russian speakers only if they pass an examination demonstrating competence in the Estonian language, a language many long-time Russian residents of Estonia had never bothered to learn.[2]

---

[2] Language differences are not necessarily bitter. Among FSU countries, the case of Kazakhstan is interesting in that while official Kazakhization has taken place, the issue does

Despite the intensity of some language disputes, a number of countries have found ways to manage them or at least to move them out of the arena of violent conflict. In Canada, for example, despite all the strident Francophone language about oppression and the strong support at times for secession, language conflict is not violent. Similarly, Spain since Franco's death has granted autonomy to Catalonia and other regions allowing them to set their own language polities. India is another relevant case. In the 1950s there were widespread language riots in many parts of the country. However, since then the situation has calmed as linguistic and political boundaries are now more aligned and each Indian state has three official languages – Hindi, English, and the language of the largest linguistic group in that state (Laitin 1997).

Holidays and ceremonies Ethnically exclusive holidays are common, but they are especially problematic in a highly divided society that has few, or no, holidays and other rituals that are commemorated across groups. This is even more the case when holidays marking the glories of one group are experienced as humiliating for another. Israeli Independence Day is for Palestinians the Nakba or catastrophe. A striking example of an exclusive holiday in Northern Ireland is the anniversary of the Battle of the Somme in which so many British soldiers died in 1916; Protestants mark this date as a solemn occasion and as continuing evidence of their loyalty to the crown while Catholics ignore it. Irish Republicans view fighting and dying in this battle as support for the British and have been unwilling to mark their own losses in a way that could communicate a shared link to Protestants. Another example from Northern Ireland is that for years St. Patrick's Day has been celebrated exclusively by Catholics although there is no religious reason why Protestants could not mark the day as well. In recent years there have been efforts to invite Protestants to march in the St. Patrick's Day parades in Dublin, Belfast, and elsewhere. While some have done so, Republicans' aggressive display of the Irish Tricolour and other Republican symbols has meant that the effort to use the parades for building cross-community bridges has not been effective to date.

Invented or redefined holidays can serve as integrative rituals, if they are defined in inclusive terms. Kwanza, an invented festival for African

not evoke the deep feeling found in the Baltics despite the large number of Russians in its population (Laitin 1998).

Americans, celebrates their African heritage; it is accepted along with Christmas and Chanukah, although Kwanza is not a religious holiday as such, as part of the American ritual calendar. Like Martin Luther King Day, its recognition of black experiences and roots is not hostile to whites and does not discourage occasional white involvement and participation. On MLK Day, a national holiday, many communities hold intergroup services and sponsor community service activities that involve people from all groups. South Africa now marks December 17, which was once the Afrikaner sacred Day of the Covenant, as the Day of Reconciliation, although it is not yet clear how successful this shift will be.

Public ceremonies can also be an important way to express more inclusive identities; narratives about them and their celebration range from solemn events to relaxed festivals.[3] In these, the joint participation and shared identities that are communicated are often more important than the explicit content of the ceremony. Reconciliation events between former opponents can be effective when they include direct physical contact or proximity between opponents, public ceremonies that receive a good deal of attention, and "ritualistic or symbolic behavior that indicates the parties consider the dispute resolved and that more amicable relations are expected to follow" (Long and Brecke 2003: 6).[4]

Symbolic landscape Inclusiveness can be powerfully expressed through expansion of the symbolic landscape as we saw in Northern Ireland, South Africa, and Richmond, Virginia, and can be understood as ritual acknowledgment and partial reconciliation. Sacred sites (which are not necessarily religious ones) are an important part of the symbolic landscape but there are also more secular representations associated with a group's identity found in the mass media, theater, literature, and public art that communicate inclusion and exclusion.

All groups have places that are sacred (Friedland and Hecht 1991) and these often are the most emotionally charged, treasured, and defended sites in the symbolic landscape, especially when they are threatened in

---

[3] Events such as inaugurations, funerals, and other state events are worth considering in greater detail than I do here. One excellent treatment from the perspective of the role the media plays in them is Dayan and Katz (1992).

[4] At the White House signing of the Oslo Agreement, Bill Clinton was keen that Yasser Arafat and Yitzak Rabin shake hands and the White House worked carefully to create the physical context to make sure they did; at the same time, Clinton did not want Arafat embracing and hugging the Israeli leader.

ways that are experienced as threats to the group itself.[5] These places mark key events in a group's past and are associated with emotionally significant victories or defeats, miracles, and the exploits of ancient heroes (Levinson 1998). Sacred places containing relics linking a group's past to its present and future often are particularly powerful emotionally (Benvenisti 2000). Often there are restrictions on admitting outsiders to them and sharing them is frequently hard to even imagine, let alone achieve.

Inclusion in the symbolic landscape offers legitimation that can both reflect and promote changes in political narratives. Such inclusion can identify and help groups mourn past losses, and also represents hopes and aspirations for the future. As symbolic statements of acknowledgment, it is no wonder that such sites and the representations they contain can become the source of intense controversy between groups but also within the previously socially invisible group. What stories do they choose to tell about themselves? How is this related to who can speak for the group? Who controls its narrative and the images associated with it? All of these issues can provoke thoughtful and heated discussion as in the case of the Holocaust Museum in Washington and the District Six Museum in Cape Town (Linenthal 2001a; Rassool and Prosalendis 2001). A more inclusive symbolic landscape is a powerful expression of societal inclusion that communicates a mutuality and shared stake in society. It renders the previously unseen seen, gives voice to those once voiceless, and can offer powerful messages to young people and help to reshape relations between groups.

Conclusion: leveraging cultural enactments and expressions

Culture cannot do all the work of bridging group differences. Real interests and institutions matter too; but it is obvious that culture and

---

[5] Group members easily feel a sacred site's power and its vulnerability. When I was in Sri Lanka in 1994 I was reminded of this on a visit to the ancient city at Anuradhapura. The area contains beautiful buildings and there are thousands of monks in flowing saffron robes and ordinary people in this important Buddhist pilgrimage center that contains a sacred Bohdi tree that is guarded day and night. It is believed to have grown from a sapling from the tree under which the Buddha gained Enlightenment in 528 BCE and was brought from India in the third century. The mood is calm and serene. A few years earlier a group of Tamil Tigers attacked Anuradhapura firing automatic weapons, killing 180 people and wounding hundreds more. On my visit there I was told about the attack but instead of focusing on the dead and wounded, my host said, "They tried to destroy our tree." For him, destruction of the tree would have been a far more deadly attack on Sinhalese Buddhists than the mortal one that took place.

institutions affect each other, although we are not always very clear how this occurs. One basic proposition is that cultural enactments and symbolic gestures can help create the political space for opponents to negotiate substantive differences, and that when such differences are successfully negotiated, an agreement's backers need to find culturally appropriate expressions to build support for its implementation and institutionalization (MacGinty 2003). So how can cultural expression be leveraged to make the most difference in enabling groups to reimagine their relationship and change behaviors and perceptions in viable and lasting ways?

In all of the conflicts considered in this book, there have been individuals and groups who have at different points made meaningful, inclusive gestures to opponents. In some cases these expressions have been reciprocated and have been part of a shift in the parties' language and the country's symbolic landscape, facilitating changes in behaviors and institutional practices. What determines when a constructive sequence follows initial gestures, as for example it did when King Juan Carlos declared the 1992 Olympic Games in Barcelona open in the Catalan language, and when are such gestures unanswered?

Inclusive gestures are unlikely to have lasting effects when they are isolated acts, unrelated to substantive efforts to negotiate and implement political and institutional changes. They are most likely to produce a positive echo effect when they are linked either directly or indirectly to specific political proposals that address core concerns and substantive differences between the parties.[6] How this is achieved will take different forms across conflicts. It some cases, it will depend on top leaders making significant, and often risky, reciprocal gestures, while in others the gestures are more popularly and community based. In some cases gestures will follow political negotiations; in others, negotiations will be made possible by a shift in climate arising from the gestures. But the gestures themselves will matter most when they create, or support, the space for meaningful substantive proposals. One path by which this can occur is

---

[6] The context in which they are offered is often fragile and sometimes when an inclusive symbolic gesture or a new political proposal is offered, outside parties immediately express their strong support for them and the supporters feel legitimated. However, these well-meaning expressions can be problematic when they leave opponents of peace processes feeling isolated and threatened so that they mobilize and provide tacit, or even explicit, support to spoilers who use inflamed rhetoric or selective violence to sabotage any possible easing of tensions.

when the reaction to prior gestures suggests to political figures that such proposals will be popular among their own supporters. Yet because many leaders in divided societies have achieved their positions as staunch defenders of their communities, it is especially hard for them to broaden their positions without fear of being accused of selling out their group. This means that the spillover (or multiplier effects) and the transfer of inclusive gestures across domains are limited unless others such as grassroots groups and opinion leaders engage actively in a discourse of cooperation and coexistence to build support for cross-group cooperation and strengthen the resolve of politicians.

While the dramatic gestures of figures such as Nelson Mandela can be crucial in leveraging cultural expression and enactments to produce changes in attitudes, practices, and institutions, smaller acts matter as well. In addition, they are politically important in engaging larger numbers of people and combating the idea that only the actions of a few powerful people make any difference. Among the modest, but potentially significant, steps that can be undertaken are those that increase the visibility of groups of people previously underrepresented in public arenas such as the mass media, political life, and artistic domains in ways that can communicate how legitimate it is for their group to have a "a place at the table." Linguistic and artistic broadening communicates recognition and "parity of esteem" that has a potential to diminish intergroup tensions. It can facilitate more inclusive identity and narratives which emphasize a linked fate, raising the prospects for self-fulfilling and reinforcing cooperative problem-solving.

I began this book by arguing that long-standing ethnic conflicts are not only about interests and structure; where primarily interests and structure are at stake, negotiated settlements can occur with relative ease. Ethnic conflicts become long standing when group identities are engaged, and in these conflicts group narratives quickly harden and promote escalation. The narratives can also, however, be powerful tools for deescalation, as they provide clues to each group's fears and hopes, and to ways to diminish perceived threat and confrontation. I end with the reciprocal argument that long-standing conflicts are not only about identity. It is by learning how to braid interest-based and identity-based efforts at conflict management that we will be able to develop examples and models of how to manage it constructively (Bates, Rui J. P. de Figueiredo, and Weingast 1998). Leveraging cultural expressions and enactments surely must be part of any strategy for reshaping narratives, weakening set positions, opening channels of communication, and imagining new courses of action that reduce destructive conflict. Bringing an understanding of how to achieve this in ethnic conflict is important in combating the strong belief in some quarters that ethnic conflict is inevitable and enduring, and in developing examples and models of how to manage it constructively.

References

Abdul-Ghafour, Yasser (2002) "No Peace for Al Aqsa." *The Jerusalem Times,* June 13.

Abu El-Haj, Nadia (1998) "Translating Truths: Nationalism, the Practice of Archaeology, and the Remaking of Past and Present in Contemporary Jerusalem." *American Ethnologist* 25: 168–88.

(2001) *Facts on the Ground: Archaeological Practice and Territorial Self-Fashioning in Israeli Society.* Chicago: University of Chicago Press.

Adamson, Ian (1974) *The Cruthin: The Ancient Kindred.* Belfast: Pretani Press.

AFP (2003) "Jacques Chirac lance la commission sur la laïcité dans la République." *Le Monde,* July 3.

(2004) "Voile islamique: une association engage un bras de fer avec les chefs d'établissement scolaire." *Le Monde,* July 1.

Agha, Hussein and Robert Malley (2001) "Camp David: The Tragedy of Errors." *New York Review of Books,* August 9.

Akenson, Donald Harman (1992) *God's Peoples: Covenant and Land in South Africa, Israel and Ulster.* Ithaca, NY: Cornell University Press.

Al-Ifrani, Imad (2001) "Jerusalem Under Threat." *The Jerusalem Times,* November 12.

Alpher, Yossi (2005) "Religion and Cynicism." www.bitterlemons.org/.

Anderson, John Ward (2006) "Catalonia Nears Autonomy from Spain." *Washington Post,* January 28.

Angelini, Alessandro (2003) "*Spaces of Good Hope: Inscribing Memory, Territory and Urbanity in District Six, Cape Town.*" Isandla Institute.

Armstrong, Karen (1996) *Jerusalem: One City, Three Faiths.* New York: Ballantine Books.

Arnold, Michael S. (1999) "Temple Mount: Layers of Dirt, History and Conflict." *Jerusalem Post,* December 26.

Atallah, Nabil (2001) "Jewish Extremists Plan Temple Foundation Stone for Al-Aqsa." *The Jerusalem Times,* October 4.

Avruch, Kevin (1998) *Culture and Conflict Resolution.* Washington, DC: United States Institute for Peace Press.

(2003) "Type I and Type II Errors in Culturally Sensitive Conflict Resolution Practice." *Conflict Resolution Quarterly* 20: 351–371.

Avruch, Kevin and Peter W. Black (1993) "Conflict Resolution in Intercultural Settings: Problems and Prospects," in *Conflict Resolution Theory and Practice: Integration and Application*, Dennis Sandole and Hugo van der Merwe, eds. Manchester: Manchester University Press, pp. 131–145.

Badinter, Elizabeth *et al.* (1989) "Profs, ne capitulons pas." *Le Nouvel Observateur*, November 2–8.

Bar-On, Daniel (2002) "Conciliation Through Storytelling: Beyond Victimhood," in *Peace Education: The Concept, Principles, and Practices Around the World*, Gavriel Salomon and Baruch Nevo, eds. Mahwah, NJ: Lawrence Erlbaum, pp. 109–116.

Barth, Frederic, ed. (1969) *Ethnic Groups and Boundaries. The Social Organization of Culture Difference*. Boston: Little Brown.

Bates, Robert H., Jr., Rui J. P. de Figueiredo, and Barry R. Weingast (1998) "The Politics of Interpretation: Rationality, Culture and Transition." *Politics and Society* 26: 603–642.

Bauberot, Jean (1998) "The Two Thresholds of Laicization," in *Secularism and its Critics*, Rajeev Bhargava, ed. Delhi: Oxford University Press, pp. 94–136.

(2005) *Laïcité 1905–2005, entre passion et raison*. Paris: Seuil.

BBC (2005) "Ex-Orange leader on parades body." BBC News. November 30, news.bbc.co.uk/1/hi/northern_ireland/4486658.stm.

Beckett, Denis (2002). *Flying with Pride: The Story of the South African Flag*. New Providence, NJ: BPR Publishers.

Belfast Telegraph (2003) "Opinion: Drumcree Roadmap Must Be Pursued.", July 4.

Bellantoni, Christiana (2004) "Senate Kills Confederate History Resolution." *Washington Times*, February 5.

Benvenisti, Meron (1996) *City of Stone: The Hidden History of Jerusalem*. Berkeley and Los Angeles: University of California Press.

(2000) *Sacred Landscape: The Buried History of the Holy Land Since 1948*. Berkeley and Los Angeles: University of California Press.

Beriss, David (1990) "Scarves, Schools and Segregation: The Foulard Affair." *French Politics and Society* 8: 1–13.

Berlin, Ira and Leslie M. Harris, eds. (2005) *Slavery in New York*. New York: New Press.

Bernard, Philippe (2004) "La préfecture de Seine-Saint-Dénis interdit à des femme violées l'access à son salon d'honneur." *Le Monde*, December 24.

Bernbeck, Reinhard and Susan Pollack (1998) "Ayodhya, Archaeology, and Identity." *Current Anthropology* 37: S138–S142.

Black, Brian and Bryn Varley (2003) "Contesting the Sacred: Preservation and Meaning on Richmond's Monument Avenue," in *Monuments to the Lost Cause: Women, Art, and the Landscapes of Southern Memory*, Cynthia Mills and Pamela H. Simpson, eds. Knoxville: University of Tennessee Press, pp. 234–250.

References

Blakey, Michael L. (2001) "Bioarchaeology of the African Diaspora in the Americas: Its Origins and Scope." *Annual Review of Anthropology* 30: 387–422.

Bleich, Erik (2001) "The French Model: Color-Blind Integration," in *Color Lines: Afirmative Action, Immigration, and Civil Rights Options for America*, John David Skrentny, ed. Chicago and London: University of Chicago Press, pp. 270–296.

Blight, David W. (2001) *Race and Reunion: The Civil War in American History.* Cambridge and London: Belknap/Harvard.

Bohlin, Anna (1998) "The Politics of Locality: Memories of District Six in Cape Town," in *Locality and Belonging*, Nadia Lovell, ed. London and New York: Routledge, pp. 168–188.

Bouzar, Dounia (2001) *L'Islam de Banlieues: Les prédicateurs musulmans: nouveau travailleurs sociaux?* Paris: Syros.

(2003) "Pas de débat réchauffée sur le foulard." *Le Monde*, April 26.

Bouzar, Dounia and Saida Kada (2003) *L'une violée, l'autre pas: Le témoignage de deux Musulmanes françaises.* Paris: Albin Michel.

Bowen, John R. (2004) "Muslims and Citizens: France's Headscarf Controversy." *Boston Review*, February/March.

(2006) "France's Revolt: Can the Republic Live up to its Ideals?" *Boston Review*, January/February. http://bostonreview.net/BR31.1/bowen.html.

Bowlby, John (1969) *Attachment and Loss: Attachment.* New York: St. Martins.

Boyle, Kevin and Tom Hadden (1994) *Northern Ireland: The Choice.* London: Penguin.

Branine, Said (2003) "Entretien avec Dounia Bouzar: Membre du Bureau du Conseil Français du Culte Musulman." http://oumma.com/article.php3?id_article=607.

Brett, Sarah (2003) "Talks in Derry Show Way for Rest of Province." *Belfast Telegraph Digital*, August 8.

Brewer, Marilynn B. (1991) "The Social Self: On Being the Same and Different at the Same Time." *Personality and Social Psychology Bulletin* 17: 475–482.

Brizard, Caroline (2003) "École: Légiférer ou pas?" *Le Nouvel Observateur*, May, 15–21.

Bronner, Luc and Virginie, Malingre (2004) "Le premier jour de rentrée s'est déroulé sans incidents majeurs, à l'exception de l'Alsace." *Le Monde*, September 3.

Brown, Roger (1986) "Ethnic Conflict," in *Social Psychology, The Second Edition*, Brown, Roger ed. New York: Free Press, pp. 531–634.

Brubaker, Rogers (1992) *Citizenship and Nationhood in France and Germany.* Cambridge and London: Harvard University Press.

(2004) *Ethnicity Without Groups.* Cambridge and London: Harvard University Press.

Bruce, Steve (1994) *The Edge of Union: The Ulster Loyalist Political Vision.* Oxford: Oxford University Press.

Bryan, Dominic (1997) "The Right to March: Parading a Loyal Protestant Identity in Northern Ireland." *International Journal on Minority and Group Rights* 4: 373–396.

(2000) *Orange Parades: The Politics of Ritual, Tradition and Control.* London: Pluto.

(2001) "Parade Disputes and the Peace Process." *Peace Review* 13: 43–49.

(2003). "Rituals of Irish Protestantism and Orangeism: The Transnational Grand Orange Lodge of Ireland." *European Studies: A Journal of European Culture, History and Politics* 19: 105–123.

Bryan, Dominic and Gordon Gillespie (2005) "*Transforming Conflict: Flags and Emblems.*" Belfast: Institute of Irish Studies, Queen's University.

Bryan, Dominic and Neil Jarman (2000) "*Stewarding Crowds and Managing Public Safety: Developing a Co-ordinated Policy for Northern Ireland.*" Belfast: Community Development Centre.

Bryan, Dominic and Gilliam McIntosh (2005) "Symbols: Sites of Creation and Contest in Northern Ireland." *SAIS Review* 25: 127–137.

Bryson, Lucy and Clem McCartney (1994) *Clashing Symbols: A Report on the Use of Flags, Anthems and Other National Symbols in Northern Ireland.* Antrim: W & G Baird Ltd.

Buckley, Anthony D., ed. (1998) *Symbols in Northern Ireland.* Belfast: Institute for Irish Studies.

Buckley, Anthony D. and Mary Katherine Kenney (1995) *Negotiating Identity: Rhetoric, Metaphor, and Social Drama in Northern Ireland.* Washington and London: Smithsonian Institution Press.

Buntman, Fran Lisa (2003) *Robben Island and Prisoner Resistance to Apartheid.* Cambridge: Cambridge University Press.

Campbell, Donald T. (1975) "On the Conflicts Between Biological and Social Evolution." *American Psychologist* 30: 1103–1126.

Cesari, Jocelyne (2005) "Ethnicity, Islam and les Banlieues: Confusing the Issues." Social Science Research Council. http://riotsfrance.ssrc.org/.

Chabal, Patrick and Jean-Pascal Daloz (2006) *Culture Troubles: Politics and the Interpretation of Meaning.* London: Hurst and Company.

Chebel d'Apollonia, Ariane (2001) "*Urban Racism in France: New Realities and Old Prejudices.*" Paper presented to the New Face of European Cities, NY: Consortium for European Studies, April.

(2002) "The Ethnicization of Immigration in France and Class/Urban Conflicts." Paper prepared for the 13th International Conference of Europeanists, Chicago, March.

Chidester, David and Edward Tabor Linenthal (1995) "Introduction," in *American Sacred Space*, David Chidester and Edward Tabor Linenthal, eds. Bloomington: Indiana University Press, pp. 1–42.

Cohen, Abner (1969) *Custom and Politics in Urban Africa.* Berkeley and Los Angeles: University of California Press.

References

(1974) *Two-Dimensional Man: An Essay on the Anthropology of Power and Symbolism in Complex Society*. Berkeley and Los Angeles: University of California Press.

(1981) *The Politics of Elite Culture: Explorations in the Dramaturgy of Power in a Modern African Society*. Berkeley and Los Angeles: University of California Press.

(1993) *Masquerade Politics: Explorations in the Structure of Urban Cultural Movements*. Berkeley and Los Angeles: University of California Press.

Cohen, Raymond (1991) *Negotiating Across Cultures: Communication Obstacles in International Diplomacy*. Washington, DC: United States Institute for Peace Press.

(2003) "Management of a Conflict System: The Church of the Holy Sepulchre." Paper presented at International Studies Association Conference, Budapest, Hungary.

Connerton, Paul (1989) *How Societies Remember*. Cambridge: Cambridge University Press.

Conversi, Daniele (1997) *The Basques, the Catalans and Spain: Alternative Routes to Nationalist Mobilization*. Reno and Las Vegas: University of Nevada Press.

Coombes, Annie E. (2000) "Translating the Past: Apartheid Monuments in Post-Apartheid South Africa," in *Hybridity and its Discontents: Politics, Science and Culture*, Avtar Brah and Annie E. Coombes, eds. London and New York: Routledge, 173–197.

(2003) *History After Apartheid: Visual Culture and Public Memory in a Democratic South Africa*. Durham: Duke University Press.

Coroller, Catherine (2004) "Pas de cérémonie pour les naturalisée voilées." *Libération*, December 22.

(2005a) "La loi sur la voile crée la paix mais ne règle rien." *Libération*, October 6.

(2005b) "Une carte de séjour refusée pour cause de voile." *Libération*, November 17.

(2005c) "La préfecture avale son voile." *Libération*, November 19.

Coski, John M. (2000) "The Confederate Battle Flag in Historical Perspective," in *Confederate Symbols in the Contemporary South*, J. Michael Martinez, William D. Richardson, and Ron McNinch-Su, eds. Gainesville, FL: University Press of Florida, pp. 89–129.

(2005) *The Confederate Battle Flag: America's Most Embattled Emblem*. Cambridge, MA and London: Belknap Press.

Crain, Robert L. (1968) *The Politics of School Desegregation: Comparative Case Studies of Community Structure and Policy-Making*. Chicago: Aldine.

Crampton, Andrew (2001) "The Voortrekker Monument, the Birth of Apartheid, and Beyond." *Political Geography* 20: 221–246.

D'Andrade, Roy G. (1984) "Cultural Meaning Systems," in *Culture Theory: Essays on Mind, Self and Emotion*, Richard A. Schweder and Robert A. LeVine, eds. Cambridge: Cambridge University Press, pp. 83–119.

Daniel, Jean (2003) "Décidément, non au viole!" *Nouvel Observateur*, May 15–21.

Darby, John, ed. (1983) *Northern Ireland: The Background to the Conflict*. Syracuse: Syracuse University Press.

 (1986) *Intimidation and Control of the Conflict in Northern Ireland*. Syracuse: Syracuse University Press.

Davis, Richard (1996) "The Iconography of Rama's Chariot," in *Contesting the Nation: Religion, Community, and the Politics of Democracy in India*, David Ludden, eds. Philadelphia: University of Pennsylvania Press, pp. 27–54.

Dayan, Daniel and Elihu Katz (1992) *Media Events: The Live Broadcasting of History*. Cambridge, MA: Harvard University Press.

de Silva, Kingsley (1981) *A History of Sri Lanka*. Delhi: Oxford University Press.

Deacon, Harriet (1998) "Remembering Tragedy, Constructing Modernity: Robben Island as a National Monument," in *Negotiating the Past: the Making of Memory in South Africa*, Sarah Nuttall and Carli Coetzee, eds. Cape Town: Oxford University Press, pp. 161–179.

Delmont, Elizabeth (1993) "The Voortrekker Monument: Monolith to Myth," *South African Historical Journal* 29: 221–246.

Delport, Peggy (2001) "Museum or Place for Working with Memory?" in *Recalling Community in District Six: Creating and Curating the District Six Museum*, Ciraj Rassool and Sandra Prosalendis, eds. Cape Town: District Six Museum Foundation, pp. 11–12.

des Deserts, Sophie, Anne Fohr, Isabelle Monnin, and Elsa Vigoureux (2003) "Enquête sous le voile." *Nouvel Observateur*, May 15.

Deutsch, Morton (1973) *The Resolution of Conflict: Constructive and Destructive Processes*. New Haven: Yale University Press.

Devine-Wright, Patrick (2003) "A Theoretical Overview of Memory and Conflict," in *The Role of Memory in Ethnic Conflict*, Ed Cairns and Micheal D. Roe, eds. Basingstoke: Palgrave, pp. 9–33.

Dew, Charles B. (2001) *Apostles of Disunion: Southern Secession Commissioners and the Causes of the Civil War*. Charlottesville: University Press of Virginia.

DiGiacomo, Susan M. (1986) "Images of Class and Ethnicity in Catalan Politics, 1977–1980," in *Conflict in Catalonia: Images of an Urban Society*, Gary McDonaugh, ed. Gainesville, FL: University of Florida Press, pp. 72–92.

Dlamini, Nsizwa (2001) "The Battle of Ncome Project: State Memorialism. Discomforting Spaces," *Southern African Humanities* 13: 125–138.

 (2003) "State Priorities and the Battle of Ncome Project: The Context of Controversial Possibilities, 1998–99." Transactions of Public Culture Workshop, Cape Town, South Africa.

Doughty, Kristin Conner (forthcoming) "Commemoration and Narratives of Community Healing: Ten Years After the Rwandan Genocide," in *African Health and Illness*, Toyin Falola and Matthew M. Heaton, eds. Durham, NC: Carolina Academic Press.

Dumper, Michael (2002) *The Politics of Sacred Space: The Old City of Jerusalem in the Middle East Conflict*. Boulder and London: Lynne Rienner.

References

Edwards, Ruth Dudley (2003) "Lessons on the Twelfth." *Belfast Telegraph Digital,* July 12.

Ehlers, Anton (2000) "Desegregating History in South Africa: The Case of the Covenant and the Battle of Blood River/Ncome." Conference on Desegregating History, Cape Town. http://academic.sun.ac.za/history/dokumente/Covenant_2000.pdf.

Eller, Jack David (1999) *From Culture to Ethnicity to Conflict: An Anthropological Perspective on International Ethnic Conflict.* Ann Arbor: University of Michigan Press.

Eller, Jack David and Reed Coughlan (1993) "The Poverty of Primordialism: The Demystification of Ethnic Attachments." *Ethnic and Racial Studies* 16: 183–202.

Elon, Amos (1997) "Politics and Archaeology." *Journal for the Study of the Old Testament.* Supplement Series 237: 34–47.

Farren, Sean and Robert F. Mulvihill (2000) *Paths to a Settlement in Northern Ireland.* Gerrards Cross: Colin Smythe.

Feldblum, Miriam (1993) "Paradoxes of Ethnic Politics: The Case of Franco Maghrebis in France." *Racial and Ethnic Studies* 16: 52–74.

Ferguson, Andrew (2003) "When Lincoln Returned to Richmond: Dispatches from an Unlikely Culture War." *American Standard,* December 30.

Fernando, Mayanthi (2005a) "The Republic's 'Second Religion': Recognizing Islam in France." Middle East Report Online. www.merip.org/.

(2005b) "Between Individual Choice and Divine Constraint: Young Muslims and the Islamic Revival in Contemporary France." Paper presented to the Middle East Workshop, University of Pennsylvania.

Firestone, David (2001) "Mistrust Foils South Carolina House's Effort to Remove Divisive Rebel Flag." *New York Times,* May 10.

Fraser, T. G., ed. (2000a) *The Irish Parading Tradition: Following the Drum.* Basingstoke: Palgrave.

(2000b) "Introduction," in *The Irish Parading Tradition: Following the Drum,* T. G. Fraser, ed. Basingstoke: Macmillan, pp. 1–8.

(2000c) "The Apprentice Boys and the Relief of Derry Parades," in *The Irish Parading Tradition: Following the Drum,* T. G. Fraser, ed. Basingstoke: Palgrave, pp. 173–190.

Fredericks, Terrence D. (2003) "Recreating Our Community: Memory, Restitution and Action." *International Journal of Narrative Therapy and Community Work.* http://www.dulwichcentre.com.au/DistrictSix.htm

Freedman, Jane (2004) "Secularism as a Barrier to Integration? The French Dilemma." *International Migration* 42: 5–27.

Friedland, Roger and Richard Hecht (1991) "The Politics of Sacred Place: Jerusalem's Temple Mount/al-Haram al-Sharif," in *Sacred Places and Profane Spaces,* Jamie Scott and Paul Simpson-Housley, eds. New York: Greenwood Press, pp. 21–61.

(1998) "The Bodies of Nations: A Comparative Study of Religious Violence in Jerusalem and Ayodhya." *History of Religions* 38: 101–149.

(forthcoming) "Place, Memory and Identity: Some Theoretical Reflections on the Power of Place," in *Culture and Belonging: Symbolic Landscapes and Contested Identities in Divided Societies*, Marc Howard Ross, ed.

Geertz, Clifford (1973a) "Thick Description: Toward an Interpretive Theory of Culture," in *The Interpretation of Cultures*, Clifford Geertz, ed. New York: Basic Books, pp. 3–30.

(1973b) "Religion as a Cultural System," in *The Interpretation of Culture*, Clifford Geertz, ed. New York: Basic Books, pp. 87–125.

Gibson, James L. (2004) *Overcoming Apartheid: Can Truth Reconcile a Divided Nation?* New York: Russell Sage Foundation.

Gibson, James L. and Amanda Gouws (2003) *Overcoming Intolerance in South Africa: Experiments in Democratic Persuasion.* Cambridge: Cambridge University Press.

Giliomee, Hermann (1989) "The Beginnings of Afrikaner Ethnic Consciousness, 1850–1915," in *The Creation of Tribalism in Southern Africa*, Leroy Vail, ed. Berkeley and Los Angeles: University of California Press, pp. 21–54.

Girshick, Paula (2004) "Ncome Museum/Monument: From Reconciliation to Resistance." *Museum Anthropology* 27: 25–36.

Glock, Albert (1994) "Archaeology as Cultural Survival: The Future of the Palestinian Past." *Journal of Palestine Studies* 23: 70–84.

Gopin, Marc (2000) *Between Eden and Armageddon: The Future of World Religions, Violence, and Peacemaking.* New York: Oxford University Press.

Gorenberg, Gershom (2000) *The End of Days: Fundamentalism and the Struggle for the Temple Mount.* New York: Free Press.

Greenberg, Jay R. and Stephen A. Mitchell (1982) *Object Relations in Psychoanalytic Theory.* Cambridge, MA: Harvard University Press.

Grundlingh, Albert and Hilary Sapire (1989) "From Feverish Festival to Repetitive Ritual? The Changing Fortunes of Great Trek Mythology in an Industrializing South Africa, 1938–1988." *South African Historical Journal* 21: 19–37.

Guibernau, Montserrat (1997) "Nations Without States: Catalonia, a Case Study," in *The Ethnicity Reader: Nationalism, Multiculturalism and Migration*, Montserrat Guibernau and John Rex, eds. Cambridge: Cambridge Polity Press, pp. 133–53.

Gulliver, P. H. (1979) *Disputes and Negotiations: A Cross-Cultural Perspective.* New York: Academic Press.

Hacker, Andrew (1992) *Two Nations: Black and White, Separate, Hostile, Unequal.* New York: Charles Scribner's Sons.

Halbfinger, David (2003) "Georgia Lawmakers Drop Rebel Cross from the Flag." *New York Times*, April 27.

Halbwachs, Maurice (1980) *The Collective Memory.* New York: Harper and Row.

Halevi, Yossi Klein (2002) *At the Entrance to the Garden of Eden: A Jew's Search for Hope with Christians and Muslims in the Holy Land.* New York: Perennial.

Hall, Michael (1994) *The Cruthin Controversy.* Newtownabbey: Island Publications.

References

Hamber, Brandon and Steve Kibble (n.d.) "From Truth to Transformation: South Africa's Truth and Reconciliation Commission." Centre for the Study of Violence and Reconciliation. www.wits.ac.za/csvr/papers/papbhsk.htm.

Handler, Richard (1988) *Nationalism and the Politics of Culture in Quebec.* Madison: University of Wisconsin Press.

Hardin, Russell (1995) *One for All: The Logic of Group Conflict.* Princeton: Princeton University Press.

Harel, Amos and Jonathan Lis (2005) "High Alert Amid Warnings of Temple Mount Attack." *Ha'aretz*, April 7.

Hargreaves, Alex G. (1995) *Immigration, 'Race' and Ethnicity in Contemporary France.* London: Routledge.

Hargreaves, John (2000) *Freedom for Catalonia? Catalan Nationalism, Spanish Identity and the Barcelona Olympic Games.* Cambridge: Cambridge University Press.

Hassner, Ron E. (2003) "'To Halve and to Hold': Conflicts Over Sacred Space and the Problem of Indivisibility." *Security Studies* 12: 1–33.

(2005) "The Jerusalem Paradox and the Rabbinical Ruling of October 1967." Paper presented at Association of Israel Studies Annual Conference, Tucson, AZ.

Hayner, Priscilla B. (2002) *Unspeakable Truths: Facing the Challenge of Truth Commissions.* New York and London: Routledge.

HCI (2000) "*Islam dans La République.*" Paris: Haut Conseil à l'Intégration.

Heymans, Riana (1986) *The Voortrekker Monument, Pretoria.* Pretoria: Board of Control of the Voortrekker Monument.

Hobsbawm, Eric and Terrence Ranger, eds. (1983) *The Invention of Tradition.* Cambridge: Cambridge University Press.

Holsti, Ole R. (1967) "Cognitive Dynamics and Images of the Enemy: Dulles and Russia," in *Enemies in Politics*, David J. Finlay, Ole R. Holsti, and Richard R. Fagan, eds. Chicago: Rand McNally, pp. 25–96.

Horowitz, Donald L. (1985) *Ethnic Groups in Conflict.* Berkeley and Los Angeles: University of California Press.

(1992) "Immigration and Group Relations in France and America," in *Immigrants in Two Democracies: French and American Experiences*, Donald L. Horowitz and Gerard Noiriel, eds. New York and London: NYU Press, pp. 3–35.

(2002) "The Primordialists," in *Ethnonationalism in the Contemporary World: Walker Connor and the Study of Nationalism*, Daniele Conversi, ed. London: Routledge, pp. 72–82.

Horwitz, Tony (1999) *Confederates in the Attic: Dispatches from the Unfinished Civil War.* New York: Vintage Books.

Howell, Signe and Roy Willis, eds. (1989) *Societies at Peace: Anthropological Perspectives.* London: Routledge.

Hughes, Samuel (2004) "Remembering the President's House: Slaves and All." *Pennsylvania Gazette*, March–April.

Huntington, Samuel (1993) "The Clash of Civilizations." *Foreign Affairs* 72: 22–49.

Ignatieff, Michael (1993) *Blood and Belonging: Journeys into the New Nationalism.* New York: Farrar, Straus and Giroux.

Irish Times (2003a) "Mood Change at Drumcree.", July 7.

(2003b) "Orangemen Reveal True Colours for All to See.", July 14.

Jackson, George (2003) "Derry Parade Goes Peacefully." *Irish Times*, August 11.

Jacobson, Matthew Frye (1998) *Whiteness of a Different Color: European Immigrants and the Alchemy of Race.* Cambridge, MA: Harvard University Press.

Jamal, Amal (2000) "The Palestinians in the Israeli Peace Discourse: A Conditional Partnership." *Journal of Palestine Studies* 30: 36–51.

Jarman, Neil (1997) *Material Conflicts: Parades and Visual Displays in Northern Ireland.* Oxford and New York: Berg.

(2003) "From Outrage to Apathy? The Disputes Over Parades, 1995–2003." *The Global Review of Ethnopolitics* 3: 92–105.

Jeffrey, Keith (2000) "Parades, Police and Government in Northern Ireland, 1922–1969," in *The Irish Parading Tradition: Following the Drum*, T. G. Fraser, ed. Basingstoke: Macmillan, pp. 78–94.

Jervis, Robert (1976) *Perception and Misperception in International Politics.* Princeton: Princeton University Press.

Jones, Will (2003) "Lincoln Statue Unveiling Ceremony, Protest Rally are Set for Tomorrow." *Richmond Times-Dispatch*, April 4.

Kaci, Mina (2003) "Sous la voile islamique, l'oppression des femmes." *L'Humanité*, April 30.

Kapferer, Bruce (1988) *Legends of People, Myths of State: Violence, Intolerance and Political Culture in Sri Lanka and Australia.* Washington, DC: Smithsonian Institution Press.

Kaplan, Robert D. (1993) *Balkan Ghosts: A Journey Through History.* New York: St. Martin's Press.

Karklins, Rasma (1986) *Ethnic Relations in the USSR: The Perspective from Below.* Boston: G. Allen and Unwin.

Kastoryano, Riva (1996) *La France, l'Allemagne et leurs immigrés: négocier l'identité.* Paris: Armand Colin.

Kathrada, Ahmed (1999) *Letters from Robben Island: A Selection of Ahmed Kathrada's Prison Correspondence, 1964–1989 edited by Robert D. Vassen.* Cape Town: Mayibuye Books in association with the Robben Island Museum.

Kaufman, Stuart J. (2001) *Modern Hatreds: The Symbolic Politics of Ethnic War.* Ithaca and London: Cornell University Press.

Keating, Michael (1996) "Catalonia," in *Nations Against the State: The New Politics in Quebec, Catalonia, and Scotland*, Keating, ed. Basingstoke: Macmillan, pp. 115–62.

(2001) *Plurinational Democracy in a Post-Sovereignty Era.* Oxford: Oxford University Press.

Keenan, Dan (2003) "Thousands Celebrate 'Twelfth'." *Irish Times*, July 12.

References

Kelly, Graine and Susan A. Nan (1998) *"Mediation in Practice in Northern Ireland."* University of Ulster, Derry: INCORE.

Kelly, James (2000) "The Emergence of Political Parading, 1660–1800," in *The Irish Parading Tradition: Following the Drum*, T. G. Fraser, ed. Basingstoke: Macmillan, pp. 9–26.

Kelman, Herbert (1987) "The Political Psychology of the Israeli–Palestinian Conflict: How Can We Overcome Barriers to a Negotiated Solution?" *Political Psychology* 8: 347–63.

(1995) "Contributions of an Unofficial Conflict Resolution Effort to the Israeli–Palestinian Breakthrough." *Negotiation Journal* 11: 19–27.

(1999) "The Interdependence of Israel and Palestinian National Identities: The Role of the Other in Existential Conflicts." *Journal of Social Issues* 55: 581–600.

Kertzer, David I. (1988) *Ritual, Politics and Power*. New Haven and London: Yale University Press.

Khalidi, Rashid (1997) *Palestinian Identity: The Construction of Modern National Consciousness*. New York: Columbia University Press.

Khouri-Dagher, Nadia (2006) "Françaises, originaires du Maghred: Elles Réussissent." *Le Monde 2*, 4 March.

Kimmerling, Bruce and Joel S. Migdal (1993) *Palestinians: The Making of a People*. New York: Free Press.

Kirshenblatt-Gimblett, Barbara (1998) *Destination Culture: Tourism, Museums, and Heritage*. Berkeley and Los Angeles: University of California Press.

Kohl, Philip L. (1998) "Nationalism and Archaeology: On the Constructions of Nations and the Reconstructions of the Remote Past." *Annual Review of Anthropology* 27: 223–246.

Kohl, Philip L. and Clare Fawcett (1995) "Archaeology in the Service of the State: Theoretical Considerations," in *Nationalism, Politics and the Practice of Archaeology*, Philip L. Kohl and Clare Fawcett, eds. Cambridge: Cambridge University Press, pp. 3–18.

Kramer, Jane (2004) "Taking the Veil: How France's Public Schools Became the Battleground in a Culture War." *New Yorker*, November 22.

Krauss, Clifford (2003) "Québec Seeking to End its Old Cultural Divide." *New York Times*, April 13.

Kriesberg, Louis (2003) *Constructive Conflicts: From Escalation to Resolution*. Lanham, MD: Rowman and Littlefield.

(2004) "Comparing Reconciliation Actions Within and Between Countries," in *From Conflict Resolution to Reconciliation*, Yaacov Bar-Simon-Tov, ed. Oxford: Oxford University Press, pp. 81–110.

Krog, Antjie (1999) *Country of My Skull: Guilt, Sorrow, and the Limits of Forgiveness in the New South Africa*. New York: Times Books.

Kruger, Cecilia (2002) "Heritage Resource Management in South Africa: A Case Study of the Voortrekker Monument Heritage Site, Pretoria." Masters Thesis. Historical and Heritage Studies, University of Pretoria.

Kuklick, Henrika (1991) "Contested Monuments: The Politics of Archaeology in Southern Africa," in *Colonial Situations: Essays in the Contextualization of Ethnographic Knowledge*, George W. Stocking, Jr., ed. Madison: University of Wisconsin Press.

Kuran, Timur (1995) *Private Truths, Public Lies: The Social Consequences of Preference Falsification*. Cambridge, MA: Harvard University Press.

Kymlicka, Will (1998) *Finding Our Way: Rethinking Ethnocultural Relations in Canada*. Ottawa: Oxford University Press.

Laitin, David D. (1986) *Hegemony and Culture: Politics and Religious Change Among the Yoruba*. Chicago: University of Chicago Press.

(1989) "Linguistic Revival: Politics and Culture in Catalonia." *Comparative Studies in Society and History* 31: 297–317.

(1995) "National Revivals and Violence." *Archives Européennes de Sociologie* 36: 3–43.

(1997) "The Cultural Identities of a European State." *Politics and Society* 25: 277–302.

(1998) *Identity in Formation: The Russian-Speaking Populations in the Near Abroad*. Ithaca and London: Cornell University Press.

Laitin, David, Carlotta Sole, and Stathis N. Kalyvas (1994) "Language and the Construction of States: The Case of Catalonia in Spain." *Politics and Society* 22: 5–29.

Lane, Christel (1981) *The Rites of Rulers: Ritual in Industrial Society: The Soviet Case*. Cambridge: Cambridge University Press.

Laronche, Martine (2004a) "La loi sur le voile a conduit à deux premières expulsions." *Le Monde*, October 20.

(2004b) "Trois autres lycéennes exclus pour non-respect de la loi sur la laïcité à Mulhouse et dans l'Orne." *Le Monde*, October 21.

Layne, Valmont and Ciraj Rassool (2001) "Memory Rooms: Oral History in the District Six Museum," in Ciraj Rassool and Sandra Prosalendis, eds. Cape Town: District Six Museum Foundation, pp. 146–153.

Lehman, John F. and Harvey Sicherman (2002) *America the Vulnerable: Our Military Problems and How to Fix Them*. Philadelphia: Foreign Policy Research Institute.

Leib, Jonathan I. (2002) "Separate Times, Shared Spaces: Arthur Ashe, Monument Avenue and the Politics of Richmond, Virginia's Symbolic Landscape." *Cultural Geographies* 9: 286–312.

Levine, Marc V. (1991) *Language Policy and Social Change in a Bilingual City*. Philadelphia: Temple University Press.

LeVine, Robert A. (1984) "Properties of Culture: An Ethnographic View," in *Culture Theory: Essays on Mind, Self and Emotion*, Richard A. Schweder and Robert A. LeVine, eds. Cambridge: Cambridge University Press, pp. 67–87.

LeVine, Robert A. and Donald T. Campbell (1972) *Ethnocentrism: Theories of Conflict, Ethnic Attitudes and Group Behavior*. New York: John Wiley.

Levinson, Sanford (1998) *Written in Stone: Public Monuments in Changing Societies*. Durham and London: Duke University Press.

References

Linenthal, Edward Tabor (1993) *Sacred Ground: Americans and their Battlefields.* Urbana and Chicago: University of Illinois Press.

—— (1996) "Anatomy of a Controversy," in *History Wars: The Enola Gay and Other Battles for the American Past*, Edward Tabor Linenthal and Tom Engelhardt, eds. New York: Owl Books, pp. 9–62.

—— (2001a) *Preserving Memory: The Struggle to Create America's Holocaust Museum.* New York: Columbia University Press.

—— (2001b) *The Unfinished Bombing: Oklahoma City in American Memory.* Oxford: Oxford University Press.

Linenthal, Edward Tabor and Tom Engelhardt (eds.) (1996) *History Wars: The Enola Gay and Other Battles for the American Past.* New York: Owl Books.

Linz, Juan J., Alfred Stephan, and Richard Gunther (1995) "Democratic Transition and Consolidation in Southern Europe, with Reflections on Latin America and Eastern Europe," in *The Politics of Democratic Consolidation: Southern Europe in Comparative Perspective*, Richard Gunther, P. Nikiforos Diamandouros, and Hans-Jürgen Puhle, eds. Baltimore: Johns Hopkins University Press, pp. 77–123.

Little, David (1994) *Sri Lanka: The Invention of Enmity.* Washington, DC: United States Institute for Peace Press.

Litvak, Meir (1994) "A Palestinian Past: National Construction and Reconstruction." *History and Memory: Studies in the Representation of the Past* 6: 24–56.

Long, William J. and Peter Brecke (2003) *War and Reconciliation: Reason and Emotion in Conflict Resolution.* Cambridge, MA and London: MIT Press.

Lorcerie, Françoise. (2005) "A l'assaut de l'agenda public: La politisation du voile islamique en 2003–2004," in Françoise Lorcerie, ed. *La politisation du voile en France, en Europe et dans le monde Arabe*, Paris: L' Harmattan, pp. 11–36.

Lucy, Gordon and Elaine McClure, eds. (1997) *The Twelfth: What it Means to Me.* Lurgan: The Ulster Society.

Ludden, David (1996) "Introduction: Ayodhya: A Window on the World," in *Contesting the Nation: Religion, Community, and the Politics of Democracy in India*, David Ludden, ed. Philadelphia: University of Pennsylvania Press, pp. 1–26.

Lustick, Ian S. (2000) "Yerushalayim and Al-Quds: Political Catechism and Political Realities." *Journal of Palestine Studies* 30: 5–21.

MacGinty, Roger (2003) "The Role of Symbols in Peacemaking," in *Contemporary Peacemaking: Conflict, Violence and Peace Processes*, Roger MacGinty and John Darby, eds. Basingstoke: Palgrave, pp. 235–44.

Maclure, Jocelyn (2004) "Narratives and Counter-Narratives in Québec," in *Québec: State and Society, 3rd edn*, Alain-G. Gagnon, ed. Peterborough, Ont: Broadview Press.

Madelin, Alain (2004) "Voilà, la loi de top." *Le Monde*, February 5.

Mahler, Margaret S., Fred Pine, and Anni Bergman (1975) *The Psychological Birth of the Human Infant: Symbiosis and Individuation.* New York: Basic Books.

Malingre, Virginie (2004) "La loi sur la laïcité: M. Fillon satisfait malgré 101 cas 'problématiques'." *Le Monde,* September 20.

Mandela, Nelson (1994) *Long Walk to Freedom.* Boston: Little Brown.

Marschall, Sabine (2004) "Gestures of Compensation: Post-Apartheid Monuments and Memorials." *Transformation* 55: 78–95.

(forthcoming) "Symbols of Reconciliation or Instruments of Division? A Critical Look at New Monuments in South Africa," in *Culture and Belonging: Symbolic Landscapes and Contested Identities in Divided Societies,* Marc Howard Ross, ed.

(n.d.) *"Visualizing Memories: The Hector Pieterson Memorial in Soweto."*

Marvin, Carolyn and David W. Ingle (1999) *Blood Sacrifice and the Nation: Totem Rituals and the American Flag.* Cambridge: Cambridge University Press.

McCaul, Kathleen (2005) "World's first Hindu theme park." BBC News. http://news.bbc.co.uk/2/hi/south_asia/4494747.stm.

McDonogh, Gary, ed. (1986a) *Conflict in Catalonia: Images of an Urban Society.* Gainesville: University of Florida Press.

(1986b) *Good Families of Barcelona: A History of Power in the Industrial Era.* Princeton: Princeton University Press.

McEachern, Charmaine (1998) "Working with Memory: The District Six Museum in the New South Africa." *Social Analysis* 42: 48–72.

McGarry, John and Brendan O'Leary (2004) *The Northern Ireland Conflict: Consociational Engagements.* Oxford: Oxford Universtiy Press.

McGeach, Mike (1990) "The Boyne". Video.

McKay, Susan (2000) *Northern Protestants: An Unsettled People.* Belfast: Blackstaff.

McPherson, James M. (1997) *For Cause and Comrades: Why Men Fought in the Civil War.* New York: Oxford University Press.

McRoberts, Kenneth (2001) *Catalonia: Nation Building without a State.* Oxford: Oxford University Press.

Meskell, Lynn (1998) "Archaeology Matters," in *Archaeology Under Fire: Nationalism Politics and Heritage in the Eastern Mediterranean and the Middle East,* Lynn Meskell, ed. London: Routledge, pp. 1–12.

(2002) "The Intersection of Identity and Politics in Archaeology." *Annual Review of Anthropology* 31: 279–301.

Millot, Sara (2003) "La République disparaît-elle sous le voile?" http://www.regards.fr/Regards/culture/voile.htm.

Minow, Martha (1998) *Between Vengeance and Forgiveness: Facing History after Genocide.* Boston: Beacon Books.

Mires, Charlene (2002) *Independence Hall in American Memory.* Philadelphia: University of Pennsylvania Press.

(forthcoming) "Invisible House, Invisible Slavery: Struggles of Public History and the Memory of George Washington at Independence National Historical Park," in *Culture and Belonging: Symbolic Landscapes and Contested Indentities in Divided Societies,* Marc Howard Ross, ed.

Monk, Daniel Bertrand (2002) *An Aesthetic Occupation: The Immediacy of Architecture and the Palestine Conflict.* Durham and London: Duke University Press.

References

Montville, Joseph (1993) "The Healing Function in Political Conflict Resolution," in *Conflict Resolution Theory and Practice*, Dennis Sandole and van der Merwe, eds. Manchester: Manchester University Press, pp. 112–27.

Moodie, T. Dunbar (1975) *The Rise of Afrikanerdom: Power, Apartheid, and the Afrikaner Civil Religion*. Berkeley and Los Angeles: University of California Press.

Morris, Benny (1988) *The Birth of the Palestinian Refugee Problem, 1947–1949*. Cambridge: Cambridge University Press.

(2001) *Righteous Victims: A History of the Zionist-Arab. 1881–2001*. New York: Vintage Books.

Moruzzi, Norma Claire (1994) "A Problem with Headscarves: Contemporary Complexities of Political and Social Identity." *Political Theory* 22: 653–72.

Mulvihill, Robert F. and Marc Howard Ross (1999) "Understanding the Pluralistic Objectives of Conflict Resolution Interventions in Northern Ireland," in *Theory and Practice in Ethnic Conflict Management: Theorizing Success and Failure*, Marc Howard Ross and Jay Rothman, eds. Basingstoke: Macmillan, pp. 143–160.

Nash, Gary B. (2003) "For Whom Will the Liberty Bell Toll? From Controversy to Collaboration." Christ's Church, Philadelphia. www.ushistory.org/presidentshouse/controversy/nash.htm.

Nash, Gary B., Charlotte Crabtree, and Ross E. Dunn (2000) *History on Trial: Culture Wars and the Teaching of the Past*. New York: Vintage Books.

Neu, Joyce and Vamik Volkan (1999) "*Developing a Methodology for Conflict Prevention: The Case of Estonia.*" Atlanta: The Carter Center.

Nic Craith, Mairead (2002) *Plural Identities – Singular Narratives: The Case of Northern Ireland*. New York and Oxford: Berghan Books.

Noiriel, Gérard (1996) *The French Melting Pot: Immigration, Citizenship, and National Identity*. Minneapolis: University of Minnesota Press.

Nora, Pierre (1989) "Between Memory and History: Les Lieux de Mémoire." *Representations* 26: 7–24.

Nordmann, Charlotte (2004) "Le foulard islamique en question," in *Le foulard islamique en questions*, Charlotte Nordmann, ed. Paris: Éditions Amsterdam, pp. 160–77.

North, Peter (1997) "*Independent Review of Parades and Marches.*" London: The Stationary Office.

Northrup, Terrell A. (1989) "The Dynamic of Identity in Personal and Social Conflicts," in *Intractable Conflicts and their Transformation*, Louis Kriesberg, Terrell A. Northrup, and Stuart J. Thorson, eds. Syracuse, NY: Syracuse University Press, pp. 55–82.

Noyes, Dorothy (2003) *Fire in the Placa: Catalan Festival Politics After Franco*. Philadelphia: University of Pennsylvania Press.

O'Malley, Padraig (1983) *The Uncivil Wars: Ireland Today*. Boston: Houghton Mifflin.

(1990) *Biting at the Grave: The Irish Hunger Strikes and the Politics of Despair*. Boston: Beacon Press.

Paige, Karen Eriksen and Jeffery M. Paige (1981) *The Politics of Reproductive Ritual.* Berkeley and Los Angeles: University of California Press.

Posner, Daniel N. (2004) "The Political Salience of Cultural Difference: Why Chewas and Tumbukas Are Allies in Zambia and Adversaries in Malawi." *American Political Science Review* 98: 529–46.

Pressman, Jeremy (2003) "Visions in Collision: What Happened at Camp David and Taba?" *International Security* 28: 5–43.

Prince, K. Michael (2004) *Rally 'Round the Flag, Boys!: South Carolina and the Confederate Flag.* Columbia: University of South Carolina Press.

Pruitt, Dean G. and Jeffery. Z. Rubin (1985) *Social Conflict: Escalation, Stalemate, and Settlement.* New York: Random House.

Pundak, Ron (2001) "From Oslo to Taba: What Went Wrong?" http:// friendshipvillage2.homestead.com/CampPundak.html.

Raiffa, Howard (1982) *The Art and Science of Negotiation.* Cambridge, MA: Belknap/Harvard.

Rassool, Ciraj (2001) "Memory and the Politics of History in the District Six Museum." Mapping Alternatives: New Heritage Practices in South Africa. September 25–26. University of Cape Town.

(forthcoming) "Community Museums, Memory Politics and Social Transformation: Histories, Possibilities and Limits," in *Museum Frictions: Public Cultures/Global Interactions*, Ivan Karp and Corinne Kratz, eds. Duke University Press.

Rassool, Ciraj and Leslie Witz (1996) "South Africa: A World in One Country. Moments in International Tourist Encounters with Wildlife, the Primitive and the Modern." *Cahiers d'Etudes Africaines*, 143, 36: 335–71.

Rassool, Ciraj and Sandra Prosalendis, eds. (2001) *Recalling Community in Cape Town: Creating and Curating the District Six Museum.* Cape Town: District Six Museum Foundation.

Redmon, Jeremy (2003) "Council: Lincoln Statue 'Symbol of Unity'." February 25.

"Ripostes" (2003) "Être musulman en France." *Le Monde*, April 28.

Roe, Michael D. and Ed Cairns (2003) "Memories in Conflict: Review and a Look to the Future," in *The Role of Memory in Ethnic Conflict*, Ed Cairns and Michael D. Roe, eds. Basingstoke: Palgrave, pp. 171–80.

Roller, Elisa (2002) "When Does Language Become Exclusivist? Linguistic Politics in Catalonia." *National Identities* 4: 273–89.

Ross, Marc Howard (1993a) *The Culture of Conflict: Interpretations and Interests in Comparative Perspective.* New Haven and London: Yale University Press.

(1993b) *The Management of Conflict: Interpretations and Identities in Comparative Perspective.* New Haven and London: Yale University Press.

(1995) "Psychocultural Interpretation: Theory and Peacemaking in Ethnic Conflict." *Political Psychology* 16: 523–44.

(1997) "Culture and Identity in Comparative Political Analysis," in *Comparative Politics: Rationality, Culture and Structure*, Mark Irving Lichbach and Alan S. Zuckerman, eds. Cambridge: Cambridge University Press, pp. 42–80.

References

(2000a) "Creating the Conditions for Peacemaking: Theories of Practice in Ethnic Conflict Resolution." *Ethnic and Racial Studies* 22: 157–78.

(2000b) "'Good-Enough' Isn't So Bad: Thinking about Success and Failure in Ethnic Conflict Management." *Peace and Conflict: Journal of Peace Psychology* 6: 27–47.

(2001) "Psychocultural Interpretations and Dramas: Identity Dynamics in Ethnic Conflict." *Political Psychology* 22: 157–78.

(2002) "The Political Psychology of Competing Narratives: September 11 and Beyond," in *Understanding September 11*, Craig Calhoun, Paul Price, and Ashley Timmer, eds. New York: New Press, pp. 303–20.

(2004) "Ritual and the Politics of Reconciliation," in *From Conflict Resolution to Reconciliation*, Yaacov Bar-Siman-Tov, ed. Oxford: Oxford University Press, pp. 199–223.

Roy, Beth (1994) *Some Trouble with Cows: Making Sense of Social Conflict*. Berkeley and Los Angeles: University of California Press.

Ruane, Joseph and Jennifer Todd (1996) *The Dynamics of Conflict in Northern Ireland: Power, Conflict and Emancipation*. Cambridge: Cambridge University Press.

Rubinstein, Danny (2001) "Stealing History: Palestinians Charge that Israel is Replacing Muslim History with Zionist Mythology." *Ha'aretz*, May 2.

Rudolph, Suzanne Hoeber and Lloyd I. Rudolph (1993) "Modern Hate: How Ancient Animosities Get Invented." *The New Republic*, March 22.

Sack, Kevin (2001) "Battle Lines Form Again on the Battle Flag." *New York Times*, April 4.

Sa'di, Ahmad (2002) "Catastrophe, Memory and Identity." *Israel Studies* 7: 175–98.

Safran, William (1985) "The Mitterand Regime and its Ethnocultural Accommodation." *Comparative Politics* 18: 41–63.

(2004) "Ethnoreligious Politics in France: Jews and Muslims." *West European Politics* 27(3): 423–451.

Salisbury, Stephan (2005) "Committee Is Put in Place to Guide Slavery Memorial." *Philadelphia Inquirer*, September 23.

Sappir, Susan (1999) "Tensions Mount." *Jerusalem Report*, http://christianactionforisrael.org/isreport/novdec99/tensions.html.

Savage, Kirk (1997) *Standing Soldiers, Kneeling Slaves; Race, War and Monument in Nineteenth-Century America*. Princeton: Princeton University Press.

Schemla, Elizabeth (1989) "Jospin: Accueillez les foulards!" *Le Nouvel Observateur*, Oct. 26–Nov. 1.

Schweder, Richard A. and Robert A. LeVine, eds. (1984) *Culture Theory: Essays on Mind, Self and Emotion*. Cambridge: Cambridge University Press.

Sciolino, Elaine (2003a) "French Threaten Expulsions After Muslim Militants Win." *New York Times*, April 16.

(2003b) "Letter from Europe: France Envisions a Citizenry of Model Muslims." *New York Times*, May 7.

(2003c) "Chirac Backs Law to Keep Signs of Faith out of Schools." *New York Times*, December 18.

(2004a) "French Muslims Protest Rule Against Scarves." *New York Times*, January 18.

(2005) "John Paul II: Paris Perspective; France Urged to Skip Papal Honors." *New York Times*, April 8.

Scott, Joan W. (2005) "Symptomatic Politics: The Banning of Islamic Head Scarves in French Public Schools." *French Politics and Society* 23: 106–27.

Sells, Michael Anthony (1996) *The Bridge Betrayed: Religion and Genocide in Bosnia*. Berkeley and Los Angeles: University of California Press.

Shanks, Hershel (1981) "Politics at the City of David." *Biblical Archaeology Review* 7: 40–44.

Shaw, Julia (2000) "Ayodhya's Sacred Landscape: Ritual Memory, Politics and Archaeological 'Fact'." *Antiquity* 74: 693–700.

Shragai, Nadav (2000) "Solving the Puzzle in the Old City." *Ha'aretz Online*, June 18.

(2001) "Barak Halts Waqf's Temple Mount Excavations." *Ha'aretz*, January 22.

Shulman, Stephen (2002) "Challenging the Civic/Ethnic and West/East Dichotomies in the Study of Nationalism." *Comparative Political Studies* 35: 554–85.

Silberman, Neil Asher (1982) *Digging for God and Country: Exploration in the Holy Land. 1799–1917*. New York: Knopf.

(1995) "Promised Lands and Chosen Peoples: The Politics and Poetics of Archaeological Narratives," in *Nationalism, Politics and the Practice of Archaeology*, Philip L. Kohl and Clare Fawcett, eds. Cambridge: Cambridge University Press, pp. 249–61.

(1997) "Structuring the Past: Israelis. Palestinians, and the Symbolic Authority of Archaeological Monuments." *Journal for the Study of the Old Testament*. Supplemental Series 237: 62–81.

Silverstein, Paul (2004) "Headscarves and the French Tricolor." www.merip.org/ mero/mero013004.html.

Silverstein, Paul and Chantal Tetreault (2005) "Post-Colonial Urban Apartheid." Social Science Research Council. http://riotsfrance.ssrc.org/.

Simon, Catherine (2001) "Hanifa Cherifi: La voile est un piège, qui isole et marginalise." *Le Monde*, December 15.

Smith, Anthony D. (1991) *National Identity*. Reno: University of Nevada Press.

(1999) *Myths and Memories of the Nation*. Oxford: Oxford University Press.

Smith, Ben (2004a) "Vote Ended Long Georgia Flag Fight; Rebel Symbolism Now less Blatant." *Atlanta Journal Constitution*, March 7.

Smith, Craig (2004b) "Voilà, the Chinese Truffle (the French Accent) is a Fake." *New York Times*, February 6.

Smith, M. Brewster, Jerome S. Bruner, and Robert W. White (1956) *Opinions and Personality*. New York: John Wiley.

Smith, Tina and Ciraj Rassool (2001) "History in Photographs at the District Six Museum," in *Recalling Community in Cape Town: Creating and Curating the District Six Museum*, Ciraj Rassool and Sandra Prosalendis, eds. Cape Town: District Six Museum, pp. 131–45.

References

Smythe, Patrick (2001) "Mississippi Votes for Flag Seen as 'Slavery Symbol'." *Irish Times*, April 19.

Snyder, Jack (2000) *From Voting to Violence: Democratization and Nationalist Conflict*. New York: Norton.

Soboul, Albert (1974) *La France à la veille de la Révolution*. Paris: SEDES.

Sole, Robert and Henri Tincq (1989) "Un sondage IFOP pour 'Le Monde'-RTL et 'La Vie' sur l'Islam en France." *Le Monde*, November 30.

Sparks, Allister (1995) *Tomorrow is Another Country: The Inside Story of South Africa's Road to Change*. Chicago and London: University of Chicago Press.

Spiro, Melford (1984) "Some Reflections on Cultural Determinism and Relativism with Special Reference to Emotion and Reason," in *Culture Theory: Essays on Mind, Self and Emotion*, Richard A. Schweder and Robert A. LeVine, eds. Cambridge: Cambridge University Press, pp. 323–46.

Stern, Daniel N. (1985) *The Interpersonal World of the Infant*. New York: Basic Books.

Stern, Paul (1995) "Why Do People Sacrifice for Their Nations." *Political Psychology* 16: 217–35.

Tajfel, Henri (1981) *Human Groups and Social Categories*. Cambridge: Cambridge University Press.

Tambiah, Stanley (1992) *Buddhism Betrayed: Religion, Politics, and Violence in Sri Lanka*. Chicago: University of Chicago Press.

Thomas, Elaine (2000) "Competing Visions of Citizenship and Integration in France's Headscarves Affair." *Journal of European Area Studies* 8: 167–85.

Thomas, Elaine (2006) "Keeping Identity at a Distance: Explaining France's New Legal Restrictions on the Islamic Headscarf." *Ethnic and Racial Studies* 29(2): 237–259.

Thompson, Leonard (1985) *The Political Mythology of Apartheid*. New Haven and London: Yale University Press.

Trigger, Bruce G. (1984) "Alternative Archaeologies: Nationalist, Colonialist, Imperialist." *Man* 19: 355–70.

Turner, John C. (1988) *Rediscovering the Social Group: A Self-Categorization Theory*. Oxford: Oxford University Press.

Turner, Victor (1957) *Schism and Continuity in an Africa Society: A Study of Ndembu Village Life*. Manchester: University of Manchester Press.

———— (1974) *Dramas, Fields and Metaphors: Symbolic Action in Human Society*. Ithaca: Cornell University Press.

UTV (2003) "Adams Offers Orangemen Talks on Parades." Ulster TV online. http://u.tv/newsroom/indepth.asp?pt=n&id=34701.

van der Veer, Peter (1994) *Religious Nationalism: Hindus and Muslims in India*. Berkeley and Los Angeles: University of California Press.

Varshney, Ashutosh (2002) *Ethnic Conflict and Civil Life: Hindus and Muslims in India*. New Haven and London: Yale University Press.

Verba, Sidney (1961) *Small Groups and Political Behavior: A Study of Leadership*. Princeton: Princeton University Press.

Verdery, Katherine (1999) *The Political Lives of Dead Bodies: Reburial and Postsocialist Change*. New York: Columbia University Press.

Volkan, Vamik D. (1988) *The Need to Have Enemies and Allies: From Clinical Practice to International Relationships*. Northvale, NJ: Jason Aronson.

(1997) *Bloodlines: From Ethnic Pride to Ethnic Terrorism*. New York: Farrar, Straus, Giroux.

Waddell, Eric (1986) "State, Language and Society: The Vicissitudes of French in Quèbec and Canada," in *The Politics of Gender, Ethnicity and Language in Canada*, Alain Cairns and Cynthia Williams, eds. Toronto: University of Toronto Press, pp. 67–110.

Wagner, Christine (2000) "Rediscovering Memorial Day: Politics, Patriotism, and Gender," in *Social Conflicts and Collective Identities*, Patrick G. Coy and Lynne M. Woehrole, eds. Lanham, MD: Rowman and Littlefield Publishers, pp. 169–88.

Walker, Brian (1996) *Dancing to History's Tune: History, Myth and Politics in Ireland*. Belfast: Institute of Irish Studies, Queen's University of Belfast.

Warner, W. Lloyd (1959) *The Living and the Dead: A Study of the Symbolic Life of Americans*. New Haven and London: Yale University Press.

Waskow, Arthur and Phyllis Berman (1995) *Tales of Tikkun: New Jewish Stories to Heal the Wounded World*. Northvale, NJ: Jason Aronson.

Wasserstein, Bernard (2001) *Divided Jerusalem: The Struggle for the Holy City*. New Haven and London: Yale University Press.

Waters, Kenny (2005) "New Memorial Gets Full Funding." *Philadelphia Tribune*, November 22.

Waters, Mary C. (1990) *Ethnic Options: Choosing Identities in America*. Berkeley and Los Angeles: University of California Press.

Weber, Eugen (1976) *Peasants into Frenchmen: The Modernization of Rural France, 1870–1914*. Stanford: Stanford University Press.

Wedeen, Lisa (2002) "Conceptualizing Culture: Possibilities for Political Science." *American Political Science Review* 96: 713–28.

Wessels, Andre (1994) "In Search of Acceptable National Symbols for South Africa." *Journal for Contemporary History* 9: 262–87.

Whyte, John (1990) *Interpreting Northern Ireland*. Oxford: Oxford University Press.

Wichert, Sabine (1991) *Northern Ireland Since 1945*. London and New York: Longman.

Williams, Michael Paul (2002) "Statue Plan Reignites Controversy." *Richmond Times-Dispatch*, December 30.

Winnicott, D. W. (1958) "Transitional Objects and Other Transitional Phenomena." *International Journal of Psychoanalysis* 34: 89–97.

(1965) *The Maturational Process and the Facilitating Environment*. Madison, CT: International Universities Press.

Wintonick, Peter and Patricia Vergeylen Tassinari (1998) *The QuébeCanada Complex*. Film, Necessary Illusions Productions.

Withol de Wenden, Catherine (2005) "Reflections 'A Chaud' on the French Suburban Crisis." Social Science Research Council. http://riotsfrance.ssrc. org/.

References

Withol de Wenden, Catherine and Remy Leveau (2001) *La Beurgoise: les trois âges de la vie associative issue de l'immigration*. Paris: CNRS.

Witz, Leslie (2003) *Apartheid's Festival: Contesting South Africa's National Pasts*. Bloomington, IN: University of Indiana Press.

Witz, Leslie, Ciraj Rassool, and Gary Minkley (2001) "Repackaging the Past for South African Tourism." *Daedalus* 130: 277–96.

Woolard, Kathryn A. (1989) *Double Talk: Bilingualism and the Politics of Ethnicity in Catalonia*. Stanford: Stanford University Press.

Woolard, Kathryn A. and Tae-Joonh Gahng (1990) "Changing Language Policies and Attitudes in Autonomous Catalonia." *Language in Society* 19: 311–30.

Wright, Frank (1992) *Northern Ireland: A Comparative Analysis*. Dublin: Gill and Macmillan.

Yack, Bernard (1996) "The Myth of Civic Nationalism." *Critical Review* 10: 193–212.

Zartman, J. William (1986) *Ripe for Resolution*. Oxford: Oxford University Press.

Zerubavel, Yael (1995) *Recovered Roots: Collective Memory and the Making of Israeli National Tradition*. Chicago: University of Chicago Press.

Zolberg, Aristide and Long Litt Woon (1999) "Why Islam Is Like Spanish: Cultural Incorporation in Europe and the United States." *Politics and Society* 27: 5–38.

Index

Index

Index

Index

Index

Index

9 780521 690324